CW00763740

They Talk Along The Deep
(a global history of the Valentia Island telegraph cables)

Published in the United Kingdom 2016 by Dosanda Publications

ISBN 978-0-9935469-1-4

v 1.1

They Talk Along the Deep

(a global history of the Valentia Island telegraph cables)

Donard de Cogan

Bill Burns (editor)

Table of Contents

Introduction

This is a history about a technology that put a small island on the south-west coast of Ireland on the world map.

The electric telegraph came into being in the 1830s and there were many who contributed to its being. In addition to the electric and business ideas of Cooke and Wheatstone there is the system of transmitting dots and dashes. This is attributed to Samuel Morse, but it was his assistant, Alfred Vail who turned it into the code as we now know it.

The electric telegraph simplified the control of the developing rail network. It also led to

- A system of uniform time (use of time balls and time guns driven by telegraph)
- Synoptic meteorology (the analysis of concurrently collected weather observations)
- Remote control of warfare (Crimea war controlled from London and Paris)
- Rapid dissemination of news (Crimea war reports of Irishman William Howard Russell),
- Insulation of copper with gutta-percha for cables (patent of Dublin man, Henry Bewley).

The trans-Atlantic telegraph cable at Valentia can also lay claim to many 'firsts'

- Demonstration of the need for high purity copper for cable core
- Clarification of the theories of electricity
- The development of uniform systems of electrical units
- Establishment of transmission and reception procedures
- Use of the cable in the determination of the precise longitude of North America
- Study of earth currents and their diurnal variation (still important for electricity distribution)
- Discovery of photoconductivity
- Improvements in electrical earthing
- Publication of all relevant results in Jnl. Soc.Tel. Engineers (now IET)
- Test-bed for new instruments and batteries
- Training ground for operators who then carried their skills all over the world
- Development of coping strategies (getting more with what you have)
- Implementation of Kelvin's siphon recorder (the first bubble-jet printer)
- Implementation of cable duplex (simultaneous bi-directional) operation on cables
- Development of short-form codes (e.g. '88' = love & kisses)
- Electro-mechanical signal regeneration (in the days before thermionic valves)
- Reduction in the number of operators by the use of cable telex
- First ever Internet connections (1922)

This book is concerned with how this all came about, about the people who were involved and what the wider effects of these innovations were. There is no doubt that the telegraph cable station at Valentia had an enormous impact on both sides of the Atlantic. The eventual reduction in tariffs (message costs) and the consequent widespread use of telegrams for business, personal and newspaper purposes had profound political, social and economic implications. The economy of the island itself was transformed by the influx of a large, relatively well paid staff. The station provided opportunities for local employment and we gradually see the indigenous population playing an increasingly important part in its running.

There have been two major omissions in previous accounts of the subject. The trans-Atlantic telegraph attracted some of the greatest names in Victorian science, commerce and politics. However when they departed to enjoy the fruits of their enterprise, the operation was left in the hands of talented but less well known people whose efforts have largely gone unnoticed. There was also the technical developments: those which eventually took much of the skill out of the operators' work, those which made for faster communications, those which made operators redundant and finally those which brought the telegraph era to an end. This book is at once a social and a technological history of trans-Atlantic communication with Valentia and its people (the Graves, the Hearndens, the Rings etc) as the common thread throughout. Distant political and economic events, which had implications for trans-Atlantic telegraphy, are treated in terms of their effect on life at the Station.

The subject material is treated in chronological order. There were very definite phases within the life of the Valentia Station and these are used to delineate chapters. Within any chapter there may well be some moving backward or forward in time in order to maintain the sense of a topic. The timescale is from about 1830 to 1973 and beyond into what might be called the 'outlook period'. Within this timescale the first chapter deals with the pressures which led to inland telegraphy, to submarine telegraphy and finally to the 1857 attempt to span the Atlantic. The text involves much quotation from a variety of sources and to avoid excessive use of quotation marks all quotes have been indented. The authors of many of the quotations used peculiar spelling/punctuation. Rather than litter the text with '*sic*' it should be assumed that any indented text is as close as possible to that given in the original. Some of these might seem strange by modern standards, except perhaps in ham radio, where for instance '=' (- . . . -) is frequently used to indicate a break as an alternative to a full stop (. - . - . -). Indeed, there is much in ham radio usage that grew out of the 'short-forms' used by the telegraph pioneers.

The first draft of the book was completed in the early 1980s and the final chapter included a vision of the future as seen at that time. When the work was restarted in 2015 it was decided that the initial draft of the final chapter should be retained as a witness of how things have changed in the intervening period. It is hoped that readers will find this as fascinating as the author does.

Acknowledgements

It has been an exceptionally lucky happen-chance that the grand-daughter of Valentia's first Superintendent (James Graves), married the son of its second Superintendent (William Hearnden) against family wishes. My first thanks must be to the late Robbie Graves (died 1990), great-grandson of James Graves. He gave me access to his extraordinary collection of papers and allowed me to take copies of anything relevant. His papers have formed the core of the archive from which this book has been researched. Without these there would still be large gaps in the story. I was so excited by this 'gift' that I immediately set about drafting this book and that was in 1984. The rapid accretion of additional archive material and the pressure of work in the employment for which I was paid meant that the manuscript was set aside with the commitment that I would get back to it sometime and that sometime is now. I must also acknowledge my late father-in-law, Arthur Hearnden (died 1989), who provided the initial impetus and who, like his cousin, Robbie Graves, supplied photographs, documents and memories.

At an early stage in this research the Royal Society made a grant of £800 to assist with a study visit to Newfoundland. It was not the era of cheap flights and the return ticket cost about £500. I am therefore ever grateful to the late Dr Patrick McManamon, his wife, Mairead and their family for having me as a house-guest and for introducing me to so many wonderful people.

Others, who should be mentioned include Derek Pawson (died 2007), boss of the London office of Western Union International who allowed me access to papers in their office. My thanks to Desmond (Sam) Breslin (died 1987) for his reminiscences of personnel and technical details and for giving a feeling of the atmosphere of Valentia during his tenure as its last superintendent. Keith Geddes (died 1998), Curator of the Communications Collection at the Science Museum, London drew my attention to their acquisition of Capt. Anderson's letter book. Lenore Symons, then archivist at the Institution of Electrical Engineers (now the IET) and her successor, Anne Locker have been unstinting in their efforts to dig out material for me. Laurie Dennett, was in charge of the STC archives before they were closed*. She did an extraordinary job in cataloguing their collections. People associated with Cable and Wireless have been most helpful. When their archives were in London the late Peter Travers-Laney was ever helpful and encouraging and it continues. John Packer of the Cable and Wireless museum at Porthcurno explained many technical mysteries to me. It has also been a great pleasure collaborating with Allan Green on the early days of submarine telegraphs. Other researchers who have been most generous in sharing their findings include David Hochfelder and Elliot Porter.

In addition to thanking many people for their help, advice and encouragement I would like to highlight the significant contribution of several others. The website created and maintained by Bill Burns (http://atlantic-cable.com/) is a treasure beyond measure. It is a first stop in any cable telegraphy research. I am generally pretty scathing about the dearth of information relating to the Commercial Cable Co, but the website created by John Crellin (http://www.cial.org.uk/) is an oasis in what is otherwise an information desert.

I have also been exceptionally lucky (some might call it good taste) to be married to the grand daughter of a Graves/Hearnden elopement. For many years she has been both my staunchest supporter and my sternest critic. However her latter role has now been superseded . In the 1984 draft of this work I recorded

> "Finally Dominic, great great great grandson of Valentia's first superintendent, who (when I started this book) never, well hardly ever disturbed me between 6 and 8 am, thus making the first drafting of this work possible."

---

* I am assured that they are now more accessible than they have been for many years

He is now the parent of a four year old. We have so far collaborated on two papers on telegraphy and as a lecturer in taxation law at Cambridge University, he is assiduous in picking up even the smallest inconsistency in my writing.

I would also like to acknowledge the contribution of Bill Burns as editor, Dick Gillman and my aunt Helen Murphy, who have had to deal with my deficiencies as a proof-reader. Ultimately however, blame for any remaining typographical and grammatical errors rests with me.

In conclusion, I have had wonderful support. I have been able to get a consensus from both the Graves and Hearnden families. If I have failed to get across some feeling for the atmosphere at the Valentia cable station, then it is my fault not theirs.

Chapter 1

The Prehistory of Atlantic Telegraphy

The need for a telegraph

In order to appreciate the wider effects of the rapid communication which telegraphy provided, it is useful to go back in time and examine the pressures which led to its development.

It is sometimes difficult from the vantage point of the early 21st century to realise just how slow the process of communication was 200 years ago. The most important posts were those of the Monarch ruling their subjects. However as the size of the royal dominions grew, so also did the problem of administration and maintenance of loyalty to the Crown. The time lapse between action and reaction had lost America for King George III and one can only speculate how different the political structure of Canada might be today if the French had had more rapid access to information than the British. There had been numerous attempts to deal with the problem over land masses. The Normans in their conquest of Ireland, like the Romans in Britain, built signalling forts within line of sight of each other. Line of sight telegraphs such as semaphores and heliographs were in extensive use by both sides during the Napoleonic wars, but of course communications were entirely dependent on the caprices of the North West European weather.

It could be said that the battle of Waterloo marked the end of the 18th century in terms of the intellectual outlook of the British people. It was followed by a period of stability on the international stage. Between 1820 and 1840 the Empire headed towards its zenith while the young industrial revolution was gathering pace. A largely agrarian population were gravitating towards the cities to partake of the financial attractions which the revolution offered. New means of transport and communications were needed if the political and industrial momentum were to be sustained.

Plentiful supplies of raw materials were needed at the lowest possible prices. Economics demanded cheap and rapid transport to the centres of production followed by efficient distribution to readily available markets. The Empire by its existence guaranteed these requirements for its infant and developing industries. However in order to protect the supplies of raw materials and ensure freedom of market outlets from foreign interference, it was necessary to back up "right" with might. Means of communication were required for colonial administration and military purposes. The faster the response to civil upheavals or intrusion by other expansionist empires, the less would be the disturbance to the general equilibrium.

Technology was now moving in the directions in which it was being pushed by commercial and political expediency. The development of steam power, which was initially used in mines and factories, did not take long to extend to land and sea transport. The first steam driven ship crossed the Atlantic in 1829. It has often been commented that the painter J.M.W. Turner, perhaps unknowingly, gave us an early glimpse of a new age in one of his pictures. One may look admiringly at the fighting Temeraire, one of the heroes of Trafalgar coming in at dusk. How often does the eye fail to notice the smoke belching paddle steamer which is towing her into port? Sunset for the age of sail; dawn of the steam era.

Within a few years I.K. Brunel was building screw and/or paddle steamers which were challenging the imagination of the early Victorians. The ss *Great Western*, a wooden paddle/sail boat displacing 2,300 tons, was built in 1837. The ss *Great Britain*, 3,675 tons, iron built, was launched in 1843. Screw and sail were used for propulsion. These ships which were built for the Atlantic trade proved to be extremely efficient. The ss *Great Eastern* (having paddles, screw and sail), which was launched in 1858, almost exceeded the technological capabilities of the time. It certainly exceeded the market for which it was planned–non stop return trips to Australia. As such it would have avoided the necessity of maintaining coaling stations along the route. Alas for its financial backers, the Australian market disappeared just before it was launched. In the long run this was perhaps to prove fortunate for the history of trans-Atlantic telegraphy.

To talk first of the *Great Eastern* and the developments in steam navigation may appear a bit previous, except that it puts many of the important issues into their world context. The single most important development during the whole era was without doubt the steam railway. It supplied raw materials, delivered products and transported people on a scale never before imagined. However, even at a time of relatively low wage costs, railways were expensive to establish and the capital investment was enormous. Many fortunes were lost by unsuccessful ventures. In terms of cost single line track systems had many advantages, but there was the question of safety and Parliament was keeping a very strict eye on all railway companies in this respect. Systems of signalling were in their infancy and different methods were still being tried out. The possibility of head-on collisions was eventually overcome using a system of batons or keys, which have been in use in many places up to recent times.

As the number of trains on a line were increased to deal with demand, further problems arose. Even on dual track some system of signalling was required to indicate to a signal man the positions of trains relative to each other. There was another situation which required a means of communication over a length of track. The early railway engines could only deal with very gentle inclines. Rope haulage over bigger inclines was often used. One ingenious system for dealing with the problem was Brunel's atmospheric railway such as the one which was used on a section of the Dublin-Kingstown railway in Ireland. There is a rise of one hundred feet over a distance of two miles between Kingstown (now Dun Laoghaire) and Dalkey. A valved vacuum tube was placed along the track and trains were pulled by means of a piston which extended from the leading coach down into the tube. Suction was supplied by a steam powered pumping house near the terminus. Remote powered systems such as this had one major deficiency. So long as there was line-of-sight between originating and terminating stations there was no problem, but to quote the words of Brunel "As soon as we can obtain good and efficient telegraph communication between the engine houses and thus ensure proper regularity in the working of the engine, we shall be enabled to test the economy of the working. At present this is impossible owing to the want of the telegraph, compelling us to keep the engines almost constantly at work". This in two sentences summarises one of the major pressures which was to lead to the development of the telegraph (although there is some indication that an electric telegraph was evaluated on this line before it went out of service).

The invention of the electric telegraph

Although there were many ingenious inventions (electrical, optical & mechanical) for communicating at a distance, credit for the development of the electric telegraph in Britain is generally accorded to the partnership of William Fothergill Cooke and Charles Wheatstone. Cooke was the son of a medical man, one time professor of anatomy in Durham. He spent several years in the army in India, resigning on health grounds in 1833. While on a holiday in Europe after his return from India, he attended a lecture where he saw a demonstration of a telegraph. He then developed an instrument of his own design, which he attempted to sell it to the directors of the Liverpool and Manchester Railway. The Lime Street tunnel was one mile long. The incline was such that trains at the Station arrived under gravity, but had to be rope-hauled out again. A means of communicating with the winch house was badly needed. The directors rejected Cooke's first instrument on the basis of complexity, but gave him sufficient encouragement to continue his work. However he had one major problem to resolve, which was to face the proponents of the Atlantic telegraph venture at a later date. It was simple enough to make needles move across a room, but would "the galvanic fluid" move over a distance of one mile? After many inconclusive experiments and uncertain advice from scientists such as Michael Faraday, he was at the point of abandoning his work, when he met Charles Wheatstone, a young chemistry professor at King's College, London. Wheatstone informed him that he too was developing a telegraph and had four miles of wire in readiness for just such an experiment. Thus in 1837 there began the partnership, which although it was eventually to end in bitterness and discord, laid the foundations of telegraphic communication in Britain

James Graves's copy of the new Morse code that was introduced while he was a telegraph clerk with the Electric Telegraph Co. at Southampton in 1853

They set up a four needle (five wire) telegraph on the Euston-Camden Town incline of the London-Birmingham Railway. This instrument was capable of indicating twelve symbols by the convergence of needles. Other railway telegraphs followed. One notable development was the two needle instrument used on Brunel's Great Western Railway, which required a specialist operator. One of the earliest of these people, Thomas Home, was the first to send messages between Paddington and Slough on behalf of members of the public for a fixed fee of one shilling. By 1845 the Government were convinced about the efficiency of the various forms of Cooke and Wheatstone telegraphs. This led the Board of Trade to insist that all railways should adopt telegraph for block signalling.

During the same year Cooke bought out Wheatstone's interests and together with some London financiers formed the Electric Telegraph Co. This was to remain the largest single enterprise up to 1870, when the Post Office took over most inland telegraph companies. The Cooke and Wheatstone instruments were inefficient in that a number of wires were required to transmit and receive information. At about the same time Samuel Morse* in America had developed a system of transmitting information in the form of a series of dots and dashes. This meant that a telegraph required at most two wires, one if the ground was to be used as the return line. The Electric Co. soon introduced Morse telegraphs alongside their needle instruments, but they adopted their own code. Thus the word 'London' read in E.T.Co. code:

.-.	-	..	...-	-	..
L	**O**	**N**	**D**	**O**	**N**

In standard Morse code this would read:

.-..	---	-.	-..	---	-.
L	**O**	**N**	**D**	**O**	**N**

The Company did not adopt the standard system until 1853, when the staff were allowed a period of two weeks to become accustomed to the change.

Railways, telegraphs and the transmission of time

The Royal Mail was amongst the first on land to be significantly conscious of time and the differences in time across the UK (easting and westing). A mail coach was operated by a staff of two. The coachman was an employee of the coach company, while the guard was an employee of the Post Office, responsible for the safety of the mails and keeping the coach to time. He carried

---

* Morse's original system was more like the code books of the Chappes' optical telegraph. A word was converted into a number by means of a code-book. The number was transmitted and decoded by the recipient. This was particularly cumbersome, but remained in use for some time for the transmission of Chinese characters. Alfred Vail, who was Morse's assistant from 1837, visited Louis Vogt's print shop in Morristown, New Jersey and on the basis of the relative frequency of type, constructed a variable byte-sized code where 'E' was represented by a dot, 'T' by a dash and so on. He had a working system by January 1838 and was transmitting up to 10 words per minute. He overhauled his system in 1843, so that only the letters E,H,K,N,P and Q were unchanged.

firearms and a time-piece. This was designed to gain about 15 minutes in 24 hours, so that when travelling eastwards it might accord with real time. For westward journeys a watch with the reverse properties was used[+]. London time came to be accepted across much of the country even if they operated to their local times. The railways moved to 'Railway Time', although the Irish Mail (train) from London to Holyhead ran to London time from its inception in 1848. Each morning an Admiralty messenger carried a watch bearing the correct London time which he gave to the guard at Euston. On arrival at Holyhead the watch was handed to officials on the Kingstown (now called Dun Laoghaire) mail-boat, who carried it to Dublin. According to Howse (*loc. cit.* p.89) on the return journey the watch was carried back to London and handed back to the Admiralty messenger who met the train[*].

The differences in time across the UK caused a major embarrassment when in 1851 a group of dignitaries travelling to the Great Exhibition, arrived at Bristol Temple Meads station at the local appointed time only to find that Brunel's excursion train (which operated to London time) had left 10 minutes earlier.

Following the invention of the electric telegraph there was a symbiotic relationship with the railways as their development coincided in time and in mutual requirements. The railways needed a reliable system for the transmission of signalling information so that they could increase the density of trains on any line while minimising the risks of a collision. However, it is interesting to note that this symbiosis was recognised even earlier than the formation of the ETC. In fact the Railway Regulation Act of 1844 says in Section 13:

"And whereas Electric Telegraphs have been established on certain Railways and may become more extensively established hereafter and it is expedient to provide for their due Regulation: be it enacted That every Railway Company on being required so to do by the Lords of the said Committee (*Lords of the Committee of Privy Council for Trade and Plantations, later the Board of Trade*) with Servants and Workmen, at all reasonable Times to enter upon their Lands and to establish and lay down on such lands adjoining the Line of Such Railway, a Line of Electric Telegraphs for Her Majesties Service and give to him or them every reasonable facility for laying down the same, and for using the same for the Purpose of receiving and sending Messages on Her Majesty's Service, subject to such reasonable Remuneration to the Company as may be agreed . . ."

Section 14 of the same Act dictates that electric telegraphs whether belonging to the railway company or some other company must be open to the public:
"all Persons alike, without Favour or Preference".

Telegraphs required way-leave for the erection of their system of poles upon which to hang their wires. Instead of having to negotiate with numerous land-owners they had arrangements with the individual railway companies. Telegraph poles ran alongside the tracks on railway land, bringing

---

[+] Derek Howse "Greenwich Time and the discovery of Longitude", OUP 1980 p. 83

[*] Even though UK and Ireland were connected by telegraph cable from 1852 onwards, this practice was continued until 1939 (P. Bagwell "The Transport Revolution from 1770" Batsford, London 1970).

signals to railway stations and to signal boxes. One of the first lines was along the Great Western Railway from Paddington to Slough and very soon the public appreciation of the potential of the telegraph was raised when it was used to send a message up the line for the apprehension of a murderer who was known to have left Slough by train. This led to the realisation that the telegraph could provide a means for the rapid dissemination of "intelligence" such as general news, financial news and betting news. With this type of traffic the Electric Telegraph Co expanded rapidly, and for those railway companies that operated to London time, the ETC provided a facility for the synchronisation of clocks.

Telegraphs go underground and under water

The extension of telegraph soon highlighted the need for insulated cables and without this development submarine telegraphy would not have been possible. Even today railway tunnels are notoriously damp places. They were even worse in the steam era. Communications along the newly built underground railways in London were suffering badly from the effects of electrical leakage. There was also the problem of the sheer density of overhead wires that could be accommodated in a city. They simply had to go underground and this required an insulating material to separate wires from each other and protect them in damp environments.

The solution to the problem was gutta percha, the product of a resinous tree, similar to the latex rubber and likewise a native of Malaysia. On exposure to the air the resin, which is collected from the tree, coagulates to give a hard material with excellent insulating properties, which is readily mouldable in hot water. The first specimens were brought to England by Dr. W. Montgomerie, a surgeon in the East India Company, who saw it to have medical applications. It is reported that a Prussian cavalry officer, William Siemens, having attended a lecture on the material, informed his brother in Germany. In 1848 Michael Faraday publicised its excellent properties but Werner Siemens claimed that he had suggested its use in underground telegraphs to the Prussian Government in 1846. In fact Siemens had patented a macaroni-like extruder, which gave reliable, continuous coatings of gutta percha around a telegraph wire. In 1847 they had laid their first underground cable between Berlin and Grosberen. During 1848, 1849 the partnership of Siemens and Halske obtained contracts from the Prussian authorities for hundreds of miles of telegraph.

In Britain the first attempts at using gutta percha as a cable covering were singularly unsuccessful. The insulator was applied by moulding rather then by extrusion and the resulting cable invariably had bare wire at the joints between the two moulds. Eventually the Gutta Percha Co. (the principal importer of the material) enlisted the assistance of a Dublin chemist and soda water manufacturer, Henry Bewley. Bewley had developed a joint-free lead pipe manufacturing process and the Company offered him a directorship in return for his expertise (see Addendum I at the end of this chapter). His lead pipe extruder worked successfully with gutta percha and paved the way for subterranean telegraphy in Britain. In 1851 the Magnetic* Telegraph Co. laid cables from Manchester to Liverpool between the tracks of the Manchester and Yorkshire Railway. An underground line was established between Manchester and London by the same Company the

---

* 'Magnetic' because they used dynamos to generate their power (the Electric Co. used batteries). The Company was run by the Bright brothers. Charles Bright was eventually destined to play a major part in submarine telegraphy.

following year. This time the cables were laid along the public road. As part of the Magnetic Co's network other lines were laid to Glasgow and throughout a large part of Ireland. In 1853 the Electric Telegraph Co. laid their first underground cables, between London and Manchester along the line of the London and North Western Railway. It was appreciated from the very earliest stages that if points were to be connected by lines of telegraph, then the problem of sub-aqueous cables would have to be tackled. The first detailed demonstration of underwater telegraphy in England was made by Col. Pulsey of the Royal Engineers in 1838. He used a wire with a tarred rope covering which was wound with pitched yarn.

Elsewhere in the Empire similar experiments were being undertaken. Dr O'Shaughnessey (later Sir William O'Shaughnessey-Brooke FRS) Director of the East India Co's telegraph ran a cable across the Hughli river in India (see Addendum II at the end of this chapter). He used a pitch-coated wire enclosed in sections of split ratan and wound with tarred hemp. Coincident with but unaware of these demonstrations, the ever inventive Charles Wheatstone was undertaking experiments and in 1840 presented a detailed plan to the House of Commons for a link between Britain and France. It was the publicity associated with this scheme that has led to his being attributed with the invention of submarine telegraphy. Meanwhile on the other side of the Atlantic the first attempts at submarine communication were also being made. In 1842 Morse set up a link across New York Harbour and in 1845 Ezra Cornell established communication between Fort Lee and New York. His telegraph, which ran along 12 miles of the Hudson river consisted of two cotton-covered cables coated with india rubber and encased in a lead pipe.

The first moves towards establishing a link across the English Channel were make by Charles West. The British were prepared to allow him to land a cable without imposing any conditions. The French on the other hand demanded evidence of the undertaking being backed up by the necessary finance. West approached the Electrical Telegraph Co. and tests were undertaken in Porstmouth Harbour by their Chief Electrician, Cromwell F. Varley[**]

Cromwell Fleetwood Varley

The wire was covered with thick cotton and insulated from the water by a mixture of pitch and resin. The ultimate failure of the experiment was felt to be due to the specific gravity of the cable, which was insufficient to ensure submersion. West was unable to obtain backing from the

[**] Cromwell Fleetwood Varley (6 April 1828 - 2 September 1883) was the son of the inventor and water colourist, Cornelius Varley. His brother Alfred Varley was also active in telegraphs.

Company and his project fell through. In 1849 C.V. Walker laid an experimental line in the English Channel which proved that transmission through submerged gutta percha covered cables was technically possible. On 23 August 1850 the Brett brothers made their first attempt to link Dover and Calais. The cable worked and messages were exchanged. However within a few hours the cable failed and the cause was subsequently found to be due to a Boulogne fisherman who raised it to the surface in his trawl. Imagining that he had discovered a fabulous eel with gold in its heart (the copper conductor) he cut out a length to bring home. In subsequent histories of the subject he was referred to as 'piscator ignobile'. The Bretts obtained an extension to their concession from the French Government and a durable link was established in September 1851. A notable feature of their new cable was the use of a sheath of iron wires to protect the insulating envelope. This was subsequently adopted as common practice in submarine cable technology.

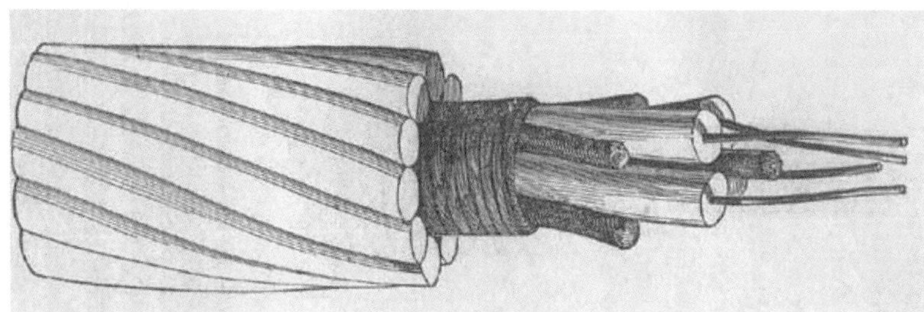

Other submarine cables quickly followed. Amongst them were three unsuccessful attempts to link England and Ireland. In one of these cases the cable was too light and did not sink. In the other it ran out too quickly during submersion; there was much to learn about paying out gear. The first Holyhead-Howth (Ireland) cable was not sufficiently durable, although it was notable as being the first to have been protected by heavy shore ends, which had a much thicker sheathing of iron. London and Dublin were successfully connected in 1853 when the English and Irish Magnetic Telegraph Co* laid a cable between Portpatrick in Scotland and Donaghadee in Northern Ireland.

The establishment of the Meteorological Department

The first international conference on meteorology was held in Brussels from 23 August to 8 September 1853, where a scheme for observational procedures at sea was drawn up. The UK Government, committed as it was to the safety of sailors at sea, proposed the establishment of a Meteorological Department which was to be under the Board of Trade. Parliament voted £3,200 with £1,000 coming from the Admiralty for the establishment of a 'uniform system of meteorological observations at sea' to help determine the 'very best tracks for ships to follow in order to make the quickest as well as safest passages' On the recommendation of the Royal Society they appointed Robert FitzRoy, late of HMS *Beagle*, and in 1854 he took up his new position as Meteorological Statist and was allowed a total staff of three.

During the night of 25/26 October 1859 the ss *Royal Charter*, returning to Liverpool from Melbourne, was destroyed in a hurricane close to the north Anglesey coast in Wales. Over 450 people were killed, some drowned and many smashed to pieces on the rocks. FitzRoy set about a

* This Company, sometimes called the British and Irish Magnetic Telegraph Co, was an extension of Charles Bright's Magnetic Telegraph Co, which had a monopoly in the northwest of England

process of what we would now call 'hindcasting'. He obtained as much information as he could about what the barometric pressure, rainfall etc. had been at different locations (land and sea) around the UK for the time of this disaster, and he was able to piece together a weather map from western Ireland and into Europe. Soon after, FitzRoy established his system of synchronised telegraph reporting of coastal observations so that he could devise a synoptic chart in near real-time. Even this was outside the remit that he had originally been given and in terms of telegram charges it was expensive. He then went one stage further. He started to transmit information about nearby weather from London to the coastal stations. We can get a glimpse of how the weather reporting scheme operated from the technical autobiography of our recurring source James Graves, who in 1859 was promoted to Clerk-in-Charge of the Jersey office of the Channel Islands Telegraph Co

"In the month of September 1860 the Board of Trade made arrangements for the Establishment of a Meteorological Station at Jersey, with a view to warning the Seafaring population of approaching storms. After some correspondence instruments (Barometers and Thermometers) were forwarded to me and I was appointed agent for Jersey - and during the time the line of Telegraphic 'Communication' was intact I forwarded every morning a report by wire to the Board of Trade, which was with others published in the "Times", "Shipping Gazette" & "Globe" newspapers (Graves was paid 3/= (15p) per week by the Board of Trade for taking and transmitting the daily weather observations). A little time afterwards "Signal Shapes" were furnished, and after some little trouble I made arrangements with the Lieut. Governor (Major Genl. Douglas) for the use of the signal staff at Fort Regent for hoisting signals when a gale was anticipated."

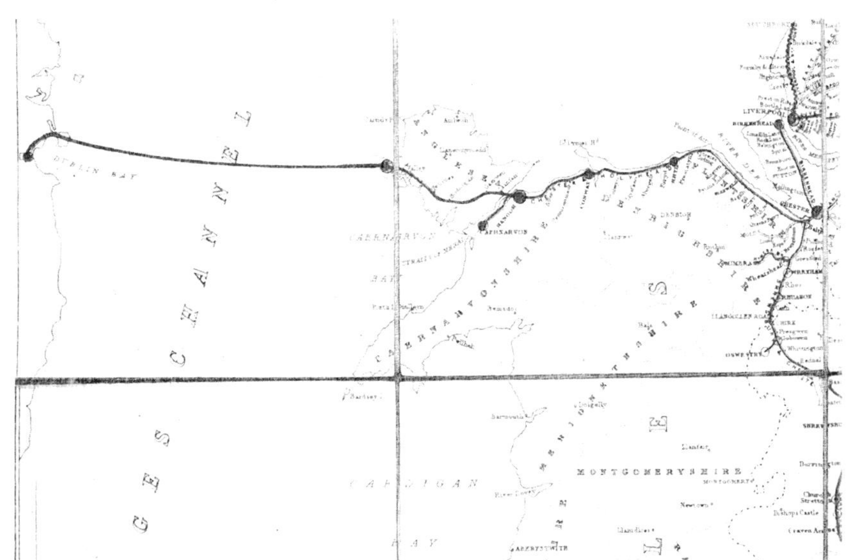

Part of an 1860 map of the network of the Electric & International Telegraph Co. showing the link between Holyhead and Dublin (Post Office Archives item 2.15)

Trans-Atlantic telegraphy on the horizon

Within a few years of the first submarine cables, experience was giving people confidence, some might say too much confidence, in the new technological achievements. All the ingredients were present for further ambitious telegraphic enterprises. Although London was connected eastwards as far St. Petersburg and Moscow to the north and Istanbul to the south, it was Napoleon III's interest in telegraphy which belatedly led the government to appreciate its full political significance. It was necessary that the Empire should excel in this as in all other subjects and a trans-Atlantic telegraph was a project worthy of its endeavours. There were good commercial as well as political reasons why Britain should wish to communicate with its recent ex-colony, now a fast growing economic power. The southern States of America were a major source of cotton, on which the industrial livelihood of many towns in the north-west of England depended. For many years the delays in communication across the Atlantic as well as uncertainty in supplies and prices had created difficulties for the trade. Prices were higher then they need have been, due mainly to the rake off by middlemen, cotton stock-holders and agents, who cushioned the industry against fluctuations in supplies. The willingness of the cotton manufacturers to bypass these people is evidenced by the amount of finance for the Atlantic Telegraph project which came from Manchester, Liverpool etc.

However, before such a project could be initiated two technological questions had to be asked and then answered. When the time came it was the American merchant, Cyrus Field, who posed the questions. His involvement in the narrative is still some short way off.

In 1850 J.T. Mullock, Catholic Bishop of Newfoundland, pointed out that his diocese formed the easternmost part of the American continent. If St. John's were connected westwards by telegraph, it would be valuable for commerce (and thereby beneficial for his flock). The suggestion was taken up by F.N. Gisborne, who was Chief Engineer of the Nova Scotia Telegraph Co.

Basilica Cathedral of St John's completed by Bishop Mullock in 1855.
Photographed by the author in March 1985

On the eastern side of the Atlantic there were those who were already making use of the fact that Ireland was the westernmost land mass in Europe. These enterprising people had offices in Cork and Kerry connected by telegraph to the industrial centres of Britain. Messages received by wire were placed in sealed containers and put aboard westbound ships that might have left port four days previously. Similarly, they collected containers from eastbound ships and relayed their contents well ahead of arrival of the vessels themselves.

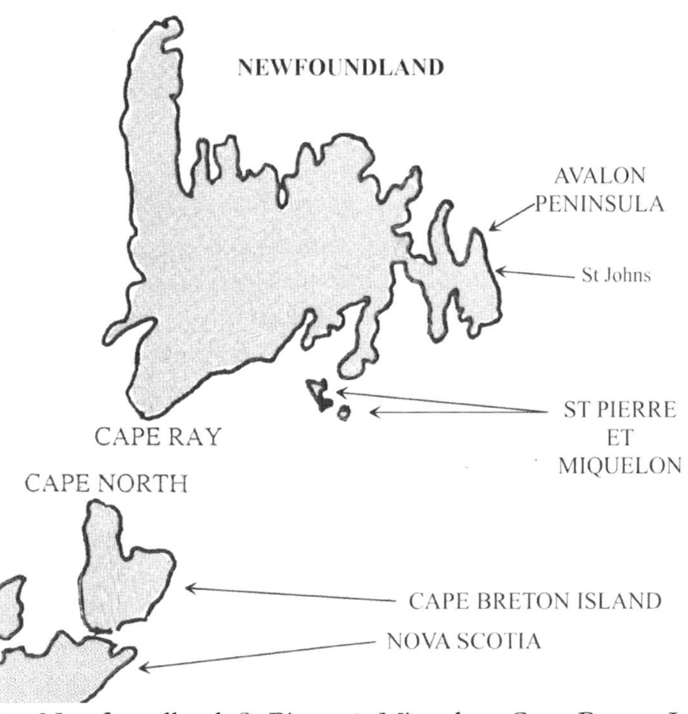

Outline map showing Newfoundland, St Pierre & Miquelon, Cape Breton Island and Nova Scotia

Gisborne planned a similar operation from St. John's. Carrier pigeons were to be used to carry the most urgent dispatches between ship and shore. Messages were to be relayed to New York via a line of telegraph, which his Company would establish. He approached the Newfoundland legislature with his plan and received a grant, whereupon he resigned his position with the Nova Scotia Co. and set about organising his Newfoundland Electric Telegraph Co.

The task which faced him was a daunting one. It required an overland line from Cape Ray to St John's, a distance of 400 miles through inhospitable and un-surveyed terrain. Cape Ray and Cape Breton were to be linked by steamboat with the long term possibility of a submarine cable across the Strait. He succeeded in undertaking a survey of the island, installing 40 miles of land line and laying 12 miles of submarine cable between Prince Edward Island and New Brunswick. The cable which had been supplied by R.S. Newall of Birkenhead, England, failed after a year. Then the money ran out. He was declared bankrupt, owing $50,000 and his staff remained unpaid. In a desperate attempt to try and retrieve something he went to New York, where he contacted the civil engineer, Matthew D. Field. Field was sympathetic and arranged for him to meet his brother, Cyrus. Thus began a new phase of trans-Atlantic communication. It was 1854.

Contemporary visiting card of Cyrus Field

Cyrus West Field was a man in need of challenges. He had amassed a fortune as a New York merchant and had withdrawn from direct involvement so that he could concentrate on other things, as yet unspecified. When he first met Gisborne he did not develop an immediate enthusiasm. Certainly the project had potential, but so had thousands of others, and although he was a rich man, he was not a squanderer. After the departure of Gisborne, it said that he was pondering the suggestion while running his hand over a globe. Suddenly he had a thought; why stop at Newfoundland; why not go all the way with a telegraph. As he saw it there were two uncertainties; fundamental questions, and if the answer to both were favourable, then the idea was certainly worth pursuing.

The first of the uncertainties was a mechanical one. Could a cable of sufficient strength be manufactured to span the width of the Atlantic? The answer to this question required a knowledge of the depths involved and the nature of the ocean floor. The depth would determine whether the maximum breaking strain of a cable would be sufficient for it to withstand submersion. When submerged a cable would stand a better chance of survival if it were laid on a flat or gently undulating surface. If the bed of the Atlantic were in fact a series of pinnacles separated by chasms, perhaps with a few submarine volcanoes, then the project stood no chance. The second question, the electrical one was in many ways the more important. If a signal were inserted into one end of a cable, what chance did it stand of emerging from the other end? The science of electricity was still in its infancy. Much had to be learnt about its underlying basis. Experience with land telegraph had shown that signals were attenuated over long distances, but the processes governing this phenomenon were not yet fully understood. However Samuel Morse had been quoted ten years previously as saying that a telegraphic communication might with certainty be established across the Atlantic Ocean.

In many ways such a link was more important for the average American than for his British counterpart. In addition to any industrial and commercial advantages that the man in the street might hear about, the telegraph was a link with the old world, with his roots. Many Americans at that time would have been little more than first or at most second generation immigrants. Many were doing very well for themselves, often achieving a standard of living that would have been inconceivable in their European homeland. However, one immigrant in America is one small man in a very large country, far away from family and childhood friends. This deep-based home sickness, which could extend over generations, and the sheer physical and psychological barrier of the Atlantic, created a voracious appetite for European news. News took a long time to arrive and anything which could accelerate its progress was likely to appeal to the American subconscious.

The morning after the first meeting with Gisborne, Field wrote to two leading authorities with his two separate questions. Lieut. Matthew Maury*, Head of the National Observatory at Washington, replied indicating that Commander O.H. Berryman had during the previous year completed a series of soundings from the shores of Newfoundland to the shores of Ireland. The sea bed consisted of microscopic shells and did not show any sign of irregularity. Samuel Morse had been the other recipient of a letter from Field. His reply was even more encouraging and during a visit to New York some days later, he met Field and outlined some of the basic physics to him.

From that point onwards Field's frenzied enthusiasm took over. It was going to take twelve years and over forty crossings of the Atlantic before the project was truly successful. His efforts were unquestioningly supported by his brothers: Daniel D. Field, a judge, acted as legal advisor, Matthew was the civil engineer and Henry, a theologian, was to chronicle the events**.

---

* Matthew Fontaine Maury (14 Jan. 1806 – 1 Feb. 1873), author of the "Physical Geography of the Sea" and an early proponent of meteorology. He gave the name 'Telegraph Plateau' to the relatively flat ocean bed between Newfoundland and Ireland.

** His book, "the Atlantic Telegraph" is one of the standard information sources for the period up to the end of 1858. A further publication, which included the period up to 1866 in its latter chapters, was intended only for private circulation

The first step was to establish a group of financiers to help spread the cost. Ten had been the initial number that Field had in mind. However when the number had reached five, it was agreed that that was sufficient. In March Gisborne was bought out and the Newfoundland Electric Telegraph Co. was taken over by the partnership. Immediately Field went to Newfoundland and obtained a charter for his enterprise, the New York, Newfoundland and London Telegraph Co. This gave them authority to establish a telegraph between Newfoundland and Ireland and granted them sole landing rights for fifty years. It also established the right to hold meetings of stockholders and directors in London, New York or Newfoundland. Once the charter was signed the debts of the old Company were discharged.

The first task was to extend the line from St. John's to New York, a distance of over 1,000 miles. It was expected to be finished within a year, but the conditions proved so difficult that it took a crew of 600 men two years to complete.

The Autumn of 1854 saw Field's first trip to London on Company business. Eighty five miles of cable was to be ordered to span the Cabot Strait between Cape Ray and Cape Breton. During his visit he met John Brett, one of the brothers who had laid the cable between Dover and Calais. He was enthusiastic about Field's proposal and even subscribed to some shares in the venture.

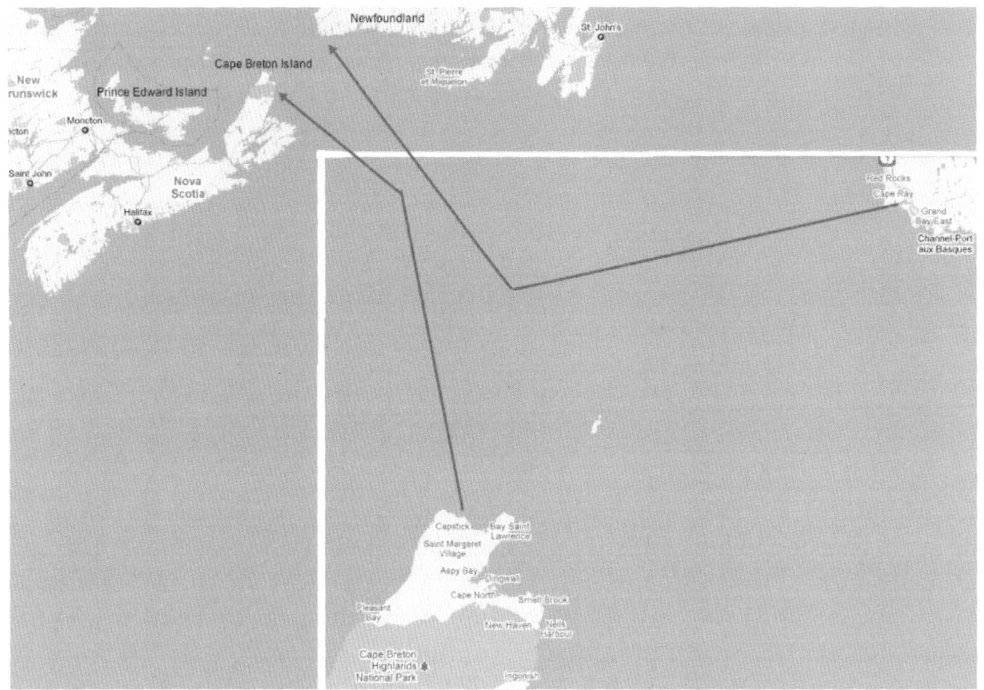

Map plus details of the Cabot Strait between Newfoundland and Cape Breton Island

The first attempt to lay a cable across the Gulf of St. Lawrence ended in failure, but a useful lesson was learnt. The cable was shipped aboard the barque *Sarah L. Bryant*, which was towed by the steamer *James Adger*. The submersion was attended by a social occasion on board the boats and all went well for 40 miles. At that point a violent storm blew up and the captain of the barque was forced to cut both the cable and the tow in order to save his ship. The failure caused some wavering of the financial backers, but the enterprise held together, the principals having learnt that submersion could only be done successfully using a steamer.

Field sailed to England to order more cable from Glass Elliot and Co., who on this occasion were contracted to lay the cable as well. A paddle steamer, the *Propontis*, was used and the cable was successfully laid in 1856 with little or no ceremony. The *Propontis* then proceeded to repair the links across the Gulf of Canso and the Northumberland Strait using recovered sections of the cable which had been lost during the previous year.

According to the American writer Bern Dibner the 1856 cable represented a technical innovation in that it was the first time that a stranded core had been used. Heretofore the cores of all cables had been solid copper. In addition to increased mechanical strength, it also reduced the consequences of fracture. If a single core broke, that was that. The loss of one or two strands of the new type of cable would not mean the loss of all communication.

In 1856 the overland work was done and there was now an unbroken telegraph network from St. Johns to New York. The cost in money and effort had been enormous. Over a quarter of a million dollars had already been spent and the next stage in the project was going to require a further injection of finance. It was also going to require a more detailed study of the ocean bed. Field first travelled to Washington and requested a further survey. Berryman was again assigned to the task and the U.S.S. *Arctic* left New York in July. In three weeks he had reached the coast of Ireland by the great circle route, the shortest distance between the two proposed termini of the cable. The existence of a submarine plateau was confirmed.

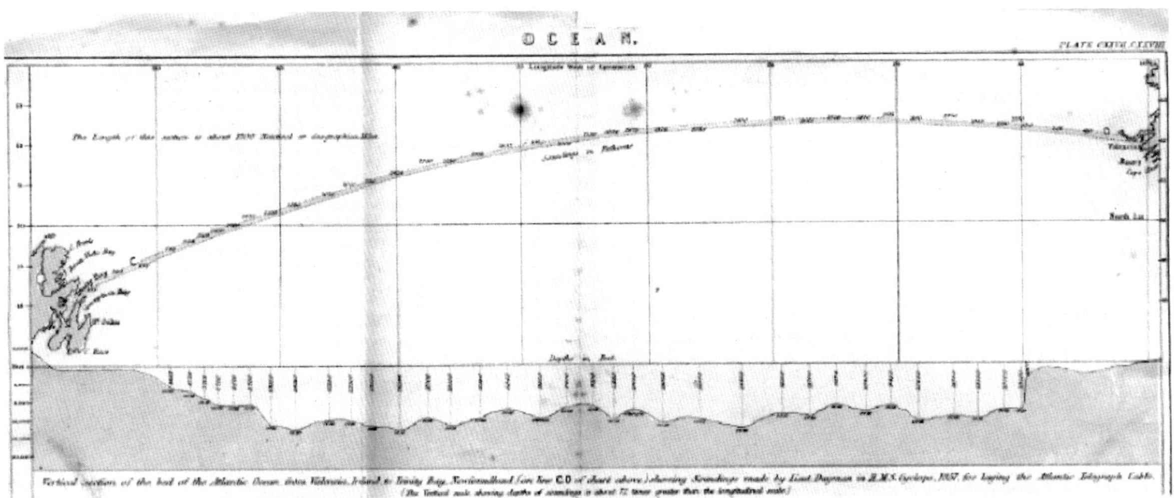

Vertical section of the bed of the Atlantic Ocean from Valencia, Ireland to Trinity Bay, Newfoundland (on line on chart above showing soundings made by Lieut. Dayman in HMS *Cyclops*, 1857 for laying the Atlantic telegraph cable)

According to his brother, Field left for England on 12 July where he requested the Admiralty to undertake its own soundings. They agreed and Lieut Cdr Joseph Dayman of HMS *Cyclo*ps was directed to sail from Valentia* Harbour along the same route as Berryman to Newfoundland. He was instructed to take more frequent soundings inshore. Dayman's expedition, slightly to the north of Berryman's line confirmed the American's observations. The maximum depth was slightly over 2 1/2 miles and the only danger was the European continental shelf, 200 miles west of Ireland, where the sea bed dropped 1,200 fathoms in a distance of 12 miles (a gradient of about 1/12)

During his visit to London in summer 1856, Field was busy pursuing the interests of his Company. He consulted with leading authorities in related subjects. Samuel Canning, Chief Engineer to Glass Elliot and Co. the cable manufacturers, advised him on the cable itself. Samuel Statham of the London Gutta Percha Co. assured him of the properties of his wonder material. He also had meetings with Robert Stephenson, son of the doyen of railway engineers; with Charles Tilston Bright, Chief Engineer to the British and Irish Magnetic Telegraph Co.; and with Dr E.O.W. Whitehouse, a retired surgeon with very definite ideas about the retardation of signals in telegraph cables. When he met Brunel he was taken down to Scott Russell's yard at Millwall to view the *Great Eastern*, then half way through construction. "There is the ship to lay the Atlantic cable" said Brunel. Neither was to know just how prophetic those words were. Brunel also offered some financial advice, which if it had been taken, might have alleviated some of the problems yet to come[+]. While in London, Field approached the Secretary to the Treasury with his proposals. A company was to be formed with a capital of £350,000. Brunel argued that this was quite insufficient. He believed that the capital should be about £2,000,000 and told Field so. How right this was to be!

---

[*] This is the first time that Valentia is specifically mentioned in connection with the enterprise.

[+] It is believed that Brunel suggested that the armouring would be better with a triple armouring as it was add to strength and reduce weight.

In approaching the Government Field obtained a response that must have exceeded his wildest dreams. They would supply ships for surveying and laying (Dayman was already at work). They would also pay a subsidy of £14,000, equivalent to 4% of working capital, for work done on its behalf. The subsidy would continue at that level until the net profits were equal to a dividend of £6/cent, when it would be reduced to £10,000 pa. However if Government traffic were to exceed this amount at any time, an equivalent additional payment would be paid. In return for this subsidy certain conditions were laid down and these were as follows:

1. That Government traffic should have priority over all traffic except that of the United States and in case of both countries claiming priority, whichever message arrived first at the station should be transmitted first.
2. That tariffs were to be fixed and changed only with the agreement of the Treasury.

The condition relating to priority was particularly generous to the United States. In view of the fact that the two termini were within the British Empire, a claim to sole priority could have been justified. There is no doubt that it was occasioned by the need for cordial relations. After all a major part of the British economy was already dependent on trade with America. Nevertheless, in spite of this generosity, the routing of the cable was soon to generate much friction and acrimony, when the matter was debated in Washington.

Field accepted the conditions on behalf of his American company. The Atlantic Telegraph Co. was born in September 1856, Field taking up one quarter of the shares for his American partners. Amongst the other subscribers were Messrs Brett and Bright, the novelist William Makepeace Thackeray, and Lady Byron. The list of Directors appointed in December 1856 included many eminent bankers and merchants from London, Liverpool and Manchester. Samuel Gurney of the firm Overend and Gurney. T.H. Hankey of the firm of bankers of that name in London. Sir William Brown, Henry Harrison, Edward Johnston, Robert Crosbie, George Maxwell and C.W.H. Pickering were all from Liverpool. John Pender and James Dugdale were from Manchester. The list also included three other names. George Peabody and Curtis M. Lampson were American merchants, long time resident in England. William Thomson*, Professor of Natural Philosophy at Glasgow University had been appointed by the vote of the Scottish shareholders to represent their interests. He was thirty-two, but probably knew more about the theory of telegraphy than any other man at that time. George Saward was appointed Secretary to the Company. Charles Bright was the Chief Engineer and Dr Edward Orange Wildman Whitehouse the Chief Electrician. With the benefit of hindsight it can be seen that the appointment of Whitehouse was a grave mistake. He appeared to be the right man in the right place at the right time. He had good credentials, having conducted important relevant experiments with Charles Bright and the Magnetic Telegraph Co. From these experiments he predicted that it should be possible to use a printing telegraph on an Atlantic cable with a reasonable word rate. This was obviously attractive as printing telegraphs did not require the same level of skill from an operator.

---

* Sylvanus P. Thompson's biography of William Thomson (later Lord Kelvin) gives a detailed account of his involvement in the Atlantic telegraph. It also lists his relevant papers and patents.

William Thomson was one of the few men of the day who could handle Fourier's mathematics, which even today forms the basis for the analytical treatment of pulse propagation in transmission lines. He had put forward his law of squares, showing that the retardation of signals depended on the resistance and capacitance of the cable. The resistance was inversely proportional to the cross sectional area of the copper core. It was also critically dependent on the purity of the metal. The capacitance varied as the ratios of the radii of the inner and outer conductors. The larger the inner diameter, the lower the capacitance and therefore the less the signals would be retarded in their progress.

Whitehouse completely disagreed with this theory and put forward his own linear law[**]. As a consequence of his law the propagation of signals would depend on the starting potential. The greater the distance to be travelled, the larger the kick the signals needed to get them on their way. He produced experimental results to support his case. Thomson in his very mild way pointed out that far from proving his (Whitehouse's) theory, the results confirmed the law of squares. Whitehouse could not see it that way. "Nature recognises no such law" was one of his chants. Although a Director, Thomson held no technical position and one can only marvel at his patience and humility in the face of Whitehouse's overbearing personality. Anyway he would put his views to the first Board meeting.

Cyrus Field was not a man to waste time. In any event he was under considerable pressure for quick results from his American colleagues. At the first meeting of Directors it was disclosed that in their haste to get things under way, the committee who established the Company had already placed orders for the cable based on Whitehouse's specifications. Like many others on the Board Thomson must have been furious, but there was little that could be done now except to continue his researches and to wait.

Field returned to America to distribute the stock and to obtain from the Government a contribution in ships and funds which would match that of the British, thus making it a truly trans-Atlantic venture. The reaction which he experienced was the exact opposite to that in England. There was a lot of genuine interest and he published a technically informative letter in response to enquiries. However the translation of interest into hard cash was a much slower process. There were also problems on the political front. The President, Franklin Pierce, favoured the project, but there was massive opposition in Congress. The Bill got through the Senate by one vote and through the House by 19. The opposition came largely from the southern States. Their case was generally based on the argument that it was not a cable between Britain and the United States, but between Britain and one of her colonies, from which she alone would reap the benefit. Both the termini were in British hands and in the event of war this would give her a tremendous advantage. At first sight it might seem strange that most of the opposition came from those most likely to gain from the link.

[**] A recent paper (D. de Cogan and A. Green "A numerical analysis of some measurements on the first trans-Atlantic telegraph cable" *IET Sci. Meas. Technol.*, 5(4) (2011) 117–124) shows that both were right, but were looking at different things. In terms of signalling Thomson's inverse square law is completely correct, but there is an initial transient in an over-damped LRC circuit (a cable) where the amplitude is proportional to the imposed voltage. It is likely that this was what Whitehead observed.

It must be remembered however that the Civil War was only a few years off and the signs of strain were beginning to show. The Telegraph Bill had been introduced and supported by the Northerners. There was particular animosity against William H. Seward, the Secretary of State, who championed the Bill. His involvement was reason alone for opposition, even if it ran counter to their long term interests. In spite of the British offer of equality the first part of their case was unquestionably valid. The section relating to war was designed to play heavily on the American subconscious mind. It was after all just over half a century since their hard won independence from Britain. In this event however Britain never held any grudge against the southern States for their opposition and the somewhat less than ambivalent attitude that it adopted during the Civil War, was later to be the source of a large volume of telegraph traffic across the Atlantic.

The Bill was signed by President Pierce on 3 March 1857, the day before he retired. It is strange that the equivalent Bill on its passage through the House of Lords, drew the same criticism on the question of war. Since both termini were on British Sovereign soil, why not make it an entirely British venture. However it passed through the House on 20 July and the stage was now set for the first attempt to span the Atlantic with a telegraph cable.

Addendum I

Transcriptions from Cavan Weekly News
http://www.irelandoldnews.com/Cavan/1876/JUL.html

Mr. Henry Bewley.

At the age of 72, at Willow Park, Booterstown, Dublin, there departed this life, on June 28, 1876, Mr. Henry Bewley, widely known in the Christian Church for his earnest spirit of evangelical enterprise and open handed benevolence.

Willow Park, Booterstown, home of Henry Bewley
Now a preparatory school for Blackrock College

The total sum that he gave away during his lifetime to charitable undertakings and works of benevolence can scarcely have been less than one hundred thousand pounds altogether. One among the numerous gifts dispensed by him was a cheque of five thousand pounds given in 1866 to the London Evangelization Society, founded by Lord Radstock and Mr. Robert Baxter; and his purse was constantly open for aiding various societies and individuals engaged in Christian undertakings.

The principal work with which his name is associated is the Dublin Tract Depository, in D'Olier-street, which has done a great work of usefulness during the past twenty-five years, and has scattered over the world English, French, Spanish, Italian, and German religious tracts and little books amounting to the astonishing number of upwards of five hundred million copies.

There is every reason to believe thousands upon thousands of souls have been converted during the past quarter of a century by the instrumentality of these religious publications, which were remarkable for the pure and pointed evangelical truth they contained; in fact, the very marrow of the Gospel. It is said that, during thee years in which is depository sold for one shilling numberless packets of tracts that cost four shillings, his gratuitous expenditure for this item alone was several thousand pounds a year.

The death of his eldest and only son at the age of 17 or 18, about twenty years ago (he subsequently had another, who now survives him), was a marked epoch in his life of generosity. He afterwards stated that he had been amassing a fortune for that son; but he looked upon his death as an indication that he should no longer thus accumulate money, but spend it in the cause of Christ, and he adhered to this determination to the close of his life.

He always possessed, however, a large amount of capital invested in his business as a wholesale chemist (Bewley & Draper, Mary-street, Dublin), and in gutta-percha and other manufactories. This business brought him into connexion with the Transatlantic cable, in which he held a large share; and the recovery of the lost cable, some ten years ago, was a gain of many thousand pounds to him. He also, at one time, received large profits from his coal-mines in Germany. He possessed marked business ability, and administrative capacity and shrewdness.

At the time of the laying of the cable at Valentia, in Ireland, he gave a banquet to some 300 people connected with that undertaking; and after the repast, hymns were sung, prayers offered up, and addresses delivered by the Rev. H. Disney and the moderator of the Presbyterian Church and others. This was an intrepid act for Christ, as many were present who were papists or infidels.

In connexion with the great religious revival in Ireland in 1859, 1860, and 1861, Mr. Bewley built Merrion Hall, in Dublin, at a cost of about £25,000; and Mr. Denham Smith, the eminent evangelist, ministered for a lengthened period to the congregations that met there.

About that period he also began Conferences once or twice every year at Dublin, and he generally sent a five-pound note a-piece to about fifty ministers and laymen, with the invitation to attend; and they were hospitably entertained during their stay. On the third day of the Conference the meetings were usually held in Mr. Bewley's conservatory, situated at his beautiful residence at Willow Park.

Remains of the Merrion Hall, Dublin following a fire in 1991. It was largely funded by Henry Bewley and used as a meeting place for Plymouth Brethren. There is now a hotel on the site.
(from the Dublin City Council Photographic Collection)

It is to be hoped his biography may yet be written; and doubtless Mr. Denham Smith, Mr. T. B. Smithies, and others, with whom he was intimately associated, might give many interesting details of his life.

The great motto of his life was, "in things essential unity; in things non-essential, liberty; in all things, charity." He loved and longed to be a peace-maker between contending sects of Christians; and none who knew him can doubt that the peculiar blessing of the peacemakers will be his.

His funeral, which took place in Mount Jerome Cemetery, in the neighbourhood of Dublin, was very largely attended by ministers and members of all evangelical denominations, thus testifying their sincere respect and sorrow for the loss of this servant of the Lord. The day was lovely; the sun shone brightly on the scene. The birds and breezes made music in the cemetery trees, and words full of comfort and hope fell from the lips of those who took part in the simple service around the grave. - Christian Herald.

Addendum II
For the benefits of people, who like me are unaware of the remarkable facets of this man, the following is included in full

(from http://antiquecannabisbook.com/chap2B/Shaughnessy/Shaughnessy.htm)

The Remarkable W.B. O'Shaughnessy

By Michael R. Aldrich, Ph.D. (Spring 2006)

Author's note: this essay is dedicated to Tod H. Mikuriya, M.D., who turned me on to the works of W.B. O'Shaughnessy more than 30 years ago, and changed my life.

Many medical marijuana patients know that Dr. William Brooke O'Shaughnessy (1809-1889) introduced cannabis to modern Western medicine, but know little else of this Irishman's extraordinary life. In addition to his pioneering work on cannabis therapy, O'Shaughnessy invented the modern treatment for cholera, laid the first telegraph system in Asia, and made significant contributions to pharmacology, chemistry, drug clinical trials, science education, and underwater engineering. There has never been a full biography of him, yet his genius shines through 19th-century science in all those fields.

O'Shaughnessy was born in Limerick in 1809 (or late 1808), and displayed such intelligence during his schooling that he was admitted to the best medical school in the world at the University of Edinburgh in 1827-quite unusual for a poor Irish lad barely 18 years old. At Edinburgh he studied medicine, chemistry, and forensic toxicology with Sir Robert Christison, and anatomy with Professor Robert Knox, dissecting cadavers supplied by the infamous grave-robbers Burke and Hare.

TREATMENT FOR CHOLERA 1831

Graduating with an MD from the University of Edinburgh in 1829, O'Shaughnessy tutored chemistry students for a year, then moved to London, but was unable to get a license to practice medicine there. So he set up his own forensic toxicology lab, doing chemical analyses of blood, feces, urine and tissue for doctors, hospitals, and the courts. (Need work? Invent your own CSI lab.)

An outbreak of cholera in 1831, possibly introduced to England by soldiers returning from India, led O'Shaughnessy to investigate the blood of cholera victims. At the time it was not even known what caused cholera, an insidious disease that kills by dehydration due to uncontrollable diarrhoea and vomiting. (Vibrio cholerae was first isolated in 1883 by the German scientist Robert Koch. Its primary vector of transmission is drinking sewage-contaminated water, as shown by John Snow in 1849. Snow plotted the incidence of cholera in London on a map, discovered that it clustered around public water pumps, and when he famously broke the handle off the Broad Street pump, the epidemic in that neighbourhood subsided. It was the beginning of modern epidemiology.)

On December 29, 1831, O'Shaughnessy sent to The Lancet "one of the shortest and yet most significant letters ever sent to the journal", presenting the results of his blood analyses. He showed that "the copious diarrhoea of cholera leads to dehydration, electrolytic depletion, acidosis and nitrogen retention," and that "treatment must depend on intravenous replacement of the deficient salt and water".

In January, 1832, O'Shaughnessy published the details of his discovery, and doctors began testing his suggestion-successfully saving the lives of nearly half their patients. Intravenous electrolyte-replacement fluid therapy is still the modern treatment for cholera, using the same principle as contemporary athletes who drink Gatorade® to prevent dehydration. Moreover it was one of the first experiments in treatment by i.v. injection, before the invention of the hypodermic needle. It was the 19th-century equivalent of finding a cure for AIDS without knowing what HIV was.

OFF TO INDIA, 1833

O'Shaughnessy's discovery came to the attention of Sir William Russell, M.D., a British physician who had returned from Calcutta to form the Cholera Commission in London. He obtained for O'Shaughnessy a commission as an assistant surgeon in the East India Company-a plum assignment for English aristocrats, much less a poor Irishman. O'Shaughnessy arrived in Calcutta in 1833.

Posted to various medical units of the Bengal Army, O'Shaughnessy moved around a lot, learned the rudiments of several native languages, made friends with local Ayurvedic and Islamic physicians, and helped found the Calcutta Medical College, where he became Professor of Chemistry and Materia Medica.

He was appointed first assistant to the opium agent at Behar and later (1840) chemical examiner for the Raj. In 1836 he married Margaret O'Shaughnessy and also arranged for his cousin, Richard O'Shaughnessy, to join him at the college. He wrote A Manual of Chemistry, in English, for his Indian students-one of the earliest textbooks of biochemistry-- and did experiments on electromagnetism and on the constituents of Indian medical plants, starting with opium. Almost as an aside, he invented a new way of extracting acids from charcoal to make gunpowder-a practical discovery much appreciated by the military.

In 1838 O'Shaughnessy discovered Narcotine (noscapine), a previously unknown alkaloid in opium, visited an opium den to see for himself how it was prepared, and wrote an elegant paper on "cases of real and suspected poisoning" in India in 1839. Then he widened his research into the Indian materia medica to demonstrate "the valuable therapeutic properties of some Indian vegetable remedies" ... (and) "to construct a pharmacopoeia for the poor to whom the costly remedies of Europe and South America are inaccessible" .

O'Shaughnessy's work over the next few years produced the first textbooks of Indian medicinal plants in English, the Bengal Dispensatory (1841-42) and the Bengal Pharmacopoeia (1844).

All three of O'Shaughnessy's books during this period were magnificent early examples of teaching science to students for whom English was a foreign language. Having textbooks in English overcame the barriers imposed by the 360 different languages spoken in India, making biochemistry and Indian medical lore available in schools and libraries throughout the subcontinent- indeed, throughout the Empire. This type of education, imperialist to the core, is one reason that English is spoken all over the world today.

INTRODUCTION OF CANNABIS, 1839

Although cannabis was mentioned occasionally by early botanists and explorers describing their travels, little was actually known about cannabis therapy in Europe and America until O'Shaughnessy read a paper to a group of students and scholars of the Medical and Physical Society of Calcutta in 1839. The 40-page paper was a model of modern pharmaceutical research. It included a thorough review of the history of cannabis medical uses by Ayurvedic and Persian physicians in India and the Middle East-some of whom (his local sources) were doubtless in the room.

O'Shaughnessy conducted the first clinical trials of cannabis preparations, first with safety experiments on mice, dogs, rabbits and cats, then by giving extracts and tinctures (of his own devising, based on native recipes) to some of his patients. O'Shaughnessy presented concise case studies of patients suffering from rheumatism, hydrophobia, cholera, and tetanus, as well as a 40-day-old baby with convulsions, who responded well to cannabis therapy, leaping from near death to "the enjoyment of robust health" in a few days.

O'Shaughnessy appended a paper by his cousin Richard on a case of tetanus cured by a cannabis preparation. He also warned that a peculiar form of delirium may be "occasioned by continual Hemp inebriation," and cautioned doctors to start with low doses. O'Shaughnessy concludes that these clinical studies have "led me to the belief that in Hemp the profession has gained an anti-convulsive remedy of the greatest value."

Exhausted from preparing three large books, and from his double duties as professor and chemical examiner, O'Shaughnessy took a "sick leave" furlough back to England in 1841. He brought quantities of hemp for the Pharmaceutical Society and specimens of Cannabis indica and Nux vomica back to the Royal Botanical Gardens at Kew, and shepherded the reprints of his article in the Provincial Medical Journal. Chemists vied with each other to make potent tinctures and extracts with O'Shaughnessy's recipes, struggling to identify and isolate the active principles of the drug-- a goal not achieved until 1964 .

Sir J. Russell Reynolds, M.D., personal physician to Queen Victoria, recommended it to his patients for menstrual cramps, and O'Shaughnessy was elected a Fellow of the Royal Society in 1843.

O'Shaughnessy's paper caused a sensation when it became widely available in England. He had introduced a wonder drug to treat some of the most awful medical conditions of the 19th century. Physicians throughout Europe and America tried cannabis for a huge variety of illnesses. As Dr. Lester Grinspoon noted in Marihuana Reconsidered (1971:15), "Between 1839 and 1900 more than one hundred articles appeared in scientific journals describing the medicinal properties of the plant."

A similar thing happened when Dr. Tod Mikuriya reprinted O'Shaughnessy's paper as the lead article in Marijuana: Medical Papers 1839-1972 (1973)-it reinvigorated medical interest in the drug and sparked hundreds more articles on cannabis therapy into the 21st century.

THE INDIAN TELEGRAPH

O'Shaughnessy had done experiments in electric telegraphy as early as 1838, without exciting much government interest. Nevertheless, his carrying of electric signals under Calcutta's River Hooghly in insulated iron wires in 1838 was the first successful underwater telegraphy in the world. O'Shaughnessy doubtless knew of Samuel F. B. Morse's successful transmission ("What hath God wrought?") in the United States in 1844, but his work was completely independent of Morse's.

When O'Shaughnessy returned to India in 1844, he effectively changed careers. Officially, he was assayist for the Mint, in charge of unifying India's dozens of different currencies with standard coinage. He also tackled a tricky problem in engineering: how to lay out telegraph lines in a country frequently ravaged by electrical storms, a land of treacherous rivers and bays, snake-infested swamps, wild jungles and arid plains, many languages, religions and cultures, dangerous assassins (the Thugs) and insurrectionist armies - Sikh, Muslim, and Hindu -- fighting desperately to keep the British from taking their lands.

O'Shaughnessy finally found his champion in Lord Dalhousie-James A.B. Ramsey, tenth Earl and first Marquess of Dalhousie (1812-1860)-who arrived as governor-general of India in 1848. Dalhousie is remembered as the man who expanded British control of India to practically its modern borders through military campaigns in the Punjab, Oudh, Kashmir, and Burma, and by annexing the lands of rajas who had no male heirs. He is even more famous, however, as the governor-general who built the civil infrastructure of modern India-the railroads, telegraph, public education (in English), cheap postage, irrigation and canals, suppression of thuggee and suttee (wives burning themselves on their husband's funeral pyre), and other programs to unite the country under the Raj.

Dalhousie learned of O'Shaughnessy's idea of stringing the telegraph across India and instantly espoused it as his own. The Dictionary of National Biography says, "The introduction of the electric telegraph was Dalhousie's idea, and was carried out entirely upon his recommendation." He named O'Shaughnessy the first superintendent (later director-general) of telegraphy, and provided funding in 1850-52 for O'Shaughnessy to try an experimental line between Alipore (south of Calcutta) and Diamond Harbour. This first line was 27 miles long at a time when the only telegraph line in England was just 18 miles long (Gorman 1971).

The real challenge for O'Shaughnessy was to invent a telegraph that did not rely on copper wires, which were used in England and America but were too fragile for use in India. He had learned this in 1838, when fierce thunderstorms tore up his copper lines. Instead, he substituted iron rods 3/8 of an inch in diameter, carried underground in cement and overground mounted on bamboo poles. These were practically immune from damage by the elements, and "are not injured, although passengers, bullocks, buffaloes and elephants trample on them." (O'Shaughnessy 1852: 5.)

Moreover, the overground lines required no insulation: "The moment the rain falls we are almost safe, as the lightning which strikes the line escapes by the wet posts to the ground." He supervised the laying of seven routes in Bengal-including re-crossing the turbulent Hooghly with this new system-and in 1852 triumphantly gave Dalhousie his official Report on the Electric Telegraph between Calcutta and Kedgeree.

DALHOUSIE'S SUPPORT

Dalhousie understood it immediately-a drastic decrease in the time it took for British military outposts to communicate with each other, as well as the potential for colonial business and trade. He sent O'Shaughnessy back to England for supplies, and ordered British officers to help him pursue his dream - the construction of lines to Agra, Bombay, the Punjab, and Madras.

While in England, O'Shaughnessy may have gone on the one-day (May 22, 1853) voyage of the *HMS William Hutt*, which laid a submarine telegraph linking Ireland with Scotland. With Dalhousie's support, O'Shaughnessy won Company approval for the project, trained 60 officers assigned to help him, wrote an instruction manual for native workers, sailed back to India, and commenced construction of the telegraph in November, 1853.

Only four months later, Dalhousie wrote: "An event has occurred which is of infinite public moment, and which almost deserves to be regarded as historical. In November last we began to lay the electric telegraph. Five days ago I received a message from Agra- 800 miles distant-transmitted in one hour and 50 minutes! ... In a short time we shall complete the line to Bombay, and thus in a few months we shall have reduced the period of communication with England from 35 to 26 days. The results of this in peace or war outrun calculation." (Baird 1910: 293.)

In January, 1855 Dalhousie added: "Yesterday the Bengal railway was opened for 122 miles... Two days before, the electric telegraph was opened to the public from Calcutta to Bombay, to Madras, and to Attock on the Indus. Fifteen months ago not a yard of this was laid, or a signaler trained. Now we have 3050 miles opened. The communication between Calcutta and Madras, direct by land, a month ago, took 12 days-- yesterday a communication was made, round by Bombay, in two hours. Again, I ask, are we such slow coaches out here?" (Baird 1910: 336.)

Another 1,000 miles were laid in 1855. It was truly an amazing feat. In less than two years, O'Shaughnessy had strung the first telegraph system in Asia, using native labour and materials, which cut the speed of communications around India from weeks to hours. In addition to bamboo posts, O'Shaughnessy used stone obelisks to carry the heavy rods over rugged terrain, and invented an insulation system using a cement of rosin and sand wrapped in pitched yarn for the underwater sections.

Copper wires were used where feasible, and O'Shaughnessy devised simple sending and receiving apparatus that native signalers-mostly teenagers-- could employ with ease. Unlike his 1838 experiments, which conveyed messages by sending a shock through the wire into the receiver's hand, O'Shaughnessy's signals activated a pointer that alternated right or left depending on the direction of the current. He later (1857) invented a cryptographic code for transmission of secret messages (military or business).

Finally, based on his years of experience with native signallers, O'Shaughnessy insisted that Morse's instruments be adopted in India, much to the distress of Cooke and Wheatstone, who had a monopoly on telegraph services in England. As Professor Mel Gorman of the University of San Francisco has pointed out, "It is impossible to imagine the foundation of a telegraph in mid-19th-century India with the complicated and expensive instruments of the Cooke-Wheatstone type." (Gorman 1971:592.) O'Shaughnessy's genius lay in designing a system that was crude, cheap, easy to learn, and appropriate for the immense distances it had to span throughout the subcontinent.

Neither O'Shaughnessy nor Dalhousie could have done it alone. O'Shaughnessy had the technical know-how, and Dalhousie the political clout, to get the project funded by the Crown. Together, they built 4,000 miles of homemade telegraph in less than two years. The introduction of the telegraph, an advanced Western technology into a colonial environment, was in some sense the opposite of his introduction of cannabis into Western medicine. O'Shaughnessy was adept at relaying scientific information in both directions, and therein lies his glory.

Dalhousie, severely ill, was forced to return to England in 1855, and in the first letter he wrote when he landed at Southampton in 1856, he notes that one officer he recommended for knighthood had already been honoured by the Queen, and "I am now going to fight for O'Shaughnessy (Director-General of Telegraphs) and Stevenson (built the first railway)." As a result, O'Shaughnessy was knighted by Queen Victoria in 1856.

While in England being knighted (March 1856 to December 1857), O'Shaughnessy met Samuel F.B. Morse and many other telegraph experts such as Charles Tilston Bright, who had led the 1853 expedition to lay the telegraph between Ireland and Scotland. O'Shaughnessy and Morse "became good friends in London in 1856 and on the 1857 Atlantic Cable expedition". This was the voyage of the HMS Agamemnon and the USS Niagara, the first attempt to lay telegraph across the Atlantic, which ended disastrously when the cable broke after only four days at sea.

The telegraph proved its worth to the Crown in 1857 during the Sepoy Mutiny, when hundreds of native soldiers rebelled against their British officers (allegedly because beef and pig fat were used to grease their cartridges) and captured the British posts at Calcutta and Delhi. A message got through to Army units stationed north and south of Delhi before the telegraph lines were cut, alerting the Raj to the uprising and enabling them to send troops quickly to quell the mutiny. Sir John Lawrence, commander of British forces in the Punjab, later wrote a poem, "The Telegraph Saved India" (for the British Empire).

UNSOLVED MYSTERIES

O'Shaughnessy returned to India to supervise the rebuilding of the telegraph lines destroyed by the mutineers, and to train his successors. He departed India for London for the last time in 1860. There he suddenly divorced his wife, married another (Julia Greenly), changed his name to Sir William O'Shaughnessy Brooke–perhaps to gain an inheritance from the Brooke side of his family–and dropped out of sight. There are many mysteries surrounding the last years of his life; we know nothing about what he actually did for 29 years before his death in 1889.

Dr. Mikuriya, following a lead that O'Shaughnessy Brooke was on the board of the Indo-European Telegraph Company, thinks that he may have travelled for them as an expert on laying lines in challenging terrains, particularly underwater. His friend Charles T. Bright was in charge of the Indo-European Telegraph to connect India to Europe through Turkey, and O'Shaughnessy's stay in England in 1857 had been extended pending arrangements for a line to India through Asiatic Turkey. One can only imagine the conversations between two geniuses–O'Shaughnessy and Bright–who fast-forwarded the 19th century into the 20th-century world of almost instant intercontinental communications, a feat only surpassed by the global Internet of the 21st century.

His gravestone in Southsea (Portsmouth, England) reads simply: "In Loving Memory of Sir Wm. O'S. Brooke, died January 8, 1889 in his 80th year."

Chapter 2

The Moves to Link Europe and America By Submarine Cable

The expedition of 1857

In the 1830s there had been an attempt to turn Valentia island into an Atlantic port. For this purpose there were proposals to link it by rail with Dublin and Wexford as transit points for the British mainland. The scheme did not materialise and the largely agricultural community of tenant farmers lived quietly for another quarter of a century before being disturbed by the frenzied activity of 1857, which would mark the uncertain beginnings of an enterprise that was to become an important part of island life during the next hundred or so years.

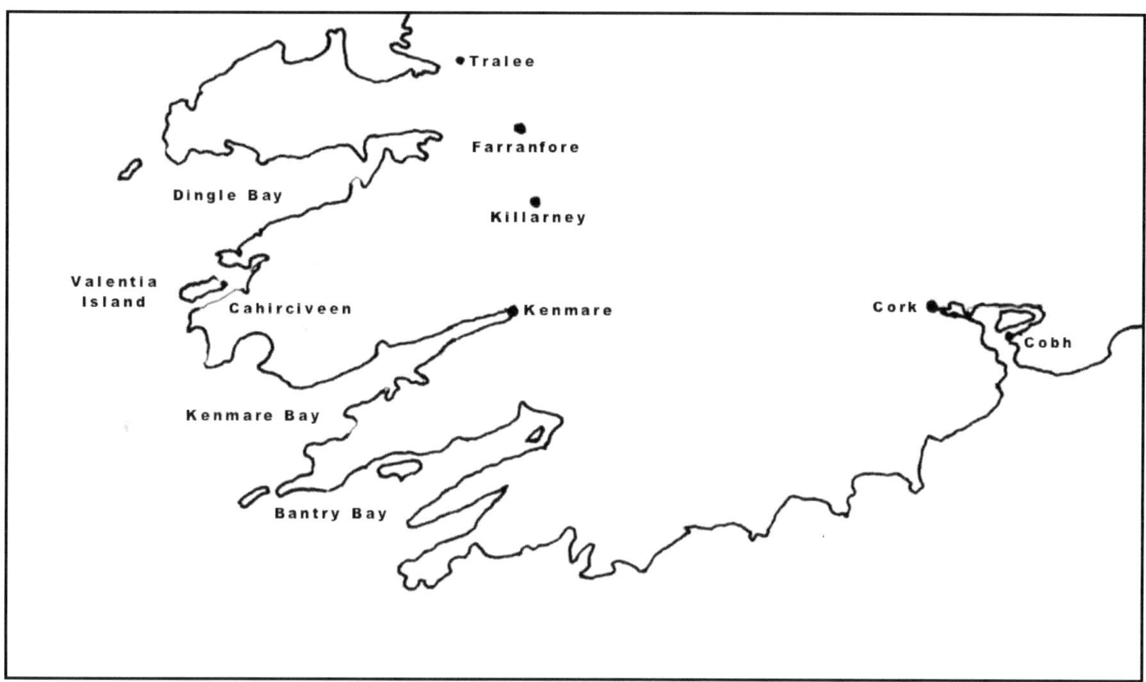

A map of county Cork and county Kerry showing some key locations in this story

The vicinity around the Iveragh* peninsula was an obvious location for a trans-Atlantic terminus, but social factors played a part. Charles Bright, in his book on submarine cables, mentions that his uncle, Edward Bright, Manager of the Magnetic Telegraph Co., together with some of his staff, visited the area and examined various harbours and beaches between Dingle and Bantry Bay. They chartered a fishing boat for the purpose and after considering the question of freedom from anchorages, rocks, soft, protected landing, together with the available Admiralty soundings, declared Valentia Bay as the most suitable locality.

John Lecky, whose father managed the slate quarry on Valentia Island, recalled much later

* The largest of the peninsulae that can be seen on the map.

> The British and Irish Magnetic Telegraph Company got the contract for the land wire and it was brought down from Killarney to the White Strand. The engineer B.D. Watlock[**] proved to be a great friend of ours, such a jovial fellow, all loved him. He erected huts for offices at the White Strand . . ."

During their investigations they would have paid a courtesy call on the local landlord, Sir Peter Fitzgerald, who held the title, Knight of Kerry[**] (Kerry is one of the 32 counties of Ireland and covers the area which includes Valentia). Valentia was fortunate to have had a man such as Sir Peter. It was he who had been the prime mover in the Atlantic port idea. He owned the slate quarry and was a good salesman for its products overseas. He had developed the Glanleam estate, which boasted many subtropical plants not found elsewhere at those latitudes. Daphne Pochin-Mould, in her book on Valentia, mentions that he was an active writer of letters on matters relating to political and religious problems of the time. She quotes the first lines of a letter to Fitzgerald from his daughter, Kate.

> Dearest Papa, I am not going to say a single word about C....h or L..D for fear you should put my letter into your book.....

We are particularly lucky that he retained most of his correspondence. One of his letter books relating to the earlier part of the cable era was subsequently in the possession of STC (Standard Telephones & Cables) and has been an important source of the information presented here.

Pochin-Mould also quotes from a letter which he wrote to the *Pall Mall Gazette* (11 Nov 1869). This summarises the problems which he had to face as an active Irish landlord and gives some insight into the reasons for his enthusiasm for the telegraph project.

> My father, on coming of age in 1795, divided the whole of his estate in this island (Valentia), consisting of (bog and mountain included) about 5,600 statute acres, among sixteen substantial tenants. This was no case of unequal bargaining between the rich and poor, the powerful and the weak. The lessee (one of whom was no less a man then the father of the late celebrated Daniel O'Connell) were quite in a position to deal on a par with the lessor, who gave to all of them leases at very moderate rents, and for terms, in no instance, of less then three lives or thirty one years, binding them by the strictest covenants to build slated dwellings, to effect other specified improvements, to reside on the lands, and not to sublet or divide. When I became owner of the property in 1853, I found every one of the stipulated dwellings in ruins or nearly so, the estate

---

[**] Benjamin Watlock was still employed by the Magnetic Telegraph Co in 1865/6. His recent passing was noted in an exchange of Christmas Greetings in 1882 between James Graves at Valentia and F. Perry at Heart's Content (see *Cable Talk: Relations between the Heart's Content and Valentia cable stations 1866 - 1886* D. de Cogan Newfoundland Quarterly, **28** (1993) 37 - 43.

[**] http://en.wikipedia.org/wiki/Knight_of_Kerry reports that " Knight of Kerry, also called the Green Knight, is one of three Anglo-Irish hereditary knighthoods, all of which existed in Ireland since feudal times. The others are the White Knight (Fitzgibbon Family) and the Knight of Glin (Black Knight)."

divided among 298 holders of land and 205 cottiers, or cabin holders, most of whom were of the very poorest class, the holdings averaging from eight to ten acres of quasi-arable land.

Without his continuous efforts the cable landing site would undoubtedly have been located elsewhere. As it was, the island, in spite of the comforts of Glanleam House and the village of Knightstown, was not the first choice of Bright and his colleagues. White Strand by Ballycarberry Point on the mainland nearby seemed to them to be the most suitable place, and the Magnetic Co. arranged to connect it to their telegraph network in preparation for the great event.

Meanwhile, ships were assembled in preparation for the expedition. The Americans lent the USS *Niagara*, a 5,200 ton single screw steam frigate under the command of Wiliam L. Hudson. It was to carry half of the cable. The *Susquehanna*, the largest paddle steamer in the US navy, was to act as escort. The British Government provided HMS *Agamemnon,* a 3200 ton man of war, which had been the flagship during the bombardment of Sevastapol in the Crimea two years previously. She was to be accompanied by HMS *Leopard.*
The *Niagara* arrived in England in May 1857 carrying Cyrus Field, Samuel Morse and two Russian naval officers, who were invited along as observers. Although there were no official arrangements for a press presence, John Mullaly of the *New York Herald* was assigned to act as private secretary to Professor Morse during the expedition. On arrival it was discovered that *Niagara's* draught prevented her from approaching the cable works of Glass Elliot and Co. at Greenwich. Accordingly she was sent to Liverpool to take on the section of cable that had been manufactured by R.S. Newall of Birkenhead. The Greenwich cable was loaded on board the *Agamemnon.*

The final loading and departure of the ships was attended by great pomp and pageantry. On 24 July 1857 the *Times* reported that the loading of the ships being complete, the occasion was marked by a fête champêtre at Belvidere House (at that time the home of Sir Culling Eardley*). Those present included all the staff who had been involved in the manufacture and loading of the cable. Three pints of beer were allowed for each man, but this ran out before the speeches, which were frequently interrupted by noises from the children. Amongst the speeches, Cyrus Field read out a letter from President Buchanan saying that he should feel honoured if the first message should be one from Queen Victoria to himself and he would endeavour to answer it in a spirit and manner becoming a great occasion.

The four ships assembled at Queenstown (Cobh) harbour on 30 July 1857 and the electricians used the opportunity to test the continuity of the cable by joining that in *Agamemnon* to that in the *Niagara* to form a continuous length of 2,500 miles (see Addendum to this chapter). The tests were successfully completed over the course of two days and the ships then moved on to Valentia harbour. There were a number of other ships waiting there when they arrived. The steamer *Advice* was to land the shore end. *Willing Mind* was to act as a picket boat and Capt. Dayman, having completed his soundings a month previously, was to lead the way. Amongst the technical men who were to accompany the expedition were Charles Bright, the Company Engineer. He was assisted by William E. Everett of the US Navy who had designed *Niagara*'s cable handling and paying out gear. Dr Whitehouse and Mr C.V. DeSauty were to be in charge of the electrical department. In the event

---

* An evangelical campaigner who died in 1863 from an adverse reaction to a small-pox vaccination.

(and not for the last time) Whitehouse pleaded poor health and remained at Valentia. Samuel Morse, who did not withstand the journey well, and William Thomson were to act as observers and technical consultants.

An historical picture of the great events just before photography largely replaced the artist can be obtained by merging the E.W. Cooke[+] drawings in the IET Archives with the details in Capt. Brine's map as is shown in the following sequence of images. The first below shows Knightstown where the 1858 cable was brought in as per the map. As an insert we can see a view of Knightstown as seen by Cooke from the mainland shore.

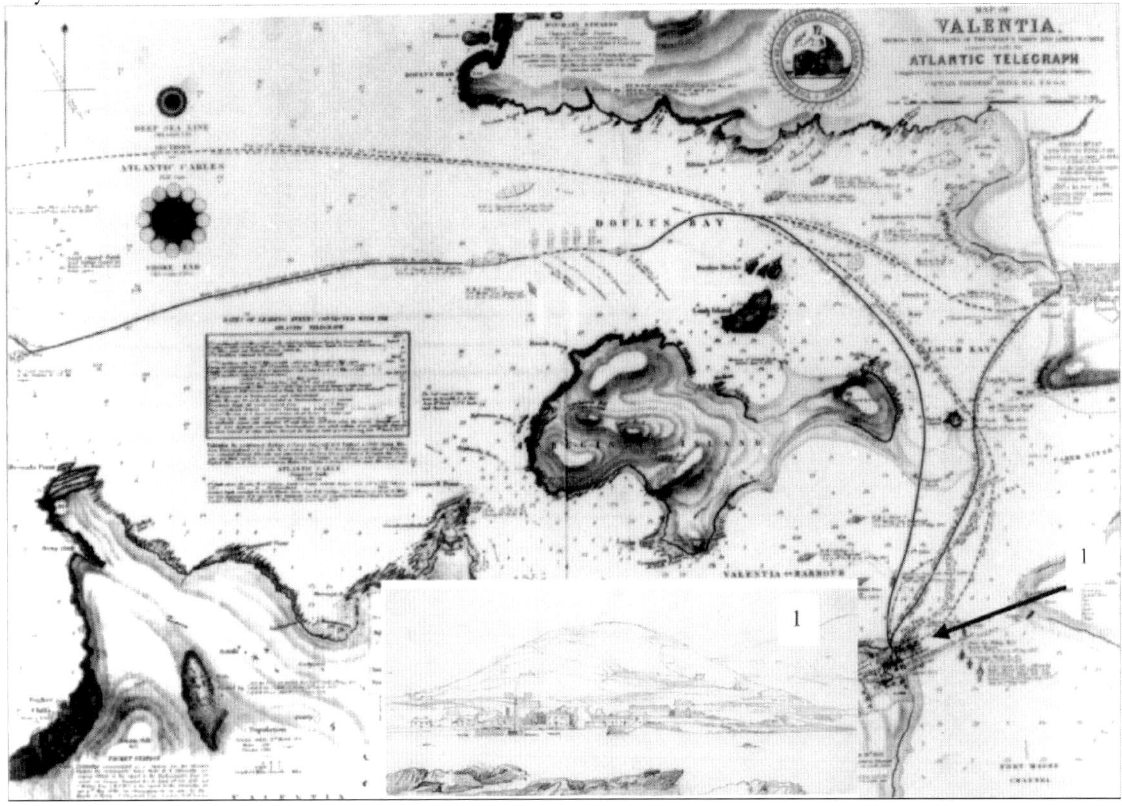

[+] So accurate are Cooke's sea-side depictions that earth scientists are now using them to determine the extent of coastal erosion (New Scientist 2 August 2008 pp 50, 51).

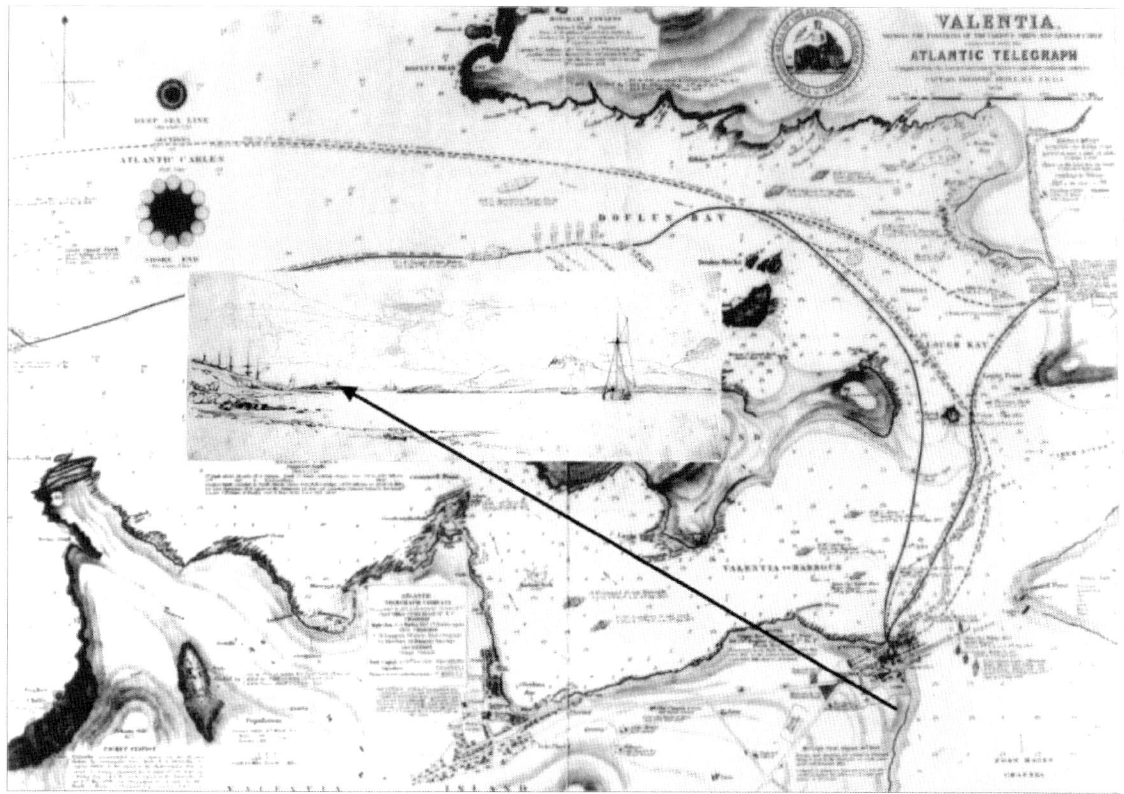

Super-position of the Cooke drawings from the IET Archives on Brine's map. The arrows show the direction of the view with the observer being located furthest from the arrow-head

Some of the ships moved around quite a lot, but the correlation of the Cooke drawing with the Brine map would suggest that HMS *Cyclops* is on the right, with HMS *Leopard* and USS *Susquehanna* just behind the Reenagiveen Point on the left.

John Lecky records

> "In 1857 when the ships arrived we had so many visitors to the Island it has always been a wonder where they all got accommodation. Our cousin Margaret Lecky came to pay us a visit and it so happened a fellow passenger on the car was a little old foreign gentleman with whom she got into conversation. He did not know where he was going and he had not made any arrangements but our cousin said Mr Lecky was sending a pinnace for her and he could come too. He was the, at one time, well known Dr Hamel who was employed by the Russian government to find out all the scientific information he could. Hence his visit to Valencia for the Atlantic cable. There was no room in the Hotel for him so my father had a bed made up for him in the little 4 roomed garden house and he had his meals with us. The garden house had no locks to the doors, only the old fashioned thumb latch so the Dr could not lock his door, but to protect himself he opened a blade of his penknife and put it through the latch on to the thumb piece, edge up, so that if anyone tried to get in he would cut his thumb badly.
>
> He was an amusing visitor but he would not give us any information. One day Father asked him how the scent of Russian leather was made. Whether or not he knew we do not know but he

said "you take one skin of your leather and you put it between two skins of Russian and press them and then your skin will smell like ours"! One day at dinner he took up the pepper caster, but it was empty. Father sent it out to be filled and gave it to the Dr who would not take it "Providence does not wish me to have pepper today". Some of the cable operators had served in the Crimea and one of them had a Crimean medal which whenever he met the Dr he took great care to have displayed prominently on his coat. Our dear Miss Maria Fitzgerald (*daughter of the Knight of Kerry*) lived at Reenglas and she entertained the many visitors as often as she could and amongst them the old Dr who being old, lonely and rather a despised foreigner elicited her profoundest pity . . . "

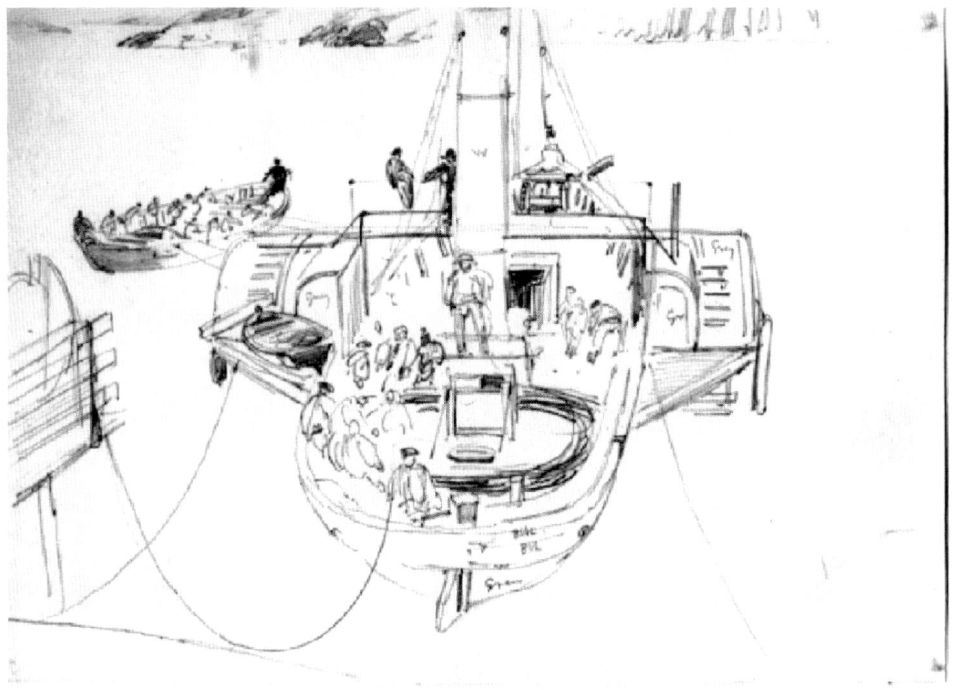

Paddle steamer, *Willing Mind* taking on the shore end of the 1857 cable for transfer inshore. Note the way in which Cooke has annotated the different parts as if he had a plan to colour the picture at some later date. (from the E.W. Cooke drawings in the IET Archives)

Shore end being taken from *Willing Mind* and transported inshore on rowed boats The small sail-boat looks particularly like one of those described by John Lecky.
(from the E.W. Cooke drawings in the IET Archives)

Shore end being shipped towards White-strand, Ballycarberry.
(from the E.W. Cooke drawings in the IET Archives)

Landed cable and cable jointing in progress. (from the E.W. Cooke drawings in the IET Archives)

On the 5th of August all was ready. The Lord Lieutenant, Lord Morpeth, stood on the shore surrounded by his staff in uniform, directors of railway and telegraph companies and a great many local dignitaries. Work started at 2 pm. American sailors waded ashore with the cable in a symbolic gesture of cooperation.

In a letter to the Times (28 May 1926) Lecky recalled

> . . . The shore end was brought and moored round six bulks of timber sunk in the sand. I wonder if they are still there? Lord Carlisle* made a speech . . .

* There is no inconsistency here. George Howard, Viscount Morpeth succeeded as 7th Earl Carlisle in 1848 and was Lord Lieutenant of Ireland from 1855 - 1858 and from 1859 - 1864.

Cable wound around timbers to isolate mechanical strains between the seaward cable and the electrical instruments on land. (from the E.W. Cooke drawings in the IET Archives)

A view of the interior of the tent at Ballycarberry Strand. The nature of dress might indicate that formal events were about to start. (from the E.W. Cooke drawings in the IET Archives)

Agamemnon's sailors were to land the westward end. At 8 pm Capt. Pennock of *Niagara* made the formal presentation to the Lord Lieutenant, who replied in a speech which according to Henry Field ended:

> Let us indeed hope, let us pray that the hopes of those who have set on foot this great design, may be rewarded by its entire success; and let us hope further, that this Atlantic Cable will, in all future time, serve as an emblem of that strong cord of love which I trust will always unite the British islands to the great continent of America.... And now, all my friends, as there can be no project or undertaking which ought not to receive the approbation and applause of the people, will you join with me in giving three hearty cheers for it
>
> (Loud cheering). Three cheers are not enough for me—they are what we give on common occasion—and as it is for the success of the Atlantic Telegraph Cable, I must have at least one dozen cheers.(Loud and protracted cheering).

The ships moved off the following morning, but the *Niagara* had only sailed five miles when the cable caught in the paying out machinery and parted. The cable was under-run[+] and spliced. After this they continued for some time at the more cautious speed of two knots. Later they increased their speed by stages to five knots. Continuous contact was maintained with Valentia for the purpose of testing continuity. Progress was reported to England and thence transmitted to America by westbound ships moving much faster then the cable squadron.

200 miles passed and a depth of 2000 fathoms was indicated when on the evening of Monday 10 August there was a sudden dead short and Valentia could no longer be contacted. After some minutes the fault cleared itself and the journey continued. Later in the night when the cable was running out at six knots, *Niagara* making only four, Charles Bright ordered the application of the brake. This stopped rather then slowed down the paying out machinery, and the cable snapped. There was little to do but return to port.

Before dispersing, Field arranged for the ships to undertake some experiments with mid-ocean laying. He also requested a meeting of the London directors to decide whether to have another try that year or to wait until the following summer. In the event, the second option was chosen and the ships stopped off at Plymouth and unloaded the cable for over-winter storage in a magazine which the Admiralty put at their disposal

Field returned to America and found his personal fortune in extreme jeopardy. The financial collapse of 1857 had brought destruction to a number of established and respected firms. However he managed to weather the storm, ready to make another attempt at the Atlantic during the following summer.

[+] The process of under-running involved returning to the shore, lifting the cable out of the water onto the deck and proceeding along the line of the cable, raising cable at the bow and lowering it over the stern until the damaged section was raised.

At Valentia, meanwhile, Sir Peter Fitzgerald was reaping the first fruits of his strenuous efforts. He had ensured that the landing of the shore end was a major local event. No one who was important enough had failed to get an invitation. His correspondence on the matter with people such as the Lord Lieutenant are still in existence. He had entertained lavishly and had looked after Whitehouse while the ships were at sea. On 7 August Whitehouse arranged to lay a cable between White Strand and Knightstown, so that on 23 August the Knight of Kerry had his first direct telegraph link with Dublin. This achievement, which must have made him the envy of all the landlords in the vicinity, was the first step towards ensuring Valentia Island's long-term prospects as the location for a permanent cable station.

Addendum

The electrical measurements of Dr E.O.W. Whitehouse

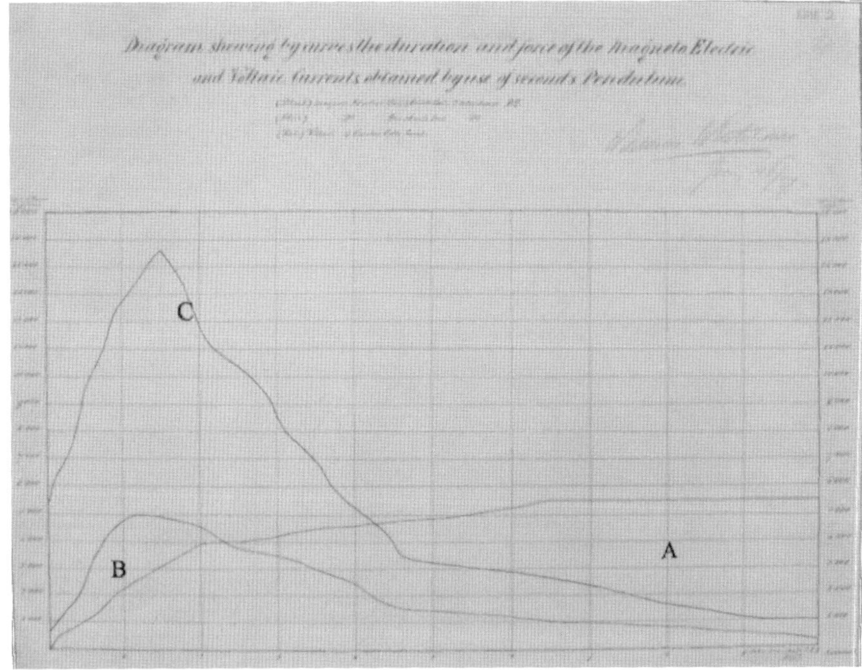

The figure above shows what are referred to as 'The Wroughton Curves' because they were discovered by Allan Green at the Science Museum Reserve Collection at Wroughton, near Swindon. It shows weight on the vertical axis and time along the horizontal. It is signed by Whitehouse, dated 16 July 1857 and probably represents one of the first recorded oscillograph traces. It is believed that it was made on the Atlantic cable, but Whitehouse gives no detail about the length of cable or the precise circuit that he used. Allan has made a 'best-guess' of the circuit which includes an electromagnet balance and a seconds pendulum. It would appear that Whitehouse applied a series of impulses (switch-on) and weighed the resulting potential as a function of time. Today we might call it a gated, or sampled measurement.

The plots are typical of a circuit which contains an inductor (L), a capacitor (C) and a resistor (R). A characteristic of LRC circuits is that the voltage/time profile is different depending on the relative magnitudes of the electrical parameters, L, R, and C.

Plot C in the figure is what would be expected from the charging of a distributed RC circuit (little or no L present), which is a perfect analogue for cables of that time. Plots A and B in the figure indicate the presence of inductance (L) and are most likely due to the large induction coils which Whitehouse used.

These hypotheses relating to the 1857/8 cables were tested using a computer simulation and the results are available in a paper by the author and Allan Green published by the Institution of Engineering and Technology (*IET Sci. Meas. Technol.*, **5**(4) (2011) 117–124).

Chapter 3

The 1858 Expedition

The promoters of the Atlantic Telegraph were now faced with a difficult task. £100,000 had been lost and during a time of international financial crisis it was going to be difficult to raise new capital. However, the Government support gave the directors sufficient confidence to order 700 miles of new cable. In order to expedite matters Field was appointed managing director with carte-blanche. One of his first actions was to request the US navy to permit Mr Everett to be seconded to the company with a view to devising an improved braking system. They agreed and Everett went to London where he was made general manager in charge of all technical operations. Using the facilities at the machine works of Easton and Amos at Southwark, he designed a paying out system with self-releasing brakes based on the invention of London engineer John Appold[*]. The brake was arranged so that it would automatically release at 1.5 tons, half the breaking strain of the cable.

William Thomson was meanwhile busying himself with all aspects of the project. He was working on the theoretical aspects and at the same time perfecting the first of his instruments that were to play such an important part in submarine telegraphy. He was already aware that if signalling were to be as fast as possible, then the amplitudes of the signals would have to be as small as could be detected. If this were not the case then time would be lost while the signal rose to its maximum value and then decayed away. He determined to design a lighter and more sensitive instrument. This was achieved by cementing a small mirror onto the deflecting coil instead of the conventional practice of using an needle. A narrow beam of light was directed towards the mirror which on deflection caused a spot to move along a graduated screen. This mirror galvanometer was protected by patent in February 1858.

On his return to Glasgow in 1857 Thomson had taken along some samples from the unlaid portion of the cable. His researches during the winter confirmed the intimate relationship between the electrical conductivity of the copper and its purity. When he communicated this information with the other directors they were quite apathetic; after all their electrician (Whitehouse) had informed them that the speed of signalling was not effected by the resistance of the conductor (how wrong he was). It was only when Thomson adopted an obstructionist attitude and opposed all other business at successive meetings that they listened to his insistence on proper testing and agreed to the insertion of a clause requiring "high conductivity" in the contract for the new length of cable. The contractors initially baulked at this clause, but eventually consented at an increased price. In order to ensure compliance Thomson arranged that the company have a testing laboratory at the factory, which is believed by many to have been one of the first examples of modern quality control in manufacture. By April he had a number of mirror galvanometers ready for use at both Valentia and Newfoundland.

---

[*] John George Appold, FRS (14 April 1800 - 31 August 1865), fur dyer and engineer, best known as the inventor of the curved-vane centrifugal pump.

On 13 April Thomson requested the directors to grant £2,000 towards new signalling instruments. On the 21st he received the reply "the directors having regard to the reports and observations of Mr Whitehouse and particularly to the financial state of the Company are of the opinion that it would not be expedient to advance so large a sum under present circumstances and therefore desire to postpone their decision upon the form of instrument to be ultimately used for working through the cable until the task of submerging it shall have been successfully completed". On the 23rd he wrote again with a request for £500 for instruments. The Board begrudgingly gave him authority to complete the instruments on hand but entreated him to keep costs to a minimum. On the 27th he sent an acknowledgement adding that he would not expect the Company to take his instruments unless they achieved a speed of three words per minute after the cable was laid. In his letter he also requested permission to be allowed to use the cable as coiled on ship to make some tests. The board, foreseeing problems, made the following formal minute:

> Ordered that Mr Whitehouse be requested to desire his assistants at Devonport to render Professor Thomson all possible attention and to follow his directions with respect to the experiments he desires to make on the cable. The same day the secretary is directed to address to Mr Whitehouse a letter, requesting him to inform the Board on which of the ships he intends to embark". On May 14 a letter is read from Mr Whitehouse advising the Board of his intention to embark on the *Agamemnon*, but expressing doubts as to his accompanying the experimental trial. "Ordered that Mr Whitehouse be informed that the Board desires his presence on board HMS *Agamemnon* during the experimental trip, and that he be requested to make his arrangements accordingly.

The experimental trial mentioned above had been the suggestion of Charles Bright. He advocated a mid-ocean splice so that each of the ships would have to travel only half the distance. This also had the benefit that any accidents or difficulties during the splice would involve the minimum loss of cable. The board accepted this and agreed to a trial in the deep waters of the Bay of Biscay. Accordingly, preparations were made for this to take place at the end of May. The United States Government once more put the *Niagara* at the Company's disposal, but the *Susquehanna* was unfortunately unable to act as escort on this occasion. She had been on station in the West Indies and had suffered an outbreak of yellow fever on board. Cyrus Field immediately went to the Admiralty and requested help from the First Sea Lord, Sir John Pilkington. In spite of their other commitments they were able to make available HMS *Valorous* and the surveying steamer *Porcupine*. Cable was loaded on board the *Niagara* and *Agamemnon*, but as the hold space on the latter was insufficient for the length that had to be carried, 250 tons were stored on deck. In the event this very nearly led to disaster.

View of *HMS Agamemnon* with cable stowed on deck
(From the Cooke drawings in the IET Archives)

The stowage took place during April and during this time the board received several disquieting reports concerning the condition of the cable. Although there is no precise mention as to the exact nature of the problem it states simply that many faults had to be cut out during transfer to the ships. The company secretary, George Saward, also put the following comment on record

> On arriving at Plymouth the condition of the electrical department was found to be such as to cause great anxiety to the Directors. They had given instructions to the electrician during the winter to employ the Company operators in constant practice upon the instruments which were supposed to be in preparation for final use in working through the cable; and as the whole of the latter was coiled in one building at Keyham, it was supposed that they would have the opportunity of sending and receiving messages through its whole length during several months and thus be prepared for all the peculiarities of a conductor so long and special in its character. The Directors were therefore greatly disappointed to find that not only had this not been done, but they found that the instruments were not in a state, nor of a nature calculated to work the cable to a commercial profit.

It is not clear what was meant by this last sentence, but it would suggest that the directors were by that time aware that the equipment which Whitehouse proposed to use was less then satisfactory.

The fleet sailed on 29 May, and in spite of the Board's specific instructions, Whitehouse excused himself at the last minute and remained on land. Meanwhile, William Thomson was almost the last man on board the *Agamemnon* as it sailed. He had been waiting for the completion of his marine mirror galvanometer which had been constructed during the previous two weeks. It was a special robust, but sensitive mirror instrument with which he planned to test the cable while at sea. All went well. Cables were spliced and buoyed and transferred from stern to bow; they also tested the practicability of paying out at the high speed of seven knots. Perhaps the most important thing which they had to test was a special splice jig that had to be designed to deal with a unique problem. During manufacture each company had built its half of the cable without regard to the other. It is usual practice for ropes to be made with a right-hand lay, but when Glass Elliot and Co. started work on the cable they found that the normal method of stowage in a ship would tend to unwind the outer serving. Accordingly, they decided on a left hand-lay, but nobody thought to inform R.S. Newall of Birkenhead of the change in direction. As one cable would have unwound the other at the mid-ocean splice, the jig, which measured several feet across, had to absorb the counteracting strains. The ships returned to Plymouth on June 3 and there was general satisfaction with the outcome of the trials.

The expedition set off in earnest on 10 June 1858. Charles Bright was chief engineer on *Agamemnon* with Messrs. Canning and Clifford as assistants, and DeSauty was electrician. Everett was engineer on the *Niagara*, which also carried Cyrus Field. Whitehouse, true to form, did not go to sea, but made his way to Valentia to await the arrival of the Irish end of the cable. One of his first actions on arrival at Valentia was to arrange to have an additional cable laid between Knightstown and the mainland. This can be seen in Capt. Brine's historiographical map with references to 1857 and 1858.

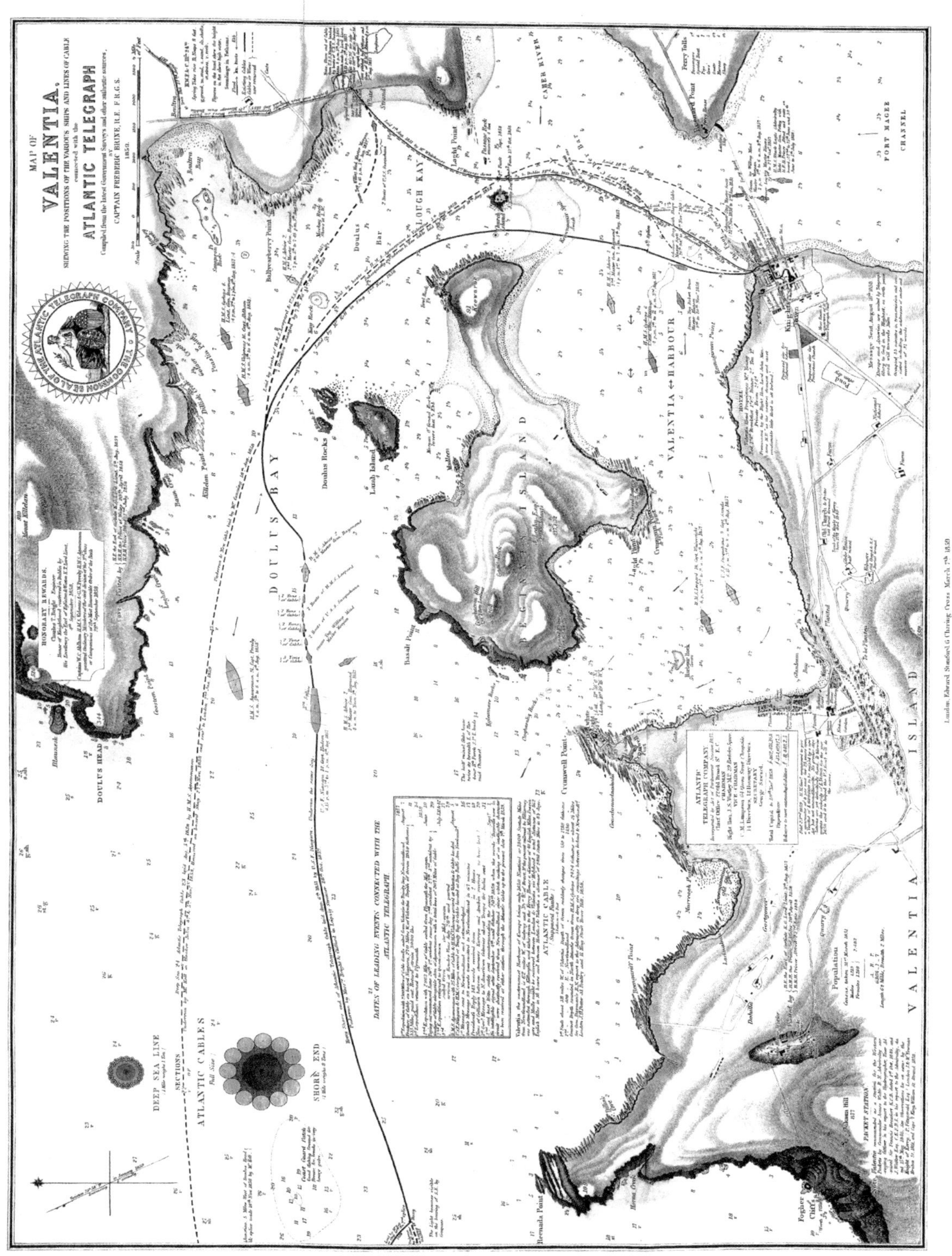
MAP OF
VALENTIA,
SHEWING THE POSITIONS OF THE VARIOUS SHIPS AND LINES OF CABLE
connected with the
ATLANTIC TELEGRAPH
Compiled from the latest Government Surveys and other authentic sources,
BY
CAPTAIN FREDERIC BRINE, R.E. F.R.G.S.
1858.
DOULUS BAY
VALENTIA HARBOUR
VALENTIA ISLAND
LOUGH KAY
CAHER RIVER
PORT MAGEE CHANNEL
ATLANTIC CABLES
DEEP SEA LINE
SHORE END
DOULUS HEAD
HONORARY REWARDS.

In anticipation of a successful outcome the artist E. W. Cooke was at Valentia with his son and his sketches (in the IET Archive) include some lighter sides to a Royal visit[*].

The upper picture show great excitement, but on the left we see buoy, presumably marking the line of cable. The Cooke collection of drawings in the IET Archive also includes a key to the lower sketch (shown below)

(From the Cooke drawings in the IET Archives)

[*] Alfred Ernest Albert (1844 - 1900), Victoria's second son, and much involved with the Navy. Created Duke of Edinburgh May 1866. Married Grand Duchess Marie of Russia 1874. In June 1893 became Admiral of the Fleet. On 22 June 1893 he succeeded to the Duchy of Saxe-Coburg and Gotha and thereafter lived in Germany where he died on 30 July 1900.

Sylvanus P. Thompson's classic biography of Lord Kelvin, as William Thomson was later to become, is worth quoting in detail here:

> At the request of the Directors Thomson consented to supervise the arrangements of the testing room on the *Agamemnon* in an honorary capacity. It was a difficult position, for he had little opportunity of making any tests on the state of the cable since it left the factory. His urgent representations as to the necessity of providing proper resistance coils and other testing apparatus on board had been ignored. Even his apparatus had only been allowed on sufferance to be inserted in the circuit on his arrival in Ireland. He was in no way responsible for the instruments provided by the official electrician for the tests on board, upon which reliance was supposed to be placed. But before consenting to go to sea he made it a condition that permission should be given to have his marine galvanometer in circuit, because by it he expected to have more definite information then he could have by watching the tests that were prepared.

Less than two days out they encountered a storm[*] of exceptional violence for which *Agamemnon* ,with 250 tons of cable on deck, was ill-suited. It was calculated that she lurched 45° to each side in quick succession, her deck planks gaped an inch apart opening and closing at every oscillation. The electrical testing room was awash. A portion of the deck cargo become dislodged and was badly damaged. One of the main beams on the lower deck broke and had to be shored up by screw jacks. At one time there were forty five men in the sick bay. The storm lasted eight days and it took two days to clear up the mess. Over 100 miles of cable on the deck had to be untangled and recoiled.

Painting by Henry Clifford of HMS *Agamemnon* during the storm. Image courtesy of J.C. Wall, Clifford's great-granddaughter.

---

[*] A graphic account of the storm was recorded by Nicholas Woods, the Times correspondent on the *Agamemnon.* It appeared in the *Times* on 11 August 1858. Woods and J.C. Parkinson were prominent correspondents in the expedition of 1866

Chaos in the cable hold during the storm (*Illustrated London News* 31 July 1858)

The ships assembled in mid Atlantic on 25 June at latitude 52° 2' N, longitude 33° 18' W. This was to serve as the rendezvous point for the four attempts of that year. Messages were exchanged between the ships and it was obvious that *Niagara* had not suffered quite so badly during the storm. On 26 June a splice was made and the paying out started. After six miles however the cable parted on board the *Niagara.* A second splice was made, but again the cable failed after about 80 miles had been paid out. On the 28th a third splice was made and all went well for a day. One hundred miles had been laid when the cable parted at the stern of the *Agamemnon*, the failure being at a point where it had been damaged during the storm. The men in the test room on the *Niagara* were immediately aware of what had happened and there was little to do but to cut, return to the rendezvous, and try again. Before ordering the cutting, Field, always ready to use the experience of failure to aid future success, decided to try an experiment. The brakes were put hard on in order to test the cable strength under real conditions. In spite of a registered strain of 4 tons and a fresh wind, the cable held for one hour and forty minutes before it eventually parted.

During the foggy days which followed, *Agamemnon* failed to find her partner at the rendezvous, and therefore returned to Queenstown to meet her, arriving there on July 12. No sooner had the ships met there than Thomson had the two halves of the cable temporarily spliced and transmitted signals through the total length, showing once more that the problems were mechanical and not electrical.

Immediately on their return to Queenstown, Field hurried to London for a meeting of the Directors, who had already been informed of the situation. Faced with a series of failures and no prospect of success they were divided in their views. The chairman, Sir William Brown, advocated the abandonment of the enterprise and the realization of the remaining assets. Against this, the men of action who had been out on the ocean advocated one final effort. Bright, Brett, Field, Whitehouse and Lampson were all eager to go on, as was Thomson, who had never despaired of ultimate success. Eventually, after acrimonious discussions which resulted in the resignation of the vice-chairman, the board ordered the immediate sailing of the fleet on what to all but themselves seemed a truly forlorn mission.

After coaling they steamed out of Queenstown. *Niagara,* with *Gorgon* and *Valorous,* left on July 17; *Agamemnon* left on the following day and used sail for a large part of the outward journey. This was done in order to ensure reasonable coal stocks for her cable laying duties. The ships met once more in mid-ocean on July 29 and paying out was started immediately. The weather was mostly bad and there were several temporary mishaps, which only the vigilance and energy of the staff prevented from becoming disasters. Because of the inertia of the paying-out wheels and machinery, the stress on the cable fluctuated with every rise and fall of the ship's stern, so that to prevent the cable from snapping the run of the wheels had to be regulated by hand at all times. Field's journey westward in *Niagara* is quoted by his brother, Henry in his history of the Atlantic Telegraph. It is interesting to see how it compared with the account of *Agamemnon's* more difficult eastward passage. From Henry Field:

> At forty five minutes past seven pm, ship's time, signals from the Agamemnon ceased and the tests applied by the electricians showed there was a want of continuity in the cable, but the insulation was perfect. Kept on paying out from the Niagara very slowly and constantly applying all kinds of electrical tests until ten minutes past nine, ship's time, when again commenced receiving perfect signals from the Agamemnon. At the same moment the same experience was going on the English ship.
>
> The next day there was fresh cause of alarm. It was found that the *Niagara* had run some miles out of her course. Comparing the distance run by observation and by patent log, there was a difference of sixteen miles and a third. With such a percentage of loss, the cable would not hold out to reach Newfoundland. This was alarming, but the explanation was obvious. The mass of iron in the ship had affected the compass, so that it no longer pointed to the right quarter of the heavens. Had the *Niagara* been alone on the ocean, this might have caused serious trouble. But now appeared the great advantage of an attendant ship. It was at once arranged that the *Gorgon* should go ahead and lead the way. As she had no cable on board, her compasses were subject to

no deviation[*]. Accordingly she took her position in the advance, keeping the line along the great circle, which was the prescribed route. From that moment on there was no variation, or but a very slight one. The two methods of computing the distance -by log and by observation- nearly coincided and the ship varied scarcely a mile from her course till she entered Trinity Bay.

It is not necessary to follow the whole voyage, for the record is the same from day to day. It is the same sleepless watching of the cable as it runs out day and night and at the same anxious estimate of the distance that still separates them from land. Communication is kept up constantly between the ships. Mr Field's journal contains entries like these: Saturday July 31st. By eleven o'clock had paid out from *Niagara* three hundred miles of cable; at forty five minutes past received signals from Agamemnon that they had paid out from her three hundred miles of cable: at thirty seven minutes past finished coil on the berth deck and commenced paying out from the lower deck. Monday, August 2nd. The *Niagara* getting light and rolling very much; it was not considered safe to carry sail to steady the ship, for in case of accident it might be necessary to stop the vessel as soon as possible.

Passed and signalled the Cunard steamer from Boston to Liverpool. Same day about noon imperfect insulation of cable detected in sending and receiving signals from *Agamemnon*, which continued until forty minutes past five, when all was right again. The fault was found to be in the wardroom, about sixty miles from the lower end, which was immediately cut out, and taken out of the circuit. Tuesday, August 3rd. At a quarter past eleven, ship's time, received signals from on board *Agamemnon*, that they had passed out from her seven hundred and eight miles of cable. In the afternoon and evening passed several icebergs. At ten minutes past nine pm, ship's time, *Niagara* in water of two hundred fathoms, and informed *Agamemnon* of the same. Wednesday, August 4th Depth of water less then two hundred fathoms. Weather beautiful, perfectly calm, *Gorgon* in sight. Sixty four miles from the telegraph house. Received signals from Agamemnon at noon that they had paid out from her nine hundred and forty miles of cable. Passed this morning several icebergs. Made the land off entrance to Trinity Bay at half past twelve. At half past two, we stopped sending signals to *Agamemnon* for fourteen minutes for the purpose of making a splice. At five pm saw Her Majesty's steamer *Porcupine* (which had been sent by the British Government to Newfoundland to watch for the telegraph ships) coming to us. At half past seven Captain Otter, of the *Porcupine*, came on board of the *Niagara* to pilot us to the anchorage near the telegraph house.

The *Agamemnon*, although her journey was shorter by 69 miles, sailed into strong head-winds most of the way. Shortly after leaving *Niagara*, there was an anxious encounter with a whale who threatened to become enmeshed in the cable. On two occasions there were near misses with American sailing ships who felt that they had right of way and were given quick lessons in maritime courtesy by warning shots from the escorts. There have been many contemporary accounts of the journey. Of these, the report by a junior member of the electrical staff (James Burn Russell, one of Thomson's

---

[*] This is of course not strictly true. All compasses on a ship are affected by deviation and corrections are applied accordingly. If indeed this was the cause of the problem, then why was *Agamemnon* not similarly troubled?

students at Glasgow University[*], which appeared in the Sydney Morning Herald gives an interesting insight into the electrical test room.

> The electrical test room is on the starboard side of the main deck forward. The arrangements have been altered several times in order to avoid the water which showers down from the upper deck. At one end of the little place the batteries are ranged on shelves and railed in. At the other end stands a table with various instruments arranged in electrical series. On one side stand the "detectors" of the old system, so called from being chiefly used in testing of faults; and Whitehouse's beautiful "magnetometer" called by some his "pet child". These are under the eye of one of the clerks on duty. On the opposite side of the table is Thomson's marine galvanometer, so called because it combines delicacy with perfect stability at sea. It is closed up in a plain deal box, which is placed on a frame, equally primitive, attached to springs. Yet this little "Jack-in-the-box", as we often call it, does the work of every instrument on the table in its own peculiar way, and a deal more accurately. The indication is given by a little mirror which reflects the light of a paraffin lamp, through a lens, on a scale. This little mirror is fixed on a very small magnet, which being influenced by the current, moves it and therefore the spot, over so many degrees. We send and receive during alternate ten minutes. The current is sent through Dr. Thomson's galvanometer to the lower end of the "orlop" coil, which will be brought to shore through all the cable on board, over the stern, under the sea to the *Niagara*, where it traverses all her cable before reaching instruments exactly similar. The most valuable observation is taken in sending on the marine galvanometer. Three seconds before it is taken the clerk at the opposite side of the table who times all the observations by a watch regulated by a chronometer too valuable to bring into so wet a place, says "Look out". The other clerk at once fixes his eye on the spot of light and immediately the word is given "Now", records the indication. This testing is made from minute to minute so that a flow is detected the moment it occurs. Indeed on one occasion, a break which happened between the taff-rail and the water was observed before it reached the sea, which of course made it at once evident enough.
>
> July 29- It is rather an exciting occupation to watch the tell-tale signals as we pay out. Even the most indifferent holds his breath for a time when their story is of dubious or ominous import. We are regarded by the engineers about the paying out machinery as birds of evil omen. If one of our number rushes upon deck or approaches with a hurried step, they look as a Roman husbandman might have done at a crow on a blasted tree. Indeed it is almost impossible to realise the anxiety and heart-interest everybody manifests in the undertaking. No one seems to breathe freely. Few but the men, even sleep soundly. Professor Thomson frequently does not put off his clothes at night.
>
> Tonight but a few hours after starting, we had an alarming crisis. We had signalled to the *Niagara* "Forty miles submerged", and she was just beginning her acknowledgment, when suddenly at 10 pm communication ceased. According to orders those on duty sent at once for Dr Thomson. He came in a fearful state of excitement. The very thought of disaster seemed to overpower him. His hand shook so much that he could scarcely adjust his eyeglass. The veins on his forehead were swollen. his face was deadly pale. After consulting his marine galvanometer he said the

[*] see http://atlantic-cable.com//Article/1858JBRussell/index.htm

conducting wire was broken but still insulated from the water. Mr Bright noticed the Professor hurrying to the electrical room and followed close on his heels. He supposed that the fault might lie in a suspicious portion which had been observed in the main coil. The cable was tested on both sides of this place but it was all right there. The fault was not on board but between the ships. There did not seem to be any room to hope;, but it was determined to keep the cable slowly going out, that all opportunity might be given for resuscitation. The scene in and about the electrical room was such as I shall never forget. The two clerks on duty, watching with the common anxiety depicted on their faces for a propitious signal; Dr Thomson, in a perfect fever of nervous excitement, shaking like an aspen leaf, yet in mind clear and collected, testing and waiting with half despairing look for the result. Mr Bright, standing like a boy caught in a fault, his lips and cheek smeared with tar, biting his nails as if in a puzzle, and looking to the Professor for advice; Mr Canning, grave but cool and self possessed, like a man fully equal to such an emergency; the captain, viewing with anxious look the bad symptoms of the testing as indicated on the galvanometer and pointed out by Dr Thomson. Behind in the darker parts of the room, stood various officers of the ship. Round the door crowded the sailors of the watch peeping over each other's shoulders at the mysteries and shouting "Gangway" when anyone of importance wished to enter. The eyes of all were directed to the instruments, watching for the slightest quiver indicative of life. Such a scene was never witnessed save by the bedside of the dying. Things continued thus. Dr Thomson and the others left the room, convinced they were once more doomed to disappointment. Still the cable went slowly out, while in the hold they were resplicing the suspected portion. The clerks continued sending regular currents. All at once the galvanometer indicated a complete breaking in the water. We all made the dread interpretation and looked at each other in silence. Suddenly one sang out, "Halloa! the spot has gone up to 40 degrees". The clerk at the ordinary instrument bolted right out of the room, scarcely knowing where he went for joy; ran to the poop and crying out "Mr Thomson! the cable's all right; we got a signal from the *Niagara*". In less then no time he was down, tested, found the old dismal result, and left immediately. He had not disappeared in the crowd when a signal came which undoubtedly originated in the Niagara. Our joy was so deep and earnest that it did not suffer us to speak for some seconds. But when the first stun of surprise and pleasure passed, each one began trying to express his feelings in some way more or less energetic. Dr Thomson laughed right loud and heartily. Never was more anxiety compressed into such a space. It lasted exactly one hour and a half, but it did not seem to us a third of that time.

As we drew nearer Ireland the storm began to abate and things became altogether so cheerful in aspect that we dared to hope. Still to the last we were never entirely free from anxiety from one cause or another. The signals failed once altogether. The only instrument which kept us from despair was Dr Thomson's. I could compare him watching the slight quivering indication, only to one holding a mirror to the lips of a dying relative to see whether so much breath remained as would dim its surface. Twice also we narrowly missed having a collision with vessels, in each case American. On one occasion the unlucky craft was a small anomalous-looking schooner. But the crew made all possible amends, as soon as they saw the cable at our stern, dipping their ensign some half dozen times and cheering lustily.

On the night of 3rd August we got into shallow water. About ten Dr Thomson came into the electrical cabin, evidently in a state of enjoyment so intense as almost to absorb the whole soul and create absence of mind. His countenance beamed with placid satisfaction. He did not speak for a little but employed himself stretching scraps of sheet gutta-percha over the hot globe of our lamp; watching them with an absent eye as they curled and shrank. At last he said : " At half past eleven you may send the 200 fathoms sounding signal." He then proceeded to congratulate those present on being connected with such an expedition, regarding its object as already un fait accompli.

When we got close inshore we threw off the cable boat. Before our prow grated on the strand her impetus had taken her ashore. The *Valorous* in the distance fired her guns. The end was seized by the jolly tars and run off with; a good humoured scuffle ensued betwixt them and the gentlemen of the island for the honour of pulling the cable up to the office. The Knight of Kerry was upset in the water. As soon as it got fairly on terra firma a bevy of ladies gave it a make believe haul- just so much as to tar their gloves or white hands, and give occasion for a nice business-like fuss in getting butter or other oleaginous matter to remove the stain. Meanwhile we were thrown rather behind. Seeing that those who most deserved the honour were likely to loose it, Dr Thomson, Followed by Anderson, a clerk and myself jumped out of the boat and waded ashore, but in time only to tar our hands ineffectually, like the ladies. The end was taken to the slate works, where the Company's offices are temporarily fixed. About five minutes to four Dr Thomson sent the first current from shore to shore to test the state of the cable. All was right. At four we received the first current (in reply).

John Lecky writing to the editor of the Times on 28 May 1926 reminisced

.... after her battering, the old wooden line of battleship, *Agamemnon* came into Lough Kay; and then the cable, instead of being taken to White Strand, was brought round and landed on the beach under the coastguard station on Valencia. I fear that my sister and I are the only people left who tarred their hands helping pull the cable up the beach that afternoon . . .

Lecky's diary, unearthed by B.K.P. Scaife* in the Quaker Library in Dublin records:

After the ships went away (in 1857) we had profound calm for a year. We heard of the new attempt being arranged and of the terrible storm that the *Agamemnon* got into in the Atlantic when she and the cable were so nearly lost. No visitors on the island, the Fitzgeralds away, Father in London. My sisters and I were all alone when one morning someone came into my room and woke me up with the news "*Agamemnon* in Lough Kay" such excitement! During the morning Capt. Lyons came down from Caherciveen and he took us 4 to go on board the *Agamemnon*. When we got out to her she was lying like a cork on the water, having laid her part of the cable from mid Atlantic and having burn all her coal as well as some of the decks, she was wonderfully light and it was a wonder how she got in without disaster. All ladders were too short and I think my sisters were slung up in chairs, how I did I forget. In the afternoon the cable instead of landing at the White Strand was brought round the East end of Begnis and landed on the Valencia beach just under the Coast guard station.

---

* Retired Professor of Electrical Engineering at Trinity College Dublin and grand-son of the fourth superintendent at the Valentia island cable station

It is obvious that the offices of the slate works provided greater comfort then the temporary hut at White Strand. The climate in the region is damp and frequently very wet. This is likely to have been one of Whitehouse's reasons for having a cable run from the mainland. The proximity to Glanleam House and the hospitality of a not-uninterested Knight of Kerry could have been another. Lecky continues:

> In the slate yard was a long narrow saw house never used. My father had the machinery cleared away and lent the house to the Company. The house was cut up and divided into rooms by bulk heads and it was at the E. end of the window overlooking the yard and pier that the instruments were assembled. The end of the cables brought in.

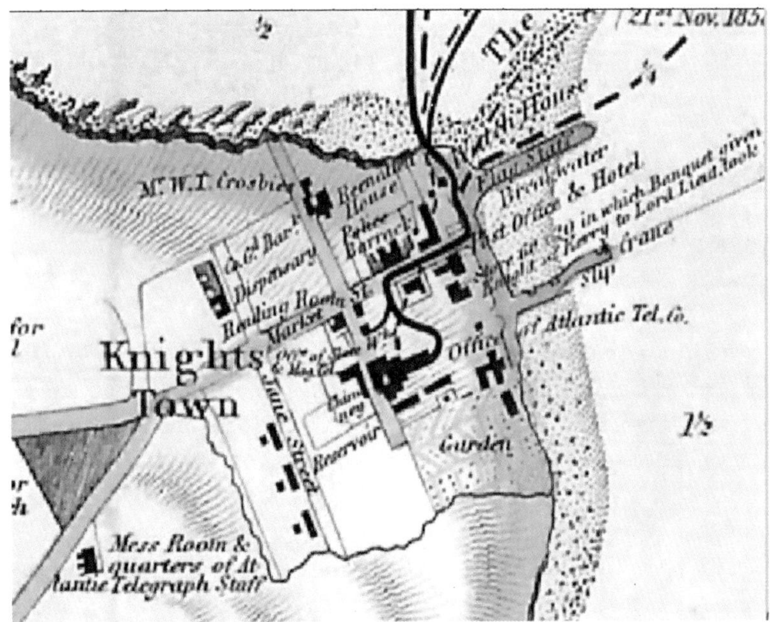

Knightstown from an enlargement of Capt. Brine's map showing where the cable was landed in 1858 and brought into an office in the slate yard.

Chapter 4

Sequel to the Successful Cable-Laying Expedition

Earlier drafts of this chapter followed the conventional format of a struggle between hero and villain (Thomson and Whitehouse) and their animosity up to and beyond Thomson's eventual triumph. This is in need of revision on account of a recently discovered document "The Journal of James Burn Russell." According to Allan Green, who was the first person to realise the significance, (http://researchatporthcurno.blogspot.co.uk/2011/02/on-front-line-in-valentia-1858.html) Russell (1837 - 1904) is best known as Glasgow's first Medical Officer of Health. He was mentioned in the previous chapter as a student of Glasgow University who responded to a request by William Thomson who was seeking assistants to accompany him on the 1857 (and later 1858) Atlantic Telegraph cable laying trips. His diary before the actual landing of the cable has yet to be transcribed, but the following section is valuable because he spent most of his time in the instrument room, and his account gives a completely different view of the relationships between Thomson and Whitehouse. It also gives the names of the operators, the clerks with whom he worked.

In this chapter we will use an amalgamation of two sources to look at the historiography: Capt. Brine's map and the drawings of E.W. Cooke (which are in the archives of the IET).

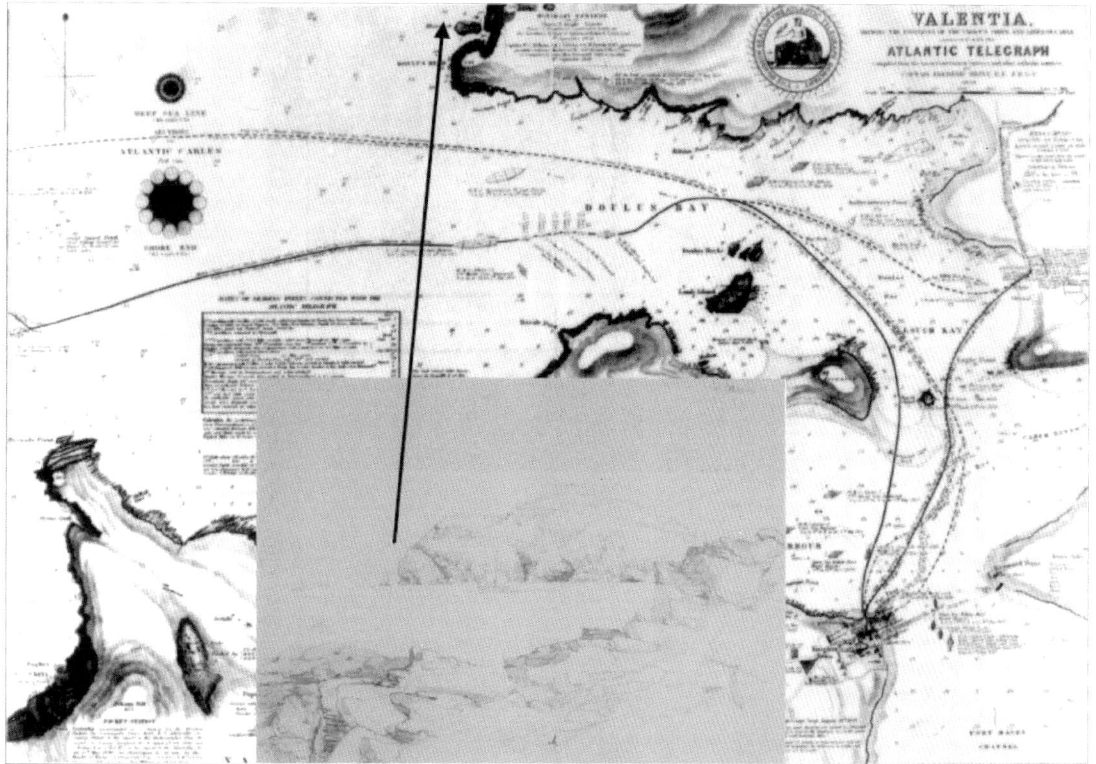

Cooke's drawing of Doulus Head from Cromwell Point Lighthouse with HMS *Agamemnon* as shown in Brine's map. (Cooke drawings are in the IET Archives)

(From the Cooke drawings in the IET Archives)

Following the failures of the past the directors were caught off guard with the arrivals of 4 and 5 August. No provisions had been made for heavy shore ends and both ships landed ordinary deep sea cable. As this was not likely to last very long, a large schooner, the *Bilboa*, was chartered to undertake the task of installing shore-end cable at both sides of the Atlantic. She was ordered to proceed to the Company's stores to take on the necessary cable.

Immediately on arrival at Newfoundland Field transmitted a message on to New York

> United States Frigate Niagara
> Trinity Bay,
> Newfoundland,
> 5 August 1858
>
> To the Associated Press, New York:
>
> The Atlantic Telegraph fleet sailed from Queenstown, Ireland, Saturday, July seventeenth and met in mid-ocean Wednesday, July twenty eighth. Made the splice at one pm Thursday, the twenty ninth and separated–the *Agamemnon* and *Valorous*, bound for Valentia, Ireland; the *Niagara*

and *Gorgon*, for this place, where they arrived yesterday and this morning the end of the cable will be landed.

It is one thousand six hundred and ninety six nautical, or one thousand nine hundred and fifty statute miles from the Telegraph House at the head of Valentia harbour* to the Telegraph House at the Bay of Bulls, Trinity Bay**, and for more then two thirds of this distance the water is over two miles in depth. The cable has been paid out from the *Agamemnon* at about the same speed as from the *Niagara.* The electric signals sent and received through the whole cable are perfect.

The machinery for paying out the cable worked in a most satisfactory manner and was not stopped for a single moment from the time the splice was made until we arrived here.

Capt Hudson, Messrs. Everett and Woodhouse, the engineers, the electricians, the officers of the ship and in fact, every man on board the telegraph fleet, has exerted himself to the utmost to make the expedition successful, and by the blessing of Divine Providence, it has succeeded.

After the end of the cable is landed and connected with the land-line of the telegraph, and the *Niagara* has discharged some cargo belonging to the Telegraph Company, she will go to St. John's for coal and then proceed at once to New York.
Cyrus W. Field

The effect on a by now sceptical public was electric. Overnight Valentia, Trinity Bay and Cyrus Field became household names throughout the American continent. Field received messages of congratulations from the President, from the Governor of Canada and from many public officials.

The *Niagara* called in at St John's, where Field, as hero addressed the Chamber of Commerce. In this he paid tribute to all who had made contributions towards the successful conclusion of the enterprise. He then hurried on to New York, arriving there to a tumultuous welcome on 18 August. There he found a public ravenous for news about the old world. At every public celebration which he attended, and there were many, he was pressed for a date when the cables would be open to traffic. His universal answer was that there must first be extensive testing and the proper protocol must then be observed. When all was ready a message would be sent from Queen Victoria to the President, who would then transmit his reply. After that the cable would be open for business assuming that all commercial arrangements were completed (he was not to know that at that moment the cable was having problems of its own). Being a man of commerce Field was ever resourceful to respond to the public enthusiasm. The remainder of the *Niagara's* stock of cable was sold to Tiffany & Company in New York, who cut it into small sections. These were sold as souvenirs+.

---

* He was obviously unaware that the location had been changed

** There is now considerable ambiguity in Newfoundland about the exact landing place of the 1858 cable. It is believed to be a place that is now called Sunnyside.

+ As the majority of *Niagara's* cargo was Newall's cable, this would account for the fact that many of the small relics which are still extant have a right-hand lay.

On the eastern side of the Atlantic the public reaction was more in keeping with British phlegm. There were congratulations all round, the two principals, Thomson and Bright, each attributing much of the credit to the other. Thomson, in his Presidential Address to the Institution of Electrical Engineers in 1889, expressed the view that "to Bright's vigour, earnestness and enthusiasm was due the laying of the cable". Bright on the other hand gave the following view of Thomson:

> As for the Professor .... he was a thorough good comrade, good all round, and would have taken his turn at the wheel of the cable paying-out brake if others had broken down. He was also a good partner at whist when work wasn't on; though sometimes, when momentarily immersed in cogibundity of cogitation, by scientific abstraction, he would look up from his cards and ask, wha played what?

For his contribution Charles Bright was knighted at the age of 26. In addition to being one of the youngest men ever to receive such an honour, his was the first knighthood bestowed on a man of the new technology of telegraphy. The investiture was carried out by the Lord Lieutenant in Dublin, the Queen being on a state visit to France. In view of the competitive relations between the two countries, it can be assumed that the success of the cable added extra Imperial prestige to her visit.

As has been mentioned previously, Whitehouse had remained on shore during the expedition and had now removed his operational base to the island. The cable was handed over to him at Valentia on the day of landing. Its insulation was much improved by the low temperature and the pressure of water over it as it lay on the sea bed. Thus the cable which he took charge of was in better condition then that on which Thomson worked during the voyage. Whitehouse was convinced that he could use a printing telegraph on the cable and had patented his own improved model based on Samuel Morse's original concept. Its operation involved the energising of relays and this required reasonably high currents. He lost no time in replacing Thomson's circuit, which had worked superbly during the voyage, by his own heavy equipment. Ever larger powers from batteries and induction coils were used in an attempt to get intelligible signals. It is reported that eventually an induction coil five feet long and capable of delivering 2,000 volts was put into the circuit. He was left undisturbed during the next week to adjust the equipment for optimum operation. Existing accounts of events report that very weak test signals crossed the ocean but were insufficient for reliable working and the rate of transmission was very low. These facts were concealed from Thomson who had remained on for five days to offer what assistance he could. During that time he was not allowed access to the instruments but was shown some signals, which it was claimed had been received on the printing apparatus. This does not quite tally with what Russell reported. The transcription of the his journal that appears on Bill Burns' Atlantic website starts on 9 August.
http://atlantic-cable.com/Article/1858JBRussell/Journal/index.htm
It mentions that one of clerks, Balcutt, was an Irish man. There is no mention of friction or rivalry. On 10 August Thomson returned to Glasgow having been absent from the University since 2 May. Before his departure Whitehouse suggested to him that the difficulties in receiving reasonable signals levels might be associated with a fault in the cable about two miles out. Thomson disagreed, saying that he believed there to be a small fault at a distance of 300 miles from Valentia.

Existing reports say that on 13 August even Whitehouse had to admit to himself that his instruments were impractical. Thomson's mirror galvanometer and Daniell cells were reinserted into the circuit and intelligible signals were received. However, Russell says

> We received and sent this morning regular messages, quicker and with stronger currents indicated at this end than hitherto. Still more to increase the quantity of our battery Mr Whitehouse at one had it divided into two series of 60 which were joined up for quantity. At 3 the series was further reduced to 40s. They still complained of unreadable signals. This shows that the fault is becoming very bad.

The directors were becoming daily more impatient about lack of news from Valentia. To all enquiries Whitehouse merely reported that everything was in order and that that it would require time to adjust the instruments for commercial use. They even sent Mr France, a skilled operator to lend assistance but he was not allowed access to the instrument room. When the directors heard of Whitehouse's theory and his intention to under-run several miles of inshore cable they sent strict instructions prohibiting this course of action.

Russell records for 15 August

> Newfoundland Station Com. 8.20 Ended 10.20
> To Saward.
> E.M. Archibald, N.Y. Telegraphs instructed by Honorary Directors, A.T.Co., and Directors N.Y., Newfoundland, and London Telegraph Co. to state that unexplained delay injures it, rest companies. I replied cause not passing messages—that instruments require great care and adjustment. Doing fast possible. You should not look on cable as on an ordinary short line, as we encounter many little difficulties, but think all soon overcome.
> DeSauty

Copy of message from DeSauty in Newfoundland to Saward, received at Valentia on 24 August 1858. Reception started at 10.30 and was completed at 11.29

On 16th Russell notes:

I was agreeably surprised on reaching the office this morning to find Mr Kingsford the clerk on duty engaged in sending the Directors message. As this was not to be done until communications was reciprocal & established it betokened good things. In referring to the record it appeared that we had been speaking with ease for some hours, showing that some change had taken place either in the cable or in the instruments on the other side. At 2.35 they desired us to send alphabet which we did. They informed us that they could read it off with but three errors. The message will be found at page 16. It was sent slowly, beginning 8.20 AM ending 11.12, so that no mistake might be made.

At 11.36 the style began to imprint its magic characters. He watched them while they formed letters & the letters words as if half-afraid to look. First came dots & at quicker speed, from which we inferred that the instructions at any rate they had read. There came V's, a letter which is often given to afford an opportunity to adjust. Soon appeared an–"Understand," repeated to make assurance doubly sure, and then came "Directors A.T.Co." We all clapped our hands and hurrahed. Thinking this sufficient to show that we understood the message, the repetition went no further, but the question came–"Will you receive one?" But Mr. Whitehouse would have the whole message repeated, besides being determined to have the Queen's dispatch before anything official from the Yankees. We accordingly answered–"No! Repeat all back faster! Queen's next." This was done with perfect accuracy in thirty-five minutes. Mr. Whitehouse immediately telegraphed the acknowledgement to the Directors in London.–At 11.47

Mr McCurley, Company's Cashier, put the Queen's message into the hands of Mr. Whitehouse. On the back of the inner envelope were these instructions. "When the connection between Ireland & Newfoundland by Electric Telegraph is established, this letter is to be opened and the message contained in it is to be forwarded immediately to Washington."

The messages of congratulations were immediately transmitted across the Ocean.

TO THE PRESIDENT OF THE UNITED STATES, WASHINGTON

The Queen desires to congratulate the President upon the successful completion of this great international work in which the Queen has taken the deepest interest.

The Queen is convinced that the President will join with her in fervently hoping that the electric cable which now connects Great Britain with the United States will prove an additional link between the nations, whose friendship is founded upon their common interest and reciprocal esteem.

The Queen had much pleasure in thus communicating with the President and renewing to him her wishes for the prosperity of the United States.

TO HER MAJESTY VICTORIA, THE QUEEN OF GREAT BRITAIN

The President cordially reciprocates the congratulations of Her Majesty the Queen on the success of the great international enterprise accomplished by the science, skill and indomitable energy of these two countries.

It is a triumph more glorious because far more useful to mankind than was ever won by conqueror on the field of battle.

May the Atlantic Telegraph under the blessing of Heaven prove to be a bond of perpetual peace and friendship between the kindred nations and an instrument destined by divine Providence to diffuse religion, civilization, liberty and law throughout the world.

In this view, will not all nations of Christendom spontaneously unite in the declaration that it shall be for ever neutral and that its communications shall be held sacred in passing to their places of destination even in the midst of hostilities

JAMES BUCHANAN

On the day the messages crossed the Atlantic Whitehouse sent a telegram to the directors informing them of the satisfactory state of working of the cable. He even sent them results from his printing telegraph. The directors were unaware that on that same day he had sent a confidential message to Samuel Canning of Glass Elliott and Co, the cable manufacturers, summoning him to Valentia to under-run the cable. According to Capt. Brine's map, Canning carried out his orders on 18 August. In Sylvanus P. Thompson's life of Lord Kelvin this was reported as being done on the 17th.

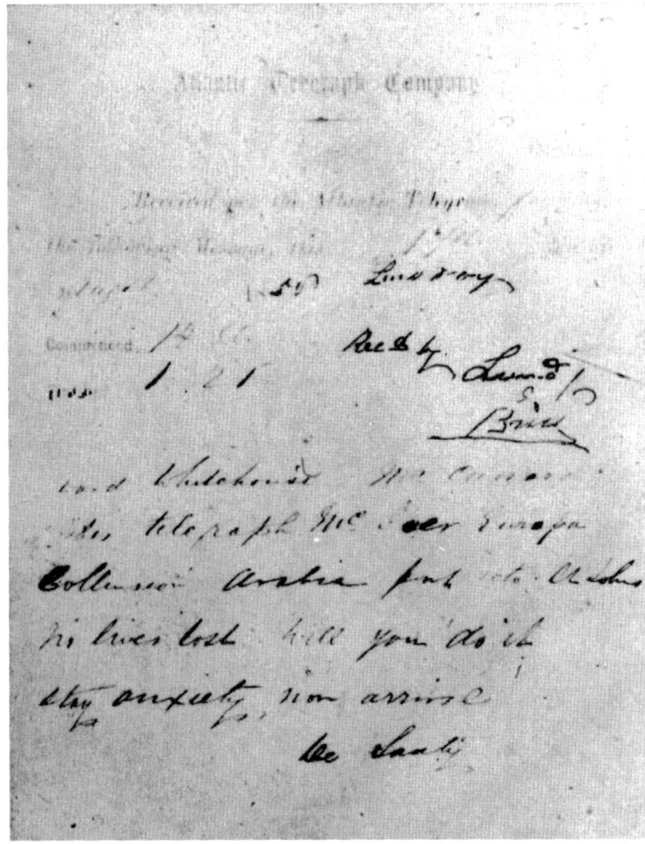

A humanitarian message reporting the collision between the Cunarders *Europa* and *Arabia* on the Grand Banks near Newfoundland

Russell's account for the 17th is as follows:

> From 8.15 to 8.49 we received the following–"C.W. Field to Directors A.T. Co, N.foundland, Monday. Entered Trinity Bay noon 5th, landed cable 6th, Thursday. Ship at once to St John's two miles of shore cable with end ready for splicing. When was cable landed at Valencia? Answer by Telegraph and forward any letters to New York."
>
> The following came 12.56 to 1.21–"Mr Bernard wishes telegraph McIvor. Europa collision Arabia. Put into St Johns. No lives lost. Will you do it? Stay anxiety–non-arrival." DeSauty. (Supt)–To receive this commercial message (*the* first of general interest) was against rule more particularly as the President's answer had not yet been sent. Still the nature of it was such that Mr Whitehouse, Bartholomew & all of us thought the Company would do themselves great good by publishing it. It would show that there was no pre-concerting requisite to get a message read off. Still Mr. W. had to submit the matter to the Directors who said they would not receive it. In the afternoon we made another attempt at under-running the cable. But the day was so squally &

wet. & the swell so great that nothing could be done. My post was with Mr Collett, a clerk on Beg Innis[*] a considerable island between Valentia I. and the mainland.

The Board on receipt of the news that Whitehouse had under-run the cable terminated his employment and immediately sent a telegram to Thomson in Glasgow.

Atlantic Telegraph Co.,
22 Old Broad St.,
London, August 18 1858

DEAR SIR–You are hereby authorised and empowered to take charge and possession (until further arrangements can be made) of this Company's office and electrical apparatus at Valentia and to issue in respect to the adjustment and working of the instruments such instructions as you may deem best. It is hereby ordered and authorised that no person whatsoever is to be allowed on any pretence to enter the Company's electrical department without your special order and permission.–

We are dear sir, yours truly,
C.M. Lampson, Vice Chairman, William Logie, Henry Harrison,
George Saward, Secretary)

Professor W. Thomson LL.D

Russell's journal entries for the next few days are set out below

18 August

Mr. Bartholomew [clerk who was extremely loyal to Whitehouse] thinking it likely that more defects would be found by further under-running sent out one of the clerks to say so to Mr Canning. I accompanied him.

20th

We were informed by telegraph to-day that the Niagara reached N. York on the 18th, and that Bull's Arms Station is henceforth to be called Cyrus station.

21st

We had capital deflections today, carrying 100 [degrees] for some time, messages being printed off at about two words and a half per minute.–The following was one rather interesting– "Mosquitoes keep biting. This is a funny place to be in. Very swampy." Mr Bartholomew received notification today from London that for the present Dr Thomson is to be in charge of the electrical department here.

21st.

Dr Thomson arrived this morning. We are still increasing our battery power; & managing arrangements in that department. Things were looking very well today. Mr Canning's labours

[*] Semaphore flags were used to maintain communications between the mainland, Beg Innis and the under-running boat.

seem to have been profitable. For the first time N.foundland receives well. Indeed they became quite bold towards evening and said "Send as fast as you can!"

The conventional narrative says that Thomson was at first disposed to defend Whitehouse; he may not always have agreed with him but he was after all a fellow scientist. His attitude however soon changed. He had not been aware that his galvanometer had been inserted instead of the printing telegraph. He was horrified to discover that the printed slips which had been sent to London were in fact forgeries. Whitehouse had had a clerk read the messages from the mirror galvanometer and then relay them by hand to his printer on the other side of the table. It is curious that Russell makes absolutely no mention of this and indeed, it will be seen that he only reports recriminations in his entries for early September.

Russell indicates that Newfoundland was using Thomson's galvanometer to read. The accepted story up to the discovery of his journal related that DeSauty having assured himself by means of Thomson's galvanometer that the cable was working satisfactorily replaced it by Whitehouse's apparatus so as to comply with orders. It is said that in their inability to read Valentia's signals, they kept asking for more battery power. It took Thomson one whole day to get Newfoundland to understand what he wanted, his equipment back in the circuit, and thereafter they were able to communicate at speeds of up to eight words per minute using no more then twenty Daniell cells (approximately 24 volts). According to Russell

25th

Mr Gurney, chairman of the Company arrived here to-day. He is M.P. for a Welsh district and a member of the Society of Friends. He is a very charitable good man, ready with his money for every laudable purpose.

Poor Thomson has great opposition to what is called–his new system. The fact of its being new I think is its chief fault. Mr Bartholomew treats the whole matter with marvellous indifference. The clerks are grievously annoyed with the Doctor's animation and impetuosity in pursuing an idea through thick & thin to the destruction of their dear old stereotyped routine.

At 12.16 received "*Persia* takes *Europa*'s passengers and mails."

26th

From 1 PM. to 11 A.M. not a signal was received. The galvanometer gave a strong, permanent deflection of 110 to 130, earth current only. At 11.22 we suddenly began to receive good signals and at 11.39 we began receiving the following. "We have had heavy storm with thunder. Cable put to earth. Hour and twenty-five minutes strong permanent deflections on galvanometer. Sending at intervals. Take message for Gurney."

I reckon this the most interesting message yet received. It is a taste of the many opportunities which the cable will open up for the study of yet doubtful phenomena. Here were the effects of a thunderstorm–a disturbance in atmospheric electricity–manifesting themselves in the two worlds at once.

28th

No sooner was it in, and the needle vibrating with the received current than the clerk watching Dr. Thomson's instrument began to complain of irregular vibrations in the spot. Dr. Th. at once explained. "Oh! Here's a discovery. Now I know why they complain of irregularities in our signals. It is currents induced in the coil of their galvanometers by the motion of the needle." He put his hands on the shoulder of a clerk standing by, jumped up on the receiving table, and by moving the galv. magnet, or bringing up & removing a separate one, proved that the current thus induced in the coil was actually stronger than that received from Newf. & therefore obliterated and blurred its indications. Other needle instruments did the same.
Sent to NF
"The irregularities you complain of in our signals are induced currents from the coil of your large Galvanometer or relay due to motions of needle or adjustment magnet. Never receive on two galvanometers at same time. Repeat last word."

30th

At 4.16 Mr Saward, Secretary, telegraphed to the Superintendent two paid Govt. messages for transmission to N.fld. They were interesting both as being the first by way of business, and as showing in a very remarkable manner what important services the cable may perform for our Govt.–both in saving money; and in knitting the limbs of empire into one gigantic frame. When we have extended these wonderful wires to India & Australia, Great Britain and her Colonies will resemble in economy the human body. London the seat of supreme intellect, whence the electric lines, the nerves, ramify and distribute themselves, the medium by which her behests are made known and executed in the remotest parts of the huge structure.

These messages ran as follows.

(1)"The Military Secretary to Commander-in-Chief, Horse Guards, London to General Trollope, Halifax, Nova Scotia,–The 62nd Regt. is not to return to England."

(2) – "The Military Secretary to Commander-in-Chief Horse Guards, London to General Officer commanding, Montreal, Canada. The 39th Regt. is not to return to England."

It is really most disheartening to have to record that it was found impossible at present to send off these messages.

31st ???
We kept asking if they could take govt. mess. At last about half past one, they said–"Try, but will try send repeat." Betwixt 1.40 and 3.41 the first govt. message was sent. It was repeated back correctly; the message being with that end split in two. At 9 P.M. the second was got through. Employed getting up a new and better observatory for Thomson's galv. I made an experiment with a bit of zinc and sixpence with paper moistened with saliva between; and the current thus generated knocks the galv. spot entirely out of range. This proves its extreme sensitiveness.

I have been much annoyed to-day with the generally prevalent disrespectful remarks regarding Thomson. Mr Bartholomew throws a slight upon him & his instruments.

Meanwhile Cyrus Field in New York was entirely unaware of these developments. The official exchanges had taken place, but the cable was not yet open for business. The public were growing impatient. At a reception in New York he read from a telegram which had been handed to him just a short while before. The directors were on their way to Valentia to arrange for the opening of the line. A footnote in Henry Field's book states that although dated at London it was in fact sent from Ireland. During the journey from Dublin to Valentia, Saward, the Company Secretary, remarked "this is the day of the celebration in New York, we ought to send a dispatch to Mr Field." At the next stop (Mallow, it was thought) it was written and forwarded, being handed to Field just as he got into his carriage.

The following day Field attended a civic banquet unaware that all effective communication across the Atlantic had ceased. As the signals had become progressively weaker the number of batteries in the circuit had to be increased, which could not have helped the condition of the insulation. After 1 September it was almost impossible to detect anything. The last message at Valentia ended with "....forty eight words. Right. Right." Newfoundland's last words were "now in a position to do best to forward".

On 5 September Russell records:

> Nothing–Anderson (one of his colleagues) left for home

By this time a total of 480 messages had been conveyed; 271 westwards and 190 eastwards*. However, the cable seems to have been irrevocably damaged. The DC working potential used by Whitehouse was approximately 500 volts and as has already been mentioned the induction coils were estimated to have applied approximately 2,000 volts across the cable.

The Company called in several consultants to advise them and to see if anything could be done to revive the cable. Amongst these was Cromwell F. Varley, chief Electrician to the Electric and International Telegraph Co, who confirmed Thomson's view that there was a fault approximately 250 miles west of Ireland. He vividly demonstrated that the failure was likely to be due to the use of excessive voltages at a weak point in the insulation. Taking a piece of cable he used a pin to completely puncture the insulation through the outer serving. The cable was then immersed in a vat of brine while a voltage similar to that used by Whitehouse was applied between the core and the outer conductor. There was a bright light generated at the point of the puncture and when the cable was removed from the brine the hole was much enlarged and the gutta percha in its vicinity was charred. It is only at this stage that Russell starts to comment on recriminations, stating that Bartholomew is blaming Thomson and he (Russell) does not like it. As the recriminations developed Saward the Secretary of the Atlantic Telegraph Co, got to hear that Russell had maintained a journal and asked to see it and further asked to be provided with extracts.

Russell's journal for 14 September records

---

* Okay, so this does not add up, but there would also have been station-to-station service messages which probably have not been included in this tally

> Mr. Phillips, Whitehouse's assistant left this morning. I went over with Mr. Walker, Magnetic Clerk to the Red house where we remained all forenoon botanizing on the sea-beach with coat & shoes & stockings off.

After that his diary appears to be concerned with different arrangements and lots of earth currents. As Thomson, Varley and others were there he may have been somewhat removed from the centre of activity. He set off for Glasgow on the 30th and in view of the fact that there is now an airport at Farranfore his itinerary may be of interest.

30th.

> I took the Mail car from Cahirciveen to Killorglin, where another car went off to the left for Tralee where I slept.

1st Oct

> Took the 3-horse coach for Tarbert. Got the railway steamer "Kelpie" for Foynes, from whence the train brought me to Limerick by 4.30 time enough to see the chief street, the "Quay", The Treaty House, the Castle, Cathedral and Exchange.

2nd.

> Started by 4-horse coach for Killaloe at 6.45. Left Killaloe at 8.30 by the "Duchess of Argyle". Sailed up the Shannon to Athlone which we reached about 4.

4th.

> Took the 9 o'clock train for Dublin where I arrived about 12.30. Mr Keating was in waiting and we at once commenced sight-seeing. We saw the Phoenix Park, Glasnevin, St Xaviers, the National Schools, Nelson's monument–Sackville Street–The Post Office, The Bank, College &c &c. At night we went to Jude's saloon.

5th.

> Started again through the city–St Patrick's Cathedral, Exhibition of Irish Industry; the chief squares, the College Buildings & museum, The Bank including manufacture of Bank notes. It was by this time close upon 1 when I took train for Belfast. The "Elk" sailed thence at 8 for Glasgow.

6th.

> After a rough passage we got to Greenock about 6 a.m. Took train there and cab at Glasgow, reaching Auburn in time to join the family at breakfast.

Although for all intents and purposes the Atlantic cable was now useless, Varley and other electricians remained on and managed sporadic communication and raising the total number of messages to 732. On 20 October the very last intelligible signals were received "two hundred and forty tk..... two Daniell cells now in circuit". This would be equivalent to 240 volts.

The reaction of a public who had celebrated the success but were unable to enjoy its fruits was understandable. In America there were many who claimed that the cable had never existed; that it was an elaborate hoax by Cyrus Field to sell shares. Fortunately for Field in that respect he had sold only one share in August and that was at a price below par value. There were those who felt that the knighthood bestowed on Bright had been a little premature.

There were also recriminations in the scientific world and these were to rumble on for some time. Throughout these Thomson attempted to behave in a chivalrous manner. During August he wrote to the Board asking them to condone Whitehouse's errors and to reconsider their resolution of the 17th. They replied on the 25th stating that his own benevolent and kindly feelings must have obscured his more reflective judgment. Their response was a short 'no'. It would appear that he continued to plead with the director after their arrival at Valentia. At a dinner given for the Board on 3 September in Killarney he spoke publicly of Whitehouse's problems of facing the unknown.

Whitehouse was less restrained. In a letter to the *Times* on 7 September he attacked the directors in a number of wild statements. Thomson inadvertently entered the argument by telegraphing the Board correcting the validity of some of the claims. He wrote a private conciliatory letter to Whitehouse. Whitehouse's response is unknown but whatever it was it drew a sharp response from Thomson.

> Valentia,
> September 23, 1858)
>
> MY DEAR WHITEHOUSE–Your reply to my last letter has made me feel how widely we differ in much that is essential for true friendship. You had surely learned long before that "no difference of opinion separated friends", in the example of our own intercourse. It is not now a question of difference of opinion, but of truth and honour that has arisen.
>
> The impression conveyed by your second letter to the *Times* is that your first statement regarding the President's reply was a mere inadvertence, attributable to your absence from Valentia, and that what you had said of it was true of other messages. I can find no evidence after the most minute investigation, that it was true of any one complete message, or that any other system than that by which the President's reply was received, was ever depended on for doing business at this station from the time when I showed you the dots and dashes on my galvanometer, on the night when the telegraphic signals first came from Newfoundland.
>
> I want no one to explain my galvanometer to the world or to boast of its capabilities. I look for no acknowledgment in the newspapers of what I have done, but I want truth. If this had been maintained not only with reference to what more immediately concerns myself, but by correction of such falsehoods as appeared in a letter signed T.S. in a Liverpool paper in which telegrams were dealt with, in a manner implying that the writer had had access to them from you, I should gladly have left to time the settlement of all questions between us, either as to science or as to the art of telegraphing. Three weeks ago I could not have believed it possible that under any circumstances you could act as you have done, and a most painful feeling of disappointment would be removed, if it could still be proved that I was not thus mistaken.
> (I remain,
> yours faithfully,
> W.T.

E.O. Wildman Whitehouse, Esq
British Association, Leeds.

This rancour was to continue on for some time with letters to newspapers, most likely to have been written by Whitehouse. These were sometimes anonymous, sometimes forged, allegedly written by Cyrus Field.

Still at Valentia on September 24 Thomson addressed a letter to the Company Secretary, George Saward.

MY DEAR SIR–
The results of experiments on the cable, quoted by Mr Varley as having been communicated to him were not, as he naturally conjectures, made at Queenstown*, but chiefly on board the *Agamemnon* during her last cruise. By a comparison which I made of them after landing, with a few hasty memoranda of observation I had made at Keyham (the last set quoted by Mr Varley), I was led to infer that the part of the cable on board the *Agamemnon* had all along been in a much worse state as to insulation then the average of the whole cable. Even the observations at Keyham alone showed that the *A*'s portion had some much worse insulation in some part of it than the *Niagara*'s. I mentioned this to Mr Whitehouse, and he said that he was aware of it and that it was owing to the improved manufacture of the cable this year which had been put on board the Niagara, and chiefly influenced the tests I applied. A thorough system of testing applied to the cable from the beginning and regularly continued during the various changes to which it has been subjected, would probably have obviated the disaster by which the whole has now been ruined. Even the doubt which is now felt as to whether the fault is 240 or 300 miles off, could not have existed if each part of the cable had been tested for inductivity. I mention this not to imply any censure on the past management, but rather to call attention to what we should aim at if we are to continue the great undertaking. The thorough testing to which I refer has not yet been fully carried out on any cable or other telegraphic conductor, but I believe that I shall be able to show that it can be done with ease and without any increased expense, but by a little beforehand.

There is one part of Varley's opinion in which I cannot quite agree with him–that the resistance of the fault is equal to at least ten miles of cable**. From observations I have made both before and after his visit to Valentia, I feel convinced that it must be much less (or the effect of the fault much greater) then he supposes. I do not think the resistance can possibly be greater than from 2 to 5 miles, but I shall repeat my observations with care, and let you know the result. It may be still that there is ground for Varley's conclusion that another fault is necessary to account for the extreme weakness of the signals, but I believe the removal of the fault about 300 miles off, if successfully accomplished, will be sufficient to restore the cable to working order. It is chiefly with reference to anticipations on this score that a more accurate determination of the resistance of the known fault is desirable–I remain yours, etc W.T.

---

* Now called Cobh

** which would explain why Kell lifted 11 miles on 19 November 1858 (see below)

P.S.–Varley's report is, in my opinion, evidence of high scientific and practical talent.

There are two items in this letter which deserve particular attention. This was the first occasion on which Thomson and Varley cooperated, and they both developed a high regard for each other. Their cooperation resulted in patents and the development of many useful scientific instruments (the author used a Kelvin (Thomson)-Varley bridge in a university undergraduate physics laboratory in the middle 1960s). In later years their friendship became somewhat strained on account of Varley's developing interest in spiritualism.

A modern view on the reasons for the cable failure

The letter also points out in post-mortem the deficiencies of the cable which had been used and this was to become the subject of much discussion. Further confirmation of this view is provided by a recent discovery. During July 1983 the author was fortunate enough to contact relatives of Capt Robert Halpin, one time master of the *Great Eastern* (v.i.). He was shown a section of 1858 cable, which had been raised from the ocean.

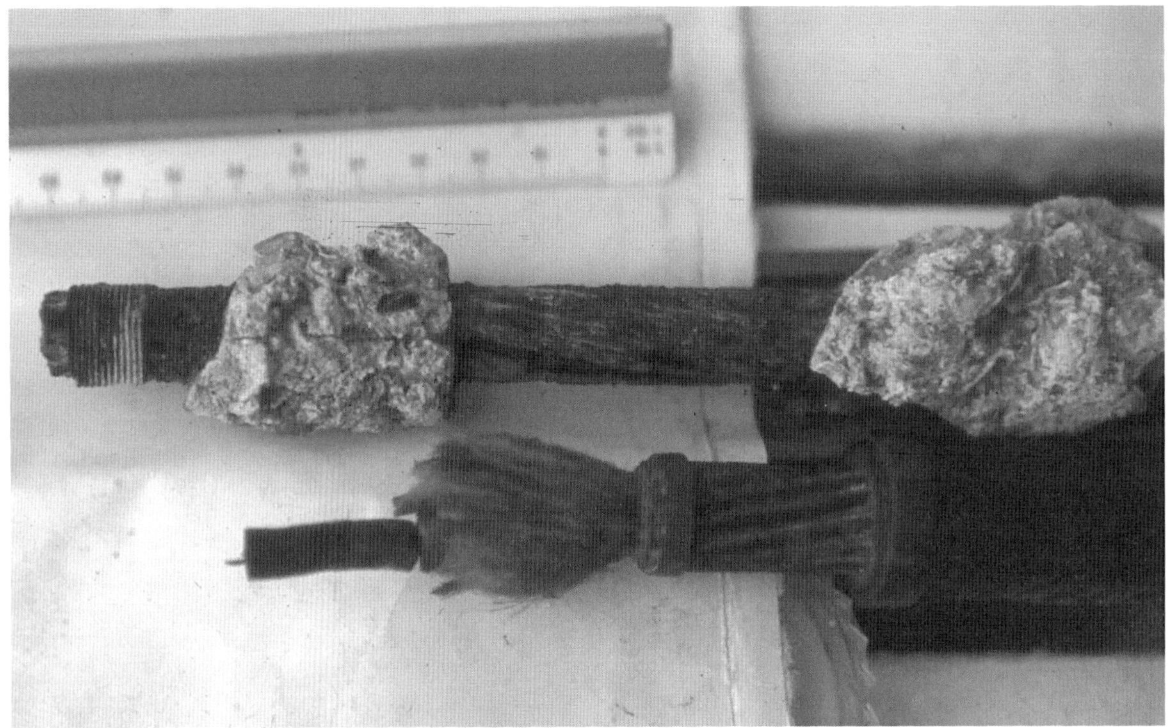

Recovered 1858 cable alongside a later cable with opposite lay

Little is known about its history but the right-hand lay of the outer serving of iron wires, which can be seen in places where the marine deposits have broken away, confirms that it was part of the section which was manufactured by Newall of Birkenhead. The most striking feature about this section of cable is the fact that the copper conductor does not lie coaxially. Corrosion and damage have exposed the core in the middle of the sample so that its position can be monitored in four places. In the worst case the strands come within less then a millimetre of the outer extremity of the gutta percha insulation

There are a number of ways in which this could have occurred. Damage after recovery is unlikely. It has been well cared for and shows no signs of maltreatment. An examination of a small section of 1858 cable which formed part of the 1983 telecommunications exhibition at the Science Museum in South Kensington, London, confirmed that its central conductor was also slightly eccentric. The extrusion of gutta percha during manufacture could have been defective, but there are no reports of this having happened. There is however another possible explanation. It must be remembered that the practice of storing cable under water had not yet been instituted; indeed there is a contemporary picture in the *Illustrated London News* which shows cable being stored out in the open immediately after manufacture. In an enclosed atmosphere, such as might prevail in a ship's hold, the gutta percha (which was far from pure) could have been effected by bacterial fermentation. This phenomenon is particularly prevalent at moderate humidity levels and in materials such as damp hay can lead to significant localised heating. Perhaps the "disquieting reports from Keyham" could have been due to this cause.

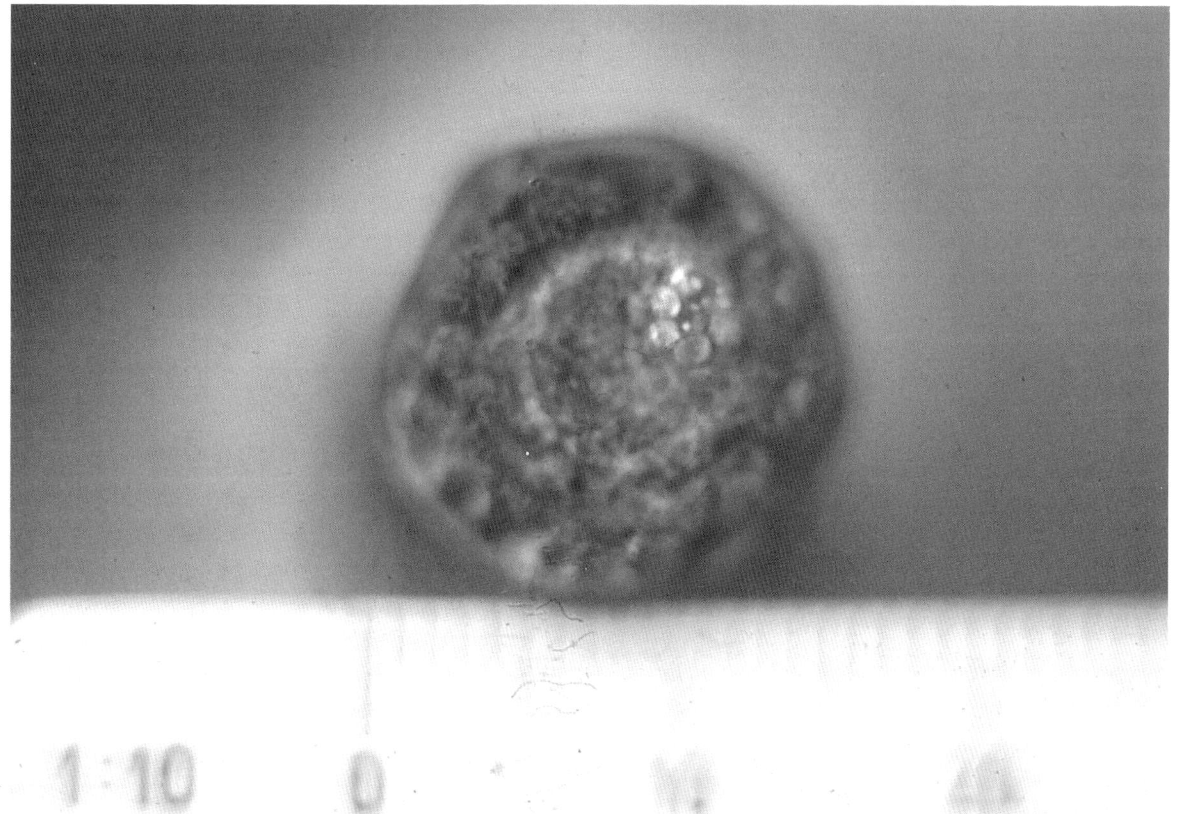

End-view of the Halpin cable with the strands of the copper conductor displaced from the centre

Meanwhile things were happening at Valentia. The *Bilboa*, which had been chartered to lay heavy shore ends, was ordered back to London to unload her cargo and was then discharged, as she was an expensive charter. The directors decided to check Varley's assertion about a fault at no more then ten miles distance from shore. The inshore section would be raised so that it could be brought to London for examination and tests. The schooner, *Stag*, under Capt. Kell was sent to Valentia, where with the assistance of a local boat, the *Julia*, the 1857 shore end was diverted to Knightstown. Eleven miles of *Agamemnon*'s cable was then lifted and cut out. The seaward end was spliced onto the 1857 shore end (see Capt. Brine's map) so that the Company could maintain a watch on the condition of the cable from its office in the slate quarry yard at Knightstown

On the basis of observations it is now suggested that the failure of the cable was due largely to inherent defects rather then Whitehouse's misguided use of excessive potentials. High purity gutta percha has a dielectric strength of 200-300 kV/cm. The gutta percha of 1857/58 was unlikely to have had anything like these voltages per unit distance. It was however sufficient to withstand 2,000 volts. This is witnessed by the fact that the cable in the vicinity of Knightstown, where dielectric attenuation would have been minimal, was found to be perfect, when it was raised by Capt. Kell and returned to London for inspection. The examination disproved both Whitehouse's and Varley's theories about inshore defects. One can also speculate that there might have been other defects further out in the ocean. The observations from Valentia were likely to have been obscured by their local defect. At that time Newfoundland did not report any problem with electrical insulation. Of course they did not have the benefit of Thomson's presence. DeSauty was the electrician there, and while technically competent he was a disciple of Whitehouse, and as will be seen later lacked the breadth of vision and originality which was necessary for his lonely task. Given that there was a weakness in the cable about three hundred miles from Ireland one can only speculate on how long it might have survived had it been subjected only to William Thomson's mild regime of a single Daniell cell used in connection with his marine galvanometer. If this had been done initially the entire development of submarine telegraphy might have been different. Whitehouse's treatment was the ultimate in destructive testing of the new technology. He defended his actions by bitter attacks against Thomson in the press and scientific literature but although he lived until 1890, he had only one further involvement in submarine telegraphy, when he acted as consultant for Glass, Elliot & Co. on the Malta-Alexandria cable of 1861[+].

In view of Whitehouse's contribution to history, could it be claimed that anyone benefited from the cable's one month of useful life? The Atlantic Telegraph Co certainly did not. Their financial statements over this period indicate just how much was spent and lost on land and sea. On the other hand the British Government did as did Cunard's shipping line. It has already been stated that many people, particularly in America questioned whether the whole thing had been a giant hoax. There is no doubt that the Company public relations policy was very bad. They had decided that no person except Thomson and Whitehouse in Ireland and DeSauty and Laws in Newfoundland would be permitted to transmit messages before the line was opened for business. It may be that having been caught off guard by the successful landings, it was realised that there had been no decision about tariff levels etc. They probably wished to avoid setting any precedent before their conditions of business were published.

Henry Field quotes a number of cases as indisputable evidence for the cable's existence. They include items of news that had appeared in New York and London papers much earlier then might otherwise have been possible. These include the death of James Eddy, America's most famous

---

[+] According to the *Electrician* Magazine Whitehouse died aged 73 on 26 January 1890 at his home in Salisbury Road Brighton.

telegraphist and the fact that the King of Prussia was too ill to visit Queen Victoria. And of course there was the news concerning the collision of the Cunarders *Arabia* and *Europa.*

The other important dispatch concerned troop movements. Following the outbreak of the Sepoy mutiny dispatches were sent by steamer to Canada recalling two regiments to England for re-emabarkation to India. While the dispatches were on their way news was received that the mutiny had been quelled and peace had been restored. On the day before the cable's demise countermanding orders were sent. One can imagine these officers' bewilderment when they received these before the arrival of their initial instructions. Nevertheless it was estimated that these messages saved the Government approximately £50,000, leaving them well pleased with their investment in the trans-Atlantic telegraph and thereby sympathetic to subsequent attempts to revive the venture.

Back on the south west coast of Ireland the principle of a telegraph station on Valentia island was now firmly established. The Company staff were engaged in monitoring what was left of the cable.

John Lecky in his diary recorded the aftermath as seen from Valentia

> All was no good and they all went away. What was left of gear and instruments an Electrician Richard Collett was put in charge of. He was a great friend of ours. He had nothing to do and was ready for anything. The Thomson reflecting galvanometer by which the messages were sent across (sic) and received was still there and Collett had some idea of recording earth currents*. He got me to sit opposite the scale and call out the variations shewn by the mirror, but I do not think anything came of this. When Collett and all had gone this instrument was abandoned and came to my father. After his death I gave it** and pieces of the shore end cable and deep sea cable to the Science Museum South Kensington where it sits alongside the similar one used at Hearts Content (sic) NFLD.

The Knight of Kerry had his exclusive telegraph line to Dublin and except for his attempts to improve the economy of his island and to ensure that nobody lured away his station, things returned to their quiet and easy going way, not to be disturbed for several years.

---

* Collett was involved in the early days of the operation of the 1865/6 cables and there was great friction between him and Graves, the Valentia superintendent. It must have been particularly galling for him when Graves subsequently published several papers on earth currents using data derived from cables when out of service.

** Recent correspondence with the Science Museum confirms that far from 'donations' these items were in fact purchased from Lecky.

Chapter 5

The Intervening Years

At first sight one might well enquire why no further attempts were made to link Britain and America by telegraph during the next seven years. There was of course a sceptical public who were unwilling to sink more money into the Atlantic. The cable itself was not showing up too well. It was mentioned in the last chapter that the seaward end of the 1858 cable had been spliced onto the 1857 shore end so that the Company could maintain a watch on its condition using their "temporary" office in the slate quarry yard at Knightstown. Their financial accounts indicate that staff were retained there until about 1861, after which all surveillance ceased. General deterioration of the cable made the continuation of the exercise valueless. Attempts were made on both sides of the Atlantic to raise and sell what could be salvaged. At Trinity Bay, Newfoundland, the state of the outer serving was such that cable could not be raised intact. Similar efforts at Valentia were hampered by bad weather. During the next few years even the deep-sea sections suffered badly from corrosion. In 1877, while carrying out repairs to the successful 1865-66 cables, the consultant engineer, Charles Hocken, recorded raising a section of 1858 cable

"\. . . . one quarter mile recovered. All iron gone–hemp and core only remaining."

America in general and Cyrus Field in particular had their own problems.

1858 was a bad year for Cyrus Field. No sooner was he back in America then his office and warehouse on Beckman Street were destroyed by fire with heavy loss of goods and records. His prospects the following year were even worse. With a nationwide depression he was forced to admit bankruptcy and his creditors were paid off at 25%. According to Bern Dibner this represented his third financial collapse in twenty years and effectively removed him from further investment in the Atlantic venture. It appears that throughout all of this he remained optimistic and following the eventual success of the telegraph he was able to sell off enough stock to repay his debts with 7% interest for the intervening years.

With the exception of Field's enthusiastic support, all US involvement in the cable came to an end. America was about to spend the next five years tearing itself apart. Henry Field reports the tragedy in terms of the Atlantic surveyors Maury and Berryman, who fought on opposing sides in the Civil War. Britain attempted to remain neutral throughout, but on many occasions financial interests took precedence over national policy.

However there were some who had been involved in the Atlantic venture and who were now doing well. William Thomson was back at work in Glasgow University, devoting himself to other matters. This time was for him what his biographer, Sylvanus P. Thompson, has called 'the strenuous years', years, in which he made some of his greatest contributions to pure science. Sir Charles Tilston Bright was busy laying cables and was about to become involved in the first attempts at achieving the dream of an Empire linked by cables.

These were not good years for submarine telegraphy; the technology was being pushed too far too fast. The British Government were looking eastwards rather then westwards and were attempting to consolidate their Empire by a telegraph to India. The Red Sea and India Telegraph Co. was founded by Lionel Gisborne in 1857. It was intended that it should link Britain with India and the Government paid it an annual subsidy of £36,000 (It is interesting to note that having been stung once they were unwilling to guarantee its dividend). The strategic problems were enormous. The telegraph would pass through several sovereign states, not all of whom were noted for their pro-British sympathies. This required inter-governmental agreements and involved payments for the use of national lines. It was then to continue overland to Suez, by cable along the Red Sea to Aden and from there to Karachi via Muscat using another cable. The total underwater distance involved was 1,358 nautical miles.

The whole exercise was a disaster from the start. There had been no proper survey of the sea bed along the route. The cable, made by R.S. Newall, was of light construction and not likely to have been suited to the conditions. A practice had also developed which was likely to stack the odds against the prospects for the long-term survival of any cable. Contracts at that time included a clause which stipulated that any surplus cable was the property of the cable laying contractor, who like any profit motivated company tried to have as little slack as possible. Thus rather then follow the contours of the sea bed, the cables were stretched straight across submarine valleys, reefs etc. in an effort to make the cable length as close as possible to the nautical length.

The Red Sea to India cables were laid in 1859 and in spite of extensive repair work in 1860 they never worked satisfactorily. This ill planned effort together with the Atlantic failure caused total loss of confidence.

The Joint Committee on Submarine Telegraphs (aka Galton Committee)

In 1859, the Government, having lost so much money in telegraphs, appointed a committee which set the model for future rigorous inquiries into scientific and technological failures. It was chaired by Captain Douglas Galton* of the Royal Engineers. The members included Professor Sir Charles Wheatstone, William Fairbairn (President of the British Association for the Advancement of Science), George Parker Bidder (who became President of the Institution of Civil Engineers in 1860), Cromwell Varley (Chief Engineer of the Electric Telegraph Co), the brothers Edwin and Latimer Clark (Civil Engineers with the ETC and later part of the cable engineering consultants, Clark, Forde & Taylor) and finally, George Saward, Secretary of the Atlantic Telegraph Co.

Between its establishment and April 1861 it sat on 77 occasions and heard testimony from key players in industry as well as those closely associated with the Atlantic and other cable failures. Whitehouse spent much of his time blaming others, including Field for pushing to get things done. Thomson highlighted the flaws in Whitehouse's approach. In spite of recriminations the Committee did much good work. In addition to the main findings in their 520 page report (presented in 1861 but not published until July 1863) they identified the need for the establishment of standardised scientific units to measure electric current and resistance. In so far as cables were concerned they

* Douglas Strutt Galton (1822 - 1899) who had a distinguished engineering and scientific career should not be confused with his cousin, Francis Galton of the Quincunx and central limit theorem.

concluded that much of the failures could have been prevented with good preparation and good care. "Field's haste was a major problem, but so also was Whitehouse's erroneous science. The Committee was optimistic for the future, stating that "a well-insulated cable, properly protected, of suitable specific gravity, made with care, and tested underwater throughout its progress...possesses every prospect of not only being successfully laid in the first instance, but may reasonably be relied upon to continue for many years in an efficient state for the transmission of signals." This did much to convince the Government at large (but not the Treasury) that trans-oceanic telegraphy was feasible in the long term. It was to be many years and several diplomatic/military disasters later before the Treasury relented and acceded to the investment of public money in cable communications.

The link with India was eventually established through the efforts of John Pender, sometimes called the 'Cable King'. Pender was remarkable in that he combined an interest in technical matters with a sharp business sense. He was as keen to promote the commercial interests of others as he was to promote his own ventures. His monopolistic approach helped to prevent international telegraphy from fragmenting into a large number of unprofitable units. He eventually provided the Empire with its "Red Line" of communication and today Cable and Wireless is a testimony to his efforts.

Pender was born in Scotland in 1815, and when still quite young was speculating on the Cotton Market, first in Glasgow and later in Manchester, where he founded the firm of John Pender & Co. In 1852 he became a director of the British & Irish Magnetic Telegraph Co, the second largest of the private inland companies. In 1856, seeing the value of an American link for his cotton and telegraph interests, he invested £1,000 in Cyrus Field's Atlantic Telegraph Co. In 1861 he founded the *Telegraphic Journal* which later became the *Electrical Review* and is still a valued publication in the field of electrical engineering.

In Britain the Electric Telegraph Co. took over the International Telegraph Co., which had been established to lay cables between England and Holland, and changed its name to the Electric and International Telegraph Co. . The new company continued this aim and in 1857 extended its operation by forming a subsidiary, the Channel Islands Telegraph Co., to connect Weymouth to Alderney, Guernsey and Jersey. The E. & I. T. C. had a line between Holyhead in Wales and Howth, north of Dublin, by 1860 and another between Pembrokeshire and Wexford in 1862. Thus the B. & I. M. T. C. monopoly on the link to Ireland was broken and the Electric were in a better position to become involved in trans-Atlantic telegraphy should it ever succeed.

The Electric and International appears to have had problems with many of their cables. The Orfordness-Scheveningen link suffered badly from anchor damage. This was in spite of the fact that four separate cables had been laid in order to avoid total loss of communication. These were abandoned and replaced by a single heavy cable. This was manufactured and laid in 1858 by Glass Elliot and Co. using their cable ship *William Cory* (1578 tons) which had been launched during the previous year.

Their Channel Islands telegraph had an even unhappier existence. The contractors, R.S. Newall of Birkenhead, had paid little attention to the nature of the sea bed on which it was placed. In addition to the hazards of the rocky coastline of the Channel Islands, the cable had been laid straight through the Portland Race, one of the most turbulent stretches of water around the British Isles. The line was repaired no less then nine times before being abandoned in the early 1860s. It did, however, have one benefit. It gave ample opportunity for the future Superintendent of the Valentia Cable Station to gain experience in difficult circumstances.

James Graves had been employed at the Southampton office of the Electric and International Co. and on account of his ability to speak French he was transferred to Jersey as Clerk-in-Charge. It was he who transmitted weather reports to the Board of Trade*, for which he was paid an additional three shillings (15p) per week. In his autobiography, which he wrote as an ongoing exercise during his life, he gives details of this, and also of his efforts to devise his own testing equipment for locating faults in the cable. This sufficiently impressed his employers that on the closure of the Jersey station he was appointed Submarine Electrician on the Company's repair ship *Monarch*.

During this period there were a number of important scientific developments. The British Association Committee of 1861-62 had on the suggestion of Charles Bright and Latimer Clark adopted names for the units of electrical measurement and recommended improved practices for electrical testing. Cromwell F. Varley had perfected an artificial cable with which it was possible to study the properties of cables in a laboratory environment. He also introduced the idea of using signalling condensers (capacitors) to sharpen electric pulses in cables and thereby augment the speed of working.

Meanwhile the Knight of Kerry was not inactive with his pen. It is true that he now had his personal telegraph line to Dublin but there were threats to his island's monopoly on Atlantic communication from home and abroad. People were discussing alternative routes across the Atlantic and also alternative landing sites. The Northern Route, much favoured by Naval officers familiar with those waters, was suggested as a series of short lines, Scotland-Faeroes, Faeroes-Iceland, Iceland-Greenland, Greenland-Labrador. None of these exceeded 700 miles, which in addition to the improved chances of a successfully laying a short length, would increase signalling speeds (nobody appears to have considered the question of the total sum of all the delays of relaying traffic from one line to the next and the additional cost of maintaining and staffing five stations). Sir Peter wrote strenuous letters to the *Times* arguing against this and against the suggestion of a direct line to the UK, which he said would add an extra 400-500 miles to the length. There were also suggestions of a South Atlantic Route via Spain, Madeira, Cape Verde, Fernando Noronha and Brazil. However, as it involved so much foreign territory, this was a non-starter. In the event neither proposal came to anything. The Northern Route, in addition to being very cold and unpleasant for cable layers and repairers, would also have been prone to damage from grounding icebergs.

A more serious threat to the Knight's aspirations came from a point much closer to home. Professor William King in a letter to the *Times* (15 November 1862) argued that Cushla Bay near Galway was a more suitable landing place for any future cable. Once more Fitzgerald went into print in defence of his island, and drew support in further letters from a number of eminent marine

---

* The Board of Trade's new weather forecasting service, set up under the direction of Admiral Fitzroy, of *Beagle* fame, were early users of this line, obtaining daily reports of weather conditions in the area.

and telegraph authorities. His defence was not limited only to the *Times*. He believed in reaching a wide audience. There were letters to the editors of the *Mechanics Magazine* (13 December 1862) and the *Daily Express* (24 January 1863). In the event he argued his case well, and even if there were certain merits in alternative suggestions, he had the goodwill and trust of the people who really mattered, the directors of the Atlantic Telegraph Co.

The fact that the Atlantic Telegraph Co. remained in existence was almost entirely due to the efforts of its vice-chairman, Curtis M. Lampson, its secretary, George Saward and of course, Cyrus Field. In 1862 the Company persuaded the Government to undertake a detailed survey of the sea bed for a distance of 300 miles off the coasts of Ireland and Newfoundland. The voyage of HMS *Porcupine* cleared up many misconceptions about the nature of the continental shelf. The soundings showed that the shelf was not a precipitous transition but rather a slope of never less than one in twelve.

There was also the general realization on both sides of the Atlantic that one or two unpleasantnesses of an international nature which had arisen during the American Civil War could have been avoided with the help of the telegraph. In this fresh climate Field made some initial overtures in Washington and was reassured by a favourable response. On 17 February 1862, Glass Elliot & Co, in reply to an enquiry from Field, said that they were unwilling to undertake the entire risk themselves but that they were sufficiently confident that it could be done that they were wiling to undertake the work and have a large stake in its funding. A definite offer with conditions was addressed to Field on 10 October 1862.

> Dear Sir,
> In reply to your inquiries, we beg to state that we are perfectly confident that a good and durable submarine cable can be laid from Ireland to Newfoundland and are willing to undertake the contract on the following conditions:
>
> First that we shall be paid each week for our actual disbursements for labour and material.
>
> Second that when the cable is laid and in working order, we shall receive for our time, services and profit twenty per cent of the actual cost of the line in shares of the Company deliverable to us in twelve equal monthly installments at the end of each successive month whereat the cable shall be found in working order.
>
> We are so confident that this enterprise can be successfully carried out that we will make a cash subscription for a sum of twenty five thousand pounds sterling in the ordinary capital of the Company.
>
> Annexed we beg to hand you, for your guidance, a list of all the submarine telegraph cables manufactured and laid by our firm since we commenced this branch of our business, the whole mileage of which with the exception of the short one between Liverpool and Holyhead, which has been taken up, is at this time in perfect and successful working order. The cable that we had the honour to contract for and lay down for the French Government, connecting France with Algeria, is submerged in water of nearly equal depth to any we should have to encounter between Ireland and Newfoundland. You will permit us to suggest that the shore ends of the Atlantic

cable should be composed of very heavy wires, as from our experience the only accidents that have arisen to any of the cables which we have laid have been caused by ships' anchors and none of those laid out of anchorage ground have ever cost one shilling for repairs.

The cable that we would suggest for the Atlantic will be an improvement on all those yet manufactured and we firmly believe will be imperishable when once laid.

We remain, sir, yours faithfully

Glass, Elliot & Co.

During the following year Field toured the big cities in the United States. In most cases he got a polite hearing and in some got an enthusiastic reception, but of financial support he got little of note. Only in New York did he manage to raise the equivalent of £70,000 and that more as a result of general admiration of his indomitable spirit rather then any confidence in the venture. He then travelled once more to England where he found a more sympathetic climate.

Only one month after the publication of the report of the Joint Committee on Submarine Telegraphs, the Atlantic Co. felt confident enough to advertise its proposals and invited bids for a suitable cable connecting Ireland and Newfoundland. Their remit was very broad: it was intended to invite a broad response, and seventeen offers were received. These were submitted to a consulting committee who after consideration recommended acceptance of the proposal of Glass Elliot & Co.

Although many of the original sources of finance were no longer willing to commit themselves there was fresh support from John Pender, now a Member of Parliament, and the railway financier Thomas Brassey. This gave confidence to other industrialists and things started to move again.
Field's strenuous efforts did not go unrecognised. At the Atlantic Co's AGM on 16 March 1864 the Chairman, James Stuart Wortley, mentioned that up to that time Field had made 31 crossings of the Atlantic on Company business[*].

On 7 April there was an occurrence of great long term significance. Largely due to the influence of John Pender the cable manufacturing company, Glass Elliot & Co, amalgamated with their insulation supplier, the Gutta Percha Co., to form the Telegraph Construction and Maintenance Co. Pender was elected its first Chairman. This move brought two very able men, James Chatterton and Willoughby Smith, into direct contact with the Atlantic enterprise.

One of the first actions of the new company was to offer to manufacture and lay a new Atlantic cable. Their terms were so generous that they may be said to have removed almost the last of the obstacles that had blocked a fresh attempt for several years.

The conductor core of the new cable was to be of a cross sectional area of copper three times that of the old cable with a weight of 300lbs per mile. The conductor was to consist of seven strands of

[*] It is rumoured that he suffered terribly from sea sickness on every occasion

18 B.W.G. set in Chatterton's Compound (a mixture of gutta percha and Stockholm tar which was less brittle than gutta percha alone and which was better at wetting and therefore sticking to the metal). The primary core was covered with four layers of gutta percha interleaved with four layers of Chatterton's Compound. The weight of the new insulation (400lbs per mile) represented a virtual two-fold increase when compared with the 1858 cable.

The outer protection was planned to have ten strands of 13 B.W.G. mild steel similar to that used by Whitworth in his design of cannon. Each wire was to be wound with treated manilla and the assembly was to be wound helically around the inner conductor which had an outer covering of hemp. The total weight of the cable thus represented 3575lbs per mile on land and 1400lbs per mile when submerged. The inshore ends would have an additional covering of twelve strands of No. 2 gauge wire giving a total weight of 40,000lbs per mile. The proposal was for a gradual transition from one cable type to another. Eight miles of heaviest shore end would stretch westward from Valentia. There would then be a splice to an intermediate type which would run for a further eight miles. This splice would be followed by fourteen miles of a lighter type until at a distance of thirty miles from land the deep sea cable would be joined on. There would be a similar arrangement on the Newfoundland side but the transitional distance would only require to be five miles.

The proposed cable represented two major improvements over its predecessor. Firstly its volume to weight ratio was larger. This meant that as it was more buoyant it would enter the water at a shallower angle. There would therefore be less strain during submersion. The tensile strength of the 1858 cable was such that it was capable of supporting five times its own weight when suspended vertically in water. The new cable was to be capable of supporting eleven times its own weight under similar circumstances.

There was also a policy decision on the subject of testing. According to Willoughby Smith[*]

> "The core of these cables was not submitted to pressure during the mechanical tests, for in no instance had pressure developed faults; but actual experiments proved that faults which would be detected under a pressure of one atmosphere became more or less concealed according to the amount of pressure applied".

The basic design of this new cable had much merit, but hindsight showed up some flaws. The cable did not withstand the test of time. The manilla soon rotted leaving a loose sheathing which quickly corroded. The resulting loss of tensile strength meant that cable repair was hampered and eventually became impossible. Nevertheless this was the design that at that time appeared to be most suited to the task, and whose manufacture was commenced in June 1864 when James Graves was seconded to the Atlantic Telegraph Co. to take charge of their quality testing laboratory at the Telegraph Construction & Maintenance Company's factory at Greenwich.

---

[*] Willoughby Smith "A résumé of the earlier days of electric telegraphy", Hayman Brothers and Lilly, Printers, 1881 (reprints are available on Amazon)

Chapter 6

Prelude to the 1865 Expedition

Things were under way, but there were several important problems to be resolved. Having had unpleasant experiences with mid-ocean splices the agreement specified the delivery of one continuous length of cable. How was such a cable to be transported? It had taken the joint effort of USS *Niagara* and HMS *Agamemnon* to carry the previous cables, and the new cable was to be so much heavier. Experience over the years had also shown the deleterious effects which the atmosphere could have on the gutta percha insulation. This cable was to be submerged in water until the moment it was paid out.

All was solved by the availability of the *Great Eastern*. How much of a coincidence this was is questionable. This ship, the last of Brunel's brain children, was to prove a disaster for its designer, builder and investors. It was built by John Scott Russell, who rented the boatyard adjoining his in order to accommodate the great ship's total length (692 feet). Nothing like it had ever been built before and the design was indeed revolutionary. Brunel's use of a cellular double hull certainly saved her from disaster when she hit uncharted rocks on the approaches to New York in 1862. However, Brunel was feeling his way in a new technology and the decision to do a sideways launch was with hindsight a mistake. It took three months to launch the ship, and during this time the strain on Brunel himself brought on nephritis from which he died shortly after the maiden voyage.

ss Great Eastern ca 1859 by Parsons. Note the five funnels
(from https://commons.wikimedia.org/wiki/File:SS_Great_Eastern_painting.jpg)

Nor did the ship fare any better once afloat. The problems with the launch, combined with delays and design changes, brought Scott Russell to bankruptcy. There was an explosion in the boilers which killed four stokers during the maiden voyage. Above all by the time she was launched *Great Eastern* was a ship without a purpose. The Australian market had evaporated and she changed hands many times in vain attempts to make her financially viable. She was no luckier with her masters, never having the same one on two consecutive voyages. The action of one in particular during a passenger voyage led those on board to experience first hand one of her design deficiencies. Because of her size her movement could develop a resonance during heavy beam seas. This led to a merciless rolling where "her unfortunate passengers were plastered up the saloon walls". Why nobody thought of inserting a fin stabiliser is a mystery. Maybe they were frightened by the fact that her draught was already 30 feet.

Only once during these years did she have a really successful if perilous voyage. "She was chartered by the war office during one of the periods of international tension during the American Civil War when she carried cavalry to Canada. This time she had a unique type of fear-nought commander, who turned right at the bottom of Ireland and ordered full steam ahead regardless, secure in the knowledge that he commanded the largest ship afloat with 14 feet of steel reinforcing in the bows against ice or collision. It is said that he left a trail across the Atlantic of skippers dancing on their quarterdecks shaking their fists after him and that he missed the Cunard liner *Arabia* by the length of her bowsprit in fog off Cape Race. With the *Great Eastern*'s usual luck, one would have anticipated a disaster on the scale of the *Titanic*, but ten days out she stood in for Quebec and disembarked her passengers.

Things after that got worse. The creditors closed in on 14 January 1864, and she was put up for auction. The reserve price was £130,000, the amount necessary to pay off all judgement claims, but as there was no interest, she was withdrawn.

There can be no doubt that Cyrus Field and Thomas Brassey had set their sights on the *Great Eastern* and when the auction failed, events played into their hands. Brassey was one of the bond holders who had legal possession of the ship. The other bond holders had not been favourable to the idea of using her as a cable layer. However Brassey convinced Gooch and Barber to join him in buying out as many other bond holders as were necessary to give them control. In anticipation of being able to purchase the ship for around £80,000 they formed the Great Eastern Steamship Co. This was done very quickly and as Daniel Gooch recorded in his diary:

> Mr Barber went down to Liverpool to attend the sale when, strange to state a ship that had cost a million of money and was worth £100,000 for the materials in her was sold to us for £25,000.

The ship was then chartered to the Telegraph Construction and Maintenance Co. in return for £50,000 worth of cable shares. If the venture were a success it was agreed that the T.C. & M. Co. would bear the cost of adapting the ship for its new task.

Her means of propulsion consisted of a screw and two 56 foot diameter paddles which gave her the maneuverability that was felt to be necessary. However it was decided to reef her paddles (reduce the surface area of each plate) to give her a maximum speed of 9 knots, 2 knots faster then the maximum cable payout rate.

Her hold had to be enlarged to allow for the volume of cable. To make room for the midships cable tank, one boiler was removed.

The paying out machinery was in the stern and the picking up machinery in the bows. This arrangement was far from ideal and was eventually to be the source of many problems. It was the only option because at that time she was incapable of going stern to windward.

Stowing commenced on 19 Jan 1865 and continued until June. Because of her draught she was moored at Sheerness, 30 miles down the Thames from Greenwich. The Admiralty made available two hulks, *Amethyst* and *Iris*, which took on 250 tons of cable per run from the T. C. & M. works. These were towed down the river and the cargo was loaded onto the *Great Eastern* at the rate of 20 miles per day. Eventually the forward tank was to hold 630 miles while the midship and aft tanks contained 800 miles each.

Another problem which had to be solved in early 1865 concerned the question of who was to command the ship during the expedition. Her previous record was no credit. Eventually Cunards were approached and agreed to the secondment of Capt. James Anderson of their steamship *China.* He was a highly experienced North Atlantic sailor and was to prove to be a very valuable choice.

In addition to the two transport hulks, the Admiralty provided HMS *Sphinx* and HMS *Terrible.* They also agreed to release Capt. Moriarty, formerly of HMS *Agamemnon* to act as navigator on board *Great Eastern.*

In the tensions of the time an approach from the American Government, who wished to provide an escort of their own, was testily declined by the Atlantic Telegraph Company's Secretary, George Saward. His action was subsequently criticised in many quarters, but W.H. Russell attributed it to overwork and ill health.

During the period of manufacture of the cable there was a disagreement between the Atlantic Co's Electrician and James Graves, who was acting as its quality controller at the manufacturer's Greenwich works. The outcome of this must have convinced the directors of the latter's integrity and was probably a major contributor to his subsequent promotion. Graves already had good reason for resenting Varley, even if he did admire his professional qualities. During 1862, while seconded to Varley's section of the Electric & International Telegraph Co., he had been demonstrating the use of recently introduced equipment. He was sent to South Wales to instruct the Superintendent at Cardiff on the use of Varley's new Universal Galvanometer. Quoting from his diary:

> While there I drew up some rough notes with diagrams for the guidance of the Cardiff officials and left them a copy. I then proceeded to Cork for a similar purpose and there extended my notes... On my return to London the Scottish district Superintendent wrote to the Engineer for a copy of the 'testing instructions' issued to the Welsh and Irish districts. The Engineer knew nothing whatever about them and having mentioned it to me, I explained what I had done, whereupon he requested me to complete them with diagrams for distribution as a pamphlet and as just at this time the first edition of Culley's Handbook was in the press under the auspices of the Board of the Company, this pamphlet which I had completed was inserted therein as an appendix, but without any clue being given as to whose work it really was. Included in the same appendix was also my description with diagrams of Mr Varley's Translating Apparatus.

His diary also indicates the basis of the disagreement which arose while he was at Greenwich in November 1864. It is quoted here because it gives an insight into the workings of the factory and the relationship that existed between the two companies.

> My hours of duty were long and trying, testing before work started at 6 am and after they ceased at 10 pm, whilst the machines were stopped for meals and from time to time during the day. There were joints to test and a record to keep of the lengths manufactured by each machine (eight in number), the temperature of air and water and other details besides the keeping of a regular record of all tests and the working out of the results upon the instructions issued by the Electrician for my guidance, sending copies of the same to London upon sheets containing about 45 columns of details for each section of cable tested, whether in course of making, completed in tanks or being shipped on board the *Great Eastern* lying in the Medway opposite the Isle of Grain on the North and Queensborough on the south of the river.
>
> As the number of sections to be tested increased I found that I needed a good assistant quick at figures and algebraical formulae to work out the results from the above tests.
>
> I accordingly applied for such a one to assist me and my request was granted by the Atlantic Telegraph Co. and the Electrician (Mr C.F. Varley) was instructed accordingly but instead of sending me a competent assistant he sent me one of his own brothers whom I found totally incompetent for the work required of him. This placed me in a very awkward dilemma. It was by his recommendation that I was appointed to my own position..... The duties were too heavy for me to perform single handed and the assistant provided was utterly useless....

He had little alternative but to report these facts to the Company and in this had the support of the contractor's staff. Following this, C.F. Varley appears to have mounted a smear campaign against him. Much of this centred around a minor fault. In the course of arguing his innocence to his employers Graves reports that:

> On Friday Dec 2nd I telegraphed Mr Varley that the fault had increased and he came to the factory in the evening and demanded from Mr Bull, the Contractors electrician on duty the faulty section of cable that he might test it. This Mr Bull refused to allow in consequence of

strict instructions from his Chief, Mr C.V. DeSauty. Mr Varley then left after recommending me to resign my appointment in the Electrical and International Telegraph Co. ....

It will be observed that a two edged sword was brought to attack me. I was to resign my old appointment in the Electric Co and a plot was already laid to put me out of the Atlantic Co to make room for his brother.... I remained at the factory that evening till 11 o clock watching the fault which still tested very variably... On Sunday Dec 4 I was at the factory all morning testing joints and overlooking splicings of cable.. The next day Mr Varley took upon himself the authority to suspend me from my duties at the factory for neglect of duty and place his brother in charge of the test room.

When Graves attempted to take with him such papers as would support his case Varley prevented him from doing so. He made instant representation to the chairman, vice chairman and secretary of the Atlantic Co., who naturally worried about the effect such a wrangle might have on the progress of the cable reinstated him pending an enquiry. They also ordered that the letter book and correspondence be brought to their offices in London.

On resuming his task he had the pleasure of discovering that the small fault had been traced and cut out and that the cable was now perfect.

The enquiry took place on 7th December.

Mr Varley was allowed to make his charges against me. He charged me with having sent him false returns of the tests at Greenwich.

I asked the Chairman if he would allow me to use my letter book which was lying upon the table and having obtained his consent I proved from my letters to Mr Varley that I had on two or three separate occasions written to him pointing out the instrumental errors and asking for his opinion and to which letters I had not up to that moment received any reply.

He then stated that I had complained of his brother as incompetent. He considered that he was as competent as I was for the duties required. I pointed out that he was not able to do correctly a simple multiplication sum without it having to be checked after him and frequently corrected, that he was unable reliably to perform the necessary calculations and that I had to do them myself notwithstanding his nominal assistance.

The Secretary, warmed with indignation said he could not sit there to hear such accusations brought against Mr Graves without any foundation whatever. The Chairman addressed Mr Varley in strong terms, which elicited from the latter the words 'Gentlemen, am I to understand that you wish me to resign?' to which the Chairman replied 'No, Mr Varley, we do not wish you to resign, but we wish you to go home and reflect how you have endeavoured without cause to injure an innocent man.' The Committee then separated and the Secretary warmly congratulated me upon the issue as also did Mr C.V. DeSauty the Contractor's Electrician who had come up to London to personally defend me if it had been necessary for independent testimony to be given on my behalf.

On resuming his duties he was instructed to send reports to Varley and also to the Board. Once this storm blew over work continued apace, but it is not clear whether Graves eventually got an efficient assistant.

Returning briefly to the peregrinations of Cyrus Field: after the purchase of *Great Eastern* he had gone home for a period of rest, but was back in England on a fleeting visit on 18 March 1865 on his way to a holiday in Egypt. As a member of the New York Chamber of Commerce he was to attend the opening of the Suez Canal as their official delegate. He returned once more to England on 1 May in preparation for the expedition.

Much of the history between 1 May and the departure of the *Great Eastern* must be deduced from correspondence in the Knight of Kerry's letter book. His tireless activities had ensured the continuance of his island as the eastern terminus of any telegraph. He was now busy organising as many of the social and technical details at Valentia. On 4 May he received a letter from Cyrus Field indicating that he and a party would be coming to Valentia to choose a landing site for the cable. An engraving from Frank Leslie's newspaper indicates that the party consisting of John Temple, B. Wardlock, C.F. Varley and Cyrus Field choose Foilhommerum Bay on June 4. The reasons behind the choice of this location are not very clear and it was eventually found to be quite unsuitable. There seems to have been a number of scientific misconceptions prevailing in spite of the progress since 1858. One view (which the Knight of Kerry vigorously supported) held that the signal would be so enfeebled after its long journey that it was imperative to land it at the furthest point west on the island. It is difficult to believe that the additional five miles to Knightstown would have had any significance except possibly for Sir Peter, who after all would receive payment for the land lines which crossed his property from the telegraph office that was now under construction. There is a letter from Richard Glass, Manager of the Telegraph Construction and Maintenance Co, thanking the Knight for his interest and stating that he (R.G.) would go into the advantages of the chosen landing site when he arrived at Valentia.

The origin of the name Foilhommerum is somewhat of a mystery. A newspaper correspondent present at the 1865 festivities on the island attempted to find out for himself. The best explanation he was offered was that many years previously a body had been washed ashore and the only distinguishing mark was a tattoo which sounded like Foilhommerum.

Field's letter to the Knight on 4 May warned him that the *Great Eastern* would not be able to enter the harbour. This of course was a severe disappointment to the Knight which was increased by the fact that the worries about draught had the Admiralty looking to their own ships. A letter to Fitzgerald on 22 June from the master of HMS *Terrible*, then at Spithead mentioned that their guns had been landed and that 100 tons of coal was being loaded on board. It continues:

> Hydrography Office advise against *Great Eastern* entering harbour. Please send list of men-of-war which have anchored there from time to time. Have you got a plan of the harbour. I cannot find Foilhommerum (what a name) marked on the chart, where is it.

Whether the Knight was able to supply a map is not known, but a subsequent letter indicated that the Admiralty had given instructions that *Sphinx* and *Terrible* were not to enter Valentia Harbour.

Returning to events in London, W.H. Russell reported that:

> On 24 May His Royal Highness the Prince of Wales accompanied by many distinguished personages paid a long visit to the *Great Eastern*, for the purpose of inspecting the arrangements for laying the Cable. His Royal Highness was received by Mr Pender, the Chairman of the Telegraph Construction and Maintenance Company; Mr Glass, Managing Director and a large number of electricians and officers connected with the undertaking. After partaking of breakfast, the Prince visited each portion of the ship and witnessed the transmission of a message sent through the coils, which then represented 1,395 nautical miles. The signals transmitted were seven words I WISH SUCCESS TO THE ATLANTIC CABLE and were received at the other end of the coils in the course of a few seconds.

The official reception to mark the occasion of the manufacture of the last mile of cable was held at the factory on 29 May and on 14 June the *Amethyst* completed her final visit to Greenwich and left to deliver the last instalment of the cable to the Great Eastern. When all the cable had been stowed various tests were undertaken. The insulation was found to be good and DeSauty's experiments showed that messages could be transmitted through the coiled cable at a rate of 3.8 words per minute. Thomson and Varley tried out a new curbed sending key which they had developed and obtained a rate of 6 words per minute. They felt confident that this would rise to 12 words per minute when the cable had been uncoiled and submerged. Their system of curbed sending employed a key that was arranged so that after transmitting a pulse, the cable would be momentarily connected to a battery of opposite polarity before being grounded. Although this idea improved the shape of the transmitted pulses and thereby increased the sending rate, it was to be a considerable time before anything like it was successfully adopted in submarine telegraphy.

Preparations were now in their final stages. The Knight of Kerry was kept busy with correspondence and making all the necessary domestic and social arrangements. He had sent letters to many people inviting them to be present at the landing of the cable. The Viceroy, Lord Woodhouse, wrote on 22 June explaining that he would only be able to attend the landing of the cable if it took place before 10 July. Saward wrote on 28 June asking the Knight to book the whole or greater portion of the hotel at Knightstown from 5 to 31 July for the Chairman, W. Stuart Wortley, W.C. Breton and Capt A. Hamilton, two of the directors in addition to Wm. McCurley, the assistant company secretary. This seems to have created some tension between the Atlantic Telegraph Co and the T.C. and M. Co., who were after all in overall control of the operation. A letter from Richard Glass explained that he and Mrs Glass would be coming ahead in the *Hawk*. It continues "Have told Saward that the rooms in Mr Jenning's will be available for his directors if not occupied by our staff". Another letter from the Viceroy several days later says that he would be there if at all possible, but he had problems with rioters in the North[*]... " I am being taken to task for not making the orange-men and the ribbon-men lie down in peace like the lion and the lamb". Robert Peel, the Secretary for Ireland wrote in similar vein. Samuel Gurney declined the Knight's invitation because he was committed to electioneering (he was not to know that his family business was soon to collapse, representing the largest failure in the City of London up to that time). He explained that his brother-in-law[**], Henry Bewley, would however be present. There were also acceptances from Robert Dudley the artist, W.H Russell the *Times* correspondent, and many others who were to attend on the expedition.

On 24 June the *Great Eastern* left the Medway for the Nore carrying 7,000 tons of cable and 7,000 tons of coal. At the Nore she took on an additional 1,500 tons of coal which she could not have taken on earlier on account of her draught. Taking all of this with the weight of her cable tanks the total dead weight amounted to 21,000 tons.

She was to have a complement of 500 men[+] for the voyage. As the duration of the expedition was uncertain she was loaded with enough provisions for a small army. The stores were not only boxed and crated but included live food: a cow, a dozen oxen, 20 pigs and 120 sheep. In addition to beef and pork there were flocks of ducks, turkeys, geese, 500 chickens and 18,000 eggs.

As can be imagined, such a newsworthy project elicited many requests for correspondents to be allowed to accompany the ship. In order to be as fair as possible the Companies decided to exclude all journalists. Instead they approached William H. Russell, the war correspondent, who had done so much to publicise the poor conditions endured by the British troops in the Crimea. He was to make a history of the expedition and Robert Dudley, the artist was to assist him by making pictorial records. In the event this was to be a very sensible decision, although others on board were subsequently prevailed on to contribute to popular magazines such as *Cornhills*, *Blackwoods* and *Macmillans* and this has provided us with several alternative insights into life on board the great ship during July and August 1865.

---

[*] There were Ulster problems even then.

[**] Curious this–Bewley's wife was not a member of the Gurney family. Perhaps one of his sisters had married Gurney

[+] According to Henry O'Neill: 500 men, no women, a black cat and a jackdaw

Chapter 7

Under Way 1865

At noon on July 15th the *Great Eastern* raised her anchor. The enormous capstan, requiring a total of 180 men (60 on deck and 60 on each of two floors below), was slow to respond at first in spite of the exhortations of Mr Halpin (the first officer) and a young fiddler whom Robert Dudley portrayed perched on top of the capstan itself. The ship moved slowly down the Thames under the charge of the Trinity pilot, Mr Moore, drawing 34ft 4ins forward and 28ft 6ins aft. The Lizard was rounded at midnight on 16 July.

Before describing the details of the expedition after 16 July, it is perhaps worth listing the known persons who were involved with the execution of the task.

<u>On the *Great Eastern*</u>

Commander	Capt. James Anderson
First Officer	Capt. Robert Halpin
Navigator	Capt Moriarty RN

Telegraph Construction and Maintenance Staff

In overall charge of the operation	Samuel Canning
Mechanical Staff	
Chief	Henry Clifford
Assistants	Mr Temple & Mr London
Electrical Staff	
Chief	C. V. DeSauty
Assistants	Willoughby Smith
	W.W. Biddulph, H. Donovan, O. Smith
	J. Clark, J.T. Smith, J. Gott

Atlantic Telegraph Staff

Chief Electricians	Cromwell F. Varley
	Professor W. Thomson
Assistants	Mr Deacon, Mr Medley
	Mr Trippe, Mr Perry

<u>At the Valentia Station</u>

Telegraph Construction and Maintenance Staff

In overall charge	R. Glass
Superintendent	J. May
Assistant	T. Brown, W. Crocker, Mr Stephenson
	Mr George, Mr Fisher

Atlantic Telegraph Co Staff

Clerk-in-Charge	J. Graves
Clerks	J. Carson, F. Tranfield, Donovan

It is interesting and informative to monitor the subsequent progress of some of the juniors mentioned here and certain individuals have been highlighted for reference.

As has been previously mentioned, the Telegraph Construction and Maintenance Co. were in overall charge, and the Atlantic staff had very little formal responsibility until after takeover. (Graves, who had been retained as Clerk-in-Charge, and his three assistants do not get a mention in W.H. Russell's history). The roles played by Varley and Thomson had been very clearly defined: they represented the Atlantic Telegraph Co and were present only as observers. Varley was not to interfere or to express his opinion on any of the operations in the test room on board *Great Eastern*. He was further ordered not to give advice even if asked for it unless such a request was made in writing. Any reply was to be given in writing and to include a distinct declaration that the opinion so given was not in any way to bind the Company which he represented. Thomson was admitted on board as Varley's aide and had joined the ship on July 14th.

There were a considerable number of other notable people on board including directors (e.g. Atlantic Telegraph Co), journalists, artists and visitors. In theory the majority of these were only travelling as far as Ireland, although some remained on board throughout the journey.

On Monday 17 July *Great Eastern* caught up with the screw steamer *Caroline*, which was carrying 540 tons of the Irish shore end of cable, and as she was making only slow progress took her in tow. However, on the 18th a gale set in off the Irish coast and *Caroline* was forced to cut the tow and make her own way, piloted by her big sister.

The two ships arrived off Valentia and Capt Anderson, having ordered the firing of a gun to announce their arrival, directed his ship to Berehaven Bay. Here there was sufficient depth of water to allay any fears concerning the ship's draught. During her stay she was visited by many people, but it was generally believed by members of the public that she would be making her way to Foilhommerum. This had never been the intention. *Caroline* was carrying 25 miles of shore end which when laid would be buoyed. So in fact only those on board or on the escort vessels would catch a glimpse of the *Great Eastern* at her work.

On Thursday morning, Anderson, in company with some of those on board, climbed Hungry Hill (2050 feet). It was his custom when arriving at a new locality to climb the highest peak in the vicinity in order to get the lie of the land. Henry O'Neill, the journalist, who went with the party, soon regretted his decision:

> After a tedious ascent, we at last reached the summit, but as is usually the case, only to find ourselves enveloped in dense fog. Before we descended, however, it cleared off for a few moments, enabling us to get a hasty glimpse of the scenery around, whilst far in the distance we

> descried the *Terrible* and the *Sphinx* entering the haven by the narrow channel at the west end. This latter fact was the signal for a hurried and over precipitous descent, from the tumbles met with in which some of us did not recover for many days.

Foilhommerum Bay where the cable was to be landed, has a rocky shore line. Behind this there is a cliff up which the cable was to be dragged. It was eventually protected in an iron pipe, but it is not certain if this was done in the initial stages or subsequently. The cable station, consisting of a long low hut, was perched a few yards back from the top of the cliff. Russell describes it as:

> . . . a building of wood much beslavered with tar and pitch of exceeding plainness and let us hope of corresponding utility. Inside were many of the adjuncts of comfort, not to speak of telegraphic luxury, galvanometers, wires, batteries, magnets, Siemens' and B.A.[*] unit cases and the like, as well as properties which gave the place a false air of campaigning. A passage led from end to end, with rooms for living and sleeping in to the right and left and an instrument room at the far extremity. Here, on a narrow platform, were the signal and speaking apparatus connected with the wires from the end of the cable, which was secured inside the house. Outside the wires were carried by posts in the ordinary way to the station at Valentia, whence they were conveyed to Killarney, and placed in communication with the general Telegraphic system over the world. The Telegraphic staff and operators were lodged in primitive apartments like sections of a Crimean hut, and did not possess any large facility for enjoying social intercourse with the outer world, although so much intelligence passed through their fingers.

---

[*]The British Association for the Advancement of Science was attempting to introduce a set of standard units for electricity, basically the volt, amp and ohm as we know them today.

Festive scene at the top of the Foilhommerum cliff.
Painting by Robert Dudley in the IET collection of works by that artist.

The landing of the cable was supervised by Samuel Canning, who had been transferred to the *Caroline* when the *Great Eastern* approached Valentia. A raft of small boats was used to bring the shore end in from the *Caroline*. The subsequent events are described by Graves in his station diary. This diary starts with a set of instructions to his subordinates similar to that issued to Varley and Thomson. It then continues:

10. 30 am	(London time) shore end of cable landed from *Caroline*
11. 15	Sufficient cable hauled ashore to reach the office
11. 45	End of cable hauled to top of cliff
12. 15 pm	All cable on top of cliff
12. 30	End reached outside of office and preparations made to speak to *Caroline*
12. 45	End stripped and brought into office

12. 47 Signals received from *Caroline* - continuity all right and signals by Morse instrument good.

12. 50 Speeches made by Sir Robert Peel, the Knight of Kerry, Mr Glass, interspersed by cheers for her majesty the Queen, the Knight of Kerry, Mr Glass, the Atlantic Telegraph Co. and staff, President Johnson, Captain White and the numerous men who assisted in laying and landing this portion of the shore end. After the Doxology was sung, the multitude separated and dispersed upon the cliffs.

1. 00 Insulation test taken by Contractors staff which gives a result of 458 millions of Siemens units per naut. mile, which considering the time the cable had been coiled dry in the *Caroline* is satisfactory.

2. 33 Gun fired from the *Caroline* as a signal for the starting and immediately she steamed away being assisted by the *Hawk*.

3. 00 Contractors staff tried to take the resistance of the conductor by Wheatstone's Bridge and mirror galv. but the magnet currents set up in the cable by the rolling of the *Caroline* quite prevented the possibility of getting a result.

4. 00 *Hawk* and *Caroline* a long distance out, say 6 or 8 miles. All going on well, sea very calm, weather fine and warm - but hazy in the distance - an apparent ground swell - short distance out judging from *Caroline's* rolling.

5. 00 Insulation of cable increased from 458 millions per naut. to 615 millions.

5. 24 *Caroline* abreast of the Skelligs

6. 00 9 miles payed out, Insn 699 millions per naut.

6. 57 12 miles payed out

8. 00 Insulation 699 millions per naut.

9. 25 20 miles payed out - Insulation 874 millions per naut.

9. 45 21 ditto ditto

10. 15 23 miles payed out.

11. 20 Insulation 1326 millions per naut[**]. All payed out 27 miles[***]

11. 30 Notice received "going to seal end and buoy cable". Shore end laid all right, the insulation having increased from 458 millions (the result when all was in the *Caroline*) to 1326 millions owing to the cooling of the gutta percha after being submerged.

Interior of the station at Foilhommerum Bay
Painting by Robert Dudley in the IET collection of works by that artist.

At 11 pm on Saturday a coastguard officer, coming overland from Valentia, made his way to where *Great Eastern* was anchored, with the news that *Caroline* was paying out the shore end. This caused great excitement on board. Steam was raised and the ship headed towards the rendezvous point at 2 am on the 23rd, followed by *Sphinx* and *Terrible*. The Station Diary continues:

July 23rd Sunday weather fine and calm

[**] There seems to have been no comment on the fact that this is a remarkable and apparently sudden increase.

[***] It was generally reported that *Caroline* was carrying 25 miles of shore end.

9. 00 am *Great Eastern* reported off Bray Head and steaming outwards towards the *Caroline* at the end of the shore cable.

The artist, Henry O'Neill, who could always be relied upon to give a light hearted treatment of the expedition, and who is generally the best source of social details, gives a view from the ship at this point:

> At 10. 30 came up with the *Caroline*, and shortly after the *Hawk*, a fine steamer belonging to the Telegraph Construction and Maintenance Company, arrived having on board a distinguished party, including Sir Robert Peel, the Knight of Kerry, Lord John Hay, Captain Hamilton, a director of the Atlantic Telegraph Company[*] and many other gentlemen connected with the undertaking. There were also some ladies on board, who were sadly disappointed at not being able to visit the ship, - a task which owing to the roughness of the sea even the gentlemen could not accomplish without a wetting. Here Mr Canning rejoined us, accompanied by Dr W.H. Russell, Mr Dean, Mr Temple and others. The paddle box boats of the *Sphinx* having taken the end of our cable on board the *Caroline*, the splice from the shore end was effected at 5.30 pm.

The *Hawk* had already returned to Valentia sometime after 2 pm, bringing correspondence from those on board for forwarding overland.

The Station Diary gives details of the process of the splice:

12 noon Insulation of shore end 1468 millions per naut.

2. 15 Notice received through shore end by Morse instr. from *Caroline* to "put cable to earth 2 hours and then commence paying- out system" going to begin splice.

4. 15 splice completed: cable insulated ashore till

4. 30 when reversals of 2 minutes duration were sent from ship for 10 minutes.

4. 40 Line put to earth for 10 minutes

4. 50 Reversals of 2 mins duration received from *Great Eastern* for 10 minutes upon mirror galvanometer, the nature of signals showed the whole cable (2,300 nauts.) to be in circuit and the changes made ashore were fully understood by those on board the *Great Eastern*.

---

[*] Hamilton had a set of test messages in a sealed envelope. These were to be transmitted through the cable prior to hand-over. Field was also carrying a set of messages for transmission from the other shore.

5. 00 Repetition of same series of changes as per pre-concerted arrangement - which will be continued.

Although the diary gives a resume of these arrangements, W.H. Russell's in his book notes that

"During the paying out of the Cable, from the moment of starting until the end is landed at Newfoundland, electrical tests will be applied without intermission."

Note that the importance of keeping to a routine such as this in the days before radio cannot be over-emphasised. As will be seen later, on the one occasion when an instrument was being changed at Valentia, the temporary breakdown in communication caused consternation on board the ship.

James Graves continues:

"The speaking through the cable will be done by Mr DeSauty's system as has been used on board the *Great Eastern* up to the time of her sailing.

Separate apparatus is fixed ready for use in case it is necessary for shore to take the insulation or conductivity of the Cable. A switch which turns 3 ways serves to connect the Cable wire to either speaking or testing at a moment's notice[*]. Five ordinary Daniell cells are used for signalling and 40 cells are kept ready for testing insulation, if necessary to be taken from shore.

Our three clerks now take 8 hours duty each and Mr McCurley and I are present during the daytime. "

Before the *Great Eastern* has gone too far on her journey, it might be worth having another look at those people then on board who were not specifically involved with the cable laying. Russell was quite specific when he wrote:

As the voyage of the *Great Eastern* promised to be so interesting to electricians and engineers, several young gentlemen who worked in the testing room and in the engineer's department received a passage, as we have mentioned, but there was no person on board who was not in some way or other engaged on the business of both companies, or connected with the management of the ship.

This was perhaps an understatement intended for public consumption which omits to mention the fact that he brought his two young sons along for the experience. Henry O'Neill gives a fuller list which mentions those such as Thomson, Field and Varley and then continues:

... nor must I forget M. Despécher[**], a French gentleman who has witnessed the laying of many a cable; a great traveller and therefore more free of prejudice than some of his countrymen.

---

[*]From what is mentioned elsewhere, it can be assumed that the third position was intended for connecting the cable to ground.

[**] Jules Despécher was the author of a scheme to link France with America via the Azores.

> There is Dr Ward and his son, who have plenty of work to do as has Mr Deane, ever busy taking notes for a history of the expedition, for which the genial and industrious Mr Dudley is preparing pictorial illustrations; and last, not least the well known Dr Russell who not only supplies the literary portion of the aforesaid work, but who also has to furnish an elaborate report of the voyage for the Company to forward to the Press. His two sons, Willie and Johnny, accompany him and are looking forward with delight to catching a cod-fish in Newfoundland. There are also many young gentlemen in the other saloon who accompany the expedition for the purpose of acquiring experience as engineers and electricians, amongst whom are Mr Gooch's son, Messrs Crampton jun. and Trench, and a most ingenious little mechanician, M. Schafer, whose good temper was proof against all the practical jokes played on him: a most useful member of the community was he, repairing with great skill and readiness any article broken on board, from a watch to a meerschaum pipe

Even in this supposedly exhaustive list O'Neill fails to mention that Sawyer of the *New York Herald* was also on board.

At 10 pm on the 23rd notice was received on shore to say that 50 miles including the shore end had been paid out. Those on board the ship not directly involved retired for the night in anticipation of a good sleep. However at 4.20 am they were awoken by the firing of the ship's gun, a prearranged signal for the escort boats to stop. There was a minor fault in the cable which was impairing communications with the land. Valentia were unaware that anything was wrong until 6.48am, as can be seen from the log.

4.00am	received a ten minute current indicating the ship to be in soundings.
6.48	Received 8 quarter minute reversals, sent back same, being the signal for speaking. Received "is all right in office" and "we put to earth for 10 minutes if signals fail to follow rules sent"
7.13	End to earth on board for shore to take copper resistance, tried but spot constantly out of range of mirror galvanometer. Sent "cannot take CR." Received "free for 5 mins."
7.38	Receiving current but could not understand their meaning.
8.59	Changed galvanometer and now all right. "put to earth for 5 minutes" received.
9.19	Cable free for ship to take insulation
10.00	Sending and receiving ordinary signals regularly
11.00	" " " " " "

12 noon	" " " " " "
12.48pm	Received signals similar to those for indicating another 50 miles payed out, but doubtful.
3.25	After several attempts to read ship unsuccessfully they told shore "to join up Morse instrument"
3.32	Morse joined up
3.37	Message received by Morse Instr for Mr Glass as follows "Send *Hawk* here lat 52, long 12 and send *Caroline* to splice". Reply sent "ships ordered off, send report of cause shortly" - no cause was however assigned, nor anything said by ship to lead to any idea of cause. These signals were evidently not through a very great length of cable, say one tank at the utmost and probably cable cut on board the *Great Eastern* judging from appearance and strength of signals.
4pm - 8pm	Ship and shore alternately taking tests. Shore's tests being taken under the direction of and according to instructions from ship. All results sent to ship but none of theirs sent to shore. Nothing definite arrived at owing to want of information from ship both as to result of their tests, the distance of ship from shore and the length of cable in circuit between us and the end of it on board the ship.
9.25	Ship in answer to question states "nothing to say". Shore's tests (minimum) Cable to earth aboard 350 Siemens units. Cable free aboard 4870 Siemens units. Showing a result for insulation of only .487 millions per naut, assuming 100 miles to be in circuit, being about 1/3000 of what it should be if perfect; leading us to the conclusion that a bad fault exists somewhere between ship and shore, but as stated owing to lack of news from ship we cannot say locality.
12 midnight	Up to this time alternate tests taken by ship and shore, but nothing new transpired and no details from ship whatsoever - *Hawk* en route to *Great Eastern*, I left for Knightstown - *Caroline* ballasts and proceeds in morning.

Hawk caught up with the *Great Eastern* at 5.30 am on Tuesday. By that time 10 miles of cable had been hauled up. The process was extremely slow and tedious and was not helped by the fact that the steam engine driving the hauling-in gear was defective. The engineers were in favour of returning to the point where the cable was spliced to the shore end, but Canning insisted on bringing another small steam engine into service and to everyone's delight the faulty part was brought on board before long. According to O'Neill:

> On examination it was found that a piece of the iron wire of which the outer covering of the Cable is partly made, had penetrated the gutta percha, thus destroying the perfect insulation of the copper wires. Some suspicion arose of foul play, such an instance having occurred some years ago in laying a cable in the North Sea, a crime which was only brought to light two years after by the confession of the culprit, who declared that he had been offered one thousand pounds if he succeeded in his diabolical attempt.

The shore log records the successful outcome: July 25

9.25am	*Caroline* started but was recalled before she got out of the harbour by telegram from ship "cable OK, stop *Caroline*"
11.00	Nothing particular has passed.
11.05	*Great Eastern* telegraphs "small fault discovered in cable and cut out"
11.14	Ship says "going to join up in one min, have you anything to say " (this by Morse inst.)
11.15	"Put cable to earth for 2 hours" signalled by ship.
1.15 pm	Cable freed.
1.40	Sent current into cable to see what was state of end on board. Result showed end to be free on board as all our current returned to us again. Cable joined to Earth through galvo.
1.45	I saw current from the ship, weak and in one direction for about a minute, then reversed to the other pole- ship apparently taking the Res. of Cond. Galvo was however in circuit and would throw their results, I saw them repeating the test & removed galvanometer.
1.55	Mirror galv. put in circuit - weak magneto currents from ship's motion observed.
2.10	On charging line found it free on board again; probably engaged in splicing.
3.45	Received steady current from ship, thinking they were taking Copper Res. put cable to earth direct.
3.50 - 4.00	Recd. several irregular reversals - thinking they were a signal for speaking acknowledged them but no reply.

4.55	Recd. 8 regular 1/4 min reversals and joined up for speaking- signals recd. but were unintelligible. On examining them closely concluded they were reversed. Changed connections at my suggestion, when signals became intelligible and "take up paying out system" was received - good signals.

This error and the associated disruption in the testing schedule caused consternation on board the *Great Eastern* as O'Neill reports:

> At 1pm the splice was being made, we again proceeded on our course but not for long. Half an hour had scarcely elapsed, when to the surprise and dismay of all a fresh fault was announced. This time the disaster looked serious, for all communication with the shore was totally lost. Patiently we watched the application of continual tests, the very mention of picking up producing a feeling of gloom and the mere sight of the machine becoming hateful. When at last we were about to have recourse to it, suddenly the signals were again perfect and soon after with much laughter at our fears we learned that the cause of all our anxiety and despair was the removal of an instrument at Valentia, for some purpose best known to those on shore and then resuming the satisfactory process of paying out of the Cable with thankful and merry hearts we again proceeded on our voyage.

From then until July 29th everything ran extremely smoothly as the shore log records:

5.5 - 7.30pm	Ordinary paying-out signals going on all night and we presume that *Great Eastern* has proceeded on her way again -
10.0pm	Signalling power changed to two cells -
11.0pm	Received signals indicating 50 more nts payed out (Total 100)
12.0 midnight	" " " " " " " "

The 200 mile signal was received at 2.50pm on the following day. At 5.0pm Graves recorded that:

> The fault which was discovered on 24th inst. from information received from Mr Glass, appears to have been caused by a small piece of wire cut off in splicing having fallen upon the cable unobserved and having adhered to it, was in passing through the machinery forced into the core. The *Great Eastern* picked up eleven miles of the cable before the fault was reached. The bare fact that during the paying out a minute fault can be localised, the cable picked up and repaired on the spot should inspire all concerned with the welfare of the expedition with the utmost confidence.

He then notes that the 200 mile indication at 2.50 was an error of interpretation as some "doubtful" signals had been received at that time. 200 miles was in fact reached at 6.50. And so it continued. The distances run were as follows:

July 27

5.50 am Total 300 miles

7.50 pm Total 400 miles

July 28

4.50 am Total 500 miles

11.50pm Total 600 miles - slack 10%

In these periods of tranquillity those not involved directly in the work relaxed in their saloon. Thomson and Varley filled sheets of paper with algebraic symbols and to the others appeared to speak a different language. They would argue heatedly if their calculations differed even in the "umpteenth" decimal place. M. Despécher was competent on the piano and Dr Ward was reputed to be an excellent performer on the violin. Much of the time was passed playing cards and exchanging reminiscences. O'Neill says of Russell:

> ... an excellent companion is he on a long voyage, ever chatty and cheerful and full of anecdotes and information picked up in every quarter of the globe. It is said that Caesar, Napoleon, and I believe our own Wellington, could write dispatches and give verbal orders at the same time; but in this respect Russell beats them all. I have seen him correct the proof sheets of a newspaper of which he is the editor, enter into the general conversation, and moreover enter into a rubber of whist, all at once, though I fear with some detriment to his partner's interests in the latter operation.

In order to gain an appetite they would promenade the deck, or Regent Street as they called it, endeavouring to avoid the effects of smoke from the four main chimneys, as well as the galley chimneys, blacksmith's forge and donkey engine. They were well wined and dined during the journey, so much so that Dr. Ward and his son did good business treating indigestion. One wit on board referring to the name of the contracting company wasn't sure about "Construction" but was absolutely certain about the fact that it was an excellent "Maintenance Company".

In order to relieve the tedium of inactivity during the journey, O'Neill and others devised a newspaper, the *Atlantic Telegraph*, which O'Neill edited and Robert Dudley illustrated. It made its first appearance on July 29 and in addition to a summary of the state of the cable gives a light hearted picture of life on board. It mentions facetiously that up to that time Mr Field had completed his 700th letter, John Deane was now forced to occupy an extra cabin because the notes which he had accumulated for his great history of the cable in 96 volumes now occupied all the space of his original cabin*. The artist Robert Dudley had completed 350 sketches. It also reported that Capt. Anderson joined in amusements and that on the Thursday (July27) evening he delighted all with a séance. The amusements of the day were given as follows:

> "12 noon - luncheon and 'Daily Navigation' (not Telegraph). 5.30 pm - dinner. 8 pm - Tea. 9-11 pm - Grog possibly with whist. From daylight to dusk, looking out for the *Sphinx*** (through the kindness and liberality of the Admiralty this interesting amusement will be open to the public free of charge. NB The above amusements with the exception of whist are gratis"

As editor O'Neill gives his address as No 14 Lower South Avenue, Middle district, which one presumes was a euphemism for his cabin.

The Station Log at Valentia pinpoints the moment when trouble next struck. 700 miles had been paid out at 1.50 pm on the 29th.

3.30-3.40pm

Shore's signals greatly increased in strength and irregular deflections observed (157 left,267 left 85 R., 250 L., 205 R. being about double the usual deflections) and showing (1) the length of cable in circuit to be greatly reduced, (2) an imperfect or variable earth connection at the sea end.

3.40-3.50pm Cable put to Earth ashore as usual.

3.50-4.00pm During this interval ship should have sent signals and would probably have signalled 650 miles ran, but nothing whatsoever was received. A very weak current was observed as if coming from the end of the cable caused by the chemical action of Copper (conductor) and iron (outside wires) in sea water. There is every evidence of the cable having suddenly parted between 3.00 and 3.30 pm, during which time the ship would have being taking the insulation test. The *Great Eastern* is probably about 645 miles from land having payed out about 712 miles and from the chart she appears to be in about 1700 fathoms of water.)

---

* John C. Deane's contribution is undoubtedly the most technically informative account of the expedition. It is suspected that his further involvement with Atlantic telegraphy during and after 1866 may have consumed all his attentions, thus preventing the publication of a magnum opus on the subject, if indeed such a work was ever seriously intended.

** At 8 am on Wednesday 26 July, being the only ship with the necessary equipment, *Sphinx* was requested to take soundings. Having stopped for the purpose, she was not able to catch up with the *Great Eastern* and disappeared from sight during Friday. She was not seen again during the remainder of the expedition

4.00-9.00pm During this time the ordinary changes were made ashore viz. insulating the cable, joining up to earth direct, and joining up through the speaking instrument with a view to get if possible some communication with the ship but without avail. Variable weak currents due either to chemical action at cable end or to earth currents are from time to time seen but nothing definite such as would be given by ship - there is everything to confirm the idea that the cable has parted for some cause unknown to us and of which we can get no notice until repaired. I fear grappling for the end will be a very tedious operation.

9.00-11.50pm Ordinary signals continued to be sent by shore but nothing whatever received from ship.

According to Russell, the fault was first noticed before 1.10pm, when 716 nautical miles of cable had been paid out. The ship was brought to a halt within five minutes. On this occasion it was a dead short to earth and was reckoned to be no more then two miles distance. The process of picking up was most cumbersome and was subsequently to prove disastrous. Owing to the problems of sailing such a ship astern (she did not have a balanced rudder), the picking-up gear was placed in the bow. The cable had to be cut and then manhandled round to the front, passing paddle boxes, rigging etc. When exactly two miles had been taken on board the faulty piece was found. It was quickly cut out, the cable re-spliced, manhandled round to the back again, spliced into the main cable and paying out was resumed.

Valentia reported

11.30-1.50pm Received from ship some signals indicating "join up speaking instrument". Repeated them back and joined up speaking inst. but unable to make out signals - joined up a vertical needle galvanometer and received a steady current.

James Graves subsequently made a transcription of the newspaper that circulated on the *Great Eastern* during the voyage. The above is his copy of the illustration showing William Thomson during his period on watch in the cable tank

When all was under way again Canning took the opportunity of calling the cable tank men together to show them the fault, another piece of wire penetrating through to the inner core. It did indeed look like sabotage, they all agreed. Accordingly, Canning and Clifford decided on a course of vigilance, and the inmates of the Saloon were requested to lend a hand by participating in a day and night tank watch. This they willingly did, with a sense of satisfaction that they were now able to make a positive contribution to the successful completion of the mission. They each took a two hour spell of duty, which was not particularly pleasant, as Daniel Gooch recorded in his diary:

> " I have to got to go on watch tonight in that wretched tank at twelve o'clock. It is anything but an agreeable job to stand for two hours in a tank of cable covered with tar and like a girl with a skipping rope, jump over the cable as it runs out, say every minute, or else sit on the edge of an iron bar with your legs upraised above the cable".

All was once more tranquil on land. The signal that 800 miles had been paid out was received at 10.50 pm on July 30th. In spite of constant vigilance Valentia do not appear to have noted that at 3.30 am on the 31st the cable in the forward tank being exhausted, the ship stopped for several minutes so that a connection to the forward tank could be made.

At 7.50 am on the 1st of August the diary notes that 1200 miles had been paid out. It the continues:

> "Subsequent to 8 am no regular or perfect signals reached shore from the ship. The line was highly charged by earth currents of variable nature, sometimes + sometimes - and of very variable strength and duration. In their mildest form they appeared to be six times as strong as the battery used for sending signals on board the Great Eastern and between 9 and 11 we saw occasional signs as if the ship were trying to send a current which had the effect (this is illegible in my copy). After 11 am we saw nothing more from the ship".

On the ship Cyrus Field had relieved Jules Despécher in the tank at 7am. At about 7.45 there was a grating noise as the cable moved out of the tank. One of the men exclaimed "there goes a piece of wire" and word was passed up the crinoline shaft to the watcher. Either he never heard the warning or he ignored it as no message reached Mr Temple who was on duty at the stern. At 8.06 the ship stopped 1,186 (not 1,200 as recorded at Valentia) miles having been paid out. The fault was a bad one although DeSauty thought that the cable could have limped along for several months. Canning decided however that it would have to be hauled in and repaired. This decision was made not without considerable apprehension. They were at that time over the deepest part of the ocean. Within 300 miles they would be back in shallow water.

While tests were being undertaken prior to hauling in one of the foremen noticed a piece of wire projecting from a flake of cable immediately below the one which had passed out with the grating noise. It tended to disprove the sabotage theory and suggested that the outer sheathing had been defective in places. O'Neill gives a particularly succinct account of the happenings of the next few hours.

> "At 10.30 am in lat 51.25N. long. 39.1W the Cable having been cut and transferred to the bow, the picking-up machine was started and had hauled in about two miles when the boiler of the capstan became short of steam and whilst waiting for a fresh supply the wind suddenly changed. In attempting to get the ships head to wind she drove over the cable causing it to pass under her fore-poop and foul of the hawsepipe at the stem of the port bow. The engines were immediately reversed and every endeavour was made to get the ship's head round but without success. As the Cable was being chafed, a stopper attached to a manilla rope was put on and line veered away until the Cable was clear of the hawse pipes, when it led away to the starboard. We were hauling in a few revolutions in order to get the chafed parts on board as quickly as possible, when at twenty five feet from the bow, with a sharp snap the Cable broke and rushing through the stoppers to which men held on bravely, was sucked into the sea and lost - perhaps forever."

The impact of such a catastrophe can well be imagined. Morale plummeted. Smoking in the saloons became commonplace and earned no reproach from Daniel Gooch or Captain Anderson. Field locked himself in his cabin to draw up a fresh prospectus. The two Russell boys were thoroughly dispirited at the thought of a quick return to school instead of a promised holiday in the New World. Even the editor of the *Atlantic Telegraph* refused to issue his journal.
At first the interruption was taken as almost routine by those on land. There had been other faults and it had taken some time for them to be repaired. Even as time went on nobody was willing to admit failure. The breakdown in communications was attributed to earth currents due to a magnetic storm which was then present over most of northern Europe and which was playing havoc with overland communications as the Diary records.

August 3rd 1865

8am — Earth currents still on land lines giving on an ordinary galvo 90° left to 90° right, very variable and changing from one side to the other 2 or 3 times within five minutes. This between Valentia and Killarney only!

In accordance with instructions in case of loss of ship's signals Cable is joined up for speaking between 30 and 50 minutes past every hour, put to Earth direct from 40' to 50', joined up for speaking again from 50 to the hour and insulated from the hour to 30 minutes. This system has been carried out rigidly during the whole time since the ship's signals first failed entirely (i.e. 11 am yesterday), but not the least indication of any signals from the ship have been received. From the very hour that signals ceased from the ship a magnetic storm set in which continued to increase for some hours and then became variable both in degree and nature- varying from 116 cells positive to 116 cells negative, this value was determined when the earth currents appeared to be at its maximum or nearly so - the change from positive to negative and vice versa was very rapid in some cases and slow in others. In changing from one to the other they were never at the neutral point (giving no deflection) for more then a few seconds.

The great strength of these earth currents buoys us up with the hope that being so much stronger then the signalling power used on board and ashore we may on their cessation hear from the Great Eastern having continued paying out during the time when it would be impossible to speak either way - as those on board must be cognisant as those on shore of the strength of the current circulating in the cable. All the testing being performed on board and none on shore, they can judge the state of the insulation and the length of the cable in circuit by their tests and act accordingly.

4 August 1865

8 am Earth currents on land lines less than yesterday - able to work from Valentia to Dublin. The following message (and private information) received by me dated 8am from London

'Deflections first appeared here 5pm Aug 2nd - continued almost without intermission till 9pm 3rd. Almost stopped lines terminating at Edinbro', Glasgow, Liverpool, Manchester, Bristol, Cardiff, Lowestoft, York, Sheffield and Amsterdam - many lines looped* greater part of day - some lines tested on which the earth current could not be neutralised with 80 cells and from a steady deflection on Sheffield wire three sparks were obtained in 15 seconds. Amsterdam to Berlin was only line affected beyond Amsterdam - deflections on these lines stronger then the working power of 70 cells

From these it will be seen that the magnetic storm occupied a very vast area and that it was variable in our cable some 8 hours before it reached London - or a rate of 225 miles an hour from W to E.

12.30 pm Received following message from Secretary -
'If you have not defective insulation does anything lead you to suppose that there is a loss of continuity at the time shore tests for resistance of the conductor does the resistance of the line become smaller.

12.35 pm Reply as follows -
Shore tests for neither insulation nor conductivity and had instructions do not permit him to do so - all Great Britain troubled last two days with earth currents,

* i.e. using a second wire for completion of the circuit instead of the earth. Normal working involved a single wire with the battery at one end of the line and the galvanometer at the other end both connected to ground.

equal in some places to 80 cells - between Amsterdam and Berlin equal to upwards of 70 cells- Westward from here equal to upwards of 100 cells- not so strong this morning but still greater then signalling power - anxiously waiting their cessation to clear state of affairs

Having shown Mr Glass the message from Secretary at 12.30 pm, I was informed a few minutes afterwards that a hurried test for conductivity had been made giving something like 5000 units, but with a + current. I suggested that it be repeated more carefully, as the earth current was still on to a moderate extent and a negative test could be ???[+]

1.30 - 1.40 pm

Conductivity test repeated in my presence, when the following results were obtained by Mr May.
Positive current to Cable, res. increasing rapidly to 5870 units
Negative current to Cable, res. decreasing to 4150 units

Each of the above tests extended over about 3 minutes only which in my opinion is not sufficient and to form a conclusive decision upon such tests would be likely to prove erroneous. Such as they are, they show the cable to be undoubtedly parted and the conductor exposed in salt water - The units used in above test average as nearly as possible 4 per naut at a temperature of 47° Faht.

1.40 pm Ordinary routine resumed

7.40 pm Received following from Secretary -
'Are the indications such as to induce you to think that the Cable is severed from the *Great Eastern* - Wire me to Camberwell'.

Reply as follows -
'Yours received – Yes - no change since my message at 1.40 pm except diminution of earth currents, which have nearly abated'. "

Things did not change very much during the next two days. At 3 pm on the 7th Graves records:

"Earth currents entirely abated - weak current from cable arising from exposed conductor. Tests taken by Mr May upon Mr Glass' instructions in my presence showing the following results for resistance of the conductor.

Negative current to Line Positive current to Line

[+] word in original document not decipherable

1st minute	4700 units	1st minute	6100 units
2	4500	2	not obtainable, varying too rapidly
3	4400	3	5950
4	4450	4	5900
5	4500	5	5900
6	4550	6	5850
7	4550	7	6350
8	4650	8	6650
9	4670	9	6600
10	4790	10	6630

The 10 minutes negative readings taken first followed by the 10 minutes positive readings

1 min. neg.	3880 units	1 min. pos.	6080 units	(loose contact)

Then

1st min. neg.	4580 units	1 min. pos.	5740 units
2nd min. neg.	4690 "	2nd min. pos.	5780 "
Again 1 min. neg	4750 "	1 min. pos.	5850 "
Lastly 1 min. neg.	4700 "	1 min. pos.	6080 "

As is invariably the case with bad faults, or breaks in seawater the negative currents give a lower result then positive, as negative cleans the conductor and so gives easy passage of current to earth, whilst positive deposits a chloride on the copper which partially insulates the conductor and therefore increases the resistance - This proves fault to be in the water.

The mean of the 15 negative readings = 4557.3 units; - these units during the manufacture of the cable averaged as nearly as possible

At a temperature* of	30°	3.82 units per naut
" "	40°	3.92 " "
" "	50°	4.01 " "

* It is assumed that all of these temperatures are given in Fahrenheit.

which gives a result for distance respectively as follows: - if the bottom of the Atlantic be at a temperature of

30° then fault = 1193 nauts from shore
40° " " = 1162 "
50° " " = 1136 "

Or, discarding the 11th reading which appears doubtful these distances would be respectively 1200 at 30°, 1175 at 40°, 1148 at 50°

Now assuming that the bottom of the Atlantic be at 39.5° at which temperature fresh water (salt) is at its greatest density - expanding with either heat or cold above or below that temperature and therefore unable to remain longer at the bottom - then the distance of the fault would be 1175 miles (or a trifle over) from shore i.e. cable paid out - provided that the whole of the testing current escapes at the fault. What may be the state of the cable beyond this fault, of course, it is impossible to say. If the cable be broken there then the tests may be taken for the distance. If the cable be not broken there and the end on board the *Great Eastern* be insulated the tests will again be correct - but if it be not broken at the fault and the end on board the ship were joined to earth the results will show less than the actual distance of the fault, depending upon the length of the cable in circuit beyond the fault. The leakage is however so bad that it offers very little resistance in itself, shown by the not very great difference in the negative tests, whatever may be the resistance of the fault itself it must be deducted from the observed tests and this would throw the fault nearer the shore.

It must be merely conjecture to presume what has happened to the *Great Eastern*, or what she is now doing, if the gale alluded to in the extract from the Shipping Gazette seriously affected the *Great Eastern* immediately after the fault showed itself - they might have cut and buoyed the cable after (as is usual in such cases) sealing up the end, in raising it again, they may have lost it either by shipping or by breaking the buoy rope, or other causes. If no bad weather has interfered with their operations and they discovered the loss of insulation as soon as the fault developed itself when they had paid out 1200 and some few odd miles which of course they would do, they might immediately prepare to pick up towards the fault, with a view to cutting it out and presuming them to have 45 miles to pick up at the rate in very deep water of say 1/4 miles per hour that operation would take 180 hours at least without stoppage of any kind an this calculated from noon on 2nd inst. would expire at midnight on the 9th. If therefore they are picking up towards fault we may hear of them again through the Cable at any hour depending upon the speed of the operation.

Following received from Secretary: -

'Your diary. Suppose there be strong earth currents, would they enter the exposed end of the Cable if fractured, or is their presence in your shore instrument an argument against fracture. Have tests been taken subsequent to the one referred to by you and do these confirm you and other scientific persons in the opinion that the conductor is severed from the ship. Have you any manifestations indicating currents formed by exposed conductor in contact with external iron - Please wire me soon and write me fully on all matters tonight'

Reply sent as follows: - St. Helier's Place or Camberwell
'Monday 5.40 pm
Yours received. Earth currents in Cable being chiefly due to induction would rather escape from than enter an exposed end of cable if fractured. Their effect on instruments here is due to escape to earth of the induced current. Weak currents are received which arise from the conductor and iron exposed to but separated by sea water. Earth currents having ceased.

Tests taken this afternoon by Mr May upon authority of Mr Glass. Results show the existence of a very bad fault equal in leakage to a dead break at a distance varying between 1175 nauts and 1137 nauts. The former calculated at a temp. of 31 degrees, the latter at 47 degrees Fahrenheit- probable extremes of Atlantic. The Cable may or may not be severed at the distance paid out by *Great Eastern* and she may now be picking up towards the leakage and may possibly be heard of at any hour'-

During the day earth currents of a very weak kind have been noticed, but nothing heard of from the Great Eastern. Mr A. Varley arrived with the Curb Keys yesterday-

August 9th 1865

Earth currents of a weak kind again today, their force varying from a maximum of 2 cells to a minimum of about 1/100 part of a cell - still nothing from ship-

Engaged all day with Mr Varley in endeavouring to adjust the new curb key to the artificial line supplied for this Station. The latter not being a facsimile of the Cable in length and inductive surface, we find it very difficult to make the key act properly as it has been made for and calculated upon the whole cable. Should we ever get the Cable handed over to us to work I have no doubt the key will answer the purpose better the it does at present on the artificial line- The mirror galvanometer appears too delicate in its movement and oscillates after each signal owing perhaps to a want of sufficient induction plates in proportion to the calculated length of the various contacts. With an ordinary delicate vertical needle galvanometer the signals are very clear, dead and easy to read. It would not be amiss to have one or two of Henley's small galvanometers here which are indispensable in an office and of which we have none-

Mr Varley leaves tomorrow morning (Thursday) for London.

No change in state of affairs. Earth currents stronger during the night, but weakened towards morning

Things remained very much the same over the next few days and the only unusual entries was a statement to the effect that a Mr Glaisher* had arrived, had visited the Cable house and had been admitted into the instrument room. He left on the 16th.

August 17th 1865
10 am Received intelligence that the *Great Eastern* had arrived off Crookhaven."

At 7.15 pm a telegram arrived from Crookhaven and its contents were entered into the Station diary.

<u>Copy of Telegram from Crookhaven August 17th 1865</u>

<u>The Atlantic Cable</u>

The cable parted whilst being hauled in for testing - attempts to pick up unsuccessful.

The *Great Eastern* arrived off Crookhaven, reports that after sailing from Valencia and making a splice with shore end on July 23rd she continued her voyage to lat. 51° 25' long. 39° 6' being 1063 miles from Valencia and 600 miles from Heart's Content Trinity Bay, having paid out 1212 miles of cable, when it parted on August 2nd at 12 30 pm in soundings of 3900 yards under the following circumstances: - A partial loss of insulation having been discovered, the ship was stopped to recover that portion of the cable in which the fault lay - the electrical tests placing it probably within 6 miles. The cable was passed from stern to bow for this purpose and after getting two miles of cable, the fault still being overboard, the cable broke about 10 yards in board, the wheel at the bows having been injured by chafing.

* Presumably James Glaisher FRS (7 April 1809 – 7 February 1903). Founder member of Meteorological Society (1850) and Aeronautical Society 1866. Famous for his record breaking balloon ascents (1862 - 1866)

> Previously faults had been discovered, the first in soundings of about 3000 yards and the second in about 4100 and had been successfully recovered and made good. In the first case 10 miles and in the second 2½ miles of cable were hauled in.
>
> After the cable parted a grapnel with 2½ miles of rope was lowered down, the ship being placed so as to drift over the line of cable- the cable was hooked on the 2nd; when over 2200 yards of rope had been hauled in, the swivel in the latter gave way; 2800 yards of rope were lost - the cable having been lifted 1200 yards from the bottom.
>
> On the 4th a buoy with flags and bell was moored with 4500 yards of rope to mark the place. It is in lat. 51° 35' long. 39° 42'
>
> From the 4th August fogs with adverse winds prevailed, no further attempt until the 7th which was made nearer the end of the cable and was unsuccessful from the same cause, when the cable had been lifted bout 10000 yards.
>
> Another buoy was placed in lat. 51° 28' long. 38° 26'
>
> A third attempt was made on August 10th which also failed, the grappling chain having fouled the fluke of the grapnel. About 800 yards of rope came up covered with ooze.
>
> A further attempt on the 11th at 3 pm also failed through the breaking of the grappling rope, the cable being raised 600 yards from the bottom-
>
> The stock of rope being exhausted it became necessary to return to England for more and stronger tackle.

These few words conceal the magnitude of what had been achieved on board the *Great Eastern.* Nobody had ever attempted to grapple for something in 2½ miles of water. Indeed it would not have been possible except for two facts. Five thousand fathoms of wire had been brought along for use with large buoys. These were intended to mark the position of the cable if it broke, although nobody had ever conceived of using them in such deep water. The weather on the day on which the cable broke had been excellent for Capt. Moriarty's task. It is not clear whether it was by coincidence or providential precaution, but just at the moment of fracture he had taken a set of fixes so that the ship's position was then known with considerable accuracy.

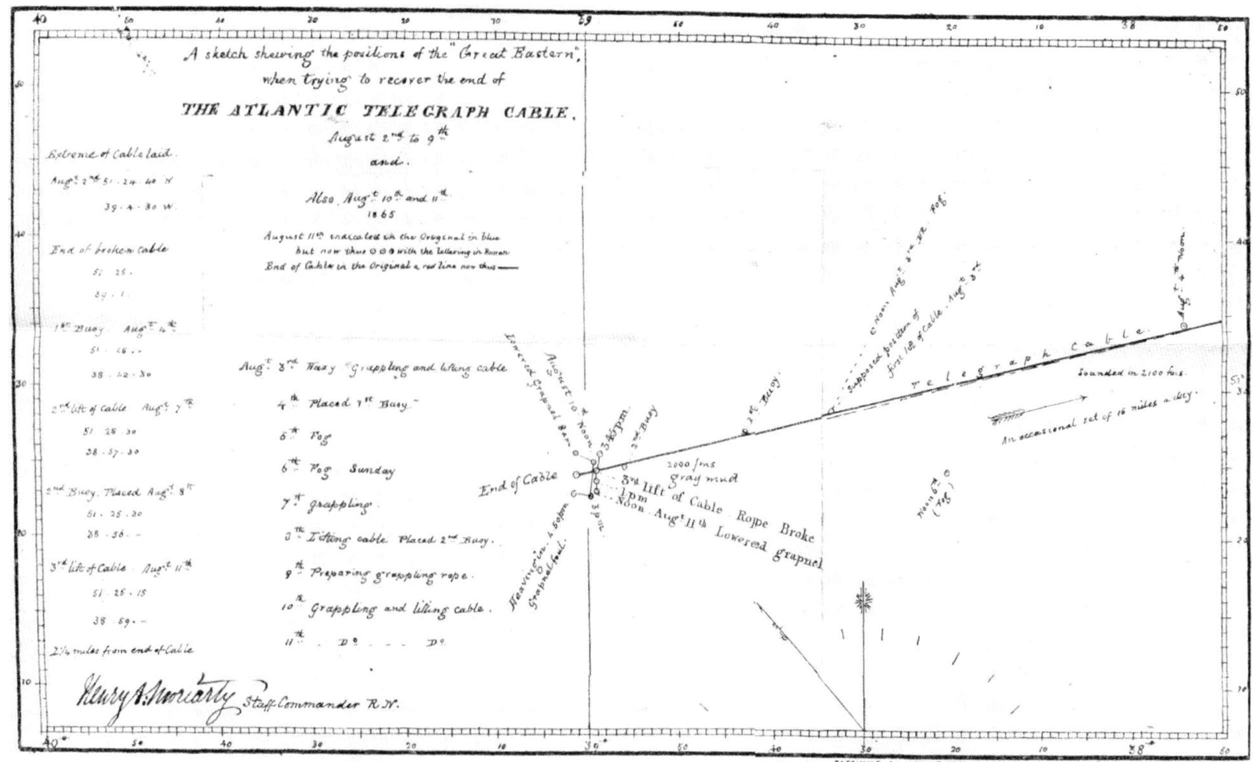

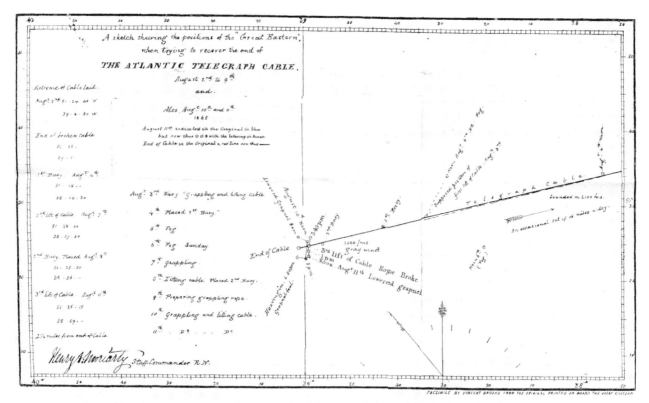

Chart produced by Capt. Moriarty showing the history of the cable fault and subsequent attempts to raise it (From the *Great Eastern* Photographs file in the IET Archives)

Faced with the loss of over a million pounds worth of investment everyone on board felt that the attempt was worth it. Anderson turned his ship back and the rope consisting of 100 fathom lengths shackled together was lowered overboard with a 3cwt five fluke grapnel on the end. The boat was then allowed to drift in the wind over the track of the cable and all eyes were on the dynamometer watching the strain on the line. They got a bite on the first attempt, but when 1400 fathoms had been drawn in one of the shackles broke and cable, rope and grapnel were lost. Immediately a buoy was lowered into the sea to mark the spot. They then steamed back to a point nearer the end of the cable in the hope that there would be less strain on the rope when it was lifting. They dropped another buoy and had to wait for favourable wind to drive them once more across the line of the cable. A navigational fix at noon on the 4th showed that they had drifted 30-40 miles off station during the foggy night. The pattern during the next few days was the same, drift during the night, steam back during the day, wind still against them so that it would cause the ship to drift along the line of the cable rather then across it. Again a gloom descended on the ship.

Another attempt was made on the 7th, but again 1500 fathoms of wire were lost, when a swivel gave way under the strain. There was still 2000 fathoms of wire on board and it was decided to make a final attempt. However before this was done there were some improvements to be made. Damaged pieces of wire were cut out (the lay of the hawser which had originally been 10 inches had in places been stretched to 27 inches by the strain during the previous attempts). Shackles were replaced with ones made on board and as the picking-up machinery had been damaged when the swivel gave way, it was decided to use the ship's capstan. Before this could be used, however, its diameter had to be increased from its original two feet six inches. It was encased in timber covered with sheets of iron which gave it the appearance of a solid drum five feet six inches in diameter. As there was by this stage only 1700 feet of wire left, a stout piece of manilla rope was pressed into service.

The first go at the final attempt failed because the grapnel had been damaged. Orders were given to haul in, a process which took 13 hours. but when the grapnel came onboard, it had on it the remnants of sea bed ooze, which Dr Ward examined under the microscope. It was found to consist mainly of shells but there was great excitement when some living matter was observed in one of the shells, thus disproving the idea that life could not exist at such depths.

At 12.30am on Friday 11th of August the grapnel was lowered for the last time, and at 8.30pm the dynamometer indicated that the cable had one more been grappled. Hauling in was commenced, but just as the manilla rope was passing through the swivel block, the 4 ton strain proved too much and the rope snapped at the splice. For a few moments men tried to hold on to it with their bare hands and then it was gone.

There was nothing to do now but return home. They did not however go defeated, but with a sense of triumph. Like the evacuation at Dunkirk seventy-five years later, something had been achieved out of apparent total defeat. They were all ready to have another go and this was in the best spirit of the Empire. With the uprising of spirits, the *Atlantic Telegraph* (newspaper), dormant since the disasters, much to everyone's delight, made its reappearance on the 12th of August. A final edition was produced on the 17th.

Their faithful escort made for Newfoundland to pass on the news and to restock with coal. *Great Eastern* set her sails and maintained a steady nine knots all the way. At Crookhaven[*] their telegram was sent forward and Russell and three others disembarked.

O'Neill ever with a sense of humour then turns his narrative to the plight of the remaining livestock on the ship.

> "Of our livestock there remained only fifty sheep, a few pigs and some score or so of fowls; but the havoc made must not be ascribed to the voracity of man. In taking my daily stroll amongst the animals I daily noticed a gap in the oxen sheds and knowing there to be plenty of fresh meat in the ice cellar, I was anxious to know the reason. The butcher (he is not an Irishman) informed me that they were killed in order to save their lives and that their gradual decay was

[*] In the interval between 1858 and 1866 a canister service had operated from Crookhaven. Late messages were delivered to/collected from passing ships. A similar system operated at Cape Race. (see http://atlantic-cable.com/Article/NewsTelegraphs/index.htm)

> owing to the water they drank. I am not sufficient of a chemist to know the properties of condensed water but however great a blessing is the discovery of turning the sea waves into fresh water, it certainly does not contribute to the prolongation of animal life. It had been death to the ducks, the cow and the oxen; nor had it improved the sheep, so destroying their natural instincts that they tamely submitted to the interested caresses of their greatest enemy, the two-legged wolf. The pigs alone have thrived, but on what will they not fatten and grunt. To dismiss these interesting creatures; the fifty sheep have been purchased by Mr Gooch and 'Billy' round whose neck the young Russells tied a pink string to save him from the butcher's knife, is to pass the rest of his days in clover."

On Saturday 19th August the *Great Eastern* stopped about two miles off Brighton and landed the majority of her passengers. To a man each one of them was certain of success. The principals of both Companies in addition to Anderson and Gooch appended their signatures to a very positive report on the progress of the voyage and of the certainty of ultimate success. Gooch proposed fitting a screw to the bow of the ship so that she could haul in while steaming astern. It is not known whether this was ever put into practice, and in any event a balanced rudder would probably have been a more pressing requirement.

The journalists and artists dispersed to propagate their message to a disappointed but enthusiastic public. Much was written by Russell in the *Illustrated London News* and the *Times*. He also published his official history of the Atlantic Telegraph, complete with engravings by Robert Dudley. J.C. Deane's authoritative and technically detailed account appeared in the October issue of *Macmillans Magazine* and *Blackwood's*, while *Edinburgh Magazine* carried O'Neill's light hearted contribution.

Russell wrote an article on the voyage, which appeared in *Cornhill's Magazine*. It is perhaps the most defensive of all that was written at the time but contains a concluding paragraph that was to be visionary and in a sense prophetic.

> "There is another consideration connected with the extension of submarine telegraphs of great importance. We have seen that cables can be grappled and caught even though it may not be possible to take them up. In the event of war therefore an enemy's cruiser could not only interrupt communication between the one portion of a belligerent state and another, in order to annoy the enemy and interrupt his connection with neutral states".

The Knight of Kerry was left frustrated but certain that if all went well there would be a permanent telegraph station on his island the following summer.

The Station Diary following the receipt of the *Great Eastern's* telegram from Crookhaven of the 17th is taken up with detailed calculations of cable length and average ocean temperature. It was planned that the condition of the cable should be monitored continuously until further notice. It is not certain whether this was undertaken by the staff of the Telegraph Construction and

Maintenance Co. The Atlantic Co's accounts would suggest that Carson, Tranfield and Donovan did not remain at Valentia to assist.

On 19 August James Graves wrote the final words of the expedition.

> "Received telegram requesting me to be in London on Monday (21st inst.). Left Valentia in the evening 9 pm and arrived in London as requested on Monday morning.

August 21st	At office in London- Board meeting held
August 22nd	At office in London-
August 23rd	At office in London- Board meeting held
August 24th	At office in London daily-

Chapter 8

August 1865 - November 1866

(The 1866 expedition: its planning, execution and outcome)

When the *Great Eastern* returned to London the enthusiasm of the public amply matched that of those who had travelled on the expedition. There had been failure, but ultimate success was now certain. Here was a ship, symbolic of its time, which everyone wanted to love, but which had never until now been allowed to show itself off. It had found a role at last. Commentaries appeared in the papers. Participants gave talks to learned societies and the contributions from the journalists who had travelled with the ship all helped to maintain this enthusiasm well into the autumn of 1865.

There was no doubt in anyone's mind about a new cable which would be laid during the following summer. The Telegraph Construction and Maintenance Company had a fresh set of proposals. It would lay a new cable at a cost of £500,000 and would not require payment unless it was successful. If it was successful it would receive a bonus of 20% of the total cost, or £100,000, to be paid in shares, It also proposed to use the experience gained during the unsuccessful voyage to raise the 1865 cable, splice it and complete the laying. For this, if successful, it would be paid an additional £137,000. These proposals were accepted by a meeting of the Atlantic Telegraph shareholders of 14 September 1865.

It had been generally accepted that the use of tar and hemp covered stranded wires had not been totally successful. In fact the tar had probably caused bits of wire to stick to the cable. The new cable was to have soft iron wire rather then stranded steel and this was to be galvanised, no doubt to the great satisfaction of those who would have to handle the cable. The weight of the proposed cable would be less then that previously used by 100lbs/mile. This would make it more buoyant and cause it to present a more favourable angle with the sea on paying out. The reduced angle would mean that the vertical forces on the cable would be much reduced.

The shore ends were also to be modified. Instead of 36 stranded wires there would be a sheathing of 12 iron wires each 5/16 in diameter. The Irish shore end, being the longer before deep water was reached, would be tapered over 30 miles. The first 8 miles would be exceedingly heavy cable, the next 8 lighter and finally 14 miles of light shore end before the deep water section was spliced on.

Cyrus Field, content in the knowledge that his dream would be pursued during the following summer, returned to America towards the end of September. It was his intention to promote the new cable during the next few months.

William Thomson went back to his University and resumed the writing of his great Treatise on Natural Philosophy. Between times he was kept busy perfecting new instruments and testing appliances for the cable.

James Graves had to face problems of his own. On his return to London he received a letter from the Secretary of the Electric & International Telegraph Co. reminding him that he had been seconded to the Atlantic Co. for the duration of the manufacture and testing of the cable and as he had not resumed his post, he must be considered to have resigned. The terms of the letter were such that he had little alternative but to tender his official resignation.

After the Atlantic Company's board meeting of 14th September 1865 it was necessary to raise further capital of £600,000. There was general uncertainty in the City. As interest rates were high it was thought prudent to offer a 12% preferential issue (i.e. preference over the 8% issue of 1865, which itself had preference over the 4% stock of 1857/8). The Secretary, Assistant Secretary, the office clerks, Graves and the telegraph clerks (F. Perry, J.H. Carson, C. Trippe and F.T. Tranfield) were all engaged during the autumn in circulating the prospectus over the whole country. Before long they had the satisfaction of knowing that sufficient applications had been made to ensure a full subscription.

Because of dissatisfaction amongst existing shareholders, who resented the preferential nature of the new share issue, the Company had sought legal advice and it had been favourable. It therefore came as a bombshell when just before Christmas the Attorney General issued an adverse opinion. It was his belief that they had no right to issue the new shares without a special Act of Parliament. However, Parliament was about to go into recess, the agenda of Government business was full. The chances of passing through a private member's bill to adjust the situation was all but zero.

Thus Cyrus Field returned to Britain on 31 December 1865 to a position of forlorn hopelessness. The Company had been in the process of calling in the new share capital, but following the verdict all subscriptions were being returned. As so many times in the past, he did the rounds of the influential financiers in an effort to raise more funds. He had firm allies in Daniel Gooch and John Pender. Gooch, a member of Parliament, suggested an expedient which would circumvent the legal difficulties. A new company, the Anglo American Telegraph Co. would be formed with a capital of £600,000. It would enter into agreement with the Atlantic Telegraph Co., issue the preferential stock and take over responsibility for laying the cable. For this it was to be paid the equivalent of a preferred dividend of 25% to come from the revenues of telegraph operations amounting to £125,000 per annum. Field's New York, Newfoundland and London Telegraph Co. would contribute £25,000 per annum from its revenues on condition that the cable was operational during 1866. The arrangements allowed the Atlantic Telegraph Co. the right of redemption; terminating the agreement on or before 1 Jan 1869 (on giving three months notice) by payment of £1,200,000 to the new Company i.e. double its share capital. If this option were exercised the Anglo American Telegraph Co would reserve the right to take £600,000 in cash and the other half in ordinary Atlantic shares at par. In the event of the Atlantic Telegraph Co. using their right of redemption, the Anglo Co. would be dissolved and the funds distributed amongst the shareholders.

Gooch, who had owned no stock in the original Company, offered to subscribe £20,000 to the new undertaking. Field seconded this with a subscription of £10,000 (in view of his financial position in the United States it is difficult to see how he could have honoured this). During his fund raising tour Field had a very sympathetic response from Thomas Brassey the railway engineer and financier, who now offered to subscribe to one tenth of all the shares.

Perhaps Gooch and Pender were not keen that Brassey should have such a large holding (and, as will be seen later they were correct in this view). Together they pressurised the other directors of the Telegraph Construction and Maintenance Co. They were each asked to contribute £10,000. Finding them reluctant to put so much at risk, Pender persuaded them by offering a guarantee of £250,000 of his own and his wife's money (his wife, née Emma Dennison, came from a very rich Nottingham family). According to James Graves the total eventually subscribed by Field, Brassey, Gooch, Pender and the T.C. & M. Co. amounted to £230,000.

On 6 March 1866 the Anglo American Telegraph Co. issued its prospectus. It did not contain any mention of Government guarantees. Unlike its predecessor it did not have any, and of course was not incorporated by any Act of Parliament. Although confidence was at a low ebb, through the agency of J.S. Morgan & Co. (an ancestor of Morgan Grenfell & Co) the balance was fully subscribed within two weeks. As part of the promotional exercise meetings were held in London, Manchester, Liverpool and Glasgow.

The meeting in Glasgow was held on 19th March. William Thomson delivered a speech in which he emphasised the improvements in cable manufacture since 1858. He spoke with entire confidence as to the success of the project and had not the slightest doubt that they would succeed in transmitting 8 words per minute in regular work.

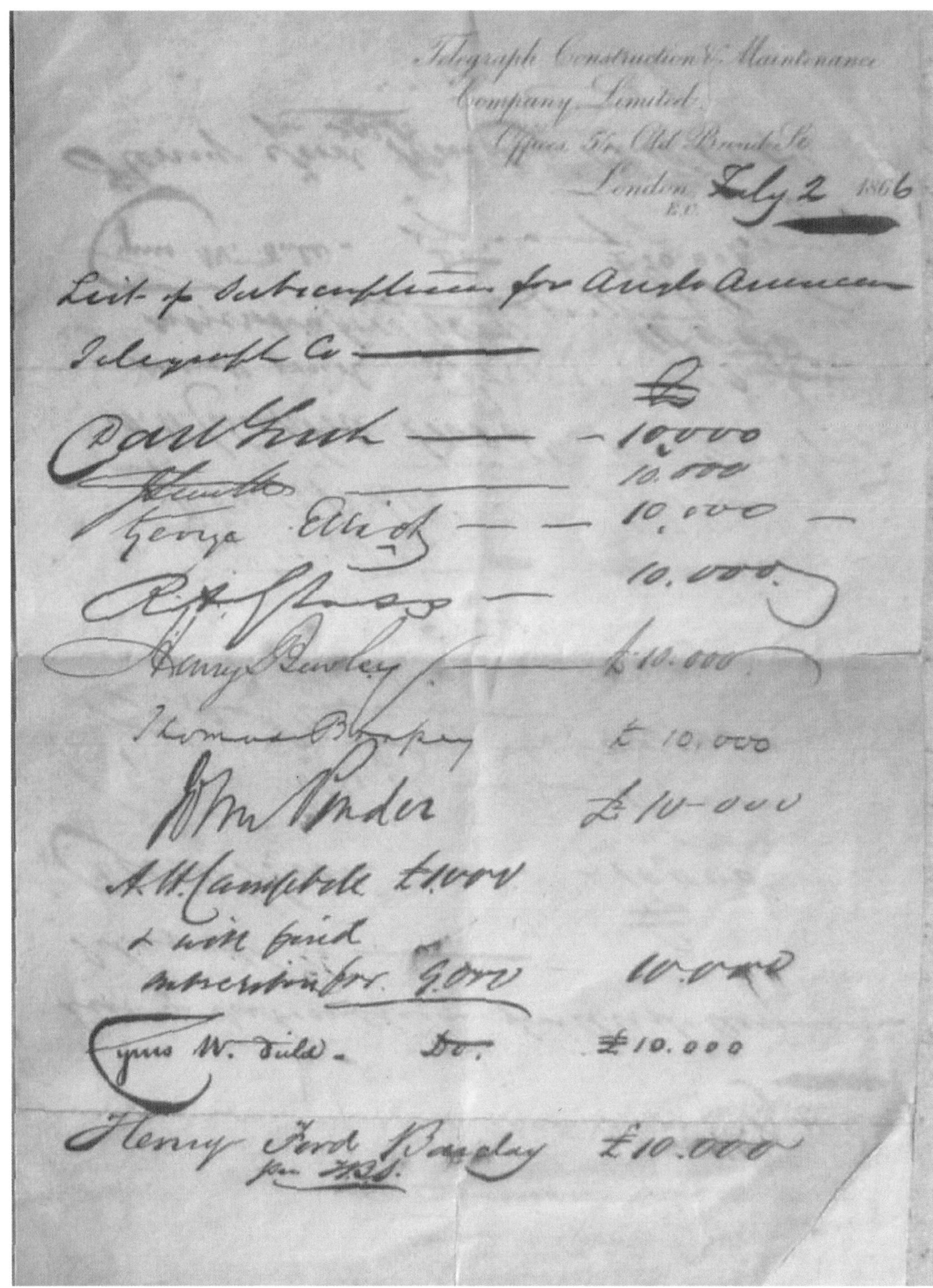

Telegraph Construction & Maintenance
Company, Limited.
Offices 58, Old Broad St.
London, E.C. July 2 1866

List of subscriptions for Anglo American
Telegraph Co

	£
Daniel Gooch	10,000
[illegible]	10.000
George Elliot	10,000
R. A. Glass	10,000
Henry Bewley	£10.000
Thomas Brassey	£10,000
John Pender	£10-000
A. H. Campbell £1000 & will find subscription for 9,000	10.000
Cyrus W. Field - Do.	£10.000
Henry Ford Barclay	£10.000

A list of subscribers to the Anglo American Telegraph Co recorded in the diaries of Daniel Gooch

CHAPTER 8

As soon as it became obvious that the Anglo would be successfully floated, work commenced at Greenwich. There were a number of important changes this time. There had been a certain amount of dissatisfaction with DeSauty's system of electrical testing, in which several miles of cable could be paid out before a fault was discovered. At the beginning of April Willoughby Smith, who had been with the Gutta Percha Company, was appointed Chief Electrician to the Telegraph Construction and Maintenance Co. and was therefore in charge of the electrical arrangements for the new expedition.

The Board of the Atlantic Telegraph Co. held a meeting on Friday 6th April 1866. Those present were Messrs Lampson, Cropper, Gurney, Hamilton and Saward. It was unanimously resolved that:

> "Mr Graves having tested throughout its manufacture the cable of 1865 and having then been appointed the Company's Station Manager at Valentia, the Directors of the Atlantic Telegraph Company feel that they can rely upon him to test and report to them on their part as to the manufacture of the cable of 1866 and as it will require two or more efficient persons to keep a proper supervision over the electrical condition of the cable, the Directors of the Atlantic Telegraph Company desire to call the attention of the Anglo American Telegraph Company to Mr C.W. Lundy their late appointed Station Manager in Newfoundland, as a person from character and experience to cooperate with Mr Graves in the work referred to and whose services in Newfoundland would be of great value in case of success. If further hands should be required, which will be the case if continuous night and day tests are made, the Board would suggest that, if agreeable to the Anglo American Telegraph Company, a selection may be made from the late operative staff of this Company."

Graves records that "Mr Cropper and Capt. Hamilton (being also Directors of the Anglo American Telegraph Company) were requested to convey the substance of this resolution to the other Directors of the Anglo. The result of this was that the whole operating staff who had been engaged by the Atlantic Telegraph Company in 1865 were temporarily employed during the manufacture of the 1866 Cable"

Cable was produced at the rate of about 20 miles per day and after testing was transferred to the *Great Eastern.* The final total length of cable on board added up to 2,400 miles, 748 miles being the remainder of the 1865 cable.

All those who were involved with this the fifth expedition to lay a cable across the Atlantic took the matter with the utmost seriousness. William Thomson, who had spent much of the winter perfecting new instruments, did much travelling up and down to London. It is told that his secretary was not infrequently sent to Glasgow Railway Station a few minutes before the mail train started with this urgent message "I have gone to White's to hurry on an instrument. The London mail train must on no account start till I come." Such was the national importance of the problem and such was the honour in which Thomson was held, that the Station Master obeyed. While the ship was being loaded with cable the public were admitted to view at 1/= per head[+]. Thomson wrote to a nephew telling him not to ask for him while visiting it. "Every moment I am on board will be more the occupied, and I cannot take friends into the electrical room. I am sure you know too much of my difficulties last year and are too entirely interested not to understand this perfectly"

The new Chief Electrician, Willoughby Smith, had devised a system of continuous testing throughout the whole voyage. This was subsequently described by him in a paper to the Society of Telegraph Engineers in 1879.

> . . . .the idea of which had suggested itself to me while on board the *Great Eastern* on the previous expedition. I placed sheets of tinfoil and gelatine alternately with each alternate sheet connected to the cable and the others connected via a very sensitive astatic galvanometer to earth (a leaky capacitor). This gave a constant deflection so long as the cable was kept at constant tension. Any changes could be immediately noticed by the observer ashore. ...current through shore astatic was .0025 of total. No deflection of the ship's marine galvo but 200 divs on the astatic[*].
>
> Tested in Feb. 1866 using the cable on board *Great Eastern.* The test equipment was housed in a herdsman's cottage on the shore of the Medway opposite to where the *Great Eastern* was moored. Thomson and Latimer Clarke gave favourable reports. Mr Laws made some suggestions for amendment.
>
> Before starting to lay the cable my plans had to be finally submitted to Messrs Thomson and Varley, as representing the Atlantic Telegraph Co. and the latter suggested certain amendments which had distinct advantages over Mr Law's. . . . .
>
> The whole of the system worked remarkably well. During the fourteen days occupied in laying the cable from Ireland to Newfoundland, 164 messages in all were sent and received between ship and shore, containing 6,437 words or 30,059 letters.

Cunards were happy to allow the continued secondment of Capt. Anderson on the same terms as before. He immediately set about getting *Great Eastern* into shape. Firstly her hull had to be scraped down. There was a coating of barnacles and seaweed which was at least two feet thick. Removing this would considerably improve her fuel consumption. The boilers were overhauled and the engines modified to allow rapid reversing if necessary.

[+] One shilling, or 5p in decimal currency.

[*] In his original idea a separate galvanometer was connected through a double action key to two unequal resistances connected to earth. The differences in deflection would represent either a dot or a dash.

According to K.R. Haigh in his book on cableships "several improvements were made both to the paying-out and picking-up gear. A 70 hp steam engine was coupled to the after-gear so that it could be used for picking up purposes and avoid the complication of transferring the cable to the bows. Modifications were made to the jockey wheels on the six sheave gear; the spindles on which the wheels were mounted on lever arms which could be loaded with weights to vary the retardation applied to the cable before it reached the main drum. An adjustable band brake was also fitted around the shaft of each V-wheel. The picking-up machine consisted of two grooved drums 5ft 7in. diameter mounted one behind the other and driven by a further 70hp steam engine. Located on the individual drum shafts were two gear wheels and a brake drum; one pair of gear wheels being engaged at any time by separate pinions on a lay shaft. All the drums and gearing with the exception of the main drive from the steam engine were mounted inside the support frames of the machine so that the cable had to be threaded around the drums. An overhanging drum outside the framework on the port side drove the holding-back gear through a belt drive. Braking power to the brake drums was imparted by manually applied compression of bands around the drums."

If it were necessary to pick up cable, the ship simply turned round, and facing in the opposite direction started hauling in. Of course a cage was placed around the propeller to prevent it fouling the cable during this operation.

The Telegraph Construction and Maintenance Co. also chartered two other ships, the *Albany* and *Medway*. The *Medway* (1,823 tons) carried shore end and 45 miles of spare deep sea cable. Both were fitted with picking-up gear similar to that described above. It was planned to use these ships to partially raise the 1865 cable, so that when it was hauled onto the *Great Eastern* there would be less vertical strain. Between the three ships there was 20 miles of steel rope of 30 tons breaking strain, heavy buoys and several types of grapnel. One type had a strong leaf spring on each of the four prongs so that when the cable was caught, it would not easily slip off the flukes.

In addition to cable and coal the *Great Eastern* carried 500 tons of telegraph gear and batteries. The ship's draught at the time of sailing was almost 32 feet.

The Admiralty once more agreed to the secondment of Capt Moriarty as Navigator. HMS *Terrible* was also made available. The expedition was also to be accompanied by HMS *Racoon*, which was equipped for taking soundings.

It is perhaps worth noting at this stage that it was perhaps a good thing that the Anglo American Telegraph Co. took over from the Atlantic Co. Samuel Gurney, one of the directors of the latter Company, was also a partner in the merchant banking firm of Overend Gurney & Co. They suspended payments on 10 May 1866 with liabilities of £11,000,000. Up to that time it was the largest ever financial collapse in the City and its repercussions lasted for years. Gurney's direct involvement with the 1866 cable could have been disastrous.

The major feature of the new expedition was the total professionalism and lack of ceremony. It was certainly the most sensible course at the time, but it has meant that the events were never chronicled with the same detail as those of the previous year. Even the Knight of Kerry was holding his breath on this occasion. Henry Bewley as one of the directors of the Anglo took responsibility for organising a service. In a letter which he wrote to Fitzgerald on 4th July 1866, he suggests that it would be better to have it at Valentia rather then on board the *Great Eastern.* He suggested that the service, which was to be held on 12th July should take place in the Coast Guard boathouse on the mainland opposite Foilhommerum. In his letter he asks the Knight of Kerry to add to the existing list the names of any parties who it would be desirable to invite. In due course Bewley and Bevan, another Anglo director, issued printed invitations to approximately 100 persons.

The departure of the *Great Eastern* and its journey to Ireland were recorded by James Graves on a loose pencil-written sheet of paper, which was found tucked into the back of the 1865 Station Diary.

1866	
Fri 29 June	Left New Cross for Sheerness by 4.50 train. Arrived off *Gt. Eastern* about 7.30.
Sat 30 June	A very hot day. *Great Eastern* left moorings at noon, anchored at the Nore 3.15.
Sun 1 July	Service on board in morning. Weighed anchor at noon. Landed pilot in tug at Dover. Accompanied by Mr Pender's yacht. Parted with yacht at Goodwin sands.
Mon 2 July	Running down Channel, past I. of W.
Tue 3 July	Passed Lands End.
Wed 4 July	At sea
Thu 5 July	Anchored Berehaven - went ashore and climbed Hungry Hill, by barometer 216 feet high.
Fri 6 July	Walked to Castletown - dined there. "*Wm. Cory*" arrived during morning. Rode back to landing place and went aboard G.E. 10.30 pm embarked on *Wm Cory* and left for Valentia - before clear of harbour met *"Terrible"*. *"Cory"* arrived off

Sat 7 July	Foilhommerum 6am. Got ashore and luggage up to Telegraph House. 9am breakfast. Prepared for landing cable. About 36 boats formed bridge and cable brought to office at 5pm. *"Cory"* started 5.20. At 10.20pm half of it payed out.
Sun 8 July	3.10am Shore end sealed and buoyed - 29 miles payed out. Tests well. Insulation increased from 200 to 700 mill per nt

HMS *Racoon* arrived at Berehaven on Thursday 12 July. William Thomson was on board, and his wife had travelled overland to Valentia. The Service took place at noon and was in fact held at Knightstown. According to a report in the *Times* it took place in a building to the rear of the Valentia Hotel where the guests had previously been entertained to lunch. Bevan had been unable to attend so that the arrangements were left to Bewley and Capt White of the local coast guard. The Dean of Ardfert read the Service. This was followed by addresses from Bewley, the Moderator of the General Assembly, Richard Glass (already in poor health) and the Knight of Kerry. The *Times*, in addition to naming the principal guests, gives a list of members of staff who were present:

> C.F. Varley (who was remaining at Valentia to represent the electrical interests of the Anglo American Telegraph Co.), W.T. Ansell, local superintendent of the Electrical & International Telegraph Co., T.H. Sanger, Supt. of the British and Irish Magnetic Telegraph Co., B.D. Watlock, Engineer, Mag. Tel. Co., Messrs May, George and Crocker of the Telegraph Construction & Maintenance Co., Messrs Graves*, Tranfield and Carson of the Anglo American Telegraph Co.

Just as the service was being held the *Great Eastern* weighed anchor at Berehaven and proceeded round to the point where the shore end had been buoyed. Graves's last available diary entry for 1866

Fri 13 3pm	Splice made and *Gt. Eastern* commenced paying out main cable- all well.

Richard Glass communicated the fact by overland telegraph at 4 pm and his regular bulletins were to be one of the features of the 1866 expedition.

Although they were not to have the benefit of the presence of W.H. Russell or Henry O'Neill, the Telegraph Construction & Maintenance Co. were fully aware of the value of good press coverage. They had on board the journalists Nicholas Woods, J.C. Parkinson and J.V. Poore amongst others and the testing system of Willoughby Smith allowed the passage of more news and information than had been possible in previous attempts. This was also the first time that there was a photographic record of some of the events. Robert Dudley was also on board and made a further

* This is the first time that Graves is mentioned in print.

series of watercolours and paintings. Details of his experiences and his reminiscences can be found at
http://atlantic-cable.com/CablePioneers/Dudley/index.htm

As before, Canning was on board, assisted by Henry Clifford. There seems to have been a certain amount of friction between Clifford and Capt. Anderson, and Daniel Gooch felt it expedient to accompany the ship and keep the peace. William Thomson was to represent the interests of the Atlantic Telegraph Co. and Cyrus Field was, in spite of the name of the new Company, the only American on board.

The convoy was led by HMS *Terrible*, charged with keeping the route clear of passing ships. *Medway* was on the port side and *Albany* on the starboard quarter of the *Great Eastern*. All were instructed to keep to their station, ready to close in for instructions if the signal gun was fired. The path over which the ships were to pass, although a great circle route, was 30 miles to the south of the position of the 1865 cable, so that when the old cable was grappled there would be no chance of interfering with the new cable.

In the main the journey was with one or two exceptions uneventful. An average of 5 knots was maintained over a quiet sea in monotonously good weather. Sabotage was still suspected and the men in the tanks, dressed in special pocketless overalls, were under constant close scrutiny at all times. However the use of galvanised sheathing seems to have completely solved the problems of the year before.

But there were one or two incidents to scare them. At 4 o clock on 17 July Willoughby Smith recorded

> "One of the electrical staff activated a switch in the test room, which caused a bell to ring in the tank room. Those in the tank room without a moments hesitation ordered the engineer to stop and it was some time before the confusion was resolved. A more serious affair happened at half past midnight on Wednesday 18th July. One of the outer sheathing wires of the cable had broken and when it came to be paid out, it caught up three or four turns of the flake below. In a twinkling the whole bundle of cable rushed up out of the tank into the paying-out machine forming an apparently inextricable mass of kinks and twists. The ship was at once stopped and all hands put to work to unravel the tangle, while a buoy was made ready in case the cable should break. In about two hours, by extraordinary exertions the cable was made straight and paying out slowly recommenced. During all this time the rain was coming down heavily and the sky was as dark as pitch. Our companion ships had gone ahead, having taken no notice of our signals"

Throughout all this the electrical signalling continued and Valentia were probably unaware of any disturbance.

The next day at 6.22am Willoughby Smith recorded an almost identical incident.

> "For the third time the ship's engines were stopped and reversed. We should have had all the trouble of yesterday had not one of the men, at risk of severely hurting himself, fortunately caught the tangle before it went out of the tank. As it was he had a pretty heavy fall on his back, but the cable was saved and everything went on as before."

With hindsight Willoughby Smith was able to recall this many years later. In an 1881 paper[*] he says of these

> "Owing to the hardness of the iron used in the cable of 1865, its adhesive compound and the long time it had been lying coiled in the tanks on board the *Great Eastern*, several exciting scenes occurred while submerging that portion ....."

The implication being that the 1865 cable was not specifically reserved for splicing onto the 1865 section, but simply used as it came from the tank.

By the end of the day the aft tank was emptied of cable. The next lot of cable was to come from the forward tank, which accessed the paying-out gear via a wooden trough 495 feet long. A watch of men was stationed from the tank to the paying out machinery with many lamps placed at short distances to watch the cable's progress. For each mile that was brought up a green lamp was passed from the tank to the stern, where its passage was recorded. During daylight a system of flags was used.

On 22nd July they passed about 35 miles south of the end of the lost cable. That night Gooch wrote in his diary

> "Now for a walk in Oxford Street and then to bed."

This was his name for the length of lighted deck (O'Neill called it Regent Street the previous year). Two days later they changed from the forward to the middle tank, prior to which Gooch wrote:

> "It will be my last walk in Oxford Street as two thirds of it will be cut off when they are paying out of the middle tank. This changeable Atlantic, (he added) when I sat down to write this I could see the moon out of my window through the fog, and it is now raining very hard; I hear it against my window."

The 'old coffee mill' as the sailors called the paying-out gear kept grinding away unceasingly. News was received regularly through the cable and was printed in a newspaper, the "*Great Eastern* Telegraph 1866 and Test Room Chronicle". Robert Dudley and the journalists on board had a tradition to maintain. Nicholas Woods and J.C. Parkinson wrote a number of masques for the entertainment of those on board. One was called "*Field-Glass being a Cableistic and Eastern Extravaganza*", with the official programme hand-drawn by Dudley and printed on the ship's lithographic press.

Communication with Valentia being maintained throughout, and assisted by Richard Glass's regular communiqués, had a tremendous impact on the public. Excitement increased daily as the

---

[*] "A resume of the earlier days of electric telegraphy" read at the Extraordinary General Meeting of the Society of Telegraph Engineers and Electricians in Paris on 21st Sept 1881.

prospect of a successful outcome became more certain. In expectation of success Field requested Valentia to gather all the latest news from the war then raging in Europe.+

Soon they were in thick fog on the Grand Banks. Although visual contact was lost, a system of whistles kept the convoy together. Two from *Terrible*, three from *Medway* and four from *Albany*. *Great Eastern* was to reply with one long blast.

Great Eastern laying the first successful Atlantic cable painted by Henry Clifford (note the four funnels)
National Maritime Museum BHC3380

The Admiralty had arranged that they were to be met 30 miles off shore and as they approached the mother ship signalled to the others to move on ahead. During the afternoon of Friday 27th July signals were received from *Terrible* to say that HMS *Niger* was on station to receive them and that there was another ship waiting at the entrance to Trinity Bay. According to Bern Dibner:

> *Albany* also signalled that she had passed an iceberg standing 60 feet out of the water. At four in the afternoon, the crew of the *Niger* welcomed the *Great Eastern* with three cheers which were as lustily returned by most of the 502 men aboard. The ships then headed for Trinity Bay with

+ The Austro-Prussian war, which heralded great changes in Europe, also established a reputation for Julius de Reuter, who was to play such an important role in the future development of trans-Atlantic telegraphy. He was able to telegraph news from both camps to London.

> signals arranged to be guided towards Heart's Content. The news had preceded the arrival of the convoy and there were signs of jubilation everywhere. British and American flags floated from such high points as the church steeple and the telegraph station.

Quoting John Deane:

> We had dressed ship, fired a salute and given three cheers and Captain Commerell of HMS *Terrible* was soon on board to congratulate us on our success. At nine o'clock, ship's time, just as we had cut the cable and made arrangements for the *Medway* to lay the shore end, a message arrived giving us the concluding words of a header in this morning's Times: 'It is a great work, a glory to our age and nation and the men who have achieved it deserve to be honoured among the benefactors of their race - Treaty of peace signed between Prussia and Austria'

As preparations were being made to splice the shore end cable, Field went ahead to make arrangements for transmission of the news to New York. He had been aware of a break in the cable connecting Cape Ray, Newfoundland and Cape North, Nova Scotia on the other side of the Cabot Strait. He was mortified to find that his instructions to have it repaired had not been carried out. The other directors of the Newfoundland Company, being sceptical of the prospect of success, had not taken any action. This was to mean a delay of 24 hours in transmitting the news to New York, because it would require a ship to relay messages to the nearest mainland telegraph post.

Gooch reported that as he and Canning stepped ashore, the cable was being slowly paid out through the shallow water:

> There was the wildest excitement I have ever witnessed. All seemed mad with joy, jumping into the water and shouting as though they wished the sound to be heard at Washington. As soon as the cable touched the land all the ships in the harbour fired a salute: the noise was something tremendous and the smoke soon hid the ships from our view. When the cable end was brought actually to the little wooden house built to receive it another wild scene of excitement took place. The old cable hands seemed as though they could eat the end: one man actually put his mouth to it and sucked it. They held it up and danced round it - nay a sight that filled our eyes with tears. Yet I felt no less then they did. I did cheer, but I could better have silently cried.
>
> Well it was a feeling that will last my life; it will be one of those thoughts which will assist to bring peace to my mind when other matters trouble it. I am glad two of my boys were present to enjoy and glory in their part of so noble a work. They may, long after I am gone, tell their children of what we did. While the cable was being coupled up with the instruments they all went into the little church in the village. There were three clergymen assembled to see the cable and all took part in the service, which was very nicely done, the clergyman of the village reading the prayers, a couple of hymns were sung and we all earnestly returned our thanks to God in the words of thanksgiving in the Prayer Book.

Field's packet of news arrived in New York on Sunday 29 July. The first message read:

> We arrived here at nine o'clock this morning. All well. Thank God, the cable is laid and in perfect working order

This was followed by a dispatch to Associated Press which included details of the voyage and his collection of European news.

The practice which had been gained by the Valentia staff during the fourteen days when the *Great Eastern* was at sea meant that they were able to transmit at high speed. The line was opened for business almost immediately and the first message from Speyer, the merchant bankers in London, to their office in New York was charged at a tariff of £20. The Queen* and the President of the United States (Andrew Johnson) exchanged greetings although the boat link across the St Lawrence slowed things considerably.

Messages of congratulations were showered on the principals of the enterprise; none more so than on Cyrus Field. The same day as he received a telegram from San Francisco, he also had a message from Ferdinand de Lesseps (the engineer of the Suez Canal) in Alexandria. These amply demonstrated the extent of the telegraph links that were opened up by the recent success.

The Telegraph Construction and Maintenance Co. had fulfilled half of their contract. There was still the 1865 cable lying at the bottom of the Atlantic. First however the *Great Eastern* had to be refuelled. Six colliers had been previously dispatched from Cardiff to Newfoundland. One foundered on the way. The remainder arrived a few days before the *Great Eastern* and work was now put in hand to transfer their stock of coal.

During this period Thomson wrote his official report to Richard Glass.

> *Great Eastern*
> Heart's Content
> 6 August 1866
> My Dear Mr Glass
> I have been thinking how many sheets of foolscap I ought to cover in my report to you, but really I cannot find that I have anything to say as to my department except that everything went like clockwork in the testing and I had the satisfaction of being a 'cypher' from the time we got our arrangements completed before leaving Berehaven. I hope by about this time fortnight to be able again to make a similar report. But if unhappily there is trouble with faults I am very confident we shall be able to avoid confusion as far as can be done by speedy and accurate enough localization.
>
> The cable as you know has far exceeded our expectations as to speed. So there will be ample time to arrange about curb keys and permanent plans for working when we are all home

*Technically the Royal message jumped the gun. It arrived in Heart's Content while *Great Eastern* was in the harbour, but before the cable had been landed.

> again. I hope before Christmas to be able to give you a recorder that will take messages through the cable with security at fifteen words per minute or more.
>
> We are all very sorry to hear you have been so poorly. I hope and trust by the time this reaches you will be perfectly well again.
>
> I owe you many thanks for your great kindness about my messages to and from my wife. They have been a great comfort to me, although I feel distressed that the accounts of my sister-in-law's health have been so bad,-
>
> With kind regards to Mrs. Glass, I remain, yours very truly,
>
> William Thomson

Capt Moriarty sailed out in the *Albany*, in company with *Terrible*, to locate and buoy the spot where the 1865 cable had been lost. The *Great Eastern* and *Medway* left on August 9 and this information was immediately passed on to Valentia. On the journey to their hunting ground William Thomson, who was particularly concerned about the health of his sister-in-law was able to dispatch a letter to his wife on the 13th via a passing steamer. The letter indicated that they intended to start grappling that night. The letter reached her on the 23rd.

When *Great Eastern* arrived, the location was marked by a line of buoys, Albany had already been grappling for a week without bringing up the cable, although she had hooked it several times and had lost a lot of rope in the process. When conditions permitted *Great Eastern* started to grapple. There were two or three unsuccessful attempts and then on 17 August the cable was raised to view. However it could not take the strain of its own weight, disintegrated and fell back into the ocean.

Days of frustration followed. There had been a lot of fog, which hampered activities and the weather showed signs of deterioration. Everyone began to lose heart. On August 31st, on the 30th attempt the cable was raised half way, then suspended from a buoy. *Medway* grappled further to the west while *Great Eastern* took station between ship and buoy. Moriarty's reckoning of the position of the cable had been so accurate that as the cable was being hauled aboard, one of the marker buoys was rubbing against the side of the ship.

The cable was secured with additional ropes before it was hauled aboard. From here on everything was a great rush just in case it started to break. The west end was cut away and the eastward side connected to the electrical instruments. There was now the anxious moments of frustrating delay waiting for a response from Valentia.

Ever since the 1865 cable had been broken, its condition had been continuously monitored on land. James Graves, who had by now been formally appointed Superintendent at Valentia, summarised the frustration which must have been felt when he wrote

> The *Great Eastern* was doing its utmost to bring life to the dead cable, whilst we on shore took turns at watching for signs of returning life upon the mirror galvanometer with the utmost impatience and anxiety as the time approached when we calculated the great ship would be on the grappling ground
>
> On the 2nd September at 5.37 am Mr Crocker* (whose watch it was came in breathless with nervous excitement and aroused me and Mr May, who occupied the same room and all he could articulate was 'ship, ship'. We both jumped out of bed partly dressed and rushed into the testing room, where with our own eyes we saw very unmistakable signals from the *Great Eastern* calling our attention. It was her first call and the instant it ceased we replied and without any further preliminary remarks the following message was sent:
>
> "Canning to Glass - I have pleasure in speaking to you through the 1865 cable - Am going to make splice"
>
> After a few enquiries about the working of the other cable and the health of the staff, the splicing was proceeded with and the paying out commenced**.

Daniel Gooch in his diary recalls:

> I think my heart ceased beating during those few minutes. God only knows the sensation of such a moment

The cable was threaded out slowly and carefully despite the storm, which had it occurred a few hours earlier would have destroyed all hope of retrieving the cable that year. Various messages were sent from the ship.

On September 3rd Mrs. Thomson in Glasgow received the following message from Valentia:

> Mr Graves has been requested by Professor Thomson to write to Mrs. T. to inform her that he is well and to request her to telegraph the latest news in full by means of the 1865 cable+. It is expected that that the *Great Eastern* will arrive at Hearts Content on Saturday next....

So uncertain was everyone of success that they had not yet prepared a significant quantity of stationery. Most of these messages were recorded onto British and Irish Magnetic Telegraph Co. chits.

---

* Crocker was subsequently transferred to Heart's Content in March 1867, but appears to have unable to stand the weather extremes. He left the Service in 1868.

** According to Merrett there were also enquiries about the state of the cable across the St Lawrence

+ William Thomson's sister-in-law, Agnes Crum in fact died before the *Great Eastern* reached Liverpool on September 18th.

The *Great Eastern* arrived in Heart's Content on September 8th to a reception which defied description. The shore end was once more landed by *Medway* which thereafter proceeded to use a piece of spare cable to lay a new line from Cape Ray to North Cape to complete the link. On the 9th the 1865 'test messages' were transmitted as follows:

> Test messages to be sent from Hearts Content to Valentia by the Cable of 1865. May the cable now recovered be a bond of peace between Great Britain and America to last for many years Augustus T. Hamilton
>
> Test message to Newfoundland from George Saward, Great Britain
> To Captain A.T. Hamilton, Hearts Content, Newfoundland
> Thank you for the proof just received from you confirming the safe completion of this work so long and ardently laboured for.

Graves then continues:

> These messages being acknowledged to be correctly transmitted the vice-Chairman of the Atlantic Telegraph Co. (Capt A.T. Hamilton) sent a message to the Assistant Secretary (Mr J. McCurley) stating that he had taken over the cable of 1865 on behalf of the Anglo American Telegraph Co. and a few minutes later the Contractor's Electrician (Mr J. May) telegraphed to Mr Canning that Mr Latimer Clark had given him certificate and he had handed over the cable of 1865 to Mr Graves

The following messages were also received:
Gooch, Hamilton and Field to Stewart, London

> Our work is finished. The *Great Eastern* started about 4.30 pm for Liverpool expecting to arrive there on the 19th September.

Shortly after the *Great Eastern* left, cableships *Medway* and *Terrible* steamed out of Heart's Content, *Medway* laying an earth cable as it went. On Tuesday they called in at St John's for coal, and the principals attended a banquet in their honour.

On the journey round to Cape Ray, the two ships stopped in at St Pierre et Miquelon, a French colony just off the tip of Newfoundland. The French had always been energetic in supporting proposals to use this island as a telegraph staging post. Accordingly, Cyrus Field, Mr Temple and Capt. Commerell of *Medway* were lavishly treated by the Governor, Col. Creu, who afterwards accompanied them along the coast to choose a suitable location for landing a future cable.

The two ships were off Port aux Basques on Saturday. The cable end was landed and paying out commenced. From this point until her eventual arrival in Queenstown (Cobh), Ireland, *Medway* suffered a series of upsets. Off Cape Ray there was a storm which caused the cable to snap 10 miles off St. Paul. It was retrieved in 250 fathoms of water and they started again, but a defect in the gear broke the cable again. However it was hauled up and on Tuesday the other end was landed in the Bay of Aspee.

The two ships refuelled at Picton, Nova Scotia, whence Cyrus Field departed for New York. The ship left there on Tuesday 27 September to replace the cable to Prince Edward Island. This was accomplished on October 2nd after which *Medway* headed for home. *Terrible* went via Charlottestown so that she could refuel before crossing the Atlantic. When *Medway* was 300 miles west of Ireland her propeller shaft broke and the propeller was lost. Although the ship was not designed for sailing, the captain was able to improvise a jury rig and she sailed into Queenstown (Cobh), Ireland on 21st October to await a tug to tow her to the Thames.

Any scepticism about the ability of electricity to travel over such distances were dispelled by two experiments which took place within a short while of the successful landing of the 1865 cable. On September 12th Latimer Clark at Valentia borrowed a silver thimble from the daughter of the Knight of Kerry[*]. He sent instructions to Heart's Content to join the cores of the two cables. Placing a drop of acid in the thimble connected through a sensitive astatic galvanometer to one of the cables, he had a piece of zinc connected to the core of the other cable. Whenever the zinc was dipped into the acid, a deflection was observed on the meter, indicating that it would be possible to transmit a signal through the 3748 miles of cable (a total resistance of 15,510 ohms according to Graves) using such small power.

Dr Benjamin Apthorp Gould (1824 - 1896) the American astronomer who used the Valentia cables to determine the longitude of North America relative to Europe.

[*] This is now preserved in the Science Museum in London.

Several other experiments were undertaken including one by Dr Gould on behalf of the Astronomer Royal (in concert with the Magnetic Telegraph Co) between Greenwich and Newfoundland for the verification of longitudes in the United States.

The *Great Eastern* arrived in Liverpool to a tumultuous reception on September 18th (it was observed passing Crookhaven near Valentia at 6 pm on the 17th). There were dinners and receptions in all parts of the country for the expedition's principals. Towards the end of September Royal honours were bestowed. James Anderson, Richard Glass, Samuel Canning and William Thomson received knighthoods. Daniel Gooch and Curtis M. Lampson were made Baronets[**]. On the other side of the Atlantic, Cyrus Field, now able to extricate himself from his financial problems by the sale of cable shares, was given the very rare honour of a unanimous vote of thanks from the United States Congress.

The largest banquet of all was held at Liverpool. The President of the Board of Trade took the Chair. Captain Anderson, Sir Charles Bright, Samuel Canning, Henry Clifford, Latimer Clark and Willoughby Smith were present. The Chairman read a letter from the Prime Minister, Lord Derby, officially announcing the list of honours.

Perhaps unknowingly, Liverpool had more to lose by the success of the cable then was realised at the time. Heretofore the delay in communication between the sources of raw materials and the centres of manufacture had led to the establishment of a breed of middle men and agents in major ports such as Liverpool. Trans-Atlantic telegraphy removed their function, particularly as telegram tariff levels came down. From this time onwards, whether by coincidence or not, a number of commercial bankers abandoned Liverpool and relocated to London.

Meanwhile at Valentia, Graves's pen was already hard at work. On 19 September he addressed a letter to Richard Glass (using Atlantic Telegraph Co. stationery).

> R.A. Glass
> Ashurst, Dorking Surrey
>
> My Dear Sir,
> We have effected considerable improvements in the working of the line since you left here, these improvements are mainly the result of experiments upon different methods of suspending the mirror in the galvanometer and the adjustment of the permanent magnets, and also in finding the best resistance in galvanometer for giving good signals with low battery power.
>
> The details of these results I have forwarded to Mr Lat. Clark in order that he may give the proper instructions when ordering new galvanometers for the Stations. At present we are

[**] Honours were also offered to Stuart Wortley and Capt. Hamilton, who declined them.

working with two odd ones belonging to the Telegraph Construction & M^{ce} Company- one of these requires the power of 10 cells at Newfoundland to work it, while the other works easily with two cells only and splendid signals.

We frequently see in the London papers references made to speed and recommendations in favour of Capt. Bolton's and Snell's Code arguing financially upon a maximum speed of 7 or 8 words a minute - adding that the by the use of the code we might get even 15 words a minute but they say nothing of the time occupied in coding and translating before the message can be retransmitted*.

Now it happens that by our latest improvements we are enabled to attain a working speed of 15 words a minute and in a trial of speed last evening we reached <u>20 words</u> a minute read by Mr Carson without abbreviations, received from Heart's Content and written down at Instrument. The speed at which messages can be sent - or I should way the limit of the speed at which the cables will transmit signals, is simply the possibility of the clerk being able to send- for the reader can now excel the sender - it is very sharp work to send 18 or 20 words a minute on the double keys, but if sent it can be read off. I think we should find it an improvement if our sending apparatus were simply the handle of a single needle telegraph instrument - which might be made specially adapted to this line - as being easier of manipulation then two keys and giving firmer contact then done with the fingers - and I am of the opinion we shall have to use this before long instead of the double keys**. This great rate of signalling is truly marvellous through such a length and while we can do this our two cables are in themselves equal to six working at the speed we a few months since anticipated and we shall be able with our two lines keep pace with the land wires unless the number is more then doubled.

Although we can work at such a high speed, there is no necessity for doing so at present with our messages, but I merely point out these facts to shew what can be done if necessity should arise - when the new receiving galvanometers arrive I expect to get a speed of 20 words a minute with a power of two cells at each end for sending.

I am happy to hear through Walter Judge such a good account of your health and trust it may continue to still further improve. All our staff desire kind regards. I am my dear sir, yours very truly
James Graves

ps I have informed Newfoundland of our improvements in order that they may follow our example - as we are compelled at present to work to them with 20 cells.

---

* At a later date codes were generally adopted to provide security for customers such as bankers, financiers etc, this apart from any government codes and ciphers.
** In fact double keys were to remain in use even when automatic transmitters sent most of the traffic.

Graves's personal reminiscences also give a good deal of information about the establishment of a permanent station.

> The correspondence during the interval between the completion of the cables and the month of October was chiefly respecting the official regulations for the traffic and the making permanent provision for the staff in the matter of house accommodation. It was originally proposed to build a station and some cottages at the western end of the island, as scientific advices had put forward the theoretical conclusion that to lengthen the cable by 5 miles and erect a station nearer the small village of Knightstown would reduce the working speed and consequently the revenue of the Company.
>
> Upon this subject in a letter dated 10 September 1866 addressed to the Chairman (C.E. Stewart Esq.) I remarked as follows-
>
> 'Upon mature consideration respecting the site for the new buildings I have come to the conclusion that they ought to be built nearer Knightstown- This place (Foilhommerum) is very bleak and exposed- As the majority of our staff are married with families, they would be far more comfortable if they were nearer to the school, church and other essentials which ought not to be overlooked when selecting a site for permanent residences of the Company's officials, and I sincerely trust that this may have some weight with the Board. The objection on account of decreased speed of working is little more then a myth, which a little management would compensate for, even if the objection had any basis, which I doubt'
>
> Upon the same date I wrote to R.A. Glass Esq (afterwards Sir Richard). Amongst other matters as follows.
>
> 'Could you possibly arrange for the offices and houses to be near Knightstown
> There are so many things which bear in favour of it - the objection as to diminished speed of working is chimerical - Out here there is neither school, church, shop, post-office, doctor nor any other convenience necessary to young families'

On 21 September Graves left Valentia for London where he made arrangements to move his household effects. Together with his wife and family he returned at 7pm on 1 October. The following day he was busy with his pen again.

> Great inconvenience was felt by the members of the Anglo American Telegraph Company's staff at their being unable to make money remittances through the post from Valentia; the fact was represented by me to the Postmaster General, Dublin, on the 22nd of August 1866, and in due course I received the following letter dated from the 'General Post Office, Dublin, 2nd October 1866
>
> 'Sir, I beg leave to inform you that your application on the subject has been laid before the Postmaster General and that his Grace has been pleased to sanction the establishment of a

> money order office at Valentia (Killarney) I am sir your obedient servant G.C. Cornwall, Secretary'

A few days later the news of the Liverpool banquet was causing him considerable indignation when he addressed another letter to the Company Chairman.

> We have just received the London daily papers in which an account is published of the Liverpool banquet, and the Valentia staff generally feel rather hurt to find that amidst all the compliments paid to the various persons employed in this great and successful expedition, not one word was said respecting the part they took in carrying out the programme of operations.

This of course was nothing more than the truth. The *Great Eastern* could not have carried out its work without the assistance of those on shore (one could argue that at that time the Company's staff were merely observers and that it was the contractor's staff who should be rewarded). Eventually the justice of his case was recognised and the directors sent an 'appreciation' to Valentia together with an award of £250 to be shared among the staff.

The festivities following the twin success were not forgotten at Valentia. Shortly after the completion of the first cable the Knight of Kerry, Sir Peter Fitzgerald, wrote around to the other land owners looking for contributions towards a special occasion. It is not known how successful he was (the Board of Trinity College Dublin* contributed £5) but the celebrations were deemed a great success. Amongst the features of the day was a boat race (a favourite sport in that vicinity). All the local landlords sent along a team. Mr Daniel O'Connell (son of the famous parliamentarian and promoter of Roman Catholic Emancipation) although unable to be present himself, sent his boat. His wife and daughters attended.

And so - what of the principal characters of the enterprise?

Daniel Gooch was created a baronet on 15 November 1866, the first engineer ever to be so honoured. He succeeded John Pender as Chairman of the Telegraph Construction & Maintenance Co. when the latter left to become more involved in the Eastern Telegraph. Gooch remained as MP for Cricklade until four years before his death in 1889.

Richard Glass, knighted by patent on 26 November 1866 retired owing to ill health as Managing Director of the Telegraph Construction and Maintenance Co. in March 1867. He became MP for Bewdley in 1868 but was unseated on petition the following year. He died in 1873, aged 53.

---

* Trinity College Dublin had a very poor reputation as a landlord in all its very extensive Kerry estates. It was very much the case of management by a committee of academics rather then by a single improving resident landlord. Its tenants fared particularly badly during the 1847 potato famine on account of the College's inability to take decisive action.

Thomson, Canning and Anderson were knighted by accolade at Windsor Castle on 10 November 1866. There had been a storm of protest at the fact that Staff Commander Moriarty had not been honoured for his part. Thomas Brassey wrote to the *Times* on 22 October 1866 suggesting that at the very least the Admiralty should consider promoting him. The authorities conceded and on 2 November it was announced in the *Times* that he had been made a Commander of the Bath. Thomson and Varley were to make a number of important contributions to telegraphy, of which more later. Capt Anderson left the bridge for the company boardroom. Like his great ship and her first officer, Robert Halpin, who succeeded him, he surfaces on a number of occasions in the subsequent history of the Valentia Cable Station. In the meantime, however, *Great Eastern*'s missing funnel was restored and she was refurbished for commercial use.

Willoughby Smith's position in the Company and his reputation as a first rate electrical engineer were firmly established. He became Managing Director of the Telegraph Construction & Maintenance Co., from which he retired in 1888. His contribution to the science of electricity was acknowledged when he was elected President of the Institution of Electrical Engineers in 1883. He died in 1891.

Henry Clifford, who served as an engineer on all five of the Atlantic cable expeditions from 1857 to 1866, at the same time drawing and painting views of the activities, was Chief Engineer at the Telegraph Construction & Maintenance Co. until his retirement in 1893.

In Valentia itself, Sir Peter Fitzgerald, though successful in at least one of his aims, had his own problems. He opposed the new Land Acts as well as Home Rule and the disestablishment of the Church in Ireland. There were also Fenian problems. His daughter, Kate, writing to him from Valentia in 1869, began her letter:

> Dearest Papa, I am not going to say a single word about C....h or L...d for fear you put it in your letter book and ignore it....

In 1871 he attempted to reorganise the patchwork holdings of his tenants, rehousing many of them on new land which had not been heretofore tilled. Although it was intended to rationalise a system that had got out of hand (one farmer had a 30 acre holding which was several miles long by a few yards wide), it met with general opposition. However his new houses were of good quality with slated roofs. He died in 1880.

Before finally leaving the sequel to the 1866 expedition and concentrating on its long term outcome, it is perhaps worth seeing what became of the Atlantic Telegraph Co., whose final destiny had been thwarted by the judgment of the Attorney General in 1865. Under the Articles the right was reserved to the Atlantic Telegraph Co. of terminating the Agreement on or before 1 Jan 1869 (on giving three months notice) by payment to the Anglo American Telegraph Co of £1,200,000, double the amount of its capital.

Relationships between the two companies had always been somewhat strained. This broke out into open warfare in the columns of the *Times* once the expedition had been successful. J. Stuart

Wortley and George Saward, Chairman and Secretary of the Atlantic Co., were ranged against C.E. Stewart[*] and J.C. Deane, their counterparts in the Anglo. Much of the argument turned on the relative values of the two companies. In 1867 the Atlantic Company obtained an Act of Parliament (30 Vic. c28) permitting them to raise sufficient cash for their purpose. So, the Atlantic Co. exercised its right of redemption and it was agreed that the Anglo should forthwith be dissolved and the funds distributed amongst the shareholders. However, one of the clauses that had been inserted into the Act stipulated that such a resolution to pursue this cause would have to be passed with the agreement of three fourths of the Anglo shareholders' votes. By this means a small number of wealthy shareholders were able to block the resolution. In view of this it was felt that the only available option was an amalgamation. This was achieved by Acts of Parliament in 1870 and 1871, when the Atlantic Company disappeared. George Saward, who had been one of its parents as well as midwife, died a bitter man in 1873.

Thomas Brassey

George Saward

[*] C.E. Stewart died in 1868. Sir Richard Glass, now returned to health, took his place as Chairman of the Anglo American Telegraph Co.

Chapter 9

1866 - 1883 The Atlantic Telegraph In Operation, Development And Expansion

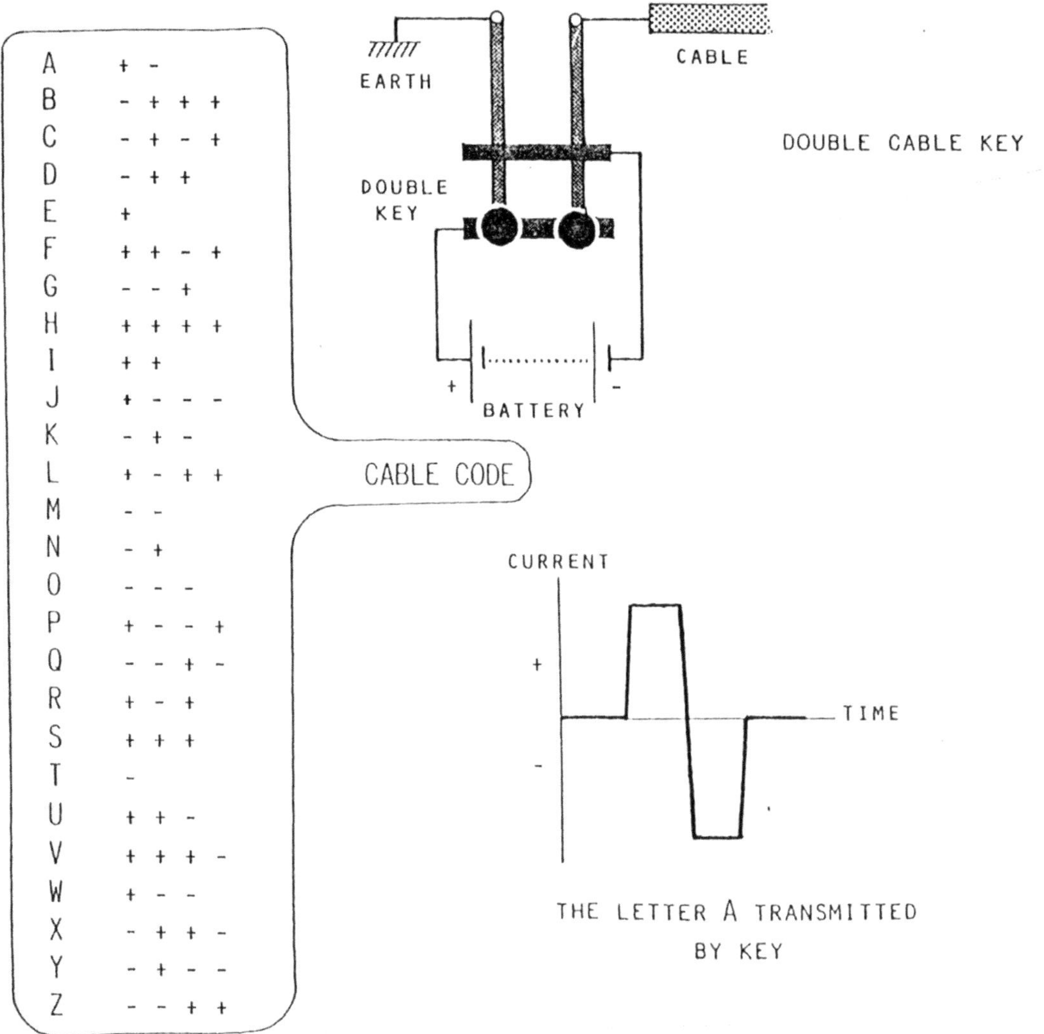

A Steinheil (double) key as used at Valentia with the translation from land-line Morse to cable code

The choice of date limits for this chapter may at first sight appear a little odd. It was a very exciting, if somewhat frustrating period, and James Graves, as Valentia's first Superintendent, was in a unique position to observe it. During this time he maintained a detailed personal record, which he undoubtedly intended to publish at some time. It therefore forms an almost unique record of events. However, by 1883 there was intense competition and the Company's financial position was far from satisfactory. It is not clear whether from this point onwards the Superintendentship became a more time-consuming job, or whether in the general depression Graves simply lost interest in his writings. His manuscript for "Thirty six years in the telegraph service[+]" is concluded in an uncharacteristically hasty manner and the subsequent history of the Valentia Cable Station must be followed from other, less direct sources.

The first commercial message passed across the Atlantic on Saturday 28 July 1866. C.E. Stewart gave clearance for its transmission, which was commenced at 1.24 pm. It was from Speyer in London to Speyer in New York[*] and the sender had to pay a £20 minimum charge for 20 words with £1 per word thereafter.

From the very beginning the Valentia Station used the call sign VA (...- .-). On the other side NF (- . ..-.) was initially used, but this was subsequently changed to HC (.... -.-.) for Heart's Content. It is believed that NF was still retained for messages from the office in St John's, Newfoundland

In the previous chapter reference was made to Graves' representations concerning the inadequacies of the station building at Foilhommerum Bay. In spite of very slack business at the start it soon became obvious that the building was quite unsuitable for other (operational) reasons. It contained the offices of three companies: the two major landline companies in addition to the Anglo. According to John Merrett, who was employed at Valentia (in the 1920s), the Electric Telegraph Company's offices were used as sleeping accommodation at night and the Anglo's private office was also a bedroom for their senior clerk, Mr George.

During the first part of October Graves sent a staff report to Head Office at 26 Old Broad Street, London. This indicated that there were three senior clerks (E. George, J.H. Carson and F.T. Tranfield). The three juniors (Endean, Gregory and Mackey)[**] were paid £120 pa plus food. While the senior clerks lived at the Station, the juniors had to travel backwards and forwards to Knightstown five miles away. The Company hired horse-drawn sidecars for this purpose. Indeed, this represented the largest single item of monthly expenditure during this period.

The beginning was a period of learning for everybody. The staff had to be trained in sending and receiving at the cable, which as previously indicated, they seemed to pick up very quickly.

[+] A copy is available under the heading 'Technical Autobiography' at http://dandadec.com

[*] Speyer Bros. were an enterprising firm of merchant bankers, active in both foreign exchange and issues. Of Frankfurt Jewish origin, they opened in New York in 1837 and London in 1861. Their early financial business consisted largely in acquiring American railroad and other investment bonds for sale in Europe, from which whey became very wealthy; in 1866 they were already reckoned to be worth around £1.0m.

[**] Names of staff are quoted where possible because they give some idea of career development of telegraph staff as well as giving an indication of staff mobility.

Meanwhile Graves and various visiting electrical consultants spent much time trying out different arrangements. A single wire cable had to be grounded at both ends to give a complete circuit.

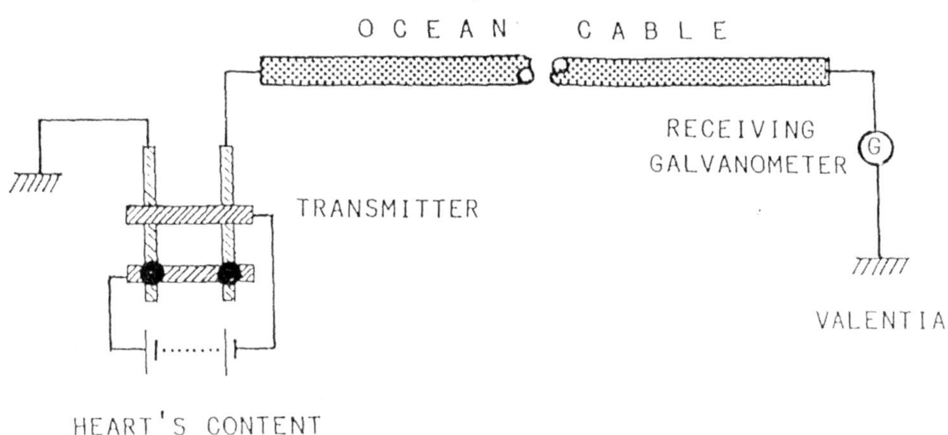

A single wire cable circuit with the transmitter and receiver end connected to ground

Such a system was prone to earth currents. Because the crust of the earth is not a perfect conductor, two points on its surface (e.g. Valentia and Newfoundland) can have different potentials with respect to each other. These earth currents, as they are called, can vary with time* and are particularly strong during periods of intense solar activity (aurorae) or thunderstorms. They had the effect of moving the light spot on the receiving galvanometer in an erratic manner, frequently sending it off scale. Any compensation by the use of resistors also reduced the sensitivity of the instrument.

It was found that by connecting both cables together to form a continuous loop, earth currents could be completely eliminated and a very high transmission rate achieved (up to 90 words per minute)

* One of Graves's major scientific contributions was to demonstrate the diurnal nature of earth currents.

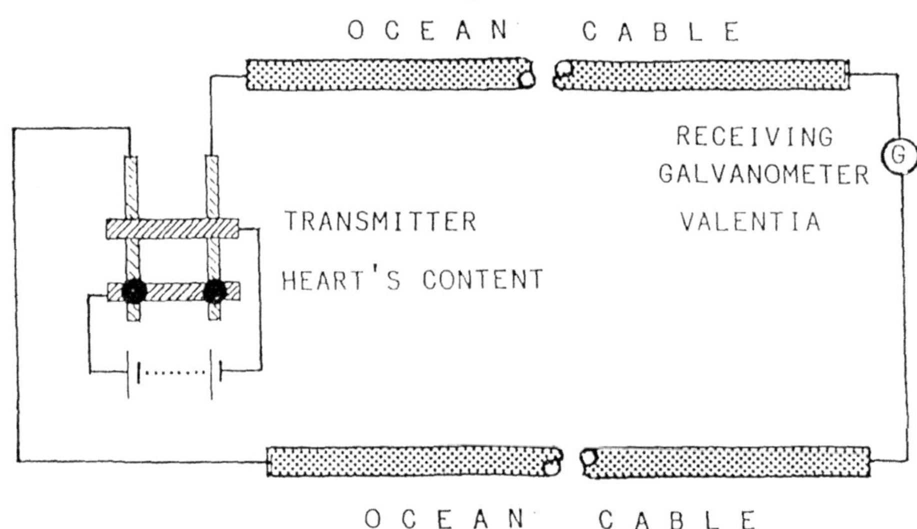

Metallic loop circuit using two cables between transmitter and receiver

A more efficient method was to attach a condenser (capacitor) between the galvanometer and earth.

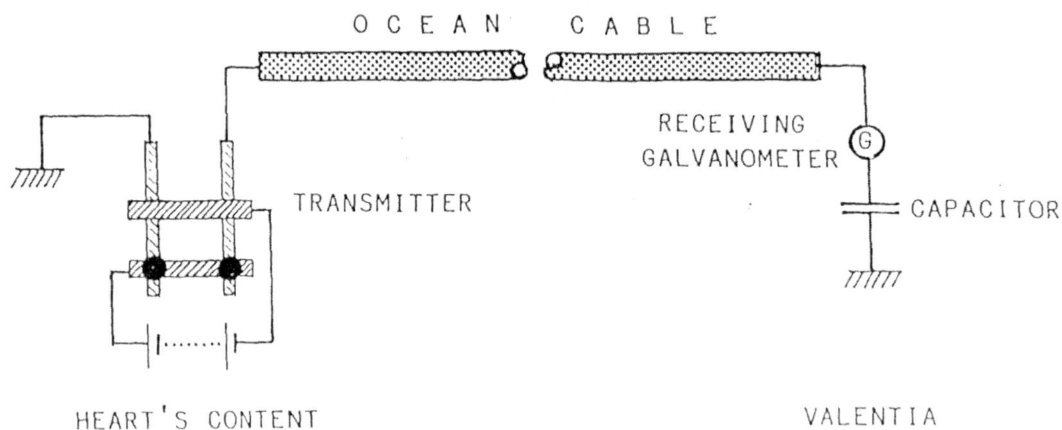

Single wire circuit with capacitor between the receiver and ground to block earth currents

The side which did not have a condenser in circuit suffered from earth currents, while the side which did was free. However unpleasant experiences stick hard in the mind, particularly with company directors. Whitehouse had destroyed the 1858 cable with condensers (under completely different circumstances). At 9.15 pm on 23 October 1867 orders were received over the land lines to discontinue using them. The word rate immediately halved and the signals were sluggish and ill defined. Earth currents frequently took the spot off the scale. They struggled along in this way until 11.30 am on the 24th when the condensers were once more inserted and the line worked well.

On the 18th and 19th October experiments similar to the thimble experiment on 12th September were carried out at Newfoundland. In the first, the cables were joined at Valentia. At Heart's Content a galvanometer was connected to one cable and a single cell to the other. The cell consisted of a copper percussion cap with, according to Graves, "one drop of sulphuric acid, a few grains of sand and a small morsel of zinc". On connection it was possible to read distinct signals.

Graves then reports that "At 11.15 on the following day the signals from Hearts Content became very small, but quite clear and distinct. Many sentences were read and on enquiry he (Richard Collett) stated that he was using a percussion cap and a small piece of zinc" This was through the 1866 cable using earth connections with a condenser in series at Valentia.

Collett was the Company's Traffic Manager and had been sent to supervise the setting up at Newfoundland. It is not clear why, but he appears to have had a personal vendetta against Graves and missed no opportunity to find fault with his work or that of his staff. His actions while at Heart's Content led to very bad feelings between the two Stations. For instance, at 1.20 am on 16 October he wired through: "Attention at your Station disgraceful, see it attended" Graves replied "When I complained of your Station (message of 29 Sept 'unless NF receives better work will be delayed'), you telegraphed the Chairman that my message created ill feeling. What can be the effect of yours? George and Mackey were on duty, the former attending fire in kitchen, latter call of nature in field. 'Wait' was given by former till return of latter to write. MY staff are competent to do their work and they do it to the best of their ability" In submitting his views on the matter to the Chairman, Graves commented on the degeneration of relations under arbitrary rule on the other side, saying that the government there is far from the spirit conveyed in the words 'tis better far to rule by love then fear'. Even if never again stated so explicitly, this was to be his style of management during the next forty-three years.

The message rate of £20 per hundred letters had the desired effect of limiting traffic at the initial stages. Accordingly, on 1 November 1866 it was reduced to £10 for a message of the same length, and it did indeed lead to an increase in business.

During the period November and December 1866 and January 1867, the cable station for the first of many occasions became a potential target of attack at a time of political conflict. The struggle for Irish Home Rule and settlement of the Land Question involved both peaceful political and violent action. The Fenians were one such group and presented the authorities with a sinister threat. Unlike previous organisations in Ireland they were a secret society broken up into cells, so that the intelligence methods so successfully used in the past were of little value. They were to a large extent inspired and financed by the large group of Irish who had emigrated to America twenty years or so previously and many of whom had acquired useful military experience during the Civil War. One such person was J. J. O Connor, a Valentia man who had attained the rank of Captain in the 28th Massachusetts Regt. In 1865, aged 26, he returned to Kerry and began recruiting for the Fenians. Following rumours of his activities, a detachment of Constabulary was lodged at the Station and a gunboat was moored at Knightstown in case the attack came from the sea; piracy was not unknown along these coasts. The Magnetic Telegraph Company's office was kept open and a secret code of signals was arranged in case the gunboat was required in a hurry.

Early in January 1867 the Knight of Kerry organised an anti-Fenian demonstration in Knightstown, which is described by Pochin Mould in her book on Valentia:

> In a flowery speech, the Knight affirmed their loyalty to the Queen, the foolishness of the Fenian cause, more especially in a time of increasing prosperity. Nor should anything be done to harm the Atlantic Telegraph Company (he had not come to terms with the Anglo American Telegraph Co.). If an Irish Republic were set up, would it do more for the Valentia people; if the land was divided among them, who would finance the slate mine?
>
> This flatulent meeting was fully reported in the papers and the 'Nation' (5 Jan. 1867) tore it to shreds. "As the crowd were all the Knight's tenants, they had duly applauded and laughed at his jokes; but all of this would be taken at its true value by anyone of sense. As to the Telegraph Station, it was worked by a few men 'with a machine made up of a few bits of zinc and copper' and when national prosperity and national feeling were to be spoken of, it could safely be ignored. Indeed it might rather be asked 'whether by the spouting of such silly addresses as that of the Knight of Kerry, the Fenian cause is not advanced rather then retarded'

Pochin Mould then continues:

> As to the safety of the Atlantic Telegraph Station on Valentia, that according to some unpublished notes of F.C. Mackey (a relative of Mackey mentioned above) (d. 1970), had its own method of protecting itself. There was 'an ever ready barrel of porter, which of course was put down to office expenses. Judging by ancient office records the Fenian boys must have been both frequent, numerous and thirsty visitors

Collett left Heart's Content for England on 14 November 1866 and immediately relations between the two Stations improved under the rule of Mr Laws at Newfoundland. However occasional attempts by the management and their consultants to operate a single cable without looping the return (through the other cable) or grounding via condensers did lead to friction. Earth currents completely obscured the signals and brought strong protests from the receiving station.

On 5 February 1867 the Queen's speech at the state opening of Parliament was transmitted to New York and appeared in its entirety in the morning papers on the 6th.

There were further rumblings of Fenian troubles in March. The sergeant of the resident constabulary informed them that an attack was imminent and that there should be a blackout of the Station at the first intimation of trouble.

Financial records which formed part of the Western Union International (WUI) collection in London in 1983 give an interesting insight into how the station was expanding. In January 1867 there was a payment of 45-5s-2d (£45.26p) to a Mr Shanahan and £25-13s-2d (£25.66p) to a Mr Murphy for transport between Foilhommerum and Knightstown. The total station costs for that month were nearly £325. The data for February has a breakdown to indicate that of a total of £255, £224.26 was for salaries. Car hire for March 1867 amounted to £17. In addition, the staff complement as at March 1867 also included: D. Murphy (houseboy), J. Devine (lamp boy), N. Murphy (cook) and M. O'Shea (housemaid). There is a further informative breakdown for December 1867. Of nearly £347 station expenditure, £187 was for the salaries of cable staff, while £36.45 was for the salaries of landline staff.

So the first few months of the Station's existence went by - not too much business, the tariffs were still very high - strained relations between the Traffic Manager, Collett and Graves who defended his staff with righteous (Collett probably thought pompous) indignation. The staff, predominantly English, were settling down to a new way of life. Valentia was certainly remote from Manchester, Liverpool and London, and the pressures and pace were correspondingly less. The weather in this area touched by the Gulf Stream was never too cold, but it could be incredibly wet for unbelievably long periods.

On 14 May 1867 the 1866 cable broke for the first of many times; it was the less fortunate of the two. The cause was almost invariably grounding of icebergs off Newfoundland. On this occasion the break had occurred two or three miles out from Heart's Content. The *Chiltern* (1,391 tons), which had recently been purchased by the Telegraph Construction and Maintenance Co., was dispatched to Newfoundland where it arrived on 17 June, and the repair was effected within two days.

There was still not sufficient work for the two cables, and on 22 June Graves suggested that connecting the cables in parallel would improve signalling and maintain continuous monitoring of the condition of both. This was agreed and worked for some time.

There were some unusual disturbances of the "spot" during the summer of 1867, and it did not take long to observe that these were connected with the working of the land lines. The submarine cable had been fitted with a very efficient earthing system consisting of two miles of cable laid out to sea and terminated in a large mass of zinc. The landlines had only a rod earth into the ground and the long, hot and unusually dry summer its efficiency had been reduced. Earth leakage through to the submarine cables was the cause of the disturbance, in spite of the two offices being at opposite ends of the building. Graves knowing that the sheathing of the cable was itself an excellent earth, arranged for the landlines to use the sea earth which had been installed on Cromwell F. Varley's insistence. It worked well and was also used at Heart's Content when they were troubled with a similar phenomenon on 15 August.

The landlines across Newfoundland had given trouble and had been a source of much delay from the very start. It was therefore a relief to all when on 30 August the *Chiltern* completed the laying of a cable which linked Sydney Mines (Cape Breton Island, Nova Scotia) to St Pierre et Miquelon and Placentia Bay (Newfoundland).

The month of August also saw a visit from the Company Secretary, J.C. Deane, to discuss plans for a new station building, which was to be much closer to the centre of population.

The 1866 cable failed again late in the summer. This time the fault was estimated at 80 miles out from Heart's Content. The *Chiltern* arrived at the spot in September but was hampered in her efforts by bad weather. This is recorded in the Valentia Station Diary.

18 September 1867

9.20am	Observed test currents from ship
2.00pm	Since 11 am observed further currents, probably while splicing. Expect speak to her soon.
7.00pm	Speaking to ship. Following from ship: "Strong wind, heavy sea, going to buoy cable and leave it - 82 miles from Hearts Content."

20 September 1867

10.43am	Test current from ship
12.14am	Ship now about to make final splice
3.15pm	Fear that ship slipped VA end of cable
6.55pm	Received signals again from ship
10.07pm	Ship now about to make final splice
10.52pm	Speaking NF on '66 cable OK

The Anglo American Company had been having discussions with the British & Irish Magnetic Telegraph Co. about the exclusive use of landlines, and on the 25th of November the landline office was handed over. Direct communication between Foilhommerum and the new Anglo offices in London started on the 30th. This may have reduced delay, but in the short term the Company now had to deal with all the problems which occurred on the landlines and these were not few. However, it was probably the best thing in the long run. When the Post Office took over all inland telegraphs in 1870, a less flexible regime was introduced. At least the Anglo had already established the principle of their right to exclusive landlines to headquarters. Much of Graves's writings during this period were concerned with the new problems which they experienced.

On 1 December 1867 the tariff was reduced to 5 guineas

A new transmission record was established in early March 1868. The aftermath of the American Civil War still rumbled on. There were still remnants of American ill-feeling towards Britain for her 'neutral' stand during the hostilities. The Queen's proclamation of neutrality at the time had given the South belligerent rights. This was viewed as an unfriendly act by the North. In addition Confederate cruisers, built or armed by Britons, not only destroyed American shipping, but did indirect damage by driving up insurance rates and forcing many American ships to operate under foreign flags. The Confederate States also raised large sums of money in the UK and fitted out blockade runners there.

The frustration felt by the Unionist States led to the boarding of a suspect British ship, the *Trent*, and the ill-feeling caused by this action nearly brought them into direct conflict with Britain. Indeed it may be remembered that the lessons of the *Trent* case were put forward as one of the arguments in favour of establishing a trans-Atlantic telegraph.

Early in the Civil War the Secretary of State, William Seward, set about seeking redress for the losses caused by the *Alabama*[*]. The Alabama Claims, as they became known, eventually became a broad generic term for all American grievances against Great Britain. At one point (April 1869) the claims amounted to $2,125,000,000, which of course could only have been met by the cession of Canada. It was not until My 1871 that the Treaty of Washington was signed, in which Britain expressed regret for the original escape of the *Alabama* and five other cruisers from British ports. The claim was submitted to an international board of arbiters and the United States was awarded $15,000,000 in gold in respect of all direct claims. All indirect claims were ignored.

The Telegraph Company was requested to transmit the Commons debate on the Claims which had appeared in the *Times*. It was agreed that this should be done when there was no other work to do. Graves records:

> On Sunday 8 March 1868 the debate on the Alabama Claims filling eight and a half columns of the *Times* was commenced to be transmitted at 11.15 am. We got off 3,941 words on the 8th, 313 words on the 6th, 1,958 words on the 10th, a good part of the evening of this day being occupied by 'banquet messages' between London and America. On 11th the debate was finished at 11.55 pm, 9,060 words being sent on this day, making a grand total of 15,272 words, which no doubt tended to develop 'Press' messages.

---

[*] Launched in Liverpool on 15 May 1862. Under Capt. Raphael Semmes she sunk, burned or captured more then sixty ships before her own destruction in June 1864.

Press messages did indeed become big business and also a source of friction. Press magnates wanted to transmit material as cheaply as possible, while the directors of the Anglo American Telegraph Co. wanted to maximise profits.

Work had been going on for considerable time to prepare the new station offices on the eastern side of the island. The site was on the shore, a short distance to the south of Knightstown.
Both the Knightstown and Heart's Content stations were designed by the Dublin architect, Thomas N. Deane, (http://en.wikipedia.org/wiki/Thomas_Newenham_Deane). The Knightstown 'complex' was designed with expansion in mind, the station being surrounded on both sides by staff quarters. The Superintendent's house, which was situated next but one to the Office was distinguished not only on account of size, but because it also possessed a bay window.

There is an interesting letter in the archives of Trinity College which is reproduced below:

> To the Registrar TCD 9 March 1867
> From Thomas Newenham Deane
> 3 Upper Merrion St., Dublin
>
> Dear Sir,
> I am requested by the Chairman of the Anglo American Telegraph Co as their Architect to apply to the Board of Trinity College for their kind permission to lay the telegraph wires in a trench of sufficient depth across the property of the College in the island of Valentia, it being proposed to erect permanent buildings at Knightstown instead of the temporary sheds at Knightstown and Foilhommerum
>
> If the Board will be so good as to grant the necessary facilities, I have no doubt that my Clients are quite prepared to indemnify the College against any inconvenience which may arise to the tenants on their property during the laying of the wire or subsequently thereafter.
>
> I am Dear Sir
> Yours Faithfully
> Thos Newenham Deane Archt.

The transfer was effected as Graves meticulously records

> "... at half past four o clock on the afternoon of 20 September 1868"

It was not, however, without its problems. Severe electrical disturbances were observed on the instruments at the new location. They were hardly to know that it was entirely due to an impedance mismatch. They had in fact used standard landline technology between the old and new stations, the wires being buried in order to protect the cables from lightning strikes. It was not until they replaced this arrangement by two five mile sections of buried submarine cable over the whole distance between Foilhommerum and Knightstown that they were able to get trouble-free working.

WUI documents indicate that the cost of trenching and installation of cables from Foilhommerum to Knightstown amounted to £185-18s-10d (£185.94p in decimal currency)

In August 1869 the station had fourteen cable staff and five land staff, plus servants, and by a curious coincidence, we know some of the staff names. There was a reference in the last chapter to Kate Fitzgerald writing to her father, the Knight of Kerry:

Dearest Papa, I am not going to say a single word about C....h . . . .

This of course was the period when the Church of Ireland was being disestablished, and feelings ran high amongst the Protestants of Valentia, particularly since the Government was not going to appoint a clergyman to replace the incumbent, who had died the previous February. This led to the presentation of a petition to the Prime Minister, William Gladstone, in July 1869[*]. It was signed by cable station staff, including James Graves, John Smythe, Robert B. Mackey, <indecipherable>, Alfred Sell, John Crilly, Henry Windeler, William Dickens, Chas. F. Thomas, Daniel Jones and Fredk. T. Tranfield.

During the whole of this period, and for several years to come, relations between Graves and the Traffic Manager, Richard Collett, were very poor indeed. Perhaps Collett was a bitter man. He had been offered the Superintendentship of the Singapore Station when it was being planned in 1860. However, on the cessation of hostilities with China, the Rangoon-Singapore cable was diverted for use between Malta and Alexandria. It is unlikely therefore that Collett was ever able to take up this appointment.

His animosity with Graves took the form of finding fault with every aspect of the operation at Valentia. One case concerned a recently appointed clerk, Ross, who misheard the word 'hoax' and wrote it down as 'oaks'. This would be an understandable error particularly if the instrument clerk reading the galvanometer were of British rather then Irish origin. The Irish are apt to place more emphasis on the letter 'h'. Perhaps if Ross was more experienced he would have queried it anyway. This happened on 16 May 1868 and on 23 May Graves received a memo from Collett requesting him to be more particular in seeing the rules and regulations carried out. "If the precautions instituted are not properly applied, the blame must fall on your shoulders. Smythe, the Clerk-in-Charge, is somewhat at fault for not having the word spelt out, but the greatest responsibility rests with you. Ross should not have been allowed to receive a paid message until you were satisfied and certain he was proficient and knew all the rules of our Service"

The minimisation of Smythe's part, if any, in the affair was largely due to the fact that Smythe, George (later Superintendent in London) and Collett had worked together prior to joining the Anglo. They formed a triad and it was evidently Collett's long-term aim to have Graves removed and replaced by one or other of his friends.

[*] A copy of this was discovered by Donal O'Sullivan in the Irish State Paper Office, Dublin.

It is true that Graves often appeared soft on his subordinates. He stuck hard by his principle of 'Tis better to rule by love....' and his juniors respected him for it. He defended his staff vigorously.

In March 1867 he had reported that three errors were made in originals and four in repetitions. In an analysis of three days' work at that time he stated that the incidence of wrong letters was one in thirty thousand, which, he claimed, compared well with many landline stations, where traffic comes in onto a printing machine. He then compared reception at the two stations (NF and VA): "In comparing the reception by NF with that of VA I think some allowance should be made for the fact that the greater part of the reading at NF is done in the daytime, whilst nearly the whole of the VA reading is during the hours when human nature is not quite so bright and wakeful as when the sun is shining"

It must have been hard for Graves to have to pass on the following note to Mr O'Sullivan** on 13 March 1869

> I regret to have to hand you the following and earnestly request you to avoid giving occasion for like remarks in the future. The Committee have requested Mr Collett through me to caution you respecting the numerous errors you make. The Traffic Manager adds that he hopes for your own sake as well as for the interests of the Service that you will in future be more correct in your work.

No opportunity was missed for needling. On one occasion (15 March 1868) copies of tests were left out of a report to London. Three days later Collett wrote

> I have on a previous occasion had to write to you with regard to disobeyance of orders and instructions for which there can be no excuse.
>
> It becomes my unpleasant duty to state that if a case of this kind again occurs I shall recommend the Committee to make a change. Its impossible for me to know what is going on if the rules are to be broken at your will and pleasure....."

The defence on this occasion was quite reasonable. With increased business and only one cable working (1866 was out), tests were undertaken as opportunities permitted. Weedon, the Heart's Content Superintendent, living on the job, was able to take his tests on Sundays. But as Graves lived in Knightstown and the Station had not yet been transferred there, Sunday was not a suitable opportunity, and his testing had to be done during gaps in traffic—always provided earth currents were at a sufficiently low level to permit meaningful results to be obtained.

From this point on Collett's invective became more virulent and more directed against Graves. He was assisted by his two colleagues at Valentia, Smythe and George, who were apparently willing to cooperate in the hope of furthering their careers. As will be seen later, their subsequent careers were in fact not particularly noteworthy. Matters continued in this way until April 1870, when Collett's 'retirement' was suddenly announced. It took some time before the facts became known.

** One of the first native Irish staff.

He had indeed approached the Board with a recommendation for Graves's removal. They submitted all relevant files to the Chairman and Secretary of the recently nationalised Electric & International Telegraph Co. in order to obtain an impartial opinion and just as in the case of Varley and Graves in 1864 the plaintiff came unstuck.

The Board then made an extremely sensible decision when they asked Henry Weaver, late Secretary of the E. & I.T.C[+]., to take over as Traffic Manager. Weaver had been a very successful company secretary and was thoroughly liked and respected by all in the Service. His appointment heralded a new era in relations within the Anglo American Telegraph Co.

The digression to complete the story of Collett has brought the story forward in time and has bypassed one or two important details of the history of the Valentia Station. C.E. Stewart, the Company Chairman, did not live to see the transfer to the new offices at Knightstown; he died on 22 May 1868 and his place was taken by Sir Richard Glass.

As mentioned in the previous chapter, any prospect of the old Atlantic Telegraph Co. taking over the operation had evaporated on 1 Jan 1869 and the way was then clear for the Anglo Co. to enter into a number of agreements with a recently arrived competitor.

The arrival of a French cable (competition or not?)

The whole question of the Société du Câble Transatlantique Français is a little odd. It was formed at a time when business was as yet very slack. True, the French desperately wanted such a cable, if only for prestige reasons. The owners of the *Great Eastern* were anxious to find work for her and, as usual, part of their service fee was shares in the cable company. However, one of the prime movers in the formation of this company was Julius de Reuter[**], whose news agency business was already well established. The existing tariff rates were prohibitive so far as he was concerned and any competition which might lead to a reduction in rates was to his advantage.

The Company, although French in name, had a largely British board of directors, many also holding directorships of the Anglo. In the Autumn of 1868 the Telegraph Construction & Maintenance Co. started work on 2,584 n miles of cable, which was to be laid between Brest and St Pierre et Miquelon, with a branch cable from there to Duxbury, Cape Cod, Massachusetts. The *Great Eastern*, now commanded by Robert Halpin, set off from Sheerness on 21 June 1869 and headed for Brest.

During the laying of the cable there was a disagreement as to whether or not a fault had been paid out. To overcome this the contractor agreed to extend their guarantee from 30 days to two years.

[+] Which was in the process of being taken over by the Post Office as part of the nationalisation of UK inland telegraphs

[**] Another was Jules Despécher, author of "Projet de télégraphe transatlantique" in 1863. He seems to have been an ardent proposer of projects.

There were no major problems on the way until the *Great Eastern* approached St Pierre, where the fog was so thick that the cable had to be cut and buoyed by guess[+].

The French Company was never truly independent of the Anglo. After working for some months in opposition, it accepted its rivals invitation to form a pool or 'Joint Purse', as it was called, made up from the net earnings of both cable systems (it would have been to their advantage particularly since they had a longer and therefore slower cable). It was eventually absorbed by the Anglo in 1873, when it went into liquidation. The French were then without a truly independent Atlantic cable until 1879.

On 11 June a banquet was held on the *Great Eastern* with Pender, Brassey, Ralph Elliot, Sherard Osborn[++], Canning, Reuter, Anderson, Varley, Jenkin, Baron d'Erlanger, Lord Hay, Lord Houghton, Mr Elliot, Mr J.B. Burt, Secretary of the Anglo Med. Co, Mr Slater, Secretary of the French Co, Mr T. Crampton and others.

The fleet left St Pierre 18 July 1869 and arrived Duxbury on the 23rd. *Chiltern* & *Scanderia* anchored off Rouse's Hummock where the cable hut was situated. Before cutting the cable on the ship a message was sent to Napoleon, and Varley sent a message to his wife.

The concession to land a cable had been granted to Reuter and d'Erlanger on 6 July 1868. The cable was not to touch non-French territory *en route* and the concession was to last for 20 years from 1 September 1869, during which time the French Government were not to grant concessions to any other party.

The capital of $6,000,000 was sold in 8 days.

The route was less prone to iceberg damage then the Anglo routes

The cable, using a four-wire core, had a higher conductivity and was reputed to be superior. Projected rate 12 wpm. In fact, the Brest-St Pierre section gave 10-12 wpm while on the St Pierre-Duxbury 20 wpm was possible.

There is a book (SHH 93:621.39) in the IET Library in London entitled "Notes from Landing of the French Cable at Duxbury" published by Alfred Mudge & son, Boston 1869. It mentions that the manager was Mr Brown and his assistant was Mr Gaines. There was a staff of 12 in the office operating the land and sea lines. It is a social record, being comprised of the speeches of the project principals and of the various local worthies. Of particular interest is a reference in Sir James Anderson's speech that the entire project was vigorously opposed by Cyrus Field.

[+] In preparation for connection to the specially armoured shore-end cable.

[++] Rear Admiral Sherard Osborn (1822 - 1875) became Managing Director of the Telegraph Construction and Maintenance Co in 1867.

German communications

The Germans were also very keen to have telegraphic communications with the New World. In addition to the benefits to commerce, there was the question of prestige and aspiration. The German Union Telegraph Co[*] was established to fulfil these desires and immediately entered into agreements with the Anglo and the land telegraph companies in Britain. The first agreement was signed in October 1869 and provided for transmission of German traffic from Emden via an appropriated line on the Indo-European cable to Lowestoft, and from there to London and Valentia. The German Company contracted W.T. Henley to manufacture and lay its own cable between Borkum and Lowestoft, and this was completed by the Henley's cableship *La Plata* in 1871. The German traffic soon became a very valuable source of revenue and played an important part in Valentia's subsequent history.

The Valentia station was now thoroughly conversant with its cables and instruments, even if they had already suffered several interruptions on the 1866 cable. There was a keen desire to use both cables to capacity, so when the French cable was in the final stages of its installation in 1869, the Anglo board seriously considered a further reduction in tariff. However, it was eventually agreed to defer any decision until the following June.

In 1870, following Acts of Parliament to nationalise all inland telegraphs, the Post Office took control and there was an immediate improvement in communications between Valentia and London. The Anglo never really had the resources to maintain such a length of overland line. The Post Office honoured previous agreements and the Company continued to have exclusive rights on these landlines.

The 1866 cable failed again in September 1869. The Company was fed up with the cost of contracting the Telegraph Construction & Maintenance Co. to undertake the repair. Accordingly the cable remained as it was while they fitted out their own repair ship, the *Robert Lowe*. This was a 832 ton single screw steamer with a schooner rig, which was owned jointly with the French Company. The ship was ready to sail to Newfoundland in June 1870 when Weedon, the Superintendent at Heart's Content, informed Headquarters that he was too ill to travel and would therefore not be able to accompany the boat during the repairs.

On 25 June Weaver, the Traffic Manager, asked Graves if he would supervise the repairs, and in spite of his own poor health at the time he willingly accepted. He left for London on the following

[*] With the Franco-Prussian war still three years in the future the author believes that *Vereinigte Deutsche Telegraphen Gesellschaft* (German Union Telegraph Co.) was probably an aspirational name and might be better translated as the United Germany Telegraph Co.

morning and spent several days discussing matters with Weaver. Having assembled apparatus for use on board, the ship set sail for Newfoundland on 6 July under the command of Capt. Blacklock.

They arrived at Heart's Content on the 19th and set about the repairs on the 27th. The first fault lay at three miles distance from the Station. Other breaks were located at 69 and 74 miles respectively. As this was an area of very uneven seabed, they sounded for a better route and inserted a bypassing loop, which was completed on 19 August. On their return to Heart's Content there was a message waiting for them:

> "Weaver to Blacklock[*] & Graves
> I congratulate you very heartily upon the successful repair of the 1866 Cable - I trust you may have good and speedy luck with the French"

The French cable between St Pierre and Duxbury was also broken, and C.F. Varley, who was now their Chief Engineer, had suggested that both jobs could be undertaken during the same trip.

The ship sailed from Heart's Content to Nova Scotia on 25 August and stopped in at Halifax on the 30th to take on cable and coal. From there they proceeded on the following day and had little difficulty in finding the cable, in spite of the fact that the *Great Eastern* had originally laid it in thick fog and its position had been plotted on the chart using a large element of guesswork. Just as they were about to complete the repair, both ends having been buoyed, they were overtaken by a violent storm. The report of their experiences occupied 18 column-inches in the *Halifax Morning Chronicle* for September 13, the day after their safe return. The report mentioned that the barometer fell 1.3 inches in five hours. The storm lasted about 36 hours but the ship had been blown well off course. Fog prevented any action before the evening of 5 September and they did not get back to their position until Wednesday 7 September. There was still too much sea for them to grapple (there is no mention of whether the buoys had been washed away; one suspects that they had). The Duxbury end was raised and spliced on the Thursday, and by midnight they had paid out cable to the position of the St Pierre end. The final splice was completed at 11.38 am on Friday the 9th and they returned to Halifax, where they received a telegram of congratulations from Capt Mayne, the Managing Director of the French Company.

They set off for England on September 28 and arrived in London on October 11 only to find that the 1866 cable was once more broken. The break had occurred somewhere between their re-routing and the Heart's Content Station. What a disappointment it must have been for men who had been away from home for close on four months. The outcome of this proved to be one of the blackest periods in the Anglo Company's history and the downfall of Collett's henchman, Smythe.

At first, on September 14th, the board decided against sending the ship out again, as the bad weather was already drawing in. However, they reconsidered their situation on the 17th and it was

---

[*] Capt. Blacklock had been the master of the Electric and International Telegraph Company's cableship *Monarch* when Graves had been its Submarine Electrician in 1864

decided to chance it in spite of the weather. Capt. Blacklock refused to go, and Graves claimed that his constitution would not permit it; he had not been in good health for several years. Smythe volunteered to go as electrician and a Captain Anderson (not Sir James) was engaged. The *Robert Lowe* left London on 31 October 1870 with intentions of stopping at the locality of the break (if weather permitted) before reaching Heart's Content. She had no success at first and put in for coaling on 23 November, where she remained until the 26th. Nothing further was heard from her until as Graves records:

> ... on 30th at 3.55 pm when the 1865 working cable failed and the tests showed the break to have occurred at the exact distance from Heart's Content at which the ship was supposed to be grappling for the 1866 cable, the natural inference was that they had grappled and broken the wrong cable.

That is exactly what happened. Valentia were informed of this via Brest and London on 3 December. Up to the beginning of February several unsuccessful attempts were made to retrieve the disastrous situation, but on each occasion they were driven back by storms.

During this time the total unsuitability of the *Robert Lowe* was well demonstrated. Her testing room was more open to the weather then would have been desirable or prudent. The testing room staff often had to work in near freezing conditions, ankle deep in water. This inevitably meant the possibility of electric shocks every time they touched the instruments. On 30 January she was driven into port by ice with her bow stove in. In a letter written on 8 February 1871 Graves commented on the uselessness of the *Robert Lowe* from his first hand experience. He also made the suggestion that it would pay the Company, in view of its cable mileage, to build a specially designed ship kept solely for the purpose of repair work. The *Robert Lowe*'s experiences had also demonstrated the foolhardiness of attempting repairs during the North Atlantic winter. The Company were now going to have to wait. Meanwhile, orders were given to have four of Valentia's best mirror clerks sent to Brest so that some level of Anglo traffic could be maintained. This was the first example of such cooperation, which was to become commonplace in the future, even amongst fierce rivals. The Joint Purse Agreement, of which the Anglo was subsequently to complain so much, had saved them on this occasion. Graves remained at Valentia to supervise the ship watch; a tedious business. At least he had the satisfaction of knowing that his cable repair voyage had been a job well done. He was awarded a £50 pa salary increase (his first since joining the Anglo) and an allowance of one guinea per day spent at sea. He occupied his spare time in scientific investigations, which in time were to establish his scientific reputation. Once it was known that the *Lowe* was no longer involved in repair attempts the ship watch was discontinued, and he had the opportunity to conduct earth current investigations during the next 78 days, from 6 March to 22 May. The results were summarised in a paper read before the Society of Telegraph Engineers in London (which later became the Institution of Electrical Engineers) and was published in Volume II of their Proceedings. In this he showed definite correlations between the sun's position and earth currents, and the coincidence between strong earth currents and earthquakes.

The tedium for those remaining at Valentia was relieved somewhat by the social atmosphere which the Company strived to provide. It was fully aware that Valentia was "well outside the pale of civilization" for their predominantly British staff (what must it have been like at Heart's Content?). There was a library at the Station and on 22 October 1870 the Board voted an additional £10 pa for the renewal of books.

Within eight or ten years many of the staff appeared to be settling down to long-term residence. On 24 February 1874 the Board authorised a lodging allowance of £20 pa for each married clerk not accommodated in a Company house. At the same meeting they agreed a grant of 5 guineas per year to be paid to the Valentia hospital. Some of the clerks were moving to other stations by way of promotion. Graves's eldest son, Arthur James, who had been trained at Valentia, was transferred to the recently acquired French Station at Duxbury, Massachusetts during December 1874. While there he was operating a landline when there was a lightning strike. The resulting detonation left him profoundly deaf for the rest of his life and has family communicated with him by hand-signing[+].

On 23 May the Telegraph Construction & Maintenance Company's cableship, *Scanderia* (1983 tons) arrived at Newfoundland and set off for the grappling ground on 2 June. In spite of much field ice in the vicinity the '66 was repaired on 3 June and the '65 on the 20th.

Land line communication between Valentia and London was still far from satisfactory. In August 1871 Mr George was replaced as Superintendent at London. This was then the end of the Collett, Smythe,[*] George trio. His place was taken by J.H. Carson, the senior cable operator at Valentia and one of the original three senior clerks, who had taken over the cables with Graves in 1866. By strenuous efforts on both sides the landline situation was much improved, and Carson's appointment led to better relations between Valentia and London.

The Word Rate and more work

In 1872 Henry Weaver introduced the 'word-rate' system, which completely changed the economics of telegraph communications. From that time onwards messages of any length would be carried, and would be charged at the rate of 4 shillings (20p) per word. It coincidentally removed Reuter's lucrative scheme of message-packing[**]. The word rate introduced a completely

---

[+] There is a family story that during the First World War Arthur James's son would always come off night-shift early so as to meet his father on his way to the Station. There was a fear that his father would be oblivious to the challenge from the military guard on the Station and might get shot.

[*] The Company continued to employ Smythe, but from this point he disappears from the history.

[**] In order to reduce his news transmission costs Reuter had a method of data compression whereby a single word might convey a much larger meaning. When there was no alternative to 20 words on the Atlantic cables Reuter's traffic might occupy only ten words in a particular message.

new spectrum of users, but although the number of customers increased the proportion of messages which comprised one or two words was very large, and as Bright said, "In due course as the use of the telegraph became more widely extended and appreciated, the increased number more then balanced the decreased average length of messages". Of course this meant more work at the Valentia station.

Graves himself had had enough of Valentia by this time and was also looking for a change. The Company were considering a cable direct from England to Nova Scotia and from there to New York and Graves was offered the Superintendentship in New York. However, in January 1873 the scheme was abandoned. The French Company had just gone into liquidation and been totally absorbed by the Anglo, and Mr Brown, their Superintendent at Duxbury, was then transferred to the Anglo offices at New York. By way of compensation Graves's salary was raised to £500 pa.

There were several internal Company changes at about this time. As part of the dismantling of the French Company, Julius de Reuter and Baron d'Erlanger were transferred onto the Anglo's Board of Directors. In December 1873 Sir Richard Glass died and his position as Chairman was taken by F.C. Bevan.

On 17 March 1873 the German Union cable in the North Sea was broken, and to compound difficulties the cable from Brest was broken on 20 April. Records show that the latter was repaired on 21 May.

During this period the directors of the Anglo American Telegraph Co. started to become aware of the health of the Valentia staff and their families. A Station Medical Officer, Edward Blennerhassett, was appointed on 1 November 1870 at £100pa. This was subsequently raised to £150 on 1 February 1874. When Blennerhassett died on 24 March of that year he was replaced by William Mark Whittaker. On 24 February 1874 the Board of Directors voted a contribution of 5 guineas towards the Valentia hospital. There is local lore that the old wooden building at the Foilhommerum cliff was dismantled and transported to Knightstown for use as a fever wing to the hospital, but when this happened is not quite clear.

Another item that was voted on by the directors at their meeting on 27 February 1874 concerned a Lodging Allowance. £20pa was available for all married staff who could not be accommodated in Company house

The word rate in 1875 was 4/= (four shillings) with a special reduction for Spanish Government traffic. The Spanish Govt. insisted that all private messages be sent in clear and subject to a tax of 40ct per ten words.

The remaining word spaces were then sold off to merchants and others who could not have afforded the cost of a full message.

Pause

At this point in the history we are presented with a problem, simply because so much is happening. For that reason we will start by concentrating on the arrival of the next competitor which made life a lot tougher for the Anglo American Telegraph Co. and its staff. We will then return to Valentia and to the changes in its cable network between 1873 and 1881.

We must start by considering someone who weaves in and out of our story from here until his death in 1905. Alexander M. Mackay was chief electrician of the Nova Scotia Telegraph Co., when at 22 year old he was appointed by Cyrus Field to be manager of his interests in Newfoundland. He was very good at this job and, indeed, used 300 linesmen to keep the landlines along the south shore of Newfoundland operational during the snows of October 1866.

When Field was realising his assets he sold his overland route from the US up to Cape Breton Island to Western Union. At the same time the Anglo American Co were taking over Field's operation in Newfoundland, with only such land as was necessary for business. The price was £864,520 in Anglo shares. The land which had been granted to Field but had not been taken up by the Anglo was sold to the Newfoundland Land Co in 43,226 x £3 shares. As part of the deal Anglo acquired Alexander Mackay, "who had had the complete confidence of Field" and who appears to have balanced allegiance to Field's interests with those of the Anglo and of the Newfoundland inland telegraphs (which also came with the sale), even when these appeared to be in conflict. It would be very interesting to know if he also had interests in the Newfoundland Land Co. Thus the Anglo had a cable station at Heart's Content with a superintendent who had control of both the land and cable operations (similar to the model at the Valentia cable station after the nationalisation of the UK inland telegraphs). They also had an office in St John's with Mackay as their manager having responsibility for the operation of the Newfoundland inland telegraphs as covered under the original agreement between Field and the Government of Newfoundland. For some reason this latter topic is almost never mentioned in Anglo American financial reports, so it is not clear whether it made a profit or a loss or whether Mackay operated it as an independent entity.

The overland route along the Newfoundland South Shore to Port Aux Basque was a continuing source of frustration. At that time the Anglo Co. were in the process of having an additional Atlantic cable landed at Heart's Content and, as this would have put an intolerable strain on the landlines, they ran a cable from Heart's Content down Trinity Bay to Rantem. This was carried across the Avalon Isthmus in a trench to Island Cove, and from there to Sydney Mines C.B.I. by way of Placentia. Mackay supervised the submarine cable trenching through Rantem Cove, and when mineral deposits were discovered during these operations, the mining rights on either side of the trench were sold off 'on behalf of his employers'. The Anglo financial reports makes no mention of this and one wonders who the true beneficiaries were: Anglo, the Newfoundland Land Co. or Mackay himself.

Just as Graves had had problems with Collett as well as several staff at Valentia, so Ezra Weedon, the Superintendent at Heart's Content, was having problems with the behind-the-scenes activities of Mackay. On 22 September Weaver in a confidential message to Weedon says:

> In all your dealings with Mr Mackay be careful and couching. Don't hint that I have asked you these questions. We have got a very difficult game to play in Newfoundland. Mr Mackay is necessary to us and we must try to keep him in good humour.

Ballinskelligs and the opening of ID

During 1873 the Company had to face their first real prospect of stiff competition with the formation of The Direct United States Telegraph Co (D.U.S.T.C). It was intended to be just that: a direct link between Europe and America with no intervening stations in Canada. However, the cable which was used was such that had it been laid as planned, its speed of working would have made it unprofitably slow. It was the first major cable undertaking by Siemens Brothers (the London Company, not the German firm of Siemens and Halske), who had provided a large portion of the financial backing. Its formation was yet another example of the symbiotic relationship between cable manufacturer and cable company.

Siemens, having had bad experiences with chartered ships, commissioned their own, the *Faraday*, which had many revolutionary features. These included twin screws, a bow rudder, twin superstructure with a through deck as well as similar cable laying gear fore and aft. This meant that it could lay or pick up a cable with equal facility. The ship was launched on 17 February 1874, was fitted out during April, and on 16 May 1874 set off on her maiden voyage to lay the cable for the Direct United States Telegraph Co. Carl Siemens was the Engineer in Charge.

It was originally intended that the cable should be connected directly between Ireland and the United States, and for that reason Siemens designed a special highly conducting cable. However, in spite of this, it was soon realised that the excessive length would result in an uneconomical operating speed (measured in words per minute) and that a nearer landfall would be needed.

Papers in the Centre for Newfoundland Studies at Memorial University in St John's show that as *Faraday* approached Conception Bay its intentions were challenged in the courts by the AATC manager in Newfoundland, Alexander M. Mackay, who was mentioned above. On 6 August 1874 the Direct company was subjected to an injunction. This they opposed, insisting that the cable landing monopoly claimed by the Anglo was void for a variety of reasons. The matter was pursued through the Supreme Court of Newfoundland. The initial injunction was removed on 26 October 1874, but reissued on 27 November 1874. It was overturned again on 3 February 1875, but that ruling was overturned on 5 April 1875. The Direct Co. appealed to the Privy Council in London, who considered the matter during January and February 1877. Their appeal was dismissed with costs and the original ruling was allowed to stand. In parallel with all of this, the UK

Parliamentarian Henry Labouchere[+] and colleagues pushed hard on the question of the Newfoundland Government exercising its right of 'pre-emption', a take-over of the telegraph operation, which right formed part of the original agreement with Cyrus Field. By creating uncertainty in the public mind, it was possible to damage the stock market value. The architects of this attack were able to buy Anglo shares at a knock-down price and sell them when it became obvious that the Newfoundland Government never had any intention of exercising its rights of pre-emption.

Once it became clear that it was not going to be possible to break the monopoly, CS *Faraday* was forced to adopt a different tactic. The cable was started in the United States at Rye Beach, New Hampshire, although it seems that there was no specific permission for this landing. The next stop was Tor Bay, Nova Scotia. From there it was taken to a point off the coast of Newfoundland, where it was buoyed while *Faraday* returned to England for more cable. This section of the operation took 81 days due to the gales, fog and ice. On the next expedition the remainder of the cable was laid and landed without any mishap at Ballinskelligs, which is just a few miles away from Valentia. The cable was tested by Sir William Thomson on 16/17 September 1875 and found to be in excellent condition, and the forecast of 9 words per minute was confirmed. At the western end it was connected to New York by landlines leased from the Franklin Telegraph Co and everything was ready.

The Direct's service was opened for traffic in 1875 amidst great acclaim and advertising. A special rate was offered to the press and other heavy users (just what Reuter had been fighting for). The Anglo tried to reduce the tariff levels in an attempt to hold their market share and try to squeeze their new opponents. This was not particularly effective and with the tariff rate at 1 shilling (5p) per word their income suffered badly and their fortunes on the stock market drifted downwards[*].

The opening of the Direct Company's service was not to the liking of Sir John Pender, the 'Cable King'. He had recently established the Globe Telegraph and Trust Co. as a mechanism to cushion investors against fluctuations in the value of telegraph stock and the financial effects of frequent interruptions due to cable failure. This was an early form of unit trust but with a difference. In

[+] Henry Labouchere 1831 - 1912), Rebellious nephew of Henry Labouchere (1798-1869), 1st Baron Taunton and one-time President of the UK Board of Trade, is probably best known as the author of the 'Labouchere Amendment' to Britain's homosexuality laws that was used to imprison Oscar Wilde.

[*] This phenomenon, sometimes referred to 'Pig Economics' was to be repeated several times on trans-Atlantic cables. During a period of boom in the global economic cycle a business opportunity is spotted, but it takes considerable time to raise the funding and to get the infra-structure into place. By the time everything is ready there is an economic down-turn so that the newcomer and the established operators find themselves in an economic battle with ever-reducing returns where only the end-customer benefits.

Hugh Barty-King's History of Cable and Wireless (*Girdle round the Earth*, Heinemann 1979) he summarises its purpose as defined in its articles of association:

> The acquisition and amalgamation in one Company of the principal lines of submarine telegraph and the land lines used in connection therewith. It is proposed, in the first instance, to acquire the shares and other securities of the companies owning them, issuing the shares of this Company in exchange for them, or to raise funds for the purpose of paying for them, and as opportunity offers, acquiring and absorbing the businesses and properties of the companies themselves".

There were those who labelled the Globe Trust as Pender's attempt to use other people's money to further his monopolistic ideals. However, as has been previously stated, he was unique in that he combined a desire for the universal availability of cheap communications (at a reasonable return on investment) with an interest in the commercial well-being of his customers.

Thus the state of affairs which prevailed on the Atlantic route in 1876 gave him cause for concern. Since commencement of service in 1875 the Direct United States Telegraph Co. was earning £143,610 on £1,300,000 (equivalent to 11% on capital). The Anglo American Telegraph Co. amalgamated with the French Company was earning £480,900 on £7,000,000 (equivalent to 7% on capital). Pender felt that this was too great a threat to the Anglo, in which the Globe Trust had a heavy investment. He sought to amalgamate the two companies. Against strong opposition, which included a High Court action[+], he succeeded in getting a resolution for the liquidation and reconstruction of the D.U.S.T.C. in June 1877. On 17 July Pender, Gooch and Sir James Anderson formed a second Direct US Telegraph Co. Its articles of association did not contain the clause prohibiting any agreement with the Anglo, which Pender had found so iniquitous in the original company and it immediately entered the Joint Purse. The history of the Ballinskelligs Station is thereafter closely linked to that of Valentia. The D.U.S.T.C. competition did have at least one long-term effect. On 1 Jan. 1876 the Anglo introduced a special press rate, half the normal tariff, which was increased to 3 shillings (15p) per word once the threat of competition was past. Mind you, throughout all of this Graves seems to have been hedging his bets. There is evidence that he had bought shares in D.U.S.T.C.

[+] *Pender v Lushington* (1877) 6 Ch D 70 is one of the most important cases in UK Company law. It confirms that a company member's right to vote may not be interfered with, because it is a right of property. Furthermore, any interference leads to a personal right of a member to sue in his own name to enforce his right.

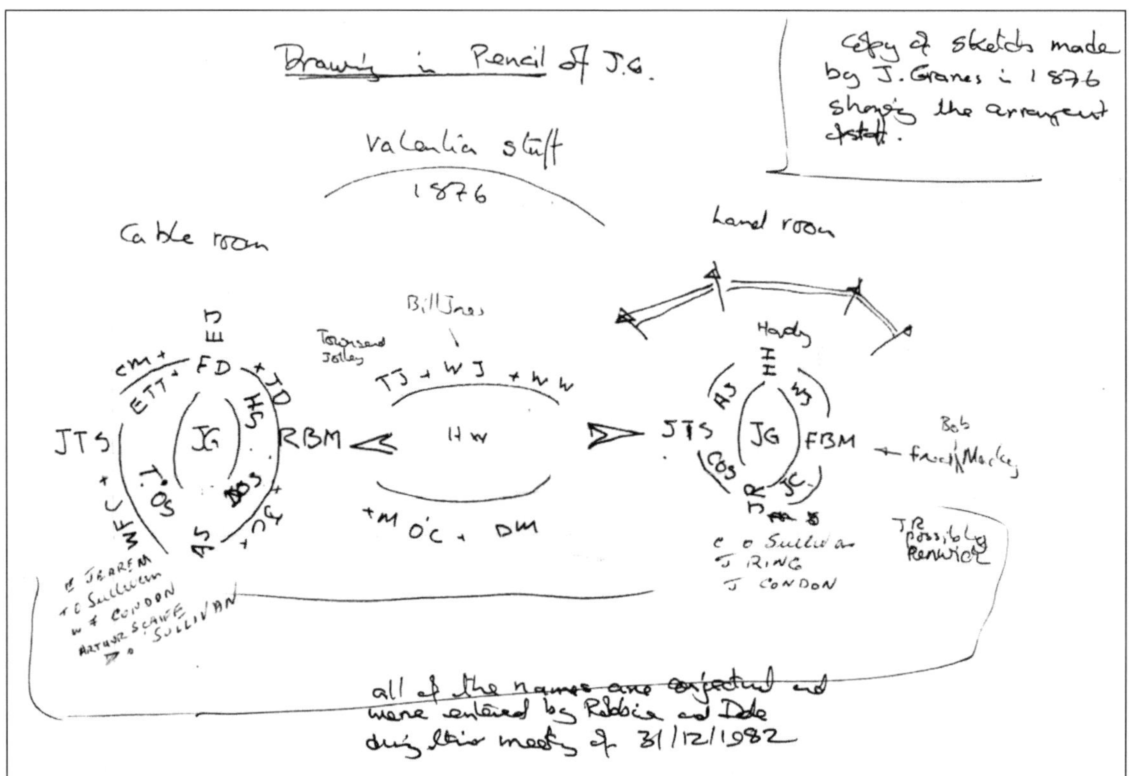

Copy of pencil drawing by James Graves showing the disposition of all staff in 1876. Only initials were given, because everyone knew who they referred to. The allocation of some names is conjectural and was made with the assistance of Arthur Hearnden.

Reduced tariffs did mean more traffic for the Anglo, but profits were much smaller. The Company had to cut overheads and reduce all areas of revenue loss. One obvious area was of course codes and ciphers.

According to Bright,[**] code systems were in vogue amongst the mercantile firms as early as 1853, possibly earlier. The first code with a published reference book was that used by Reuter for the economic transmission of news material. Regulations relating to the use of code were laid down at the Rome International Telegraph Conference of 1870. The St. Petersburg Conference of 1875 decided that code words should not contain more then ten characters.

Bright cites some examples of the economies afforded by the use of codes: "ELGIN= every article is of good quality that we have shipped to you. PENISTONE= cannot make an offer; name lowest price you can sell at". Remembering that his book was published in 1896, the following paragraph is worth quoting in full:

[**] Charles Bright, "Submarine Telegraphs", Crosby, Lockwood & Sons, London 1896, pp. 171-177

The fact is, but for the code system, the existing number of cables would in many cases, be quite inadequate for the demands of the present traffic (unless as is likely would have happened, the absence of code, or its suppression by unwise restrictions on the part of the companies had starved and stunted the natural development of the trade itself. All commercial traffic, practically is nowadays coded. Seeing that this custom began to grow up with the establishment of trans-Atlantic telegraphy, it is difficult now to estimate where we should be without it) This remark applies most conspicuously to the case of the North Atlantic (itself), and will be readily understood when it is stated that whereas prior to the universal recognition and adoption of code transmission, the average length of telegrams used to be 35 words. It is now 11. In other words but for code the cable companies might by now be asked to transmit more then three times as many words as they are transmitting in the same time. (This is to a great extent assuming that the total traffic gauged by the number of messages would still have gone on increasing at the same rate) More probably the proportion would not be so great in practice for the reasons already given. But even an addition of only half as many again would be embarrassing to the operators and indeed to all concerned excepting telegraph engineers and contractors, who would in consequence have extra cables to lay".

Now back to Valentia

On 11 March 1873 the 1865 cable failed for no apparent reason at a distance of 580 miles from Valentia. The break occurred in over 2,000 fathoms of water and its repair was going to present problems even for the *Great Eastern.* It had been decided to lay another cable between Valentia and Heart's Content and it was now suggested that the *Great Eastern* should repair the '65 on the return journey. Graves with his experience of splicing cables at sea wrote to Weaver on 18 March suggesting that the new French cable, to be laid in two parts should be done as early as possible in the year. On the return its should pick up the '65, splice on and land at Valentia in much the same way as it had done with the '65 at Newfoundland seven years previously. It could then go out again, pick up the eastern end of the '65, and after splicing proceed to Newfoundland with what would be in effect an entirely new Valentia-Heart's Content cable. Circumstances, however, altered the plan. On 9 April another fault occurred in the same cable about 1,125 miles out from Valentia. The Company, having totally absorbed their French partners, decided that the new French cable should be diverted from its original purpose and used between Valentia and Heart's Content.

The *Great Eastern* set off from Portland on June 8 in the company of the new cableships *Hibernia* and *Edinburgh.* The *Robert Lowe* had arrived at Valentia on the previous day with the shore end. This was landed on the 14th and 90 miles of cable laid. The *Great Eastern* spliced onto the buoyed end on the 15th and arrived off the coast of Newfoundland on the 27th. However, weather conditions prevented the cable being landed until 4 July and the contractors handed it over on 5 August. This cable was thereafter known as '73.

During the latter part of July 1873 the trench between Foilhommerum and Knightstown was opened and four cables were buried; two for that summer's work and two as spares for the future.

However, the summer was to yield only one cable. The attempts by the *Great Eastern* to raise the '65 on her return journey were unsuccessful. The old ship made another run the following summer on what was to be her last major cable-laying expedition. This time she set off from Heart's Content on 26 August, and on 6 September arrived off the Skelligs rocks, where 8 miles of shore end had been laid by the contractor's ship *Investigator.* The cable (thereafter known as '74) was completed on the 7th and represented the quickest passage and the shortest length of cable laid up to that date.

The increased number of cables coming ashore presented certain difficulties. Each time a repair had to be effected the correct cable had to be lifted and a new piece spliced in. This invariably introduced slack into the cable; the increased length reducing the operating speed of the cable. Graves reports one example during 1874. The shore end of the '66 cable had failed off Valentia and the T.C. & M. Co's cableship, *Minia* was sent out to repair it. On this occasion it was found necessary to replace 64 miles of cable from the landing place.

So far as was practical it was standard practice to fan out the cables as soon as possible, so that within a short distance from the landing place the cables would be sufficiently separated to avoid accidental lifting of the wrong cable during repairs. John Merrett mentions that the later cables often had a distinctive marker wire wound into the sheathing so that a particular cable could be recognised before it was cut.

There was also the problem of effecting repairs in the shortest possible time, and having the correct materials to hand. Arrangements were made to have several miles of grappling wire as well as grapnels stored at Valentia. The lawn in front of the Station was lifted and a long length of submarine cable was stored underground for emergencies. Whenever it was required the lawn was lifted again and the cable could be easily passed out to any ship lying off the shore.

1873-74 saw a number of technical developments as well as a tragedy. The *Robert Lowe* had just completed laying a cable between Placentia, Newfoundland and Sydney, Cape Breton Island when she struck Shag Rock near Cape St. Mary in late November 1873.

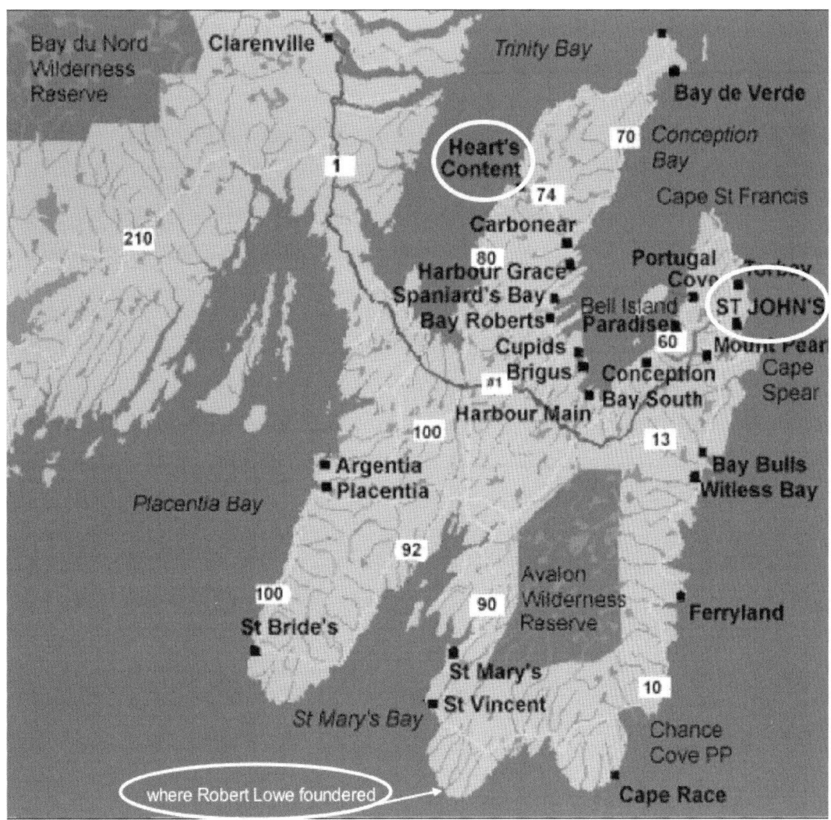

The *New York Times* of 24 November 1873 reported on the wreck:

WRECK OF THE ROBERT LOWE.
CONFIRMATION OF THIS SAD RUMOR—EIGHTEEN LIVES LOST

TORONTO, Nov. 23.--The following particulars have been received regarding the Anglo-American cable steamer Robert Lowe from the surviving officers: After connecting LaManche and Placentia town by cable, the steamer left the latter port at 4 P.M., on the 19th, bound for St. John's. At 4 A.M., on the 20th the weather thick and the wind high, the ship struck heavily near St. Shotts, and in a very few minutes filled and settled down so fast that it was impossible to get the life-boats afloat. Three other boats, containing twenty-three people, succeeded in getting clear of the wreck, and remained by it till daylight. Capt. Tidmarsh was on the bridge at the time of the disaster, perfectly cool, and took in the whole situation at a glance. He ordered the boats to be cleared away, and perished by sticking to his vessel to the last.

Five minutes after striking the ship's poop was under water. Mr. McKenden, of the Heart's Content staff, and Day, the second steward, were drowned in the cabin. The rest were swept off the decks by heavy seas, which, in a few hours, reduced the steamer to atoms. On Friday five bodies were picked up and buried. The following are the names of the lost:

J. Tidmarsh, Commander; F. Powlain, Chief Engineer; Pargent, Third Engineer; Pugh, Fourth Engineer; Bublock, Engineers' Storekeeper; McIntyre, carpenter; Quartermasters, Young, Slackwards, Warren, and Anderson; able seaman, Wagstaff; Day, second, and Benares, third Steward; Gales, chief cook; Doolin and Gallagher, firemen; McKenden, electrician, and G. P. Wilkins.

Saved—Chief Officer Denton, Second Officer Hawson, Second Engineer Stafford, Boatswain Collins, Storekeeper Richardson, Quartermasters Robinson, Payne, Chauncey Williams, Burton, and Hooston; Able Seamen Sullivan, Reid, Cunningham, Dickenson, Welch, and Higgins; Fireman Lowden, Chief Steward Jacklin; a boy; the butcher, and Miller, a passenger.

Siphon recorder (effectively the first bubble-jet printer)

The initially more significant of the two technical innovations in this period was the introduction of Sir William Thomson's siphon recorder.

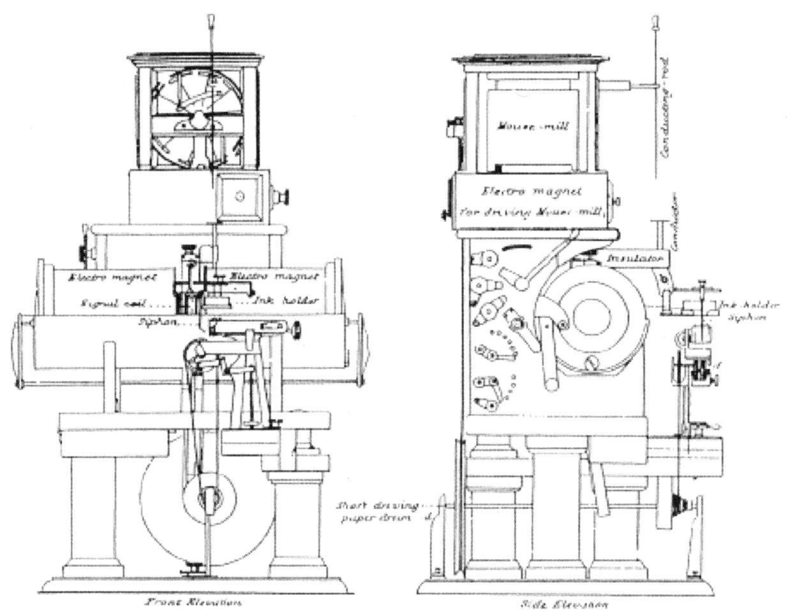

Sir William Thomson's Siphon Recorder. *From The National Encyclopaedia, 1870*

The French Company had had one in operation at St Pierre as early as 1870, but on 21 July 1874 Valentia took delivery of their first, which according to Graves was a considerable improvement on the French Company's model. Incidentally, Heart's Content took delivery of one at about the same time. They arrived in kit form and were provided with a set of printed instructions for assembly and adjustment. This machine represented a revolution in oceanic telegraphy. The drudgery of hours spent at the mirror was now gone; in fact, since it gave a printed record of each message, it did not require the same level of operator skill.

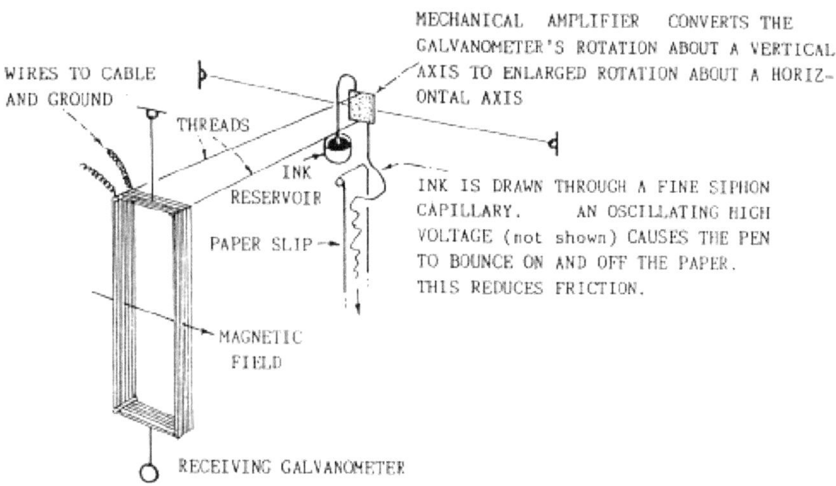

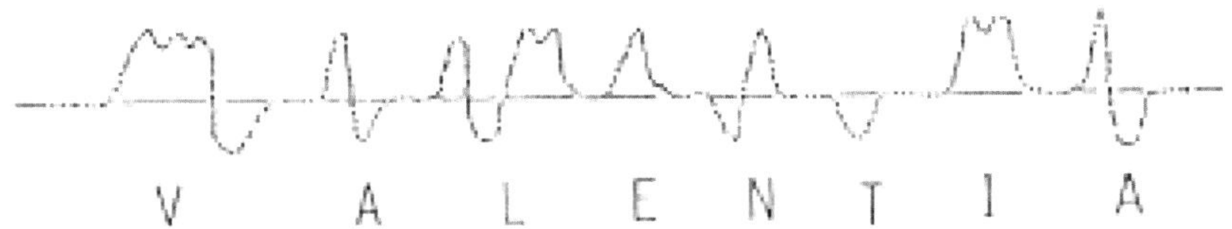

This example from a siphon recorder is quite easy to read. The example below is both attenuated and distorted and indicates the difficulties which the operators sometimes had to face

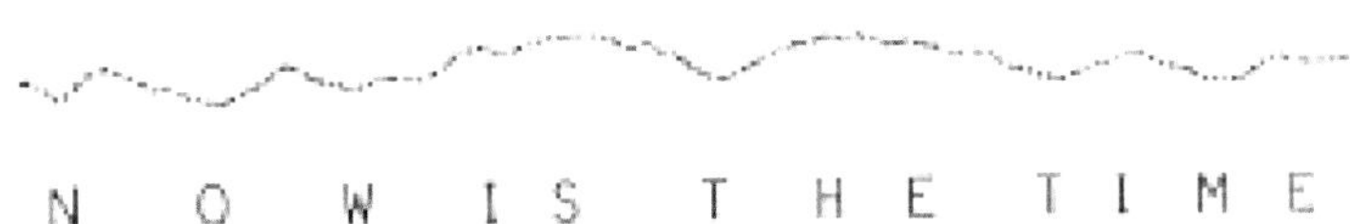

Cable Duplex

The Duplex system of J.B. Stearns was first introduced on the landlines during July 1873 and Graves, always a cautious man, seems to have been enthusiastic about it from the start. The system involved the landline as one arm in a bridge, with a differential galvanometer acting as detector. An artificial line (designed to mimic the real one as closely as possible) was placed in the other arm. By this means the local or sending station would not detect any signal on its galvanometer during transmission. There would, however, be normal deflections from signals received from a remote station. The major difficulty was of course to "balance" the artificial line. This exercise occupied Graves and Stearns in several months of strenuous effort, but once successful left the company with plenty of spare capacity on its land lines.

Stearns was already turning his mind to the question of duplexing the submarine cables themselves. This was quite a different problem. The signals on the landlines were transmitted by conventional Morse, consisting of dots and dashes. They could be amplified by a series of relays and finally recorded on a printing telegraph. The signals through the cable were transmitted using the Steinheil technique; a dot was represented by a positive pulse and a dash by a negative pulse. By this means the average electrical charge in the cable over a period of time would be approximately zero. Stearns, like many others at the time, appears to have overlooked this important point. Graves, writing to him in July 1873, explained why relays would not work: "Although it is not difficult to make a relay which will record regular reversals across the Atlantic, it is a very different matter to get a relay to register a sentence such as 'she sees she is his sister[*] in as much as every current in the same direction is weaker then the preceding one and the reversal (at the letter t) comes with such a rush. In this irregularity in mechanical force lies the difficulty in mechanical recording by means of a relay".

Nevertheless, once the value of duplex working had been amply demonstrated on the landlines, the Company then started thinking about the possibility of increasing the efficiency of its cables by the same method. Once again Stearns was retained to implement his system. His original patent specification had been sufficiently wide in outline to cover a number of alternative systems. The Company was naturally in favour of adopting the cheapest of the alternatives. This proved to be a mistake and Stearns spent many months at Valentia assisted by Graves trying to get a steady balance on the artificial line. He arrived there in September 1875 and left the following July with little to show for their combined effort[**].

Their experiments were resumed again in May 1878 with an improved arrangement. After some tests Stearns returned to London to construct a second apparatus for the other end of the cable. Having obtained an approximate balance at Valentia during August, he proceeded to Heart's Content on 4 September with the intention of returning to Valentia to finalise adjustments. This was achieved after a fashion on New Year's Day 1879, but by then the competition had stolen a march. The Direct Cable Co. had succeeded in duplexing their cable using a Taylor-Muirhead

---

[*] All letters up to 't' in sister are represented by a series of dots.

[**] The superintendent at Heart's Content was so sceptical of duplex that his actions amounted to obstruction. Much to the annoyance of Anglo headquarters in London, Valentia received no assistance from Newfoundland. Nevertheless, in a letter "Weaver to Weedon 23 Sept 1873", discovered by David Hochfelder in the Smithsonian Library, Weedon observes that Graves has got duplex going at Valentia without assistance from Stearns.

system (which was in fact superior to Stearns') during 1878. The working speed on the Direct's cable was now 20 words per minute in each direction, almost double the simplex (one way) rate.

There was now an urgent need for duplex at Valentia, but there were still delays. The recording instruments required modifications. To add to their problems the Brest cable failed and all traffic was diverted through Valentia. In order to cope with this the artificial line was adjusted as well as possible, and the Station made its first cautious steps at Duplex operation which Graves recorded

February				
22nd	duplex	used	for	2 hrs 30 mins
25rd	"	"	"	7 hrs 15 mins
26th	"	"	"	14 hrs 24 mins
27th	"	"	"	15 hrs 15 mins
28th	"	"	"	13 hrs 20 mins

The introduction of duplex working required that the Company's rulebook for employees had to be rewritten to include all the new procedures[+].

Just as the skill of the mirror clerk had been overtaken by the siphon recorder, a new and very exacting skill came into its own; that of balancing the artificial line (the in-office facsimile of the ocean cable). In early January 1880 an artificial line was constructed for the 1873 cable, and much to the surprise of Graves he achieved a balance and had the cable working duplex within two weeks. They also took delivery of a replacement artificial line for the original duplex unit and sent the old one back for rebuilding. The intention was that it should then be used on a new cable which was to be laid that summer.

The minutes of the meetings of the Anglo board of directors for this period have been abstracted from holdings in the Smithsonian by David Hochfelder.

8 April 1879

- Joseph Stearns gives his cost estimate for artificial lines for duplexing the 1873 cable and Duxbury cable at £1700 and £1200 respectively.
- The Company then paid Stearns £1540 for duplexing the 1874 cable.

23 May 1879

- There was also an agreement with Stearns to pay him £1500 a year during life of his patents from 1 March 1879.
- Graves at Valentia and Windeler, the Valentia mechanician, were to get £100 and £50 respectively as bonuses.

[+] James Graves's personal rule book is still in existence. His margin notes are an important source of information about the Station's history after 1888.

4 July 1879
Thomson, Varley, and Jenkin were to get £1500 a year for siphon recorder until their patent expires in 1885.

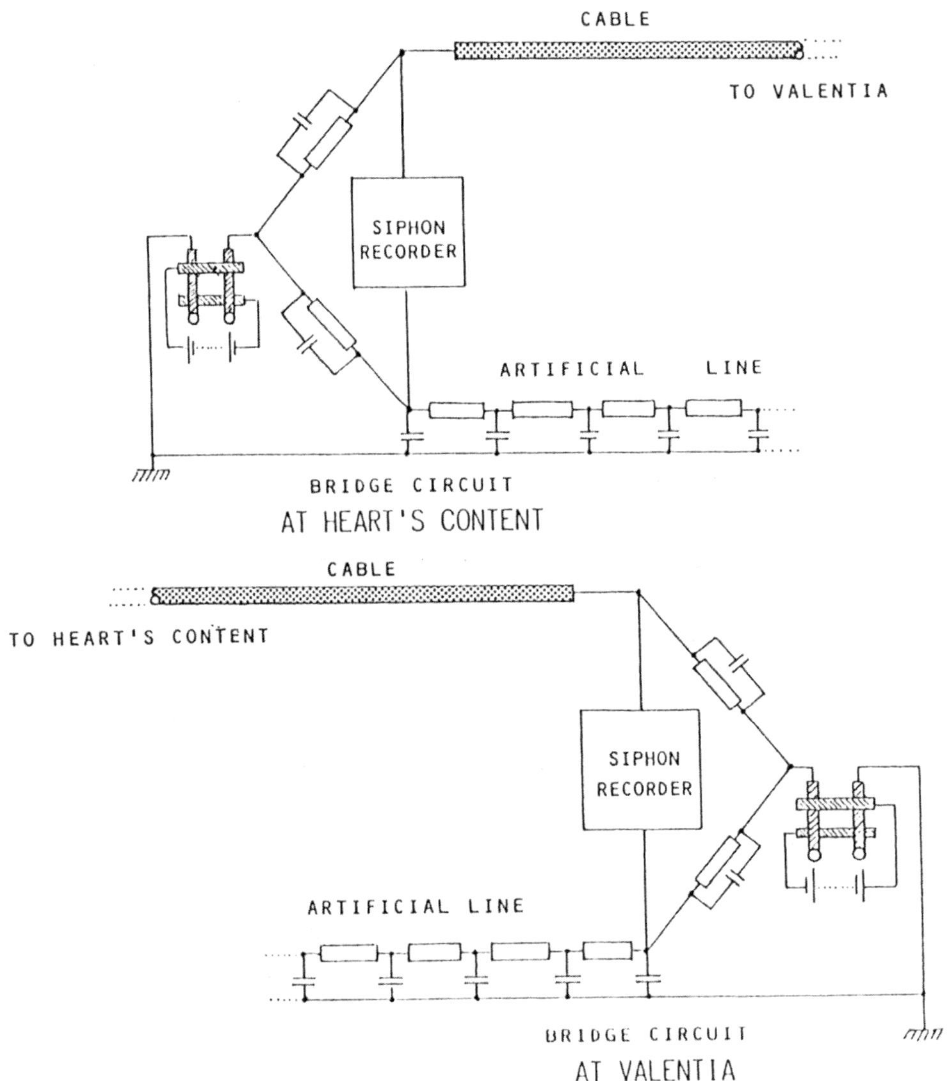

Duplex circuits at opposite ends of the Atlantic. Each is effectively a Wheatstone bridge. When the electrical properties of the artificial lines and the cable are identical then any signal generated at one station will not affect their recorder, but will cause a deflection on the recorder at other station.

However, all was not rosy. On 18 July the Directors received a letter from Dr Alexander Muirhead asking the Board to ascertain whether Mr. Stearns' duplex now working on the cables of this Company is or is not an infringement of his patent. Board says it is in no position to ascertain. It is not clear what became of this, but because it was demonstrably a superior system, eventually all duplex equipment on Anglo cables was sourced by Muirhead's company. This probably did not help Graves's career, as unlike the superintendent at Heart's Content, he had been absolutely committed to implementing Stearns' system.

Yet another cable

In 1877 there had been an expedition to repair 1865/6 cables. cs *Seine* and cs *Calabria* were involved. A copy of the report, written by Charles Hockin of the engineering consulting firm Clark, Forde and Taylor, was in the WUI collection in London. It mentions the lifting of one quarter mile of 1858 cable on 15 July "All the iron was gone, only the hemp and core remaining." It is not clear how effective these repairs were, because we find the Anglo deciding that the bulk of the 1866 cable, which had effectively ceased functioning in 1872, should now be abandoned. It had been repaired so many times that the additional lengths had made its operating speed uneconomically low. The shore ends were still in good condition and the Company ordered 1,500 nautical miles of new cable to replace the deep sea section. It is an indication of the general development of the industry that Graves devotes only two lines in his technical autobiography to the installation of the 1880 cable which "was laid in due course and the duplex system applied to it without any difficulty."

The 1880 cable was in fact a technical landmark in its own right. As early as 1861 Willoughby Smith had suggested the use of Chatterton's compound [a derivative of gutta percha] as a coating for the outer sheathing wires. This material was normally used in direct contact with the copper core and between the covering layers of gutta percha. Prior to 1880 Smith's suggestion had never been taken up, as it was considered to be too expensive. Nevertheless, that is what the Anglo American Telegraph Co. ordered, and although it is the only known example of this application for Chatterton's compound, its use could be deemed to have been justified. It still had three quarters of its original manufactured length in 1949 when it finally failed and was abandoned. The 1873 and 1874 cables were still in operation in 1963 although there was no original material in the '74 and only 100 nautical miles in the 1873, the remainder having been cut out during progressive maintenance.

Another competitor

During 1879 the French once more entered the North Atlantic Telegraph business. After several abortive attempts La Compagnie Française du Télégraphe de Paris a New York was established by the French financier Pouyer-Quertier and was thereafter generally known as the 'PQ' Company. An order was placed with Siemens in early 1879 and during that summer the *Faraday* laid cables from Brest to St. Pierre and from there to Cape Breton Island and Cape Cod (USA). During 1880 151 nautical miles of cable was also laid between Brest and Cornwall. Shortly after opening for business the PQ Company entered the Joint Purse.

Prince Alfred's first visit to Valentia in 1858 (from the Cooke drawings in the IET Archives)

In1880 the Station at Knightstown entertained a Royal visitor, its second in eleven years[*]. Prince Alfred, Duke of Edinburgh and of Saxe-Coburg, who had last visited the island in 1858, was touring the Irish Relief Mission on the west coast of Ireland in HMS *Lively* and called on 29 April, when he was introduced by the Knight of Kerry. He was shown over the Station by Graves and "was highly gratified by his visit and took great interest in the apparatus used both for working and for testing purposes".

Prince Alfred, Duke of Edinburgh and of Saxe-Coburg,

Further innovations

There were various attempts from time to time to introduce new apparatus, some of which proved to be successful, others less so. During the late 1870s the sending key came in for attention. In 1877 the automatic curb sender of Sir William Thomson was submitted to Graves for tests. This involved following each key press by a series of short pulses of alternating polarity. Thus a +v (dot) would be followed by -v, +v, -v, +v and so on. The intention was to sharpen up the shape of the

[*] The Duke of Connaught had called on 23 April 1869

pulses and thereby increase the sending speed; this would permit the use of automatic equipment at both the sending and receiving ends of the cable. In theory, however, a true curb key should apply an infinite series of such reversals of diminishing amplitude after each key stroke and according to Graves this shortcoming was obvious in the poor results which were obtained.

One innovation that was very successful was the introduction of Wheatstone's automatic apparatus on the landlines. For several years the landlines had been under considerable strain. The Valentia traffic alone utilised them to full capacity. Whenever one of the other Joint Purse companies suffered a major cable fault their traffic had to be shared out under the terms of the agreements. This proved too much for the landlines even working duplex. The Post Office were unwilling to give the additional space on their Irish Sea cables as they were only sufficient for their needs. The alternative of a third land wire and another cable across St. George's Channel was considered but would have been too costly. Weaver then decided that the automatic system should be adopted to make better use of the existing wires, and this was done in January 1882. This introduced new work practices which met with some opposition at first. The signals from London were extremely clear and it was a waste of manpower to transcribe them into manuscript form for the cable instrument clerk to read and transmit. From this point on the slips from the land wire printer were gummed onto the transmitting forms and sent from there by the cable clerk.

There had been some respite for Graves in 1881. Up to this point he was required to personally test each of the Valentia cables once per week and of course this had to be fitted around the volume of traffic. Hereafter, testing was done once per month.

A direct link from Germany to Valentia

The German Union Telegraph Co. had been sending traffic via Valentia to America since 1869. As mentioned previously, they used two cables between Germany and Lowestoft; one of these had been laid in 1866 (and later came under the control of the Post Office) and was appropriated for the purpose. The other, laid in 1871, was wholly German owned. According to Haigh, it was, however, maintained by the Post Office on behalf of the Germans. The German Company was never wholly satisfied by the delays imposed by the relay of messages through Britain and Ireland for transmission at Valentia, so during the spring of 1882 a new cable was manufactured to link Emden and Valentia directly. Felten & Guilleaume of Köln manufactured the section between Emden and Greetsiel, while the Telegraph Construction & Maintenance Co. undertook the entire section between Greetsiel and Valentia[*].

[*] The cable was frequently damaged by ships' anchors and fishing boats, and the delays in transmission, as will be seen, continued to be a source of intense frustration to the Germans.

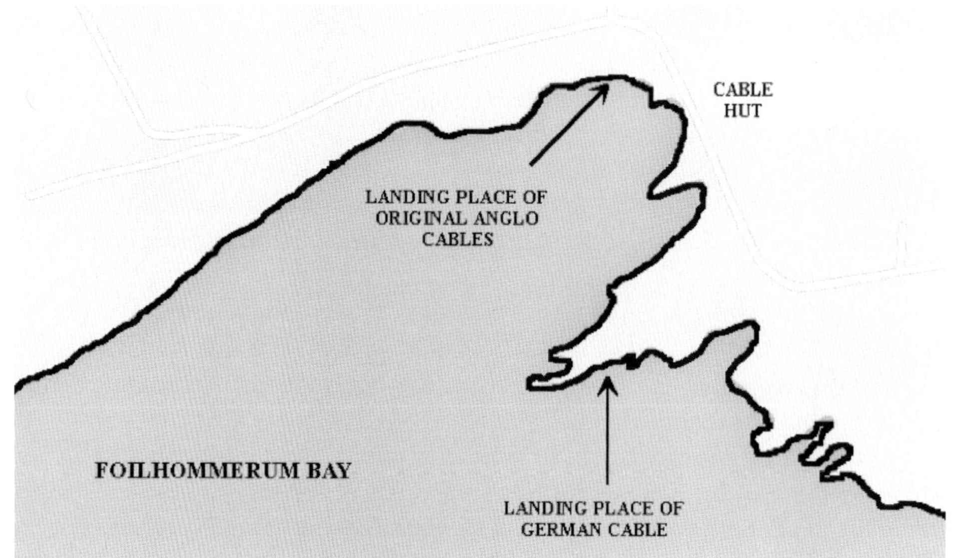

The landing site of the Valentia-Greetsiel cable in relation to the original landing site at Foilhommerum Bay

The sea cable was landed on 15 April and was nominally opened for business on the 17th. The official opening took place on the 22nd with the exchange of congratulatory messages between the Emperor and the President of the United States. For the duties of superintending the German cable at Valentia and the relaying of its traffic through the Atlantic cables, Graves received a salary of £100 pa paid by the Germans with the approval of the board of the Anglo American Telegraph Co.

Although operations at Valentia appear to have run very smoothly from this point onwards, Graves records with some annoyance that the recent Jay Gould (Western Union) cable was taking away traffic from the existing six cables and thereby reducing their proportion of gross revenue. In fact his few words completely effaces the first of several seismic changes in trans-Atlantic communications. According to Coggeshall[+], during the period 1866-1880 Western Union had been content to act as the American feeder for the Anglo American Telegraph Co. However, in 1880 the financier, Jay Gould (1836-1892), often vilified as an archetypal 'Robber Baron', had other ambitions. He had secured control of many US railroads and took control of the telegraph companies that used line-side poles, even though many had long-standing contracts with Western Union. In 1879 he created the American Union Telegraph Co with the intention of forcing Western Union and the companies for whom it acted as feeder to dance to his tune. The war did not last long, and the Western Union Board capitulated in January 1881. Meanwhile, Gould had approached John Pender to see how the Anglo American Telegraph would respond to his demand for concessions. Getting a negative response, he set about ordering two new Atlantic cables.

[+] Ivan S. Coggeshall's "An Annotated History of Submarine Cables and Overseas Radiotelegraphs: 1851-1934" (a copy of this work can be downloaded from http://dandadec.com)

Siemens completed the first cable from Canso, Nova Scotia to Sennen Cove, Cornwall in May 1881. The project was viewed with consternation by the 'Joint Pool' (companies led by Anglo). Their stock went down. Gould bought. Just as they were ready to start operations Gould announced a rate 50% higher than the Anglo's, so their stock rose. Then rumours went about that the Gould cable was faulty and that it was too light to repair. The Anglo's stock continued to rise and then Gould sold, making a handsome profit. Once Siemens had completed the second cable Gould was ready to go but was not going to have a tariff war with the Anglo and its associated companies[**]. However, since he now controlled Western Union, which acted as the feeder for Pool traffic, it was made clear that this might not continue. The value of Anglo stock plummeted and they had to accept Gould's terms. Gould's cables were now leased to Western Union who started operating as a member of the Pool in May 1882.

At this stage one has to ask how different things might have been had Anglo called Gould's bluff and established their own system of feeding, possibly by means of cables from Newfoundland to New York? But then, the Anglo American Telegraph Company appears to have lacked inspiring leadership during its entire existence and were never able to see the big picture.

James Graves

[**] It is interesting to note that an Anglo Board minute of 5 August 1881 records: "in view of impending competition, it is proposed to discontinue publication of traffic and receipts; other two pool companies to discontinue likewise"

There was a near catastrophe at Valentia in 1883. At 3.30 am on 14 March a petrol lamp was accidentally knocked over in the land instrument room. The ensuing fire was not brought under control for 20 minutes and the rest of the night witnessed feverish activity while they attempted to sort out the mess of melted wires and charred instruments. By taking temporary wires between the battery room and the nearest pole outside the building land communication was re-established on one wire at 5 am. During subsequent repairs they took the opportunity of completely re-modelling the office, with wires under the floor rather then along the ceiling as had been the case hitherto.

Although Graves's technical autobiography claims to run to 1888, it is quite clear that by the early 1880s he was losing heart. He records that, "On 21 May 1882 another change in working the cables was introduced as an experiment on one cable and after a fair trial was introduced on the other two Atlantic cables worked from Valentia Station. There were difficulties, unforeseen, met within these alterations, but they were all traced out and remedied one by one." This is entirely uncharacteristic of the man, for whom the recording of minutiae was almost a mania. One can hypothesise about the cause. Although he was extremely well paid even by today's standards, there was the sense of isolation at Valentia. There was also the importance of promotion. He had struggled to raise himself from his humble origins and promotion was one way of proving that this process was continuing. He had also witnessed the dispersal and promotion of men who he had trained. Some of these were now in more senior positions then he[*].

There was also the question of competition. Each new arrival reduced the Anglo's share of revenue. This had dropped from 100% in 1866 to 48% in 1883. There was talk of new cables and although some attempts at establishing new enterprises had not been successful[**], the Commercial Cable Co. did arrive on the scene the following year. In this environment shareholders were frightened and the Anglo's shares dropped to 40%of their original value. There was no doubt that at that time the Anglo was the largest single operator on the route, but it did have one major disadvantage, namely its enormous share capital, amounting to nearly £7,000,000. This included the capital for the 1857/58 failures, for the 1865 attempt as well as all subsequent share capital for which dividends had to be paid. The competitors, having the benefit of experience and improved technology, were generally set up with very much smaller capital.

Thus, Valentia's apogee was past, and it would now continue, with the exception of a few periods of heightened activity, on its gradual decline until closure in 1963.

---

[*] Fuller was now Supt. and General Manager of the Direct Cable Co. while J.H. Carson was his boss in London

[**] The American, British and Canadian Cable Co. and the Heuston-James Cable Co.

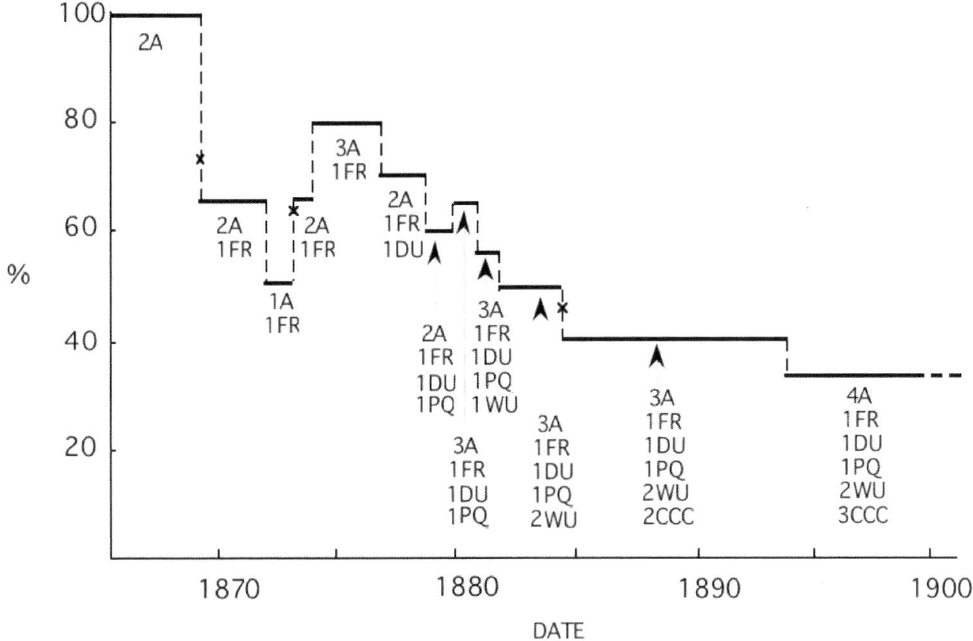

Anglo American Telegraph Co. share of the total cable installation, shown as a percentage over the period 1866 - 1900. The 'x' marks are Anglo's actual traffic share as indicated in Graves' writings. Key: FR = La Société du Câble Transatlantique Française, DU = Direct United States Telegraph Co., PQ = La Compagnie Française du Télégraphe de Paris a New York, (founded by Mr Pouyer-Quertier.), WU = Western Union Telegraph Co., CCC = Commercial Cable Co.

And finally, 1883 saw the death of Cromwell Fleetwood Varley, for whom James Graves wrote the following eulogy

> Upon the death-roll of last year appears
> A name familiar to our earlier years
> For who, among the "Old Electric" crew,
> Can say he C.F. Varley never knew?
> With penetrating mind he much foresaw,
> Conclusions drew, which years it took to draw
> By other minds of less perceptive ken
> E'en though they too were reckoned clever men.
> Peace to his dust - his work and toil are done-
> Trace faults in sand - few men can boast of none -
> Emblazoned on the scientific page
> His works will ever shine from age to age

Chapter 10

1883 - 1914 The Difficult Years

Before proceeding into this new era it might be useful to quickly review the senior management personalities of the Anglo American Telegraph Co. Weaver was now Managing Director, Wells was Company Secretary and Carson was Traffic Manager. This latter appointment must have galled Graves, as he had at one time been his subordinate and one of the original triumvirate who had come to Valentia in 1865.

Robert Blenkinsop Mackey - Founder of a Valentia dynasty

There was now a large and fairly well established staff at Valentia and although there were still many there who had maintained ties with the English mainland, there was a growing number of locals, and people of Anglo-Irish extraction, who did not. These people were evolving into a new middle class and as their situations improved so their requirements for additional income increased. In 1882 there had been a series of Company memoranda on the subject of holidays. People were now attempting to surrender holidays and have them paid as overtime. A memo of 27 December 1882 states "4 weeks leave of absence allowed to staff at Va each year, but not allowed to accumulate". By 1885 the increase and composition of the staff required that these rules be adjusted. Staff returning to England would be allowed four weeks holiday, which would take account of travel time. Those remaining in Ireland were allowed only three. It was, however, conceded that the Superintendent would get a month's holiday under any circumstances*. Clerks returning to England were not to receive cash for travelling expenses, but were to have their tickets purchased and handed to them prior to departure.

There were other related directives. The Company were paying 50% contributions to staff life assurance premiums and on 27 October 1874 Mr Mackey had been prohibited from using his policy as a means of raising a bank loan. There were a number of applications for loans to the Company itself, even from the Station Medical Officer. They seem to have been sympathetic at first, but when the situation threatened to get out of hand, all further requests were refused.

The Station records give an interesting insight into the working of the Joint Purse Agreement in relation to cable failure. On 5 July 1883 a meeting was held at which landline protocol was discussed. In the event of failure of the Direct Company's cable the staff at the Ballinskelligs Station (whose call sign was 'ID') would be transferred to Valentia. All their work would carry the prefix 'D' and would be transmitted by them to London (DUSTC call sign 'TG') and Liverpool (DUSTC call sign 'LC'). Valentia clerks would transcribe all eastbound traffic from the recorder slips.

The definition of staff duties was a matter of some importance during this period. It is evident from comments from Headquarters that Graves was incapable of delegating responsibility and that taking all on his shoulders was certainly not good for his health, which was never the most robust. Perhaps this was a legacy of the period when Richard Collett was his boss in London. In April 1883 Carson wrote to him:**

> I am much obliged for your memo and list, but I must beg you will not do as you proposed and as I have noticed you have hitherto been doing. Why should you make out work of this kind? You have Cs-in-C, superior men with superior salaries who in my opinion have ample time

---

* The tone of this modification to the rules could be interpreted as an indication that the ties binding Graves to his family in England were declining, although he still had contact with his older brother, John James, who had in 1871 been elected first President of the National Union of Elementary Teachers, now the NUT. He was still teaching at Lamport near Northampton, although Anne Louise (Nan) Hearnden remembers him as a visitor to Valentia. She did not like him "He was an old man with a grey beard who used to ask me difficult sums."

** giving the Company address as 23 Throgmorton St., London

> within the regulation 8 hours for important work of this nature. Therefore let them do it. All I ask is that having arranged how you wish it to be done and by whom: you now and then kindly look at the daily and weekly lists to check that the work is really being carried out.
>
> My opinion of our Cs-in-C (as perhaps you may have gathered) is that we don't give them enough to do, for I am sure that they have not only the ability but also the time to do many things which would tend to their own education and advantage and to the Supt's and MD's comfort.

This memo seems to have had some effect. An annotation in Graves' personal rule book dated 17 November 1884 defines the C-in-C's duties:

> Morning 6 - 2 CC held solely responsible for all apparatus and duplex balances.
> Evening 2 -10 CC held responsible for proper handling of stock work and general business.
> Night 10 - 6 CC held responsible for night traffic, clerical and examination work and postal parcels

This was revised on 3 October 1885

> Morning 9-5 CC responsible for getting the cable duplex balances adjusted before noon. The mills and recorders cleaned and in order ready for the traffic and also for keeping the land apparatus, transmitters, recorders and perforators in order.
>
> Evening 12-8 CC responsible for proper handling of stock work and general traffic
>
> Night 8-4 CC responsible for all clerical returns, examination of messages, registrations, translations, delays etc and postal parcels to leave by morning post at 9 am.
>
> Senior Clerk in cable room to be pro-temp CC from 4-9 am and in case of difficulty to send for the CC on at 9 am.

The clerks-in-charge were to check messages for errors and missing letters, In case of a missing letter a report was to be made by handing a slip to the key clerk marked "MDX missing ...." The definition of the procedure then continues "The key clerk after announcing to the sending station will hand the slip to the gummer, who will be held responsible for the delay until he has an answer 'wf' or 'wc' or some reason for its non-arrival. This is to be turned and affixed to the message. It is not for the sending station to supply proof of receiving this enquiry, but for the receiving station to show that he did ask and receive a reply"

Not all clerks-in-charge were assiduous about their clearly defined duties. On 22 September 1885 there is a note to say

> Tranfield C-in-C fined 1/6 day for neglect of supervision and examination of messages, the duty being clearly defined.

He had left it to his junior clerks. It may have been a characteristic of the man which could explain why he, of the original three clerks at Valentia had not been promoted further.

Amongst the duties mentioned above is the analysis of reasons for delays. We see that in the case of missing letters the responsibility for any delay was clearly defined. As traffic increased and the competition became tougher, the avoidance of delays became even more important. Ignoring cable failure, electrical storms and landline problems there were a number of reasons for traffic delays and from time to time the Company made attempts to regulate these as far as possible.

Although the introduction of duplex could and generally did double the working speed, it often happened that a change in the electrical characteristics of the cable (with changing sea temperature) would cause the artificial line at the sending and/or receiving station to go out-of-balance. The Company Rule Book states

> If duplex out give BAL. If it is not possible to restore the balance within a reasonable time - 15 minutes, give NO DUP.

Under these circumstances the cable would have to be worked simplex (one direction only) until a lull in traffic permitted another attempt at restoring the vital balance.

Service messages were another source of delay. It was natural that the Stations would wish to communicate with each other and with Headquarters on matters of Company business. However unless the matter was extremely urgent, this was to be done outside prime traffic time (mid afternoon GMT). In 1883 orders were issued that all service messages were to carry the prefix BQ. In 1866 there was a further modification of the rules.

> All service messages to be placed on a spike on CC's desk. No one but C-in-C (or in his temporary absence, the next most senior man) must answer them. Instrument clerks are warned <u>not</u> to forward service messages made by junior.

The source of delay which the Company worried most about (perhaps because they had little real control) was of course private communication between the instrument clerks. In March 1886 a directive from London had stated

> Remarks of any kind are forbidden on lines. Remarks must not be replied to, but reported with (recorder) slips.

It is obvious from replies received from London during the following months, that Graves had attempted to defend a certain amount of innocent communication across the ocean. He was informed that little remarks led to more offensive ones and that they were a large source of delay. Of course there was no way by which they were going to totally eradicate the problem and its frequent occurrence will be cited from time to time in succeeding chapters.

The Commercial Cable Co

The reasons for the Anglo's paranoia about delays were twofold. Firstly, they had a new and very active rival in the Commercial Cable Co. It represented the keenest of any of their competitors and it maintained an aloof and impregnable independence until the very end of the telegraph era and beyond. It was established by two Irish-Americans: John W. Mackay, a mining magnate, and

Gordon Bennett, proprietor of the *New York Herald.* John William Mackay was born in Dublin on 28 November 1831, and his family emigrated to America in 1849. He worked as a miner and later as a mining financier. In 1864 he joined forces with other Irishmen, William S. O'Brien, James C. Flood and James G. Fair (from Belfast). They developed the Comstock Lode and other mines in Nevada. Mackey owned two fifths of all shares and when the greatest ever vein was opened in 1873, the partners extracted more than $150,000,000 in gold and silver. It was said of Mackay (*New York Sun*, 21 July 1902) that "of all the bonanza millionaires he was the only one who could be called popular." His wife, Marie Louise Mackay, did not enjoy the life in mining towns and, like many wealthy Americans in the latter part of the 19th century, she lived most of the time in Paris and London. With echoes of today's emails and telephone texts, Mackay and his wife communicated with each other by cable.

James Gordon Bennett (Junior, otherwise known as 'Commodore') was born 10 May 1841. He had a totally spoilt upbringing - reared by nannies and tutors, much of his youth being spent in France. His father, also James Gordon Bennett, the founder of the *New York Herald,* was a Scots Catholic. The son, who behaved outrageously, took over the *Herald* in 1867. In most cases New York society enjoyed his pranks, but at a party in the house of his fiancée he went too far. Let's just say that thereafter he was ostracised, and feeling aggrieved, went into self-imposed exile in Paris, where he stayed for the next 40 years. He managed his paper from Paris by cable. Incidentally, it was he who sent Stanley to find Livingstone.

So both men were large users of cable, and being resentful of the cable rates at the time, they saw their arch-villain as Jay Gould, the dominant force in John Pender's trans-Atlantic cable Pool and a member of an old New England family. Today we can easily discern the classical ingredients of Catholic/Protestant, American(Irish)/British antagonisms. Gould was frequently vilified by Bennett through the *Herald*, but there is now fair evidence to suggest that Gould had a controlling interest in Whitelaw Reid's *New York Tribune*, which publicly supported him.

It is said that in 1883, while horse riding in the Bois de Boulogne, Mackey and Bennett were discussing the Gould stranglehold and decided upon setting up a competing service. One of Gordon Bennett's biographers identifies the major feature of the Mackey-Bennett cable system: "It was funded with solid cash of these two men. There was no financing, although there was some small involvement from Mackay's ex-mining colleagues. There was no dead-weight of investors, and with their financial reserves they could afford to withstand strong competition." Mackay already owned a small land-line company (the Postal Telegraph Co.) which was to be expanded to provide land-line connections in the US. Immediately after its establishment the Commercial contracted Siemens Brothers to manufacture and lay its cables. Working flat out they were able to produce 50 miles of cable every 24 hours. Their ship *Faraday* undertook the laying during 1884, with the route as follows:

New York - Dover Bay (Nova Scotia) 826 miles
Nova Scotia - Waterville (Ireland) 2,399 miles
Nova Scotia - Waterville (Ireland) 2,281 miles

Waterville - Weston-Super-Mare (England) 300 miles
Waterville - Le Havre (France) 514 miles

Thus in one year a total and efficient network was established, opening for business on Christmas Eve 1884. There was remarkable foresight in the choice of route. By having a Waterville-Weston cable the company avoided delays in the Post Office landlines across Ireland. Additionally the Waterville-Le Havre cable gave the French some confidence that their traffic was not being inspected while in transit over the Irish and British landlines. The maintenance of the cables was to be in the hands of the Company, and their first repair vessel, the *Mackay-Bennett*, was launched the same year[*]. There were much complaining among the Anglo management when the new Company unabashedly head-hunted Valentia staff[+]. Tranfield, whose career, unlike the other Valentia clerks from 1866, had not advanced significantly, moved to Waterville along with his working sons. His loss to the Valentia cricket team was much regretted.

Valentia staff cricket team

Competition between the two rivals was fierce. Carson, writing to Graves in 1886, informed him in moaning terms that the Commercial Co. had announced its intention of reducing their tariff to one shilling (5p) per word.

[*] According to Haigh the *Mackay-Bennett* was in service in various capacities until 1965. During its period of operation one of its less pleasant tasks was to pick up bodies from the sea after the *Titanic* disaster.

[+] Of course there was nothing new here. Graves frequently moaned that Valentia seemed to be used as a training ground for operators who were then taken on by other companies and posted across the world. Indeed, this diaspora of Valentia staff would continue right up to the Second World War.

What neither Graves nor Carson could see was that they were pawns in a much larger game that was being played out in America. In September 1885 the *Electrical Review* had observed that: "John W. Mackay and James Gordon Bennett are said to have done more than any other two men to lessen the evil influence of Jay Gould. The Commercial Cable is the sharpest thorn in Jay Gould's side. Rates have been much reduced and the service greatly improved." Gould reacted to the Commercial by leading a tariff war, but in order to achieve this Western Union had to make such cuts as had them running at a loss. Instead of following suit, Mackay and Bennett decided on a propaganda war. The Commercial's manager, George Ward, announced that they would not be reducing their rates to match the Pool. He said that they had a cadre of loyal customers who knew that they were getting a good deal and knew that if Gould forced them out of business or into the Pool then the tariffs would rise again. Bennett used his newspaper to campaign for their policy declaring the 'war' to be one of "monopoly and extortion against independence and fair prices." Gould countered via the New York Tribune, but large bodies of industry and commerce as well as some US Government offices supported Mackay.

Fred Tranfield, the founder of another telegraph dynasty

At some point Gould got wind of problems with the Bank of Nevada who where bank-rolling Mackay. With Mackay otherwise occupied the bank vice-President had became involved in a wheat deal that went wrong. The *New York Tribune* went to town over the affair and very nearly caused a run on the bank. Bennett's paper claimed that this was a "Stock-Jobbing Attack", typical of

Gould's dirty tricks. However, many of Mackay's associates thought that Gould had won this time. Mackay had to move fast, and with the assistance of his old silver mining partners he avoided disaster. The cable war ended on 11 July 1888. Gould's telegraph and cable earnings were well down and Western Union had been losing $750,000 a year. Mackay was the clear winner, although his staff had to do a lot of convincing that it was not otherwise until the formal agreement was signed on 30 July. Gould took it badly, but what could he do? According to Michael J. Makley, Gould observed "that there was no point in beating Mackay 'If he needs another million or two, he will go to his silver mines and dig it out.' " Gould died in 1892.

Another feature of this was the development of industrial secrecy. Up to the arrival of the Commercial Cable Co. Graves had been undertaking scientific observations of the various phenomena which affected the speed of operation of the Valentia cables. Some of these were quite significant and, indeed, are still relevant in modern communications. In addition to popular magazines such as the *Electrician*, where he wrote under the pseudonym 'Old Electric', he submitted his results for reading at meetings of the Society of Telegraph Engineers (later the Institution of Electrical Engineers and now the Institution of Engineering and Technology) and publication in their journals. In 1875 his paper 'On vibrations due to earth plates' appeared in volume IV of the *Journal of the Society of Telegraph Engineers* (p. 34). This summarised the difficulties which were encountered following the opening of the new station at Knightstown. What he described were vibrations, quite distinct from earth currents, which appeared as rapid fluctuations on the receiving instrument and interfered with normal working. They could not be eliminated by the use of capacitors. The cables of 1865 and 1866 were connected to Knightstown using a pair of gutta percha covered wires (one each for the 1865 and 1866 cables) laid through iron pipes buried in a trench alongside the road. Thereafter, signal reception became a major problem. There was cross-talk between the wires, and, regardless of the nature of the earth, a continuous fluctuation with an occasional kick was observed on the mirror galvanometer[*]. In his paper he also included a sketch of the arrangement of earth connections that were used at the station. Up to that time the normal practice had been to sink a copper rod into the ground (Graves published a paper on why that was unsuitable, given Valentia's geology) or to have a heavy zinc plate submerged in the sea nearby.

[*] This author is of the opinion that the original problem was an electrochemical one. Zinc in sea water forms an electrical half-cell, and in cases such as a ship's hull, the steel forms the other half. Corrosion is prevented by the zinc acting as a 'sacrificial anode'. Now the dots and dashes which transit a telegraph cable are comprised of positive and negative pulses. However, Morse is an 'unbalanced' code; the number of dots exceeds the number of dashes. So, on average the zinc earth-plate will have a net positive charge applied to it from the cable. This could lead to the build-up of a layer of hydrogen on the surface (polarisation). The efficiency of the earth would drop, but if a bubble of hydrogen were released from the surface, its efficiency would jump and the observed effect would be current fluctuations on the receiving galvanometer.

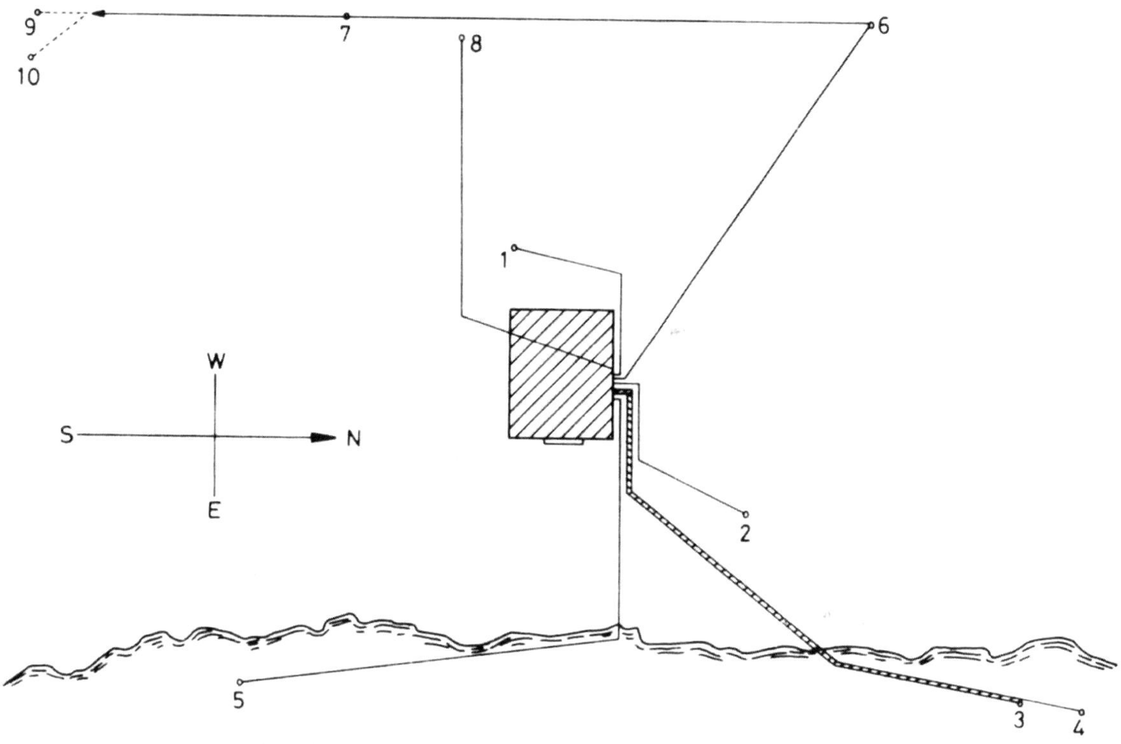

Arrangement of earth connections at the Knightstown station from Graves's 1875 paper

1 Buried thick copper wire
2 Buried thick copper wire
3 Iron of cable buried in beach north of the station
4 Copper plate on conductor of cable buried to low-water mark north of the station
5 Copper plate on conductor of cable buried to low-water mark south of the station
6 Aerial wire on pole $\frac{1}{8}$ mile distant
7 Aerial wire on pole 1 mile distant
8 Iron pipes to water cistern in field
9 Aerial wire on poles 5 mile distant
10 Aerial wire on poles joined to shore end of the ocean cable

In his 1875 paper Graves stated how they had overcome the problem by a method that had been in use at Valentia since 1868, namely to connect the earth return wire to the outer armouring of the cable, thus making a distributed sea-earth. In the late 1880s Arthur Edwin Kennelly, later a doyen of electrical engineering in the United States, had been working as an electrician for the Direct United States Telegraph Co when the cable was diverted from Torbay, Nova Scotia into Halifax. He encountered a similar problem and developed a similar solution. His paper 'On certain phenomena connected with imperfect earth in telegraphic circuits was published in Volume XVIII of the *Journal of the Society of Telegraph Engineers* in 1889 (p. 129). He had left the Pool company and joined Thomas Edison in his West Orange laboratory in 1887 and thus avoided the prohibitions that were heaped on Graves when he attempted to publish a paper 'On vibrations due to earth-plates (2)' restating his priority on the development of the distributed sea earth.

W.H. Preece, Chief Engineer of the Post Office, attempted to intervene on Graves' behalf, but Henry Weaver responded:

> I have strong objection to such matters being made public.
>
> From a scientific point of view it is no doubt desirable to let everyone know what everyone else is doing, but from a commercial standpoint to let 'all the world and his wife' know how the business of the Company is conducted is lunacy.

Commercial secrecy had arrived and Graves's paper was not published by the professional body, of which he was a founder member, until 1987.

Another source of worry for the Anglo was the rumblings of dissatisfaction from Germany[+], one of their most important customers. The German Union Telegraph Co's links with Valentia were always subject to some problem or another. The landlines across England could be slow and could not be deemed to be free from surveillance. Their submarine cables through some of the busiest sea routes in the world were continuously being fouled by anchors. Naturally they were not willing to suffer further delays across the Atlantic link and various memos to Graves during the 1880s indicate their general discontent. In February 1883 the Germans were to have preference on the 1873 cable so long as two cables were in service. If the 1880 cable was out for longer then 15 minutes (this was extended to 1 hour in October) then Anglo business was to take precedence on the 1873. As a measure of the importance of German business to the Company it is interesting to note that during the first fifteen days of February 1883 German traffic amounted to 71,861 words. London traffic was 149,082 words for the same period.

In spite of the apparent generosity of the Company, they were not averse to bending the agreements slightly to their advantage. The agreements had not specified duplex working, and although the Germans apparently had priority on one of the trans-Oceanic cables, this only amounted to the equivalent of simplex working. The fact that by working duplex the cable could carry double the traffic was apparently not disclosed.

Nevertheless complaints continued, and they often appeared to come from the German Postal authorities via the German Union Telegraph Co. rather then from itself, which seems to have been a easy-going operation. The Company was in a difficult position. The world order was changing, but it was unable to extricate itself from the terms of its agreement with the Anglo American Telegraph Co. In addition to this, the British Government was about to nationalise the Submarine Telegraph Co., which managed German Union interests on the British side of the Emden-Lowestoft cable. As this cable now carried German-English traffic (American traffic going via the Valentia-Greetsiel cable, it seemed only right that the German authorities would have to take over the cable. They saw that the best way of undertaking this was to buy out the German Union Co. However, from the outset of negotiations the Company made it a condition that the Government would have to buy them out entirely, i.e. the sale would have to include the Valentia-Greetsiel cable (there was no indication that the cable was frequently out of service due to anchor damage. A

[+] Remember that Germany had only been a united country since 1872

report in the German Postal Archives indicates that at least officially the authorities saw it as a profitable undertaking rather than a political expedient. A contract was drawn up between the two parties whereby the Imperial Postal authorities would buy out the entire company (including working cables) on 1 Jan 1890 for 6.3 million Marks. All staff would be retained except the directors. Dr Adolph Lasard and (retired director with the rank of a PostRat) Gustav Steiner, who would receive golden handshakes out of Company funds. On the basis of this agreement Parliament would be approached to provide the required funds.

Picture showing some of the staff of the German Union Telegraph Co.

Emden post office (final terminus of the Valentia-Greetsiel cable)

Meanwhile, the tariff war between the Anglo and Commercial Cable Companies had damaged both parties, even if the customers benefited greatly from a rate of 6d (2.5p) per word. It was not until the Gould/Mackay agreement that the word rate was raised to something more profitable. Nonetheless, low rates and new attitudes meant that the volume of traffic continued to increase, so that there really was room for both. The French PQ Company found itself as 'pig-in-the-middle', and made to remove itself from the Pool (Joint Purse agreement). The wider details of this will be discussed later.

The increased traffic must have put a strain on the staff at Valentia, and Graves in particular. In 1887 William Hearnden from London was sent to the station to act as Assistant Superintendent. His role will also be discussed later.

In February 1892 the Company Secretary, T.H. Wells, sent a memo to Graves "I have sent by book post tonight some errors for investigation, made on the Emden-Valentia cable. Will you kindly return them to me promptly as the papers have to be sent to the Imperial German Authorities.

There is one further memo available on the subject (dated 2 February 1893), which deals with German traffic. It spells out the Anglo's worries about long term German intentions. There had been talk about a new German cable but the discussions did not include any mention about the Anglo. For contractual reasons the Commercial Cable Co was debarred from competition with the

Anglo in Germany[*]. This was in spite of the fact that it was handling 30% of German traffic from America.

The memo continues:

> Commercial Co. will not slacken efforts to get share of German traffic. Be good enough to do all in your power to reduce delay - not only on the Emden-Valentia section, but also on the 80 cable (it is not now clear when the German priority been moved to the 80 cable)
> 1. Maintain speed
> 2. Maintain duplex
> 3. Relay as much work both ways as possible
> 4. If the average delay is not warranted by the amount of traffic press for an explanation to prevent recurrences.
> 5. Check everything

It is also not clear how much was due to dissatisfaction with the Anglo and how much was due to the emerging German desire to be independent of foreign cable manufacturers and operators. Independence from the cable companies was achieved quite quickly. A new company (The German Submarine Telegraph Co.) was formed by the brothers Guilleaume with the support of German bankers and the Imperial Postal Service. The plan was to lay a cable from Greetsiel, through the Channel, to Vigo in Spain, and thence to New York via the Azores. Cable laying started in 1896; however, on arrival at Vigo, where the Eastern Telegraph Co. also had a station, it was found that the volume of German traffic which now wanted to use this connection to the Eastern Co. network was so large as to justify the cable's existence on these grounds alone.

The Guilleaume brothers formed another company, the German Atlantic Telegraph Co. (DAT) The Telegraph Construction & Maintenance Co. supplied the cable, as the Germans were not yet in a position to do so. The first section of the Azores route was opened for traffic on 26 May 1900 and the complete route on 28 August. A completely German-manufactured cable was laid along the same route by the cableships *Stephan* and *von Podbielski* belonging to the Norddeutsche Seekabelwerke, and after this time they were truly independent of foreign companies.

---

[*] It must be remembered that the original agreements with GUTC had been made when there was only one cable operator on the Atlantic. It is clear that the Imperial Authorities wanted to free themselves from these restrictions.

The original cable office at Fayal (Horta, Azores)

At first sight a section dealing with the development of the German submarine cable network may not appear immediately relevant to the Valentia Cable Station. However, within ten years of the laying of the second German cable much was to change, and Valentia was to play an important part in the events of the war, a war which started with the destruction of the German cable network.

It is perhaps opportune at this stage to mention some of the innovations, both local and international, which were occurring during this period. Competition had led to lower rates. This had in turn led to more traffic. However, the return was less, and therefore funds available for extra cables were limited. One way round this was to increase the traffic volume through existing cables. The system in operation at stations like Valentia was to take signals coming in on the landline printing telegraphs and manually retransmit them on the Ocean cables. This could be speeded up considerable if the relaying could be done electrically. Indeed, one sees Graves being told to relay as much as possible in the memo of 23 February 1893. Relays had been in use on landlines since the earliest days of telegraphy, but they were too insensitive for use on submarine systems.

There is an undated letter to Graves from Williams, 71 Old Broad Street:

> The enclosed may interest you. Complete diagram of our No. 1 set with the addition of Brown's apparatus for direct working with Heart's Content.

These pressures brought further technical developments. In 1894 two cables were laid, one for the Anglo and one for the Commercial Co. These were the fastest cables available at the time. According to C. Bright, the Commercial's cable regularly managed 37 to 40 five-letter words per minute using automatic transmission. The Anglo cable had an ordinary working speed of 47 words per minute. It had a theoretical maximum of 48.8 wpm, although press work was frequently sent at 50 wpm.

Perhaps the greatest development of the era was one which was not exploited for another 30 to 40 years. Oliver Heaviside, the eccentric genius (noted also for the Heaviside layer in the atmosphere), had started his career as a telegraph engineer. In a series of papers during the 1880s he showed that the expressions for arrival current were more complex then those which had been developed by Kelvin. Kelvin had considered only cable resistance and conductor-to-sea capacitance. Heaviside showed that there were four, not two, terms which were of importance. In addition to the two mentioned above there were also the conductor inductance and the conductor-to-earth leakage. He predicted that the signalling speed would be increased dramatically by increasing the cable inductance.

It is interesting to see Bright writing in the late 1890s:

> We do not yet know in practice how to construct a core having the properties of Mr Oliver Heaviside's 'distortionless' circuit. In the absence of this a step in the right direction was made in the design of the latest Atlantic cables by liberally increasing the size of the Conductor.

In fact it was not until new magnetic materials were developed that a 'distortionless circuit' was built. Western Union had such a cable laid between Penzance and the Azores in 1924 and this gave an eight- to ten-fold increase in traffic capacity - but more of that later.

One must return somewhat in time to see what was happening at Valentia. There was a general realisation that perhaps Foilhommerum was not the best place to have landed cables. It was exposed to the direct impact of the Atlantic, with very little protection, and the shore was very rocky. Graves, in his writings, commented that there were copper deposits in the sea and that these might have reacted electrolytically with the cable armouring, which was heavily corroded. A subsequent examination of a 'Geology of Ireland' map does indeed show the existence of copper deposits on the mainland nearby.

Details of the number and nature of inshore repairs do not seem to have survived, but the shore ends of successive cables appear to have been made increasingly more robust. A decision was taken during 1886-87 to alter the landing point, and a place called Cooscroon (Conscroon in some documents) on the mainland was eventually chosen. There is in existence a copy of an indenture dated 29 July 1887 between the Company and Sir Maurice O'Connell and Daniel Ross O'Connell of Lake View, Killarney. This granted landing rights to the Company in perpetuity on payment of a sum of £500. The agreement also allowed for the erection of a cable hut and guaranteed access for Company staff at all times. The arrangement, which was soon put into effect, was to have all cables taken from the cable hut along the side of the road to White Strand near Ballycarberry Point, and over to Knightstown along much the same route as the British and Irish Magnetic Telegraph Co's line for the Atlantic cables of 1857/58. However, over the years it became evident that Cooscroon, while better than Foilhommerum Bay, was not a particularly good landing site for the cables. The approach was very rocky and the shore ends required frequent replacement. It would appear as if the '94 cable was brought straight into Knightstown Harbour and thereafter as each shore end came up for renewal, it too was brought in along the same route. By 1898 only '74 was still at Cooscroon.

It will be noted that in spite of these changes the Emden cable remained at Foilhommerum. The reasons for this are not quite clear at this stage. Did the shore end fail as often as the Atlantic cables did? Were the German authorities, with a mind to the future, unwilling to pay for re-routing? The fact is that the German cable came in at a slightly different place to the Atlantic cables and it could be that there were no copper deposits to electrolyse the outer armouring of the shore end.

However, once the Germans had completed their own cable to America via the Azores, the contracts with the Anglo American Telegraph Co were allowed to lapse and the cable was no longer used. Anglo records show that the last quarterly payment of £25 to Graves was made in September 1900. The same records show that the German cable hut at Foilhommerum was maintained by a caretaker until approximately 1904.

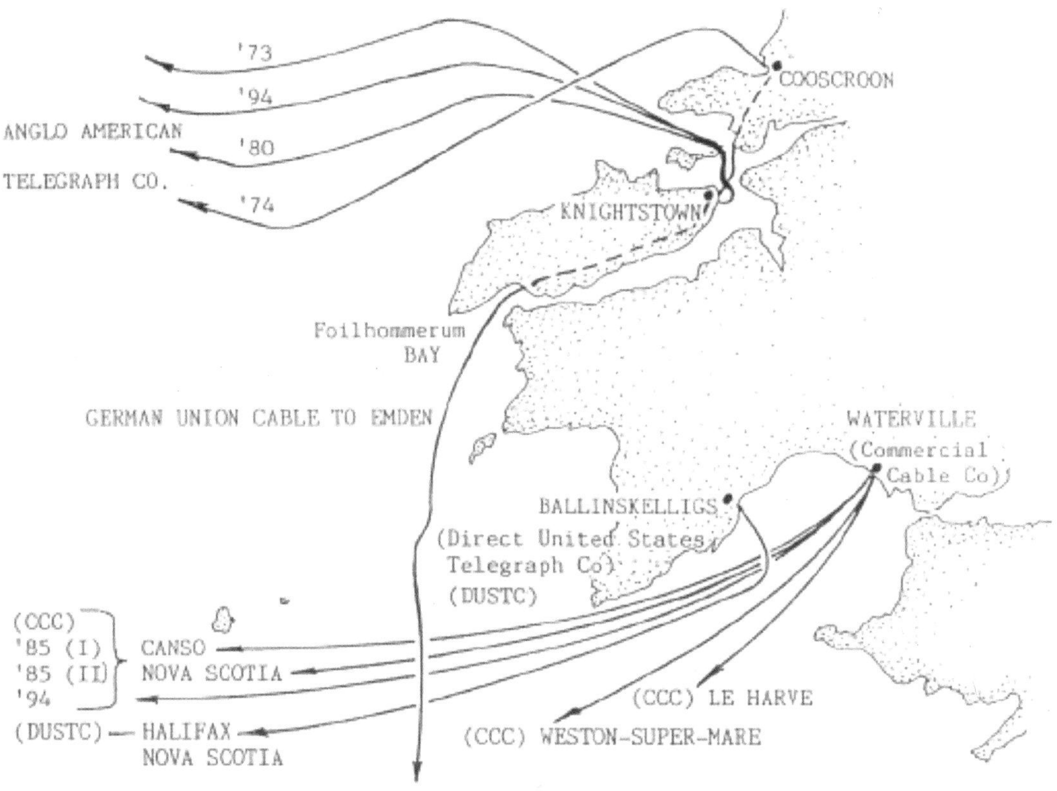

Fraud in Newfoundland?

There were indications that the Anglo's manager in Newfoundland, Alexander M. Mackay, was involved in fraudulent activities, and a commission of enquiry was appointed to investigate his misappropriation of funds. In 1891 he had been involved in a Newfoundland government contract to maintain and operate its system of telegraphs, and from the beginning of 1892 he was appointed general supt. of government lines. In sworn testimony on 4 October 1892, Smith, book keeper of govt. telegraphs (also accountant for Mackay and Anglo American Telegraph Co), said:

> Prior to opening of government telegraphs in April 1892 government telegraph accounts were kept in the Anglo books....Both sets of books had been destroyed by the fire of 8 July 1892.

In any event, Mackay would not have been alone in the murky depths of Newfoundland politics[*].

Valentia staff matters

Telegraphy was approaching maturity and now had to wait for technical developments in other fields before it could progress. Accordingly, as the records of technical developments at Valentia decline, the staff records increase. One such correspondence appears in detail about a poor soul named Smith:

> "1 March 1889 sent off duty 11.30 pm incapable, having come on sober at 5.30
>
> J. Graves Esq.
> If this man will agree to take the pledge and stick to it I will give him one more chance.
> If he ever offends again, I authorise you to discharge him and then report the matter to Head Office
> Let Smith read this
> H. Weaver 7 March '89
>
> Supt. Carefully read and noted"
> Smith's signature appears after the word "noted"

The document, which seems to have plied its way back and forth to London, acquiring more correspondence as it went, is typical of many. It also gives some idea of the extent of the discretion which the Station Superintendent was permitted to exercise.

[*] It is reported that a barrister named Morine ,who was a Member of Parliament in Newfoundland, was forced to resign when it was pointed out that he was Minister for Transport while representing the Government in a case against the Reid Shipping Co.

Dr Patrick Letters - Station Medical Officer during this period

There is another correspondence which indicates the measure of Graves's support of his staff. It concerns a young clerk, Arthur Scaife, who had absented himself for one day on account of a sore throat. He was docked a day's pay and felt that this was unjustified. In spite of the advice of Graves and his father (who became Superintendent in 1919) he sent a note to Head Office:

> "3 Oct 1904
> re. stopping of my pay for one day's absence.
> I was very ill for some days before I remained off duty and returned after one day and didn't recover for another two days. I was quite unfit for duty on this day. Under the circumstances perhaps the management will grant me my pay"

Graves, probably against his better judgment, supported young Scaife's case, but as the Station Medical Officer, Dr Letters, was not convincing in his report, full pay was not returned.

This memo highlights two of the preoccupations at the Station at that time: health worries, and a lack of confidence in the Company's doctor. The south west coast of Ireland can be very damp indeed and the weather there can aggravate respiratory disorders. Fred Mackey's notes on life in Valentia includes the following:

> When an epidemic of sickness descended on the little colony, the small staff were hard pressed to maintain the round-the-clock service expected of them. Some took advantage of the opportunity to indulge in poteen, a ferocious, locally distilled firewater which had a great reputation for killing microbes. It sometimes killed the patient as well, viruses were then of course only in their teething stages. The alternative to poteen was to take to one's bed, and let the rest of the world go by, few choose the latter.

Some memos from the period will illustrate these points:

Board order 18 March 1892
"If Mr ------ chooses to employ an outside doctor, no objection will be made, but in all cases which render absence from duty necessary, the certificate of the Co's doctor will be required before pay is returned"

Managing Director's memo 5 April 1892 (in essence)
Any member of staff suffering from a contagious disease must isolate himself until the Company's doctor certifies that the disease is eradicated from the sick house"

This seems to have applied even to children's ailments.
Supt's memo to staff 6 September 1897
I am informed that an infectious disease has appeared in the house of Mr Ring.
Every precaution should be taken to keep all children[*] apart from that house and its inmates until the danger of infection is over.

It would appear that Mr ----- , the subject of the Board order of 18 March 1892, was still causing trouble and turning up for work while ill.

Managing Director's memo 8 June 1892
"If Mr ----- neglects or ignores the order of 11/3 last again, I shall report the matter to the Board and recommend that his services be dispensed with, or in fact the services of any other member of staff, who may be ill advised enough to act in a similar manner.

One gathers that the Superintendent himself was not in the best of health during this period. A letter dated 2 June '03 from R.B. Mackey, one of the clerks-in-charge, states that he (Mackey) would not be back at the expiration of the holiday period as he was undergoing a course of treatment at Harrogate and that this would take a further two weeks before a definite medical opinion could be expressed. Its final sentence reads:
Hoping that you are feeling better

There is a note on the back of the letter to the Manager:
For your information and instructions. W. Hearnden 4/6/03

A further note on the same letter from the manager says
to Supt VA. Deal with it under rule 32

---

[*] It is interesting that children were now a large component of Station life. In the 1890s two generations of many families were now working for the Company and the third was growing up. There is a charming memo (7 November 1892) from Graves to his staff which indicates how children playing near the Station building got on nerves.

Rule 32 of the staff rule book dealt with serious or protracted illnesses "up to one month full pay, second month half pay and after that no pay"

This could well explain why Mr ----- had been so anxious to put in an appearance at work.

Bill Hearnden

Mackey's letter is the earliest available document that bears the name of William Hearnden, who was to succeed Graves as Superintendent in 1909. He worked in London and it is believed that he was sent to Valentia as Assistant Superintendent because of Graves's ill health. There is no official record of the date of his transfer, but there is a letter sent to him from London by his boys Arthur and Fred, and this is dated March 1887. It can be assumed that once he had settled accommodation in Valentia, he made arrangements for them to follow.

The arrival of Bill Hearnden at Valentia marks the earliest period of contemporary recollection by people who were alive when this book was first drafted. There is no doubt that Hearnden and Graves did not get on. Time and technology were overtaking the old man or "Boss" as his staff always called him. Hearnden was one of a new breed of professional business men. According to family rumours, Hearnden was sent from London because Graves was too soft with his staff and there may be an element of truth in this. Certainly the tone of familiarity in Mackey's letter to Graves of 2 June '03 would not have been tolerated by Hearnden. It is reported that Graves was not pleased when his grand daughter, Anne Louise[*], ran away to Cork to marry young Fred Hearnden, the author of the letters to his dad, who had joined the staff in 1894.

The Anglo-American Telegraph Company Limited.

Valentia STATION,

April 20 1894

Memorandum to Manager.

Holidays -

These have now began & will last up to the End of the year.

In order to minimize the Overtime, to afford the necessary relief, it would be advisab[le] to appoint Fredk Hearnden ~~to~~ a Junior Clerk on @ £48 a year so that he may take a regular duty with other Junior Clerks.

He has been here as a Supernumerary for several months & has qualified himself for a Junior Clerkship. I therefore recommend his appointment as from 1st April 1894.

This will still leave two vacancies upon [illegible] Staff

Jas. Graves

[*] Anne Louise Hearnden died in July 1982 aged 95

Some Valentia Staff in a photograph from the early 1900s. Fred Hearnden is identified as '6' while his brother, Arthur is '1'. Arthur was not a member of staff at the station and subsequently became an Inspector with the RIC

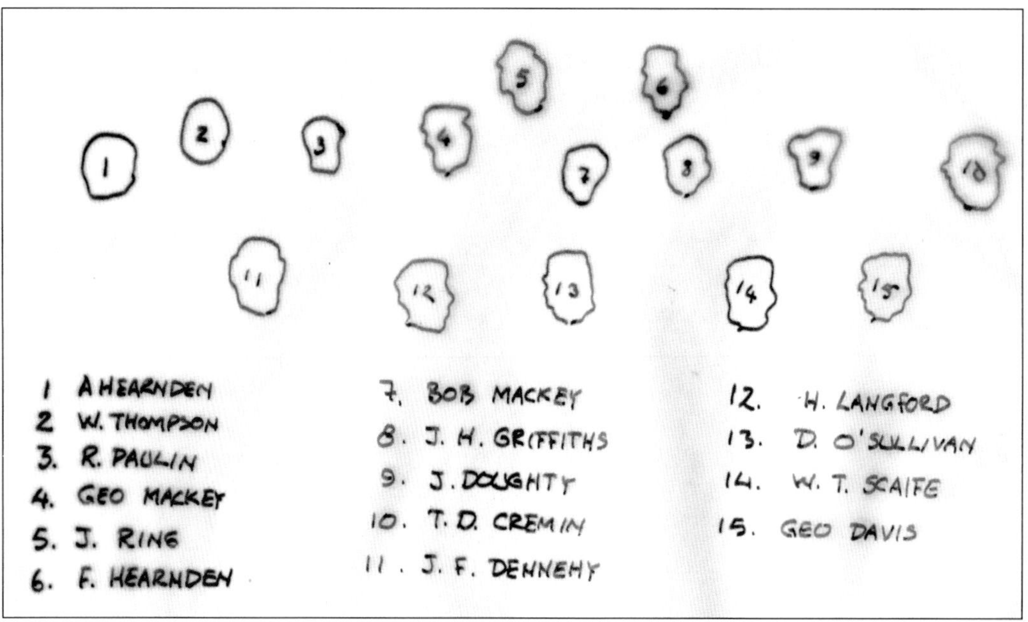

Key to the above photograph as supplied by Fred Hearnden's son, Arthur

Threats of injunctions against Marconi

The Government of Newfoundland ultimately regretted the assignment of the cable monopoly and its unwillingness to preempt. Elsewhere, cable operators were charged for the right to land cables, and if many competitors were to land cables in Newfoundland then this would have been a tidy source of income. Anglo's continued assertion of its monopolistic rights via Alexander Mackey made it very unpopular, and never more so than the near riot when he attempted to use the legal stick to prevent Marconi continuing with his experiments in St John's in 1901. It would have been interesting if it had gone to court. Wireless was not a cable and thus Marconi was not in breach of the landing monopoly. Mackay might have been able to use the Anglo's control of the inland telegraphs as his basis, although if the Government had become involved, or if Marconi had merely used Newfoundland as a relay point, then it is difficult to see what he could have achieved.

The end of the NF monopoly

The monopoly under the 1854 Act came to an end in 1901. In spite of unpopularity and questions about his methods, Mackay was appointed Superintendent of Telegraphs when the island telegraph system was reorganised under the Newfoundland Postal Telegraph. He died in 1905 and thus did not witness the legal wrangling between the Government of Newfoundland and the Commercial Cable Co. There had been initial discussions in 1906, but the Waterville/Canso cable was not re-routed for another three years. Shortly after the final agreement to divert had been made in February 1909 there was a change of Government, and before the agreement could be submitted to the Legislature the contract was repudiated by the new administration. They saw each cable in transit to America as two distinct cables and demanded $4,000 per landing. The Commercial Co. refused to pay and took legal action for breach of contract. The matter dragged on for years.

From the turn of the century onwards Hearnden senior was effectively Acting Superintendent. According to rumours the Company made repeated attempts to retire Graves on a pension, but they did not succeed until 1909.

Two pictures of Graves and his staff ca 1900. Given that he is sitting in one and standing in the other we might assume that the picture on the left was his senior staff while that on the right was his junior staff

A memo to the Acting Superintendent dated 5 May 1909 shows Graves demonstrating the same lack of confidence in the station medical officer as the other employees. It also shows that some of the Company's inflexibility had softened.

> No employee of the Company at Valentia is bound to consult the Company's doctor, but in cases of absence from duty he must provide a certificate from the doctor whom he does consult and in cases of prolonged absence periodical certificates.
>
> If the Company is not satisfied with the certificate given by the doctor consulted or even if it requires confirmation of the same, the employee must permit an examination to be made by the Company's doctor (if there be one) or other medical man it may appoint for the purpose with a view to the return of pay, continuance in the Service or retirement on a pension.
>
> The Board has authorised payment of the Superintendent's salary up to the end of April- Will you kindly ask him for a further certificate.
>
> Carson[*] Manager

[*] Carson can't have been that young himself!

Shortly afterwards the Company got their way. Graves, who had been recently widowed[+], retired and moved into a large house in a beautiful setting overlooking the bay through which the first Atlantic cables had been taken just over fifty years earlier.

End of an era. James Graves leaving the station for the last time

[+] His wife, Anne Charlotte (neeé Smith of Hoo, Kent) died in March 1909.

Four generations. The baby in arms is Robbie Graves, born 1909. To the left of the picture is his grandfather, Arthur James, and to the right his father, Charles James. Robbie was an Irish rugby cap in the late 1930s and provided a large volume of the information that is contained in this book.

Bill Hearnden, in charge, was about to preside over the first phase in the Station's forthcoming years of turbulence. The Company had contracted the Telegraph Construction & Maintenance Co. to lay yet another cable. This time both Valentia and Heart's content were to be bypassed. The cable ran from Bay Roberts at the head of Trinity Bay, Newfoundland to Penzance. The reasons for this choice of route are not clear at this stage, but at least on the eastern side of the Atlantic, they are likely to have been associated with the problems of getting additional Post Office lines across the Irish Sea. This represented the last act of a tired company weighed down by the burden of its enormous initial capital.

The Western Union takeover of the Anglo cables

At this stage we need to consider Theodore Newton Vail (1845-1920), who had an early association with Western Union but was an early convert to the telephone. In 1878 he became the General Manager of the American Bell Telephone Co. and defended his Company in the 1879 patent lawsuit, which Western Union lost, forcing their exit from telephones. The Bell companies became American Telephone and Telegraph Co. (A.T. & T.) in 1885, and Vail was elected President, but was forced to retire due to ill-health in 1887. He was re-appointed President in 1909 and oversaw a rapid expansion of A.T. & T. as it bought up smaller companies, one of these being Western Union, which was taken over in 1910 with Vail as its President. The circumstances of the acquisition of Western Union are as follows: During the Gould era the Company had been running at a loss. While competition between the Pool on the one hand and Commercial on the other had no effect upon rates between 1888 and 1911, it did produce marked results in improved service, and between members of the Pool there was more than a semblance of "house-rivalry". The public got good trans-Atlantic service. Nevertheless, Western Union's affairs were not in good order - in fact there was no adequate system of book-keeping or records and the company had no balance sheet. Competition with the Postal had almost forced Western Union into bankruptcy. Vail thought it would be a national calamity if Western Union defaulted and so in 1908-1909, A.T. & T. bought a controlling interest in Western Union by acquiring the holding of the George Gould family for $30 million. It was Vail's idea that the landline telegraphs and telephones should be co-ordinated for the common purpose of giving the public better communication service and of reducing the costs by the joint use of plant facilities and service organization: his ideas were essentially monopolistic. This being the case, it was perhaps natural for him to look upon the cable Pool not only as socially justifiable, but quite worthy of being strengthened and unified by making of it a single corporate body under his own control

As part of the US Government's attempt to thwart Vail's plan to gain a total monopoly on all telephone and telegraph business, the government put pressure on A.T & T. to force Western Union out of the British Cable Pool. Coggeshall contends that there were behind-the-scenes promptings by the Commercial Cable Co., which led the US Attorney General to indicate that if Western Union did not leave the Pool, then it would be forced out using the Sherman Act[*]. Coggeshall continues: "Vail thus was balked in his desire to amalgamate the companies both home

[*] During this time he US government was very concerned about this monopolistic growth of certain key companies and with the formation of cartels. The Sherman Anti-Trust Act of 1890 was an attempt to curtail such behaviour, but it really did not achieve bite until the Presidency of Theodore Roosevelt (1901-1909). It still forms the basis for most Federal anti-trust litigation.

and abroad into a world-wide telephone, telegraph, cable system, but making opportunity out of the turn which events had taken, he seized upon the Sherman Act as an excuse for withdrawing Western Union from the Pool forthwith[**] - leaving the Anglo and D.U.S.T both high and dry upon the beach with no landline support. The *Electrician* **67** (1911) 1022, quoting the proceedings of a DUS board meeting, says Vail informed them in February 1911 that the 1882 Pool contract would be terminated on 1 March 1911. After withdrawal of the traffic, Anglo and D.U.S.T were at first inclined to combine and fight, but court action seemed futile and there was little hope of getting any American traffic outside of New York and Boston."

According to the *New York Times* of 18 December 1910, the nature of the take-over (purchase or lease) would not become clear as quickly in Britain as it might in the US. It was suggested that this was because the stock ownership was largely divided into small-holdings, and no sale of the Company could be effected without a meeting of shareholders. From the Western Union point of view there were also difficulties because most land-lines connected to the cable landing sites in Britain and Europe were state owned. Accordingly, agreement with each of the telegraphs services as well as the assent of the International Telegraph Convention would be required.

On 3 May 1911 there were questions in the House of Commons[+] (*HC Deb 03 May 1911 vol 25 cc437-8*). The Postmaster General replied that he was taking steps by arranging for the Government to have certain powers of control over the rates for trans-Atlantic cable messages and by other measures to secure that no British interests suffer from the control of the Anglo American Cable Company's business being in effect transferred to the Western Union Cable Co.

Given these obstacles we can assume that leasing became the least-troublesome option for the takeover. The Anglo lease by Western Union was arranged by Executive Agreement in July 1911, and by Indenture of 1 March 1912, for 99 years from 1 April 1912. According to the *New York Times* of 11 October 1911, Anglo and DUS stockholders had ratified the lease on 29 September 1911. The annual meeting of Western Union was to be held on the day the paper reported and it was expected that its stockholders would do likewise.

All cables laid after the takeover date were to be the property of the Western Union Telegraph Co. The agreement also stipulated that at the end of the leasing period Western Union would return working cables and a cable repair ship to the leasing company. In the interim the Anglo went into dormancy; its shareholders receiving a guaranteed dividend from the proceeds of the lease.

However, all of this did not wash with the US Government. According to Coggeshall:

> The AT&T connection with Western Union was short-lived, being terminated in 1914 by the sale of the Gould Western Union stock to the public. This action was taken in anticipation of a

---

[**] The *Electrician* **67** (1911) 1022 - 1023 reported that Vail had made his first merger overtures in May 1910, but they were not acceptable to the Anglo or DUST

[+] see http://hansard.millbanksystems.com.

monopoly suit in the US courts. Newcomb Carlton became president of Western Union on 17 April 1914 and held that position until 1933.

Thus Western Union regained its independence in 1914, although during the period of the first world war it was virtually taken into state ownership and its operation was overseen by the US Postal Service.

Death of James Graves and succession

Meanwhile, James Graves, so long Superintendent, died on 14 Jan 1911. The publication of his will brought to light many details about Cable Station society, which had grown up during three generations. Graves himself had had a number of eligible daughters. The community in which they found themselves, mainly British and Anglican, was isolated both socially as well as geographically. They were not sufficiently upper class to associate easily with the local ascendancy (landed classes) and yet were definitely superior to the indigenous Catholic population. The influx of Post Office staff in the 1870s represented new blood, and of course there was the slow influx of new staff from England. A Superintendent's daughter or even grand-daughter seemed to be a good catch for any young man; a guarantee to promotion in the Company and thereby long-term social advancement. This of course was to place Graves in a very difficult position on a number of occasions. Indeed the case of Percy Langford, who had married into the Graves family was typical of many.

Memo from J.G. to Manager 20 November 1901

> "In this case P. Langford, whilst playing football was pushed in front of another man running, neither being able to avoid collision.
>
> "In May 1897 two cases of bicycle accidents occurred, unfitting them in each case for three days duty. In these cases half pay only was returned them.
>
> I submit it to your ruling whether in this case full or half pay should be returned for the six days during which, from inability to use his leg, Langford was unfitted for duty, being unable to walk to the Office"

Carson's reply in his characteristic red pen said

> "Production of certificate- full pay. Previous decision very reasonable"

In this isolated community the wives and daughters all contributed to create their own social microcosm, with its clearly defined structure. They even had their own magazine 'Fun at Va'. According to family sources Anne Louise Hearnden (Graves's grand daughter) not infrequently sent orders to Fortnum & Mason and of course London was the capital complete with its own social season.

Such aspirations required money and everyone knew how well the Boss was paid. So when he died they all anticipated a share in the great handout. What a shock.- There was virtually nothing there. It is true that his estate amounted to £8557-11s-8d for the purposes of duties, but the majority of it had been lent to his sons, daughters and sons-in-law.

Poor William Hearnden did not stand a chance. As an outsider he had upset the anticipated line of succession within the Station. He was a strict authoritarian, and was now attempting to rectify the easy-going attitudes which had developed during Graves's tenure. For this he was hated both by the staff of the Station itself and by their families. Of course he contributed to his own isolation; after all the superintendent and his family had standards to maintain. The Graves family, now with four generations on the island, were much more relaxed with the other staff and with the indigenous population. It is not unlikely that this sense of isolation within an already isolated community led to the early death of Hearnden's wife, Fanny.

Hearnden retired an embittered man in July 1913 and went to live with his son, Arthur, who was an Inspector in the Royal Irish Constabulary in Belfast. He was succeeded by Horatio Hardy, who had a long record of service in the Station. In fact it would appear that Western Union may have learnt something from the rancour associated with Hearnden's period as Superintendent. One thing is quite clear: for the remainder of the life of the Station most of the Superintendents were drawn from amongst long-serving staff.

With Hearnden's departure people reverted to their relaxed way, even if things would never be the same again. His name would be completely forgotten were it not for his son, Fred, who had married Graves's grand daughter, Anne Louise (Nan). Fred was an affable and easy-going sort of person who painted in his spare time. He was universally liked and had now been promoted to the rank of clerk.

Fred Hearnden beside one of his paintings.

Fred's wife Nan was one of the few people who seems to have had close contact with Bill Hearnden. She adored him and looked to him for guidance and help more than to her own father or her husband. She remained in correspondence with him right up to the time of his death[*]. The letters which have survived shed light on some important details during the wartime period. The extract below, dated 13 February 1914 confirms much of what has already been said about the man and his tenure as superintendent.

> "....... one can't meet people familiarly so nourishing doubts as to their bona fide. I have little respect for anyone who toadies to those above. My principle throughout life has been to demand explicit obedience and authority in office and in office only and I despise a man who tries to ingratiate himself in my esteem by rolling my lawns, playing old word games and talking high tea with apparent pleasure, when anybody with a grain of sense would know that it was not genuine. I may have been wrong in my convictions but I never wavered from the precept that situated as I was in Valentia, I should be civil and strange to one and all- showing no favour and bearing no ill-will to anyone. That in my humble opinion is the only way to command proper respect and what is of much greater importance I never allowed any official matters to reach my private house. Consequently my wife could never command anyone to high tea, croquet or any other damned thing. Thus jealousy amongst the women was avoided and hints and innuendoes of favouritism could never be brought against me. I am still of the same conviction and therefore can only conclude that there will be a great smash-up one of these days and very unpleasant things will come to the surface ...."

---

[*] He died in Belfast in 1919 and is buried beside his wife in the cemetery at Knightstown, Valentia island.

He was right. A 'great smash-up' was only six months away, but it was going to be on a much larger scale then he could have imagined. The First World War was to be the greatest upheaval in the Station's history and was going to consume all the energies of the staff for several years to come.

Addenda

Less than a month later another break with the past was recorded in an obituary published by what was by then the Institution of Electrical Engineers. John Gott, born Kendal 1840, was first employed by the Electric and International Telegraph Co. In 1863 went to Tripoli for the first Mediterranean cable. He was selected to travel on the *Great Eastern* in 1864 [??] and in 1869 was appointed the superintendent of the French cable station at St Pierre; he resigned this position in 1884 to take the post of Chief Electrician of the Commercial Cable Co. (how this must have galled Graves!). He held that appointment until his death in Brighton on 8 March 1914. Amongst his several achievements was the transmission of wireless through three miles in 1870, in which year he also developed a fault-searcher coil. In 1881 he introduced a modification for Kelvin's formula for the capacitance of cables.

And finally, another coincidence: on 10 September 1914, James Gordon Bennett (a lifelong bachelor), at the age of 73 married Maud, the widow of George, son of Paul Julius de Reuter.

James Gordon Bennett at his villa on the French Riviera at about the time of his marriage

Chapter 11

1914 - 1922 The Years of Turmoil

The important role that telegraphy was likely to play in an inevitable future war was well appreciated by strategists from its very beginnings. The mechanics behind the actions that were about to come into force were in place for a very long time. The Railway Regulation Act of 1844 contained a particularly relevant element:

> "And whereas Electric Telegraphs have been established on certain Railways and may become more extensively established hereafter and it is expedient to provide for their due Regulation: be it enacted That every Railway Company on being required so to do by the Lords of the said Committee with Servants and Workmen, at all reasonable Times to enter upon their Lands and to establish and lay down on such lands adjoining the Line of Such Railway, a Line of Electric Telegraphs for Her Majesties Service and give to him or them every reasonable facility for laying down the same, and for using the same for the Purpose of receiving and sending Messages on Her Majesty's Service, subject to such reasonable Remuneration to the Company as may be agreed . . . ."

After the *Times* war correspondent W.H. Russell witnessed the *Great Eastern*'s trawling for the severed Atlantic cable in 1865, he was aware that cables could be cut in time of war. His insight was prophetic. According to Daniel Headrick:

> The International Cable Convention of 1885 contained a clause, inserted upon Britain's insistence, recognizing the right of belligerents to cut one another's cables. Cutting cables, however, was no easy matter. Near the shore, where they were most vulnerable, they were often protected by powerful guns. At sea the operation required cable ships with grappling equipment and exact knowledge of the cable's location. As British firms had laid all British and most non-British cables, and owned 21 of the world's 30 cables. .....
>
> In the spring of 1898 the United States went to war against Spain. Spanish communications with Cuba via the United States were stopped. American ships attempted to cut the other cables to Cuba, but only succeeded in breaking the French one to Haiti. Meanwhile, in the Far East, Admiral Dewey seized the Hong Kong-Manila cable for his own use.

The British Cabinet appointed a committee in 1898 "to consider the control of communications by submarine telegraph in time of war". This 112-page report set out precisely what should be done. And this was indeed done at the outbreak of the Boer War. According to Headrick:

> On November 17, 1899 the Postmaster General informed the International Telegraph Bureau in Bern that all coded telegrams were forbidden south of Aden, and all clear-language telegrams subject to censorship. To other European countries it meant their

communications with Madagascar, German East Africa, Mozambique, and Somalia were subject to the veto of a British clerk in the Aden cable office.

Just as the Boer war was winding down, the Committee of Imperial Defence became an important ad hoc part of the government of the United Kingdom and the British Empire from just after the Second Boer War until the start of the Second World War. It was set up in 1902 and was responsible for research, and some co-ordination, on issues of military strategy. Under the guidance of Maurice Hankey it had, by 1914 become effectively a defence agency for the empire. In 1912 they agreed that interference with the submarine cables of belligerent states would be an important part of British wartime policy.

There was another weapon which was also planned: censorship. It had been used during the Boer war and from that time onwards schemes were evolved for the implementation of censorship on all relevant empire telegraphs in the event of hostilities. A document entitled "Regulations for censorship of submarine cable communications throughout the British Empire" was issued by the War Office on 5 December 1913. The five aims of British censorship, which covered military and economic aspects were:

(1) To deny naval or military intelligence to the enemy.

(2) To prevent the spread of false reports etc. likely to affect the morale of the civil population.

(3) To collect and distribute enemy information to Govt. Depts.

(4) To deny the use of British cables to any person or firm, British, allied or neutral for commercial transactions with the Enemy.

(5) To interfere as little as possible with legitimate British and neutral trade.

The implementation of the regulations was the responsibility of the War Office and the Post Office, the former being responsible for bringing the scheme into operation; for serving the warrants on the Post Office and the various cable companies; for appointing the Censors at home and abroad; and for supplying the necessary instructions and documents required in connection with the censorship.

The Post Office was responsible for issuing, at the request of the War Office, the necessary notification to the International Telegraph Office; the issue of a notification to the public; the establishment of temporary censorship at the Central Telegraph Office pending the establishment of the censorship by military officers; maintaining a watch at the various cable repeater stations (whether belonging to the Post Office or the Cable Companies) with a view to guarding against any telegrams being sent or received at these places; providing assistance to the Chief Censor and the Deputy Chief Censor at the Central Telegraph Office and generally taking all steps necessary to ensure that telegrams to and from places abroad passing over continental cables should be submitted to the Censors.

Many years later, as Chairman of Cable and Wireless, Sir Edward Wilshaw recalled that moment: "It must have been a thrilling moment in the Central Telegraph Office as midnight approached on 4 August 1914, when the British ultimatum expired. One after another of the British wires cleared their traffic and shut down. On the stroke of midnight a telegraphist in Berlin passed a signal 'GN' the telegraphic abbreviation for good night and for five years those wires were silent".

It is perhaps not an exaggeration to say that when Britain entered the "war to end all wars" all the seeds of victory were ready to be sown. Under the supervision of Lieutenant (later Admiral) Somerville (http://en.wikipedia.org/wiki/James_Somerville) all vessels in the Royal Navy were secretly fitted with high-power Poulsen arc wireless transmitters. Meanwhile Germany was about to lose vital lines of communication. There were several German trans-Atlantic cables through the Channel; one to Brest, one to Vigo, one to Tenerife and one to New York via the Azores. In spite of Germany's developing cable laying industry, the majority of cables had been laid by British companies. Thus the British had exact information of the whereabouts of German cables. In spite of their appearance on Admiralty charts, the Germans did not have the same intimate knowledge about British cables. Before dawn that morning, the cable ship *Telconia* reached a point some miles off Emden. In the darkness the German cables were raised and cut. Only when all links were severed did she return and raise up the seaward side of the cables and coil several miles of each into her tanks in order to thwart German attempts to repair them. The subsequent correspondence in the Post Office Archives concerning the appropriation of the severed German cables is immense. When one file is placed flat upon another and yet another, the stack is nearly shoulder high.

The communications isolation of Germany from its colonies and from the United States was almost total, and could have been critical were it not for one technical development: wireless. With wireless, Germany was able to communicate with her forces, her diplomatic missions and agents in neutral countries. Wireless, however, had one disadvantage: there was no way of preventing the enemy from listening in. One's communications were then only as secure as one's encryption system. The British response to the wealth of airwave information was the formation of Room 40 in Admiralty House, Old Building. Here, under the supervision of Admiral Sir Reginald Hall (Director of Naval Intelligence), a staff, initially of two, set about breaking the German ciphers and decoding the intercepts. The destruction of the light cruiser *Magdeburg* by the Russians and the handover of its code book had given them the naval codes by October 1914. Two further code books, one from Brussels in April 1915 and another from Persia two months earlier gave the staff at Room 40 most of what they needed.

By the latter part of the war a staff of 70-80 cryptographers and clerks were working on intercepts obtained by 800 wireless operators. Their work led to the arrest of Indian revolutionaries, Sir Roger Casement[*], Mata Hari and much else, as will be seen later.

The cable ships that were involved in appropriating German cables performed many acts of heroism. The *Dacia*, later sunk by torpedo, picked up approximately 150 miles in 1600 fathoms and relaid it as part of the Brest-Casablanca-Dakar cable. The Post Office cable ship *Monarch* was destroyed off Folkstone in 1915. It is believed that she hit a German mine. The *Telconia*, which had cut the German cables, was later attacked in the North Sea and narrowly escaped destruction.

The German attempts to destroy British cables were more isolated and far flung. The Atlantic Fleet inhibited such action in home waters, but on 7 September 1914 the German cruiser *Nürnberg* bombarded the Pacific cable station on Fanning Island (now part of the Republic of Kiribati) and cut and towed away the cables. However the staff were able to undertake makeshift repairs and communications between Fanning and Fiji were quickly restored. On 9 November 1914 the cruiser *Emden* approached the station at Cocos Islands. The staff had time to send a warning to the Admiralty in London, who were able to transmit a wireless message to HMAS *Sydney*, which was in the area. The *Emden* was subsequently sunk.

Cable censorship had started just before the outbreak of war. Initially it was done on a station-by-station basis. The shortage of censoring staff, the prohibition of the use of codes and the priority of Government messages meant that commercial traffic was severely restricted. In Newfoundland for instance the Chief Censor directed that all messages in transit either east or west bound should be censored in the UK. The general system was that all censored messages would be transmitted with a code which would confirm to censors further along the line that it could be allowed past.

At the outbreak of war the censors were mainly retired officers. Their main disadvantage was their lack of knowledge of commercial methods and phraseology. Practically none had experience of cable communications and technicalities. Although at a later stage some civilians, such as retired colonial governors, were employed, it was felt that a military background and an ability to make decisions on personal initiative was more important then any technical knowledge. Some idea of the operation can be obtained from this extract of the report of Lieut. Col. Ostrehan, Censor in Charge of the Western Union group:

> At outbreak of war there were eleven cables from Newfoundland to the American Mainland and there were ten cables from Newfoundland to UK. Telegraph and cable

[*] Hall was a key player in the circumstances that led to the execution of Casement

operators were all British subjects, so it was decided to appoint operators as assistant censors.

Censorship was imposed on 2 August 1914 at 5.30pm. These were at St John's, Government Telegraph, Anglo and Commercial (office at Cuckold's Cove), Bay Roberts (offices of Western Union Telegraph Co.), Heart's Content (Anglo Offices) and Port aux Basques.

The Report also lists stations where cable censorship was established. In some cases this was done well before the War.

Location	Chief Station	Sub-Station	Remarks
UK	Central Telegraph Office (CTO) London	Western Union office London	
		Commercial Cable	
		PQ (Compagnie Francaise)	
		Liverpool	For terminal traffic with America only
		Waterville, Ireland	For traffic to or through France by LeHavre-Waterville cable only
		Newcastle	Closed - traffic diverted to CTO for censorship
		Anglo London Office	After amalgamation traffic censored at WU house London
		Direct London Office	ditto
		Va, Id, Pz	censorship of provincial terminal traffic transferred to Liverpool in October 1914
NF	St John's	Bay Roberts	Closed 26/11/1914
		Cuckold's Cove	Closed 26/11/1914
		Heart's Content	Closed 26/11/1914
		Port aux Basques	Closed 26/11/1914 Actual censorship at St John's

As can be imagined, the volume of commercial traffic declined drastically and it took several years to recover. It was assisted by the gradual relaxation of regulations relating to the use of codes. The relevant page in the Report on Cable Censorship 1914 - 1919 (PRO DEFE1 350) is summarised as follows:

Recognising that the censorship load would increase with every additional code authorised, they decided against allowing other countries to specify their own codes. At end October 1914 a small number of published codes were to be chosen by Government Departments in collaboration with UK commercial interests. This would apply to telegrams in approved codes between British or Allied territory whether in Europe or outside and any British, Allied or neutral territory outside the European telegraph system. It did not include any two countries in the European Telegraph System or any neutral country in the European Telegraph system and any other country. Countries allowed this privilege would be informed privately so as to avoid complaints from countries that were still required to use British cables in-clear only.

As of 1 November the following four codes were permitted to be used:
1. A.B.C., 5th Edition (not including the "Improved" Edition).
2. Scott's 10th Edition.
3. Western Union (including the Universal Edition, but not including the Western Union Travellers' Cable Code or the Western Union Five-letter Code)
4. Lieber's (not including Lieber's Five-letter Code).

The following three codes were added in December, 1914 :
5. Bentley's Complete Phrase Code (not including the Oil and Mining Supplements).
6. Broomhall's Imperial Combination Code.
7. Meyer's Atlantic Cotton Code, 39th Edition.

And the following in January and March, 1916, respectively:
8. Broomhall's Imperial Combination Code (Rubber Edition).
9. Riverside Code, 5th Edition. "

As will be seen later, the working of censorship required that copies of these code-books would have to be available at every British censorship office throughout the world, and as this took time to achieve, the introduction of these privileges proceeded piecemeal.

Naturally this required the employment of decoding clerks in the censorship offices, but it would seem that commercial concerns were prepared to tolerate delay rather than sacrifice the confidentiality of their telegrams.

There had initially been censorship at all stations and offices, but by a process of rationalization censors were transferred from Valentia and Ballinskelligs to Company Offices in mainland Britain in October 1914. It was then the duty of Post Office staff at the stations to ensure that all messages were sent via the censors prior to transmission. A censor was maintained at Waterville to deal with the Company's traffic between France and America. This was consistent with the original decision of the Committee for Imperial Defence, that all cables, even those just touching the shores of the Empire, would be monitored. Col. Ostrehan's report (in PRO DEFE 1/350), written at the end of the War is enlightening. The section of the which deals with 'Method of Working' describes the layout of the Censor room and the mode of operation of the staff there. One gets the impression that the description is for a major UK-based office, where there were four tables, labelled A, B, C and D, plus a copying table. Two directors occupied table A and two military censors were at table B. Table C had two Eastern Telegraph cable censors. It must be remembered that Eastern Telegraph were responsible for the majority of the Imperial 'All Red' cable routes; cables which originated or landed in part of the Empire or in the territory of a friendly neutral (Portugal). There were two scrutineers at table D. These were cable telegraphists who received all messages from tables A, B and C. The report continues:

> At each table there is a *set* of books, i.e. Orders for *the Censor* staff, Parts A and B, and a Cable *Censor's* Handbook. All other books of reference are within reach of Censors.

The 'other books of reference' referred to above included: Post Office Directory with County Suburbs, Sell's Telegraphic Addresses Directory, Trow's New York Directory, Kelly's Merchants and Shippers of the World, Whittaker's Almanack, Lloyd's Register of Shipping, Lloyd's Weekly Index of Shipping, Berne List of Telegraph Stations, Telephone Directory, English, French and other Dictionaries, Copies of all authorized codes, Daily Bulletins.

All correspondence was categorised and details were filed according to date. The files included

a. Officers, Eastern Telegraph Cable Censors, Post Office staff, &c.
b. Cable Censor's Office, Central Telegraph Office and Companies,
c. Western Union Company, correspondence and instructions.
d. Enemy Banks under supervision.
e. Correspondence with firms.
f. Traffic Returns.
g. Local instructions issued by Officer in charge
h. Post Office Circulars
j. Supplementary Trade Terms.

The whole of this correspondence was indexed with reference to file and date. There was a letter book which contained the gist of all correspondence that had been censored. They also kept a record of all messages that had been either held or stopped which included details of the sender/addressee, and the reasons for the stoppage or release. Security for particularly sensitive material was the responsibility of the duty Censor-in-Charge and the Director.

The number of Post Office staff and the part they played in these operations are also described. Attached to the Censor office there were four Post Office cable telegraphists. Three of these were intended to advise the censors on technical matters and also to act as scrutineers. The fourth telegraphist acted as a confidential clerk to the censor-in-charge and had additional responsibility for keeping the records of the office as described above. There were also five Post Office inland telegraphists whose duties were in the instrument room. They were to act as supervisors, and ensure that the lines were not being used for any unauthorised purpose. They were also to censor all service messages and to ensure that no message was forwarded without being censored. Finally the office had the service of six Post Office staff to act as decoders. Four of these took messages that had been sent/received in authorised code and provide an in-clear version for the censor. They were also required to enter particulars of their copies in the copy book for transfer to the Central Telegraph Office or the War Office. The remaining two were intended to act as assistants to the scrutineers and to support the process of copying when necessary.

The Censor's reports give some insight into details of the history of the telegraph companies which have not been chronicled elsewhere. While Major Hunter Blair, in charge of the Commercial's office in London, was fulsome in his praise of the staff there, Lieut. Col. Wilmott at Waterville was less so. He complained about the cramped conditions available for the censors, the delay in forwarding of Government messages, postal delays and above all the fact that the Censor was in charge of issuing security passes for Company staff. This he said placed an unnecessary load on the Censor and should have been done by the military.

Col Ostrehan's report on the Western Union system, which is more comprehensive than any of the others, mentions that there was an amalgamation during April and May 1916. Up to that time the three Companies had separate identities and offices in London. WUTC's offices were in 1 Old Broad Street, Anglo's were at 63 Old Broad Street and Direct's were in Mark Lane. In each the accommodation for the Censor's staff was "very limited and unsanitary". All the Companies moved into one large office at 22 Great Winchester Street and the amalgamation was complete by 8 May 1916. In the new premises the Company was able to make available a schoolroom and a small waiting room and this was felt to be adequate. The report concludes with the following two paragraphs:

> The establishment of censorship could not fail to prove irksome to the Company, as it entailed giving up accommodation which they could ill afford; extending the system of carriers to include the Censor's room; the withdrawal of a portion of their already depleted staff from purely company work to special work in connection with the censorship; and considerable interference in matters of detail which broke up the course of established routine, &c. Notwithstanding this, cordial relations have always existed between the company and the censorship. Mr. Goddard, the European representative, from the first instructed all the officials on his staff that they were to co-operate in every way possible with the censorship, and I, for my part, have always made a point of avoiding, as far as possible, any interference with company routine, and in cases where such avoidance was not possible, of consulting the officials concerned before issuing any instructions, with the result that no friction has ensued.
>
> Owing to competition the company officials are exceedingly alive to the necessity of giving the public the best service possible, and 1 have the greatest admiration for the persistent and untiring efforts which they make, under very unfavourable conditions

owing to loss of capacity, want of experienced staff, sickness, etc, to keep their staff and instruments up to high level, and to lose no time in correcting and improving faults which are continually coming to the fore owing to constantly changing conditions.

Destroyers on patrol (painting by Fred Hearnden)

Life on the southwest coast of Ireland could not present a stronger contrast. Remote from the European theatres of war and from the arrangements mentioned in the previous paragraphs, they saw matters in a more relaxed way. True, they would have seen frigates patrolling the sea areas close to the line of cables.

In many cases, war, in a country where conscription had not been introduced, brought substantial benefits. The Blaskets, clearly visible from Valentia, are a group of islands, now largely uninhabited, which lie at the north side of Dingle Bay. Maurice O'Sullivan, who died in 1950, was born on Great Blasket and was a schoolboy there during this period. His book "Twenty Years a Growing" tells the story of his childhood and the following extract conveys an atmosphere that would not have been too different to that at Valentia:

> I looked south to the Skelligs and saw the curraghs making for home full of wreckage and waited till they reached the Point, when we all ran down towards the quay, like the gulls themselves, and had great enjoyment dragging the timbers up the slip. Soon the light of day was quenched and the wreck gatherers had put their curraghs on the stays, well satisfied with the day's work and their bones aching after all the rowing since morning.

Next day the quay and the strands were a grand sight, big timbers lying here and there and not a curragh with less then a hundred planks. 'By God' one man would say 'war is good'. 'Arra, man' said another, 'if it continues, this Island will be Tir na nOg'.

The war changed people greatly. Idle loiterers who used to sleep it out till milking time were now abroad with the chirp of the sparrow gathering and ever gathering. There was good living in the Island now. Money was being piled up. There was no spending. Nothing was bought. There was no need. It was to be had on the top of the water, - flour, meat, wax, margarine, wine in plenty, even shoes, stockings and clothes. Not a house in the Island but a store room was built beside it to keep the gatherings, and, without any exaggeration, when you entered one of them you would think you were in a big town, with all the barrels of flour piled on top of one another, tins of petrol and every sort of riches; and when the old man or old woman came round, all they had to do was to make for the barrels of wine and help themselves to a draught. Buyers were coming from all parts of Kerry to buy the wood, to buy the wax and every sort of oil, so that money was being made rapidly.

The miserable survivors of torpedoed ships[*], such as the *Lusitania* and the bodies of the dead washed up on their shores seem to have been unable to bring home to them the horrors of war.

Station under military guard

[*] Two Valentia operators were lost when the *Leinster* was sunk by U123 in Dublin Bay on 10 October 1918. A third operator who was on board survived.

Things would have been quite different at the cable stations. Each was now surrounded by barbed wire and kept under military guard. Admission was by pass only and it seems that, at Valentia, the guarded area included many of the staff houses.

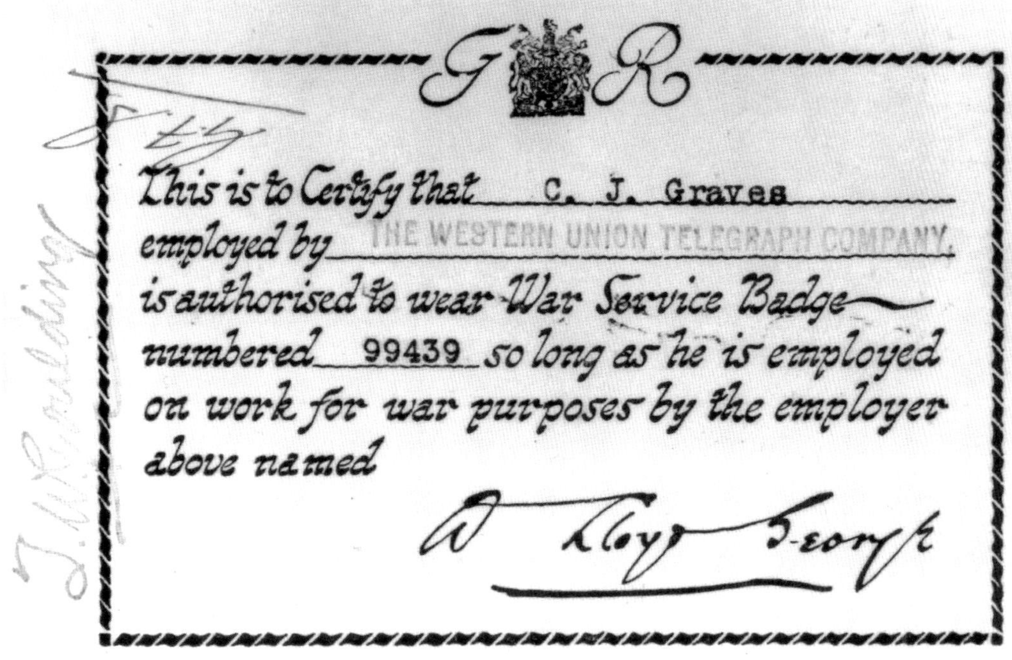

G R

This is to Certify that C. J. Graves
employed by THE WESTERN UNION TELEGRAPH COMPANY.
is authorised to wear War Service Badge
numbered 99439 so long as he is employed
on work for war purposes by the employer
above named

D Lloyd George

Entry pass which had to be shown at the military checkpoint outside the Station

Arthur Hearnden, Bill Hearnden's grandson, recalls how as a child returning from school , he had always to show his pass. More then once the guards (for fun) refused to recognise the pass and marched him into the guard room to be identified. He says that he was always terrified. The guards mostly on a rest tour from the front, took their duty seriously. Robbie Graves, James Graves's great grandson, tells that his father and grandfather's duty hours generally did not coincide. The younger man always made a point of intercepting the old man, Arthur James, as he came on duty. The effects of a lightning strike while he had been working at an instrument at the Duxbury Station, USA, had caused total deafness. There was always the danger that he would not hear a challenge from the guard on duty and so it was advisable to see him through the gate.

Some station staff, probably early in the First World War. Arthur Hearnden identified those that he could remember and these are given in the numbered table below

1	Ed O'Sullivan	7	O'Sullivan
2	J. Condon	8	Shanahan
3	J. Shanahan	9	A. Scaife
4	F. Mackey	10	W. Scaife
5	Eugene Ring	11	H. Sullivan
6	Tim Ring		

Although the censors had departed, there was a large Post Office technical staff involved at the stations. This was later increased for reasons which will soon become obvious. So that towards the end of the war there were eleven at Valentia, three at Ballinskelligs and six at Waterville. Nevertheless, in spite of their official title and function, the Station staff at Valentia always referred to them as censors and although there a was fairly cordial relationship (Robbie Graves remembers two 'censors', May and Arnold, who were friendly with his father), they maintained their distance.

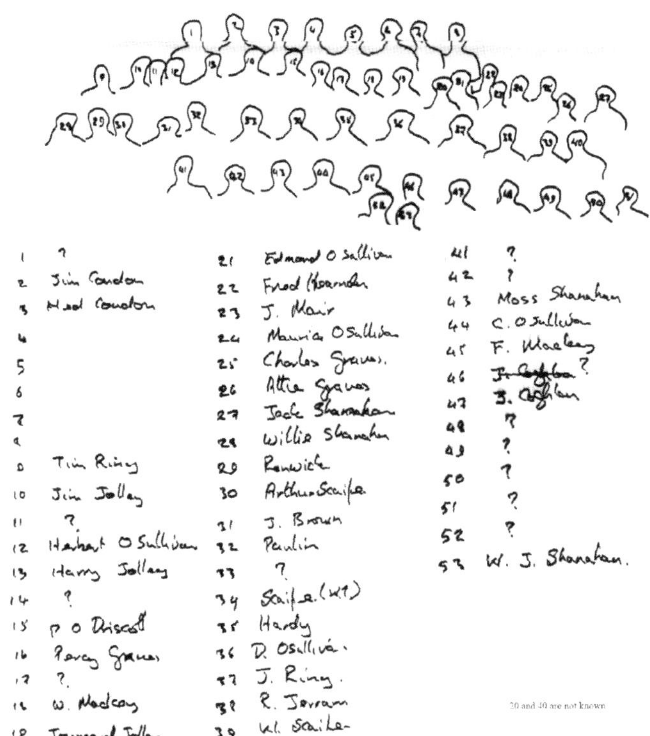

Station staff in a picture that must be before Easter 1916. The key was constructed by Arthur Hearnden. Tim Ring (No 9 in key) can be seen standing on the left, second row from top. The seated man with arms folded next but one to Horatio Hardy (Superintendent) is Jeremiah Ring (No 37 in key).

Of course the other way in which the war impinged on the staff at the cable stations was the sheer volume of work that had to be handled. For security reasons most Government traffic went by cable, although there was a wireless station at Valentia. It seems that many highly confidential messages, rather then being transmitted over land wires, where they could be tapped, were brought to Valentia by courier. Robbie Graves remembers "Moore the Courier" and how one night, when all was blacked out, they could see him signalling from the mainland with his Aldis lamp. His father signalled an acknowledgment and then informed Hardy, the Superintendent, who arranged for a boat to bring him over.

A large volume of traffic required a large staff. Hearnden and Graves family recollections suggest that there was a total of about 200 employed at Valentia. On its own this might seem an enormous number and hard to believe without corroborating evidence. The fact is that extra accommodation had to be built and if the reports of the Waterville Censor are taken at face value, the number may not be too far off the mark.

The staff had to work long hours. Twelve hour shifts (6am - 6pm and 6pm - 6am) were the norm. Bill Hearnden writing to his daughter-in- law, Nan, in July 1917 said:

> 94 being down must come as a relief to Fred (his son) and his long hours - I am afraid there won't be much chance of repair while the war is on.

He was quite right. It was not repaired until after the war. However it was the fastest Valentia cable and had the fault occurred six months earlier, the consequences for the war effort could well have been critical.

One outcome of the war was the complete change in attitudes between the cable companies. There was now enough work for all and the important thing was to keep the lines open. In 1915 CS *Faraday*, belonging to Siemens (the British Company), rerouted the western landing place of the cable it had laid in 1881 between Sennen Cove (Cornwall) and Canso (Nova Scotia). The new landing place was Bay Roberts, Newfoundland and the corresponding reduction in cable length would have meant an increase in speed and therefore traffic density. However, all did not go well. On the return journey to England, the ship attempted to effect a repair to the same cable in mid-ocean. This was unsuccessful and it was forced to return to England on 8 December 1915, and to continue the effort the following spring. From here on cable company ships were contracted to undertake repairs for their competitors. Perhaps the best known cable ship of all time, CS *Lord Kelvin* was built for Western Union to replace the ageing *Minia,* which was not in fact scrapped until 1922. The *Lord Kelvin* was a frequent caller at Valentia and was in active service right up to the close of the Station in 1966.

There were two important telegraphic events during this period which in their different ways altered the course of modern history. The first definitely involved Valentia and the other, which brought America into the War, may well have done so. The news of the Irish Rebellion of Easter 1916 was first publicised in America. The efforts by members of the

Ring family in getting this news past the censor has never been sufficiently acknowledged, except in official documents, and these have only recently been declassified. The Report on Cable Censorship during the Great War (PRO DEFE 1 350) devotes several pages to the subject and it is perhaps best to quote the essence of the text:

> During the early stages of the war, the general spirit of the staff at the Irish cable stations (of which the great bulk were of Irish origin at Valentia and Ballinskelligs and about half at Waterville) was sympathetic to the Allied cause. Some months before the Easter 1916 Rebellion it became known that a large number of operators at Valentia were Sinn Féin supporters.
>
> The Ring family, twenty in number, connected by relationship or marriage, formed an important element in the life of the Station. They included a number who were senior supervising officers.
>
> The Censorship authorities were unaware of any problem; there were no Censors there, but the Station was under the control of the Waterville Censor. There was of course the Post Office technical staff.
>
> Some days before the rebellion Eugene Ring sent an irregular message over the cable to Heart's Content. This was detected by the Post Office Checker (Dickie according to other sources) and reported to the Superintendent. The message did not arouse suspicions, as it merely asked the operator at the other end if he wished to buy a bicycle. It is obvious that this was a trial message intended to test how tight the security system really was. The fact that it was detected confirmed to them that it would be impossible to use the cable directly for the transmission of their message.
>
> Shortly before the Rebellion, a message was sent by Tim Ring using an assumed name to an address in New York. It was not sent from the Cable Station but from Valentia Post Office[*]. The message 'Tom successfully operated on today' was passed as an ordinary private message by the censors in London.

With the publication of the news in New York, it proved impossible for the authorities to hush the matter up, and America, not yet in the war, was able to focus full attention on the Irish question. The Report states that the New York address "was subsequently discovered to be the offices of the Irish Extremist Movement". The message had in fact been sent to

[*] Popular reports say that the message was dispatched on the instructions of the Republican organiser, Austin Stack, from Fermoy Post Office. This author is inclined put more credit in this version. Except for the fact that the Valentia post mistress, Miss Cremin, was his aunt, Ring would most certainly have aroused suspicions by using an assumed name in his own post office.

the housekeeper in the home of a former Fenian, John Devoy, who was active in organising Irish matters in America

Eugene Ring was dismissed from the service for contravening regulations on the passage of private messages. Together with his brother, Tim, he was arrested on 15 August and held under the Defense of the Realm Act. Company records indicate that Tim was released on 1 May 1917 and applied to be reinstated. Under pressure from the authorities he was appointed to the Accounts Dept. in the London office, where he remained until 1 January 1920.

The military in Ireland wanted all cable staff with Irish sympathies, particularly the Rings, to be replaced by operators in the service of the Government. Western Union were prepared to acquiesce to these demands but only if the Post Office or Army Signals Corps were able to make up the loss in manpower. As neither could provide the necessary staff of experienced operators, things remained as they were.

The Irish continued to be a problem for the security forces. When the Company found it necessary to transfer some of its Irish operators to Penzance, there was a flurry of official activity. Security was strengthened and three additional Post Office operators were drafted in as scrutineers.

The other event, which may have involved Valentia, but certainly involved one of the Western Union stations, was of even greater international significance. By the beginning of 1917 Britain was almost drained of all the resources that would permit the continuation of war. Germany was not much better and war-numb Europe was in a stalemate situation. Thousands of men could be sacrificed at once for the acquisition of a few yards of enemy trenches, only to lose them within a short while. Throughout all of this America had remained neutral. True, she was sympathetic to Britain and was sending military and other supplies. The Kaiser had also been attempting to create an American diversion for many years. From the beginning of the century the Mexicans and Japanese had been nurtured, so that in the event of a war in which America might become involved, a Japanese incursion into California and a Mexican incursion into the States north of the Rio Grande would keep the US fully occupied. These schemes had not yet borne fruit and Germany, playing for time, had an unwitting ally in the person of the President. Woodrow Wilson, fervently neutral, not even swayed by the sinking of the *Lusitania*, was trying desperately to arrange peace between the belligerents in Europe. He was prepared to allow all sorts of concessions to achieve his aim. The German ambassador, Count von Bernstoff, complained about the difficulty of communicating with his Government and obtained a concession from Wilson to use the State Department cable for communication with Berlin in German cipher. The understanding was that this route would be used for the transmission of messages relating to peace terms.

To the Germans this was a blessing. In order to accelerate the end of the war in their favour they now proposed to institute unrestricted submarine warfare and it was of the utmost importance that American attention should be diverted. They set about sending instructions through Bernstoff to their missions in Mexico. Up to the time of the Presidential concession there had been two routes of communication: the wireless from Nauen in Germany to Sayville, USA, which was subject to American censorship, and the 'Swedish roundabout'. This latter method involved the use of Swedish diplomatic lines of communication. From the point in time when the British censorship authorities had relaxed some of the rules on the use of ciphers and codes, it had been possible for neutral governments to communicate with their missions without scrutiny. Berlin had simply to hand their encoded messages to the German mission in Stockholm. They were surrounded with a few Swedish code groups and sent via the UK across the Atlantic, where Swedish envoys handed them over to their German counterparts.

In January 1917, after the German high command had taken the decision to initiate unrestricted submarine warfare, the Foreign Minister, Arthur Zimmerman, sent a telegram to Bernstoff in Washington. This was for his information and for forwarding to Eckhardt, their Ambassador in Mexico. In order to be sure of its arrival, Zimmerman sent it by the three routes of communication that were available. The message was first intercepted by the British wireless monitoring station, and its significance was not lost on Admiral Hall and his staff at Room 40. It was subsequently intercepted on the American cable and the 'Swedish roundabout'.

Before disclosing the contents of the telegram to his superiors, Hall set himself the task of arranging to procure a copy of the telegram as sent between Washington and Mexico. This would mean that in the event of disclosure, the Germans would be less suspicious of leaks in their communications system close to home. He was anxious that when revealed to the Americans, it should have the greatest impact with the least exposure for Room 40. The final step before official publication of German intentions was to ensure against the possibility of Presidential disbelief. If Wilson demanded proof, this could be found amongst Western Union records. It took some time and effort to prise a copy out of Western Union, but this was eventually achieved. The story broke in the press on 1 March 1917 "Germany seeks alliance against US. Asks Japan and Mexico to join her. Full text of her proposal made public".

The effect on the American public was instant. It was further assisted by the sinking of three American ships on 18 March and within a month America was tipping the balance of war in Europe.

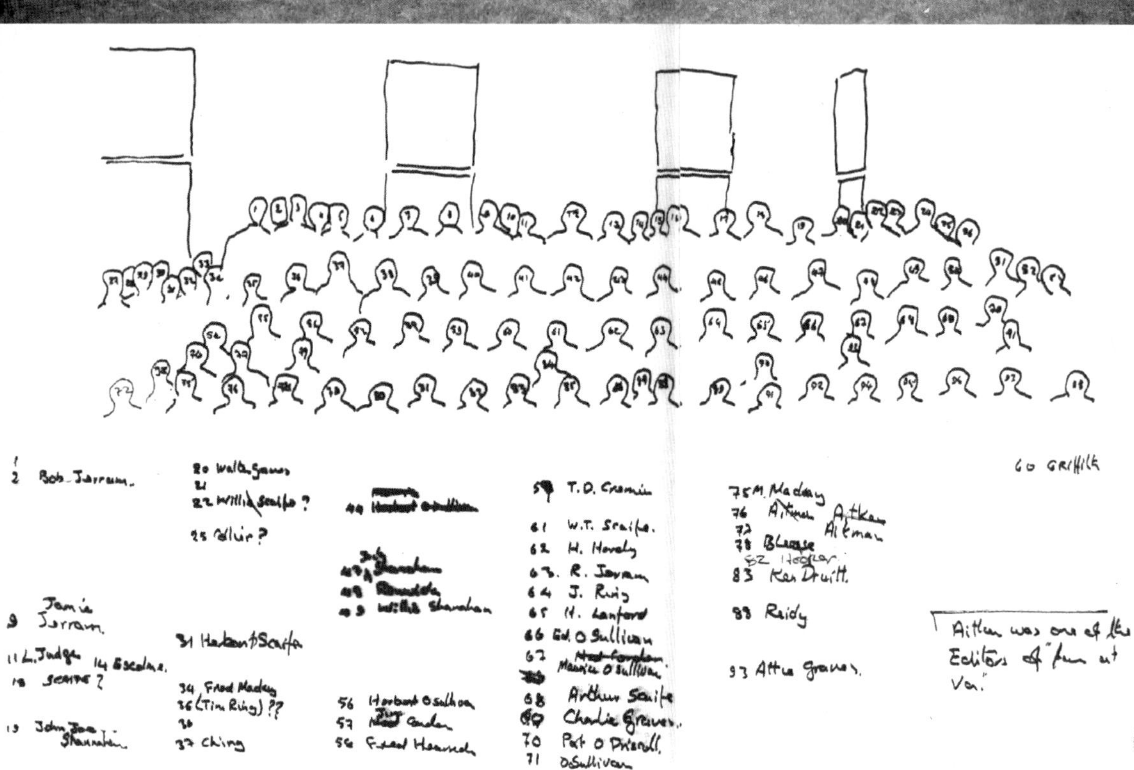

Some staff, possibly after 1916. Key derived from the memory of Arthur Hearnden. Tim Ring is absent, although his father is present, seated third on the left of the Superintendent. The person, between Hardy(No 62) and Ring (64) is Robert Jerram who later became Superintendent.

The importance of Room 40 and the cable intercepts was such that even today much of the information has not been released. Admiral Hall, who died in 1943, was prevented from publishing his memoirs, in case they might reveal the extent of British knowledge of foreign codes and ciphers. It is interesting to note that Barbara Tuchman's book on the Zimmerman telegram (published in 1959), while quoting American documentary sources as well as personal reminiscences of British people who were involved, does not contain a single item of British documentary origin. Even the secret report on telegraph censorship contains only a few dry paragraphs relating to Sweden's questionable neutrality in the Roundabout Affair. To conclude discussion on this episode, one might speculate about the contents of the messages carried by Moore the Courier. Perhaps the contents of his bag on the very night when Robbie Graves had seen him signalling from Renard's Point were about to change the course of modern history.

It must be remembered that most of the people supplying recollections of Valentia at this time would have been quite young. Only the more striking occurrences remain in memory. For Arthur Hearnden and Robbie Graves one of these occasions was the celebrations at the end of the war. Everyone went wild. The staff of the Station removed everything wooden that could be spared and lit a huge bonfire on the lawn. The frigates, which had spent the war protecting the cables, sent up salvo after salvo of star shells, while people danced happily around the bonfire.

It took several years for the effects of peace to percolate through. The Treaty of Versailles, reparation, etc. resulted in plenty of traffic for some time. In May 1919 W.T. Scaife took over as Superintendent with Robert Jerram as his Assistant. It is interesting to note that Scaife's initial salary as Supt. was less than that of James Graves in 1890.

During 1919 the Post Office supervisors were withdrawn, and the number of staff at the Station began to diminish over the next few years. This was not always a painless process; many like Walter Graves[*], grandson of James Graves, were made redundant following the introduction of new equipment such as the Brown-Allen relay. To offset this, there was a series of substantial pay rises over the next few years. The Superintendent's salary in 1920 was £750 pa. The diffusion was, however, a two way process. While many moved away to telegraph service in other parts of the world, others like Tim Ring returned again to the island.

During 1920 an operator named John Moores was transferred from the Commercial Cable Co offices in London to the Waterville cable station. He quickly displayed an entrepreneurial talent. The author's late father-in-law, Arthur Hearnden remembers Moores travelling round

---

[*] Wally was one of the first people employed to operate Italcable's new line from Anzio to New York via Malaga and the Azores.

by bicycle selling items that were otherwise in short supply. He was eventually to found the Littlewoods football pools and retail empire.

Returning to the wider scene for a few moments, we encounter some matters that still have a resonance today. While the censorship of telegraphs and mail during time of war might seem justified, it may appear strange to some that the interception and surveillance of all traffic continued in peacetime. To paraphrase from James Bamford's book "The Puzzle Palace":

> . . . The actions of Britain's Royal Mail Openers seems to have been directed by an earnest and faithful desire to adopt that course "which appeared to be necessary, either to promote the ends of justice or to prevent a disturbance of the public tranquillity, or otherwise to promote the best interests of the Country." Wisely, there was total avoidance of any discussion on how or from where the government's authority to raid the mails derived, except to note that it had been doing it for a very long time.
>
> This authority was later used to justify the interception of telegrams and, shortly after the first telephone exchange was established in England in 1879, telephone conversations. Just how far that authority extended was discovered on December 16, 1920, when Western Union President Newcomb Carlton shocked a US Senate subcommittee with the revelation that the British government secretly required that his company turn over to Naval Intelligence every incoming and outgoing telegram received in Britain. The charge was subsequently confirmed in testimony by John Goldhammer of the Commercial Cable Company and Clarence H. Mackay of the Commercial Cable Postal Telegraph Company. "In July, 1919," explained Goldhammer, "when British censorship ceased, we were ordered (by the British Government) to turn over to them all messages passing between our own offices, 10 days after they were sent."
>
> Minnesota senator Frank B. Kellogg, chairman of the subcommittee, asked Carlton whether he had ever challenged the British on the matter. "We thought that it would be misunderstood and we thought it was a source of irritation to American cablers," the Western Union chief responded. "They replied that they wanted those messages only for such supervision as might give them an inkling of pending disorders within Great Britain, I assume having to do with Irish unrest, and also to do with the Bolshevik propaganda."
>
> Chairman Kellogg then pressed Carlton as to whether there was any way to prevent the British actions. "No; we cannot prevent it," he said, but added that it was not for want of trying: "We took rather a firm stand about delivering them. We said that we would not be responsible for receiving and delivering messages destined to the United States unless we were certain that they are uncensored, so far as their contents are concerned, and we would prefer to shut down our cables as a protest if this thing was being done surreptitiously. We could not put it much stronger than that . . .

> "And I went so far as to instruct our vice president in London not to deliver the messages to the British Government and see what would happen. The British Government then explained exactly what they did with the messages; they gave us their assurance that the messages would not be deciphered; the reason why they wanted to keep general track of who was cabling; and, furthermore, they guaranteed that no information of any kind would be issued."

Caught off guard by the embarrassing revelation, the British embassy sent off a letter denying the charges directly to Senator Kellogg rather than through the State Department, a serious breach of diplomatic protocol. At the same time, the British government came up with weasel-words which satisfied the Americans, while they continued as they always had done. More on this later.

The Irish Question

One thing, however, that would not go away was the Irish question. It polarised people and created great difficulties for the Valentia staff, who were either British or of British extraction. As individual people they were generally liked and respected, but as a group they were lumped in with "the British oppressors". They in turn had their own problems with the emerging new order. They believed in the Crown and the Empire. However could the Irish people manage to govern themselves? With Home Rule, their standards of living were going to be much reduced. Not unnaturally many gravitated towards "safe ground". Some returned to England. Those with fewer ties to Britain moved to Belfast, but this was, for the moment, a gradual process.

In the larger sphere of trans-Atlantic communications both the British authorities and Western Union saw Irish independence as inevitable and took steps to hedge their bets. Western Union contracted the Telegraph Construction and Maintenance Co. to lay a series of new cables. In 1918 Valentia was connected with Penzance and a further cable was laid in 1923. Of that, more later. This meant that the Company could sacrifice speed and bypass Valentia, if for any reason political changes made it unusable.

The British Government, realising the wartime importance of trans-Atlantic telegraphy, decided to enter the field itself. By arrangement the Western Union lease on the Direct Cable Co's operation was terminated. The Company was purchased by the UK Government in 1920 and operated by the GPO. The cables which ran from Ballinskelligs to Tor Bay and Rye Beach (Nova Scotia) had been diverted during the period of Western Union tenure into Halifax, Nova Scotia, and Harbour Grace in Newfoundland. With the political uncertainties, in 1922 the GPO decided to divert the cable into Penzance and the Ballinskelligs Station[*]

---

[*] The Irish Post Office maintained the building on a caretaker basis and this author believes that it was still there when he visited Ballinskelligs in 1970. There is nothing left of it now.

was closed forever. Document S3157 in what was the Irish Cabinet Paper Office in Dublin Castle has a communications map of the area at the birth of the Irish Free State. The details can be summarised as follows: Valentia (VA) which had four cables to Newfoundland and one to Penzance (laid in 1918) had a landline to Cahirciveen and a landline through Cahirciveen and Killarney to the outside world, all on its own set of poles. It also had two landlines on a separate set of poles which it shared with ID and WV. The document shows overheads to Ballinskelligs (ID) and Waterville (WV), but does not show the cable for the ABC telegraph to Ballinskelligs. Waterville had two cables to St John's and two to Canso, Nova Scotia. It also had one to Fayal (Azores), one to Le Havre and three to Weston-super-Mare. Its landlines comprised two wires on poles which it shared with ID's wire and one of the Anglo wires.

The gloom of war had been followed by the euphoria of peace. This in turn led to the uncertainty of the 1919-1921 period. The dreaded Black and Tans[+] had visited the island for one day and had done their share of shooting up the place. There were then the Treaty talks and the Final Treaty with its special provisions for telegraphy, which will be mentioned later. The Treaty created strong divisions amongst the Irish. There were those such as deValera who believed that there had been a sell-out; nothing less than 32 counties was acceptable. The formation of the Free State only made things worse, and within a short period the country was engaged in a bloody civil war; ample proof for those who believed the Irish incapable of governing themselves.

Independence arrived and on 25 June 1922 Heart's Content received a message from J.F Richards, Superintendent at Valentia from 1922 - 1934:

> Please note starting immediately westward Irish traffic handed us direct by Free State Government will bear Itq prefix Vc. See our Vc 143 russcornostlms

The last sentence of the message contained code to which only the station superintendent had access and could well have covered some sensitive issue such as the re-routing of traffic to London for surveillance.

The outbreak of the Irish Civil War in June 1922 led to a general breakdown in communications throughout Ireland as telegraph wires were cut. Although an inconvenience, the cable stations were relatively unaffected, since there were direct underwater connections to Britain from Waterville and Valentia. The Island turned out to be largely sympathetic to the Republican (de Valera's) cause. At the outbreak of hostilities it was taken over by the IRA and was effectively cut off for two months. There were between four and six people actively

---

[+] Officially the Royal Irish Constabulary Reserve Force, but so named on account of the colour of their uniforms, this was largely comprised out-of-work veterans who were not subject to strict discipline and were hated for their arbitrary attacks on people and property. Their commanding officer, Henry Hugh Tudor, later took refuge in Newfoundland and died in St. John's on 25 September 1965.

involved. Between them they had one rifle and one uniform, although according to Arthur Hearnden, the uniform only fitted one of them. The rifle was passed on as one came on "duty".

Picture reported to show some of the Republicans who interrupted the operation of the station

Several of the Western Union management came from Ireland. The traffic manager in New York W.J. Blenheim had been Superintendent at Ballinskelligs some time before 1910 and was obviously worried. On 7 July 1922 he received assurances via Newfoundland:

> Id says no trouble there whatever, and Waterville have not heard. Everything quiet there or would have heard.

Nevertheless, he was still concerned. On 22 July he put out a request:

> When opportunity occurs please ask Richards personally on cable how conditions are both at Va (the station) on the Island and at Id. Have there been any disturbances in the neighbourhood?

The following day he received the reply from Richards:

> There is absolutely no trouble here or at Id up to now and none in the immediate vicinity, but cannot say when the Free Staters may visit Cahirciveen, then there will be trouble there, but do not anticipate any here. Only trouble seems to be a shortage of provender. Local shops give notice that they are not going get (sic) any new supplies after end this week. They say that they can't afford to stock goods to be commandeered by IRA. That's the only doubtful thing here. Id absolutely quiet too. If any sign of trouble I have only to wire Admiralty and they will have destroyers here within six hours.

In spite of these reassurances, the Station diary at Heart's Content (HC) in Newfoundland indicate that things started to go wrong on 6 August 1922:

6th		
	9.45pm	Lost Va's coming slip. We ask him keep it running
	11.20pm	Va to Co. Office dismantled here. No engine or any power
7th		
	1.25am	We again see Va
	1.38am	Va says will call later, don't call us
	5.04am	HC sees someone calling but unable get them see us
	5.30am	We get following 'Have joined 94+Pz and 74+2Pz direct'
	5.31am	Va says 'We can't read you, if you get what I said send some dots, if not, reversals'
	5.34am	(Va asks) Is Mr T or Mr B there? HC answers - no
	5.43am	(Va says) Have put thro Pz direct. Is there anything doing. Sig- Rds (signed Richards) HC waiting Pz call on 2Va and 4Va. Rds advised
	5.46am	Va- HC -OK, keep on trying - GB (goodbye) Keep watch
	6.46am	Va calls HC - calls x and sigs k
	6.47am	Va - HC Is Mr B. down yet? ford replies - Yes, here. Ford
	6.48am	Va - HC - What's your second christian name Have taken every precaution - HC replies Nathaniel
	6.50am	Rds sends report to Mr B., which forthwith copied and handed A.T.M. (American Traffic Manager)
	6.54am	Va - HC -GB will call later.

The IRA was known to have sympathisers amongst the staff at Valentia, and this last exchange indicated concern that there might also have supporters in Newfoundland. This message indicates that others were trying to use the line, but whilst unobserved, Richards joined up two of the four Atlantic cables directly to the shorter Valentia-Penzance sections. This gave the Western Union some operational capacity and was to prove very useful later.

On 9 August there was a flurry of messages between Newfoundland and London:

> Following just received- Tell Mr B. IRA have been here again and smashed all our accumulators. Think help should be sent. Threats of worse tonight. Richards.

There was an immediate reply from New York to Newfoundland:

> Thanks. From now on please have some one watching on 3Va as well, with normal magnification so that weak signals could be read.

This instruction was so that any messages sent from Valentia on their normal chatting cable (laid in 1880) would be picked up immediately. Other managers joined in. Tranfield[*] in Newfoundland asked whether the Western Union President, J.J. Welch, had been informed. Blenheim replied affirmatively, and asked that sensitive messages be forwarded in code.

In addition to the superintendent's clandestine use of the cable, there were individual acts of bravery. Tommy Smith is shown below in his battery room at a much later time. When the IRA handed him a bomb with orders to destroy the engine room of the station he said "I am a small man with a big family and shoot me if you wish, but I will not do that." The engine room was smashed, but no bomb.

Tommy Smith checking batteries

A member of staff who had been present at Valentia recounted to the author that at 2am on 9 August the Republican censor, armed with a revolver, took away some components from the

[*] A brother (?) of F.T. Tranfield, ex of Valentia and later Waterville (grandfather of Jack Tranfield, of whom more later), Charles Tranfield was Superintendent at Heart's Content during this period.

power plant. Next morning five Republicans arrived and moved the staff into the mess. A group was then taken out and set to destroy the batteries.

Picture of the damaged batteries

The intention may have been to inhibit international communications but there may also have been a more immediate reason. As Free State forces were gaining there was a developing paranoia. Late one night there was a knock on the door of F.W. Hearnden's house, which was situated next door to the Rings' house. The light[*] in his front window had been seen to flash. He or Wallie Graves, who was living with the family, was obviously communicating with the enemy on the mainland. In fact it had a fault and kept flickering, but it took a considerable time to convince the IRA of this fact. Nevertheless, the destruction of the Station electrical supplies would ensure that communication with the enemy did not happen.

On 14 August Richards was in touch with Newfoundland:

> Please code following to A.T.M. for E.T.M. (Eastern Traffic Manager R.J. Paulin in London). Monday. No change, do you require any operators for temporary transfer to Ldn (London) or Pz (Penzance), if so can spare as many as you wish. Only difficulty be transportation and would suggest chartering steamer and land them suitable port your side. It will be some time before we can resume operations here. Will endeavour to keep you

[*] The electrical supply at the station was also used to provide lighting in the staff houses

> fully advised but have to be very discrete in speaking HC owing to IRA spies. Personnel all well but getting anxious re provender.

Paulin replied on same day:

> Doing nicely at Penzance with some assistance from London and in no immediate need transfers from Valentia at present. To charter steamer this purpose expensive job, also doubtful whether get any one undertake from here under present conditions.

Nevertheless the staff were now receiving much encouragement per wire. Blenheim asked Tranfield in Heart's Content to use caution when next speaking to Richards:

> but give him my regards and say he is by no means forgotten.

The Western Union President instructed Richards that if emergency requires:

> Do not hesitate to charter vessel on your own initiative or do anything else you deem advisable for the welfare and safety of staff.

If the state of war could be ignored, the entire event was a wonderful enforced holiday. According to Arthur Hearnden it was a most beautiful summer with ample opportunity for sailing and fishing. The staff were merely required to visit the office once a day and sign in. He said they made good use of it. Together with their father (now promoted to Assistant Supervisor) the boys had a splendid time fishing and sailing.

On 15 August Richards was able to report:

> Things gradually improving. Free Staters gradually wiping out opposition. Shouldn't be surprised they be down to Cahirciveen today or tomorrow the way Reps, are fleeing.

On the 17th Government forces were reported to be within 16 miles. As the Free State forces took control of the mainland in the vicinity of Valentia, there was also much Republican frustration over the apparent involvement of the British Navy, whose frigates sent up star shells to light the hills during night actions. It is told that one day one of the IRA on the island left headquarters (a commandeered Coast Guard hut near Knightstown) and moved down the shore until he was closest to one of the naval vessels at anchor. He then discharged a shotgun at the boat before returning to HQ. There was no immediate reaction, but on the next tide, anchor was raised and the boat drifted gently down the coast. As it passed the Coast Guard building, all guns were turned towards land causing general panic, not only to the Republicans but also to other people who lived in the vicinity and who would have been in the direct line of fire.

There was also time to look towards the future. On 18 August Paulin in London wired Newfoundland requesting that they relay the following message to Richards:

> Is firm James Shiel, solicitor Ctg query Cvn (Cahirciveen) still in existence and can they be recommended as agents for pursuing our claims for damages against Irish Government?

There was a reply the following day:

> James Shiel not available to act for Company being District Councils solicitor dealing with all claims on their behalf. Recommend P. Rosney who promises and very anxious do all possible in our interests. On receipt quick reply will go Ctq interview Rosney and retain his services

On 20 August Richards sent a message to Paulin in London (via Newfoundland):

> Walsh (Superintendent at Waterville) paid me a visit yesterday. Apparently they are worse predicament than we. Their engines absolutely out of action, even bolts in concrete beds taken away and all oil feeds smashed. Batteries all sulphated. All cables long (to America) and short (to Britain) earthed at Wv (Waterville). All personnel OK and he would be obliged if you would inform his headquarters.

Liberation

The Free State forces arrived at Valentia on 23 August and according to the late General M.J. Costello the invasion force comprised four chartered ships, two for landing troops and two to provide covering fire, if needed. There then began a mopping-up operation interspersed by heavy counterattacks. This account is somewhat at variance with an eye-witness account.

> . . . During our isolation, the island had been kept from starvation by the arrival of various provisioning boats. One of these was the Spillers boat and on a particular midweek day, we were out in our boat, when we saw it coming across. We thought it somewhat strange, since it had called by two days previously. We thought it even more strange when it sailed on towards Alter Rock, (situated between Atlantic Villa and Glanleam House). Suddenly the boat, now out of sight of the Coast Guard hut, was full of Free State soldiers. We headed back for home as fast as we could row. The Republicans, disturbed at their breakfast of bacon and eggs had made off across the fields. As we arrived at our road, we met the Free Staters rushing along. It was a hot day and they were dripping with sweat on account of their great coats. They took these off and left them in a heap by the side of the road and told us to look after them.

The following day Richards wired Newfoundland with a message for Blenheim and Welch

> Arrival of National troops yesterday solves food problem. We will now be able to get supplies from Cork by *Nobby*. Reported Cvn captured early this morning, this will also help considerably. Three wounded nationals brought here last night from Cvn assault.

On 25August 1922 he was able to report that a magneto had been borrowed, batteries were now being charged and their generator was again operational, so that the married quarters would be able to have two lights per house from dark till 12.30 each night. He also responded to various queries by saying that there were 26 Free State soldiers billeted at the ex-Coast Guard station on the island and that on the previous evening the Station had been put under guard. This consisted of five soldiers, one NCO and four privates, one of whom was a local who would assist with the identification of staff. The size of the garrison seemed to increase steadily. A later message said that there had been a requisition of blankets, pillows and mattresses for 28 men from Station stock and an official receipt had been received. The number had further increased by the next day as Richards reported to Newfoundland:

> For Welch - Tell him status at Id* normal. There has been no attack there but Id has no landline outlet as yet. Cable is OK. Re Wv we hear that place has been occupied by nationalists but fancy can't afford to leave more than 50 men as garrison. They are chasing the enemy. Part of the F.S. troops are those who landed here. Heard this morning that Commercial were starting get things going again as quickly possible . . . Re Va things now normal and we have garrison of about 35 men; constant guard kept on Station. There are few, about half doz irregulars left hiding here but Nationals expect capture them shortly.

Counter attacks

Counter-attacks were expected, but first news of any in Western Union records was an enquiry form New York to Newfoundland:

> Trippe - Tranfield Aug 29/22
>
> Press message from London News Association, Nyk (New York) - Motor-boat loaded insurgents landed Va attempt wreck Va station. Cut one wire, then driven off. Any news from Richards. Rush reply

There is no record of a response from Richards in Valentia and no record of a cut cable. There is some mention of an incident involving the Valentia wireless station, but this was thought to be an attempted looting incident. "... Three unarmed men endeavoured break in some buildings but flew on approach of National scouting party. Firing was done by Nationals".

Independent evidence suggests that Erskine Childers did organise a boat party to cut a cable. This is discussed in more detail below.

On 30 August Newfoundland records make further mention of the Valentia wireless station, which seemed to have escaped most of the troubles. There were suggestions that until the damaged cables was reinstated, incoming traffic could be passed to Valentia wireless for re-transmission to Lands End in Cornwall. There was some disquiet about this from the wireless station which claimed that they had great difficulty communicating with Lands End; presumably they sent all messages by telegraph.

On 5 September Richards wired Newfoundland:

---

* Remember that Id was the code for the Ballinskelligs station, just as Va was the code for Valentia

> Serious ambush last night on Wv road directly opposite our station, casualties both sides. Reported Irregulars landed on Island opposite Portmagee. Great activity all night. More later.

His next message recorded that one free State officer and two soldiers had been killed:

> . . . Irregulars not known but believed to be heavy. No troops landed on Island.

More action followed.

> Pz Su-Ldn - Supt. Va via Pz +HC Sept 10th/22
> Following for Captain O Donoghue, Valentia-
> Quote - Kenmare captured. Commandant (Scarteen) O'Connor dead. Inform Foley at once. Irregulars boarded the *Shark* at Kenmare yesterday evening and are advancing towards Waterville and Cahirciveen wearing the uniforms of the captured garrison. Valentia Wireless Station is to get in touch with the nearest destroyer at once to hold up the *Shark* and take all on board prisoners. Signed Commandant Griffin[*], Cable Station, Waterville.

This was relayed to Valentia and shortly afterwards there was another message, this time from Capt. M. Hegarty at Waterville:

> Please deliver Valentia Wireless Station - Please inform Capt O'Donoghue to communicate with Capt. of destroyer and tell him to hold up the *Shark* and all on board, or any other steamer as the irregulars are disguised in our uniform (sic) coming from Kenmare to Cahirciveen or Waterville.

The outcome of this is uncertain and there was continuing anxiety. The next day Blenheim was in touch with Tranfield in Newfoundland:

> "... speaking him (Richards) this morning, quote - Business Kenmare serious and whether we can cope with it or not remains to be seen. British destroyer left Va this morn (sic) and joined outside by another. Will keep you in touch everything, unquote".

The garrison on the island remained worried and the following day (12th) there was a message:

> Richards-Tranfield for Foley Please ask CCC say to Walsh Wv (the Superintendent there) "quote Commandant Griffin in Va waiting for the goods to arrive unquote". This was answered with a message from the Superintendent at New York to Richards: "Following received via Commercial Cable Co quote to O/C national Troops. Va reinforcement of fifty me have landed at Wv. Advise O/C Cahirciveen, signed D. Hegarty".

Valentia then enquired from Waterville:

---

[*] According to the late Gen. M.J. Costello, known to his military colleagues as 'Speccy' Griffin.

> For Capt. Hegarty quote- are the fifty men that landed still in Wv? Did the Cumbria land any troops in Kenmare. Had the Cumbria troops on board leaving Wv and where was she bound. Send by wire communications from Chief of Staff. Reply immediately. Signed O/C Va island unquote.

One of the most fascinating features of this series of messages is the way in which the new army of the Irish Free State was using this technology to maintain contact under very difficult circumstances. The headers at the top of many of these telegrams indicate that they were sent from Waterville to Weston-super-Mare and thence to London, where the Commercial Cable Co passed it over to Western Union, who relayed it to Bay Roberts (Newfoundland) via Penzance. It then travelled overland to Heart's Content and from there back to Valentia. Other service messages during this period confirm that the military commanders were able to maintain contact with the Chief-of-Staff in Dublin by similar ingenious routing.

In spite of the troubles some people seemed to get around. F.T. (Jack) Tranfield, in a discussion with the author reported that he had a safe-pass from both sides. During his travels he encountered Erskine Childers:

> Where are you going? - where are you from?- asked Childers. On being told, he said
> Oh that's OK - they are an American Company aren't they?

Another person who appears to have had a pass from both sides was James Dennis who had joined Valentia in 1917. He had a motorcycle and he told the author that during his travels, he too met Childers.

Although things had started to subside, the IRA visited Ballinskelligs Station on 20 Sept. They enquired whether there was communication with Valentia. During the next day the cable linking these two stations was cut. There is every reason to believe that this was masterminded by Childers.

Map of the route of the ABC cable between the Valentia and Ballinskelligs stations. The point 'x' marked on the map shows where Tim O'Shea retrieved a section of this cable, shown below

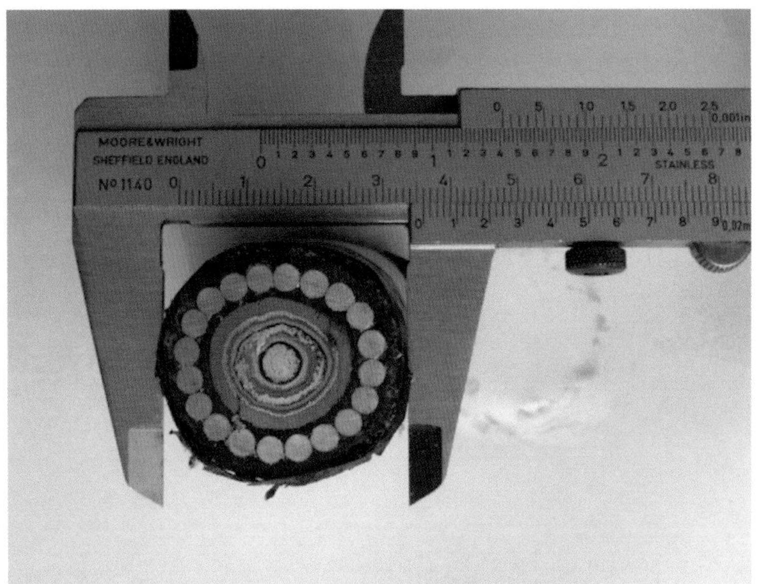

Dimensions of the ABC cable given to the author by Tim O'Shea

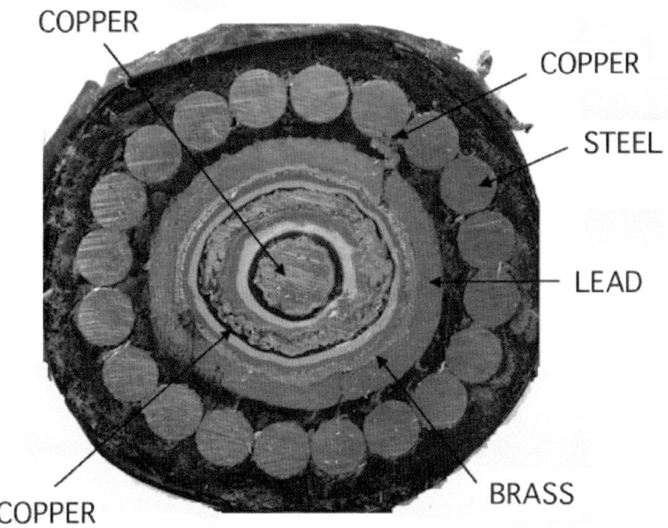

Composition of the various parts of the ABC cable

There was also an exchange of messages on 24 September:

> S. Va - S. Wv
> MOVF for Comdt Griffin quote Reported here desperate attempt to be made on Waterville tonight. Look out. Cahirciveen attacked last night-signed Comdt O Donoghue Valentia.

This may have been a timely warning which thwarted an attack. Certainly, there is no record of further disturbances at either Waterville or Valentia.

A return to guarded normality

The claim against the Irish government was also progressing and it looked as if Western Union was going to seek a full compensation. On 17 October Blenheim asked Tranfield in Newfoundland to prepare a statement of all expenses incurred at Heart's Content since August 7th due to the non-operation of the Valentia station and the interruption of the Irish cables and Irish landlines. This statement was to include any overtime, as well as salaries, bonuses, house allowances, etc. of all cable traffic employees whose positions had been rendered redundant on account of these events. This statement was to be made up by months and was to be continued each month until normal service was restored.

It would appear that the Valentia Station was back to normal by 1 December 1922. It was reported that local army conditions were favourable and that there was a 24 hour guard on the Station with additional men at night.

An outsider's view of happenings in Valentia in 1922

Another witness of these events was the Irish yachtsman, Conor O'Brien. In his book "From Three Yachts" he records:

> On this earlier passage conditions must have been quite favourable, for I remember nothing whatever about it; early in the evening we got in to Valentia, and, seeing that the alternative was cooking for ourselves, went for dinner to what was then the best hotel on the West Coast. So long had the placards "Do not talk to Strangers" disappeared from the railway carriages that I forgot this advice was equally sound in an Irish and in a German war, and I did talk to a stranger. I haven't an idea who he was, or whether he was, as I expected, afterwards shot as a spy; he rather seemed to have bought the hotel, but nobody knew anything about him. He was amusing, and not so obvious as some spies I have met, but evidently he aroused the suspicions of the Free State Army, which was in possession, for an officer and a sergeant came off to the ship late at night and accused us of being in conspiracy with him. Apart from him, all appearances were against us; we had been in Brandon last night, and that was a Republican stronghold; we came in a yacht, and it was well known that all hostile acts were performed by or with the aid of yachts; there were two Englishmen in the yacht, and Childers, who was an English yachtsman, had recently cut the cable here (Valentia lives on its Cable Companies). Altogether a black indictment, to which I could offer no defence, for it was two years since I had last seen anyone connected with Valentia and, according to the common practice, I might have changed the colour of my coat several tunes in that period. I was a good deal relieved when the gentleman left, for he was very rude and rather drunk, and emphasized his arguments by banging the muzzle of his revolver on the cabin table; which spoiled the table and is, besides, a dangerous trick, because if a gun goes off when the muzzle is choked it is liable to burst. But when they left they took my dinghy, ostensibly to land some men at Waterville, where she was broken up, as I could have told them would happen, and I never got any compensation for her.

Chapter 12

Decline 1923-1945

Although the years of turmoil had come to an end, they were not followed by tranquillity. Rather there was a sense of uncertainty at all levels. At the Station, the Protestant staff were unsure of how they might fare in a Catholic-governed country; not too badly in general, but things were never going to be the same again. Added to this, technological advances as well as economic depression meant that fewer staff were now required and the number of employees declined steadily[*].

The first of the technological advances was the automation of retransmission of messages over landlines. Up to this time it was customary for operators, mostly juniors, to manually perforate messages onto tape using mallets. Tape from several operators was then gummed together and passed sequentially through a high-speed transmitter. The introduction of the Kleinschmidt perforator, which was essentially a typewriter keyboard with a tape output, speeded up the process considerably. Another innovation was the Heurtley hot wire magnifier. Heurtley is believed to have visited Valentia in 1917. The basic idea was to pass a current of the order of milliamps through a fine platinum wire. The centre of the wire was suspended across the end of a very sensitive galvanometer which responded to the incoming signals on a cable. If the deflection was to the left, as shown in the picture below, then a portion of the wire entered a stream of warm air. As a result of the temperature rise the resistance of the wire went up and hence the current in the platinum wire went down. If on the other hand, the galvanometer was deflected to the right the platinum wire would enter a stream of cold air which would cause the resistance of the wire to go down and hence the current in the wire would rise. Thus the device formed an electromechanical amplifier whose output was directly related to the minute deflections of the receiving galvanometer.

---

[*] Indeed, there are rumours that some of the damage inflicted on the Station had been done by disgruntled employees who were about to be replaced by new technology.

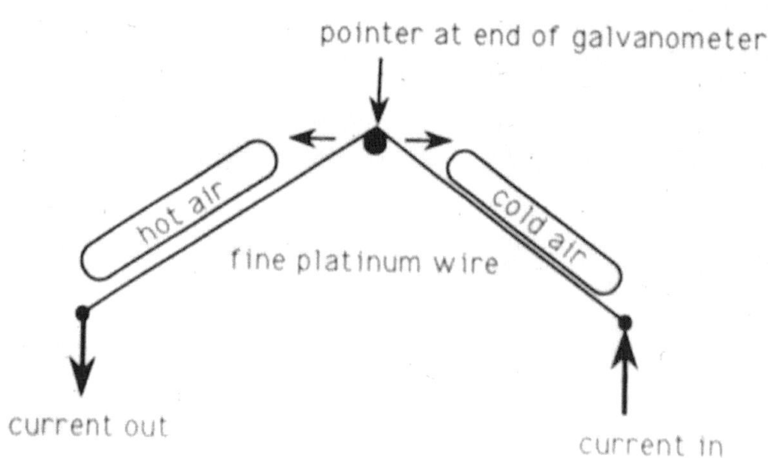

The basic concept of the Heurtley hot-wire magnifier

Of course, although the concept appears both simple and ingenious, the practical implementation was much more complicated and the photograph below shows a magnifier as might have been used at Valentia.

Heurtley hot-wire magnifier as supplied by Muirheads

With this and some other signal improving apparatus it was not long before telex on ocean cables became possible. However, telex needed a slightly different signalling system. Up to this time a form of Morse had been used, but the byte-length in Morse is variable (dot = e, dot-dot = i, dot-dot-dot = s and so on). The introduction of the Murray code and later the ITA-2 code meant that all characters had exactly the same byte-length (see below).

A	●	●			
B	●			●	●
C		●	●	●	
D	●			●	
E	●				
F	●		●	●	
G		●		●	●
H			●		●
I		●	●		
J	●	●		●	
K	●	●	●	●	
L		●			●
M			●	●	●
N		●	●		
O				●	●
P		●	●		●
Q	●	●	●		●
R		●		●	
S	●		●		
T					●
U	●	●	●		
V		●	●	●	●
W	●	●			●
X	●		●	●	●
Y	●		●		●
Z	●				●

Western Union and the British Government were uncertain how things would develop following Irish independence; whether in fact the Free State would manage to govern itself in a way which would present minimum hindrance to the existing economic order. As already mentioned, provisions for alternative lines of communication were made.

Nowhere perhaps was this sense of uncertainty more acute than in the 'collective mind' of the Free State Government itself. The administration was new and well aware of the pessimistic views about its long term ability to govern. Above all they had a Treaty document, with its provisions not always crystal clear, which they strived to adhere to.

A social gathering aboard *HMS Waterhen*[*] during a visit to Valentia

The Treaty, while allowing a high level of independence, sought to minimise the effects that any transfer of administration might have on British security. Memories of some of the naval problems of the First World War were probably responsible for the insistence by Winston Churchill and Admiral Sir David Beatty that certain strategic ports and anchorages as well as airfields were to remain under British control. They are listed in the Annex to Appendix D of the Treaty. Section 2 of that Annex contains the following words:

> "A Convention covering a period of five years shall be made between the British and Irish Governments to give effect to the following conditions:
>
> (a) That submarine cables shall not be landed or wireless stations for communication with places outside Ireland be established except by agreement with the British Government: That the existing cable landing rights and wireless concessions shall not be withdrawn except by agreement with the British Government and that the British Government shall be entitled to land additional submarine cables or establish additional wireless stations for communication with places outside Ireland....."

[*] HMS *Waterhen*, built in 1918, was transferred to Royal Australian Navy in 1933. On 29 June 1941 it was bombed while acting as a ferry for men and materials during the siege of Tobruk, and sank the following day. There were no casualties.

Thus the Irish could collect landing revenues and grant licenses but only with British approval. and Britain maintained overall control (to the author's knowledge this situation remains unchanged). It is not clear what was meant by the opening words relating to a Convention. Perhaps it was an example of Churchill's brilliance at confusing his opponents. By creating ambiguity Britain was maintaining all options. Perhaps wireless would take over. On the other hand technological advances might lead to such cable speeds that Ireland would become irrelevant in the North Atlantic cable network.

Confusion there certainly was. Cables and cable landing rights were of little importance compared to other pressing matters, that the new Free State Government had to face. With little or no guidance on the exact meaning of the relevant Treaty provision, they considered the matter from time to time. Irish Cabinet documents of that period indicate the degree of frustration which must have existed, particularly for the cable companies.

In early July 1923 Western Union applied for permission to land a new Valentia-Sennen (Penzance) cable. It could be argued with the benefit of hindsight that this was amongst its long term precautions. Irish landlines could be bypassed, and, if necessary, Newfoundland could be linked directly to Britain, omitting Valentia. This of course would have resulted in a considerable reduction in cable speed. The Commercial Cable Co. had made an application to land an Azores, Waterville, LeHavre cable a month earlier. The Executive Council of the Irish Government considered the matter but deferred any decision pending enquiries into the existing conventions and contractual forms, under which the British had hitherto granted such licenses. There were no developments during July, the best cable laying month. By the end of August both companies were pressing for decisions. This elicited a response on 31 August to say that the matter was in the hands of the Attorney General, who was away at the League of Nations. It would not be possible to grant even a provisional permit, as the Executive Council did not meet until mid September.

Following correspondence with the British Board of Trade and GPO, the Irish Cabinet now felt confident enough to state on 23 October 1923 that all applications for landing licenses would first have to be submitted to the Imperial Communications Committee, who would impose such conditions as the UK Post Office and UK Board of Trade advised. On 28 October it was reported to the Cabinet that both companies had landed their cables, claiming that they had informal permission from the British Post Office. This led to all nature of recriminations. In answer to questions the Post Office claimed that they had spoken by telephone to Mr MacDunphy (Assistant Secretary to the Executive Council) and that he had said that in view of the urgency, he saw no objection to the Post Office granting provisional permission. A pencilled margin note on the original document simply says "not true - Mac D". The Council was incensed but felt powerless to do anything about it and the matter rumbled on during January 1924. Meanwhile the Attorney General was still sitting on the question. It was not until 1927 that he stated that legislation would be necessary before licenses were granted, but he failed to specify just what that legislation should be. A curious coincidence during this period features the further involvement of the Bewley family in trans-Atlantic communications. The Attorney General in arriving at his decision had sought legal advice from Charles Bewley KC, a son of Henry Bewley[*], who had perfected the method of extruding gutta percha and had invested heavily in the original ventures.

In the middle of all of this the various government departments within the new administration started to wrangle amongst themselves. The establishment of the Free State required a completely new civil service. Many officials of the British Administration remained on, special provisions being made to ensure their safety and standard of living. Many expatriate Irish working in the Colonial Service returned to take part in the new venture. The new service was stable, responsible and essentially incorruptible, although many of the administrative regulations and procedures were arrived at by gentlemanly agreement in the clubs of Dublin and not by public debate in the Dail[**]. Each government department was still cautiously feeling its way and determining the extent of its authority. As the landing of cables was a matter of communications, *Post & Telegraph* felt that it came under their sphere of operation. *Industry & Commerce* claimed that as Board of Trade powers over the foreshore were now vested in their Minister, *Post & Telegraph* had no part in the matter. A letter of August 1926 suggested that it was the Minister of Finance who should grant licenses, and so it went on.

The companies suffered badly from this indecision. As an example, during 1924 the Commercial Cable Co. wished simply to alter the landing place of three of their cables from a point near Hotel Waterville to a point one mile to the north west. The Company may not have had much joy from the delays that they had to endure, but the map, which accompanied their application is informative, as it gives some idea of the complexity of their inshore cable network at that time.

Only once was this indecision turned to advantage. Western Union wanted a line of their own between Penzance and LeHavre. Their application to the British Government was turned down. In its way this was understandable. There was heavy Post Office investment in cross-Channel cables and with competition from wireless there was now spare capacity. As an alternative Western Union, and indeed the Commercial Cable Co., were offered leases on special circuits on Government cables to France. This would be in addition to their leases on circuits to Belgium, Germany and Holland. Western Union claimed that they wished to

---

[*] Charles Henry Bewley (1888 – 1969) later caused much difficulty as Ireland's ambassador in Berlin from 1933 to 1939.

[**] This approach required a high degree of conservatism with consequent slowdown in operation. Even in the 1922 Civil War it produced a very stable climate. In fact the first government lasted 10 years and was replaced by the Republican Fianna Fail party, which remained in office for 15 years.

expedite New York-Paris traffic and that exclusive lines on Government cables did not get around the problem of landline delays.

An application to the Secretary of the Free State Department of Post & Telegraph was received in July 1926 from S.J. Goddard, European Vice President of Western Union. It was clear that the Company wanted to circumvent Britain's refusal to grant a landing license. They proposed that one of the Valentia-Penzance cables would become a Valentia-LeHavre cable. The British authorities approached the Irish Government and requested that the application be refused. The request was based entirely on inter-governmental cooperation and it was stressed that the British could offer no objection under the Treaty. The Irish, in reply, stated that the Western Union application appeared quite reasonable and that it would be difficult for the Irish administration to refuse it unless better objections were presented. Thus the Valentia-Le Havre link came into existence when the Penzance cable was cut just outside British territorial waters and diverted to its new terminus.

It could be said that this period of uncertainty led both the British Government and the cable companies to omit Ireland from their considerations in the technological developments which were about to take place. Ireland was ideally situated as a landing place and even if it did require extra relaying through the country and across the Irish sea, there was the advantage of shortest distance. There was also the advantage of tradition. No modern communications engineer would have sited a station at Valentia, and yet it was the only suitable place in 1857-58. Once there, there was the investment and commitment. Removal to the mainland would have required effort, the relocation of staff and offices, and the disposal of the existing site, not an easy task in a rural area. Perhaps the same could have been said for Ireland itself. The extra distance to the English mainland would have resulted in a reduction in cable speed and under different circumstances the status quo might have been maintained. However, technological changes were about to accelerate the marginalisation of Ireland from international cable communications, a process that had started before 1922 and would continue until recent times.

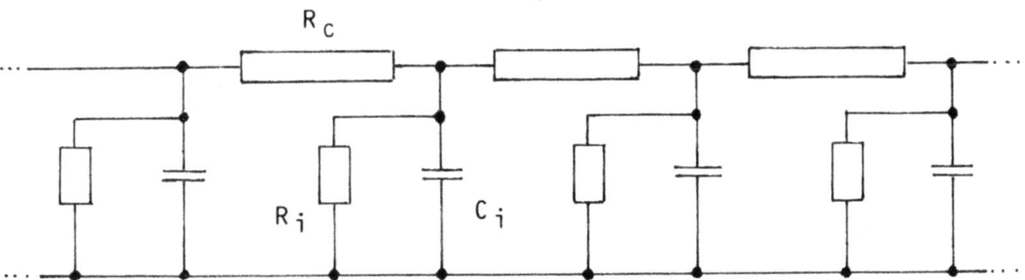

Early models for a submarine cable: The model used by William Thomson (Lord Kelvin) comprised the conductor resistance (R_c) and the capacitance across the insulator C_i. It subsequently became obvious that the resistance of the insulator played a major role.

During a previous chapter reference was made to the work of Oliver Heaviside and his suggestions for a distortionless cable.

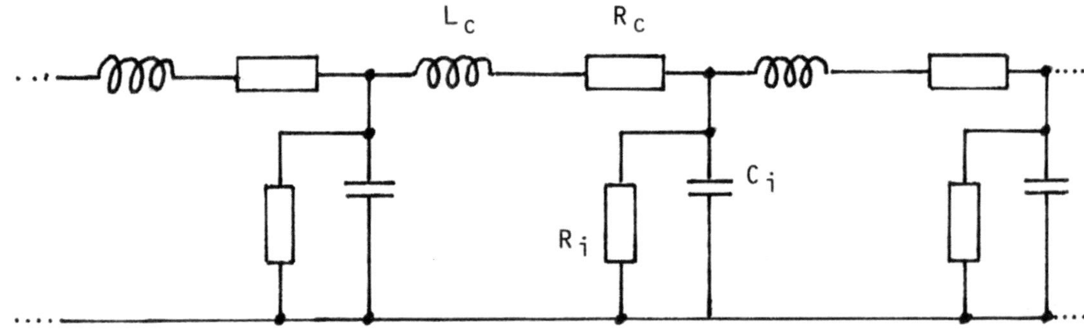

CABLE IS 'DISTORTIONLESS' IF $\frac{R_c}{L_c} = \frac{I}{R_i C_i}$

Heaviside's model for a submarine cable: This model includes inductance L_c in the conductor. For early cables L_c was not sufficiently large to achieve the distortionless condition. Hence cables were slow

The first attempts to produce 'loaded cables' as they were called, were made at the beginning of the 20th century. A series of inductance (Pupin) coils were inserted along the cable. Continuous loading of cable was first achieved by the Danish engineer, Krarup, using a helical winding of soft iron around the cable core. These were used in short cable lengths between Germany and Denmark. The Telegraph Construction and Maintenance Co. laid such a cable across the Straits of Dover in 1911-1912, and there was a definite improvement in signalling speed.

The true potential of loaded cables was not realised until the invention of Permalloy by the Western Electric Co. in America. This high permeability nickel-iron alloy had just the right characteristics. Tests were undertaken at Bermuda in February 1924 on behalf of Western Union. They were so impressed that an immediate order was placed for a New York-Azores cable, which was laid in September of the same year. A further cable was laid between New York and Cornwall via Newfoundland in 1926. Valentia was now bypassed. A Newfoundland-Azores cable was laid in 1928 and used different weights of loading throughout its length. Mumetal, not Permalloy was used for loading and the phenomenal speed of 1500 words per minute was achieved.

The loaded cables using Permalloy had been constructed by the Telegraph Construction & Maintenance Co. using tape brought in from the United States. Once they became aware of the developments and the potential for the future, they set to work on their own loading material. They were one of the first companies to employ a group of research scientists and "the Chemistry" as the laboratories were called, was a forbidden area for most employees. Mumetal, a copper-nickel-iron alloy was the result and it eventually superseded Permalloy in most applications. It was generally produced as wire and wound helically around the central conductor.

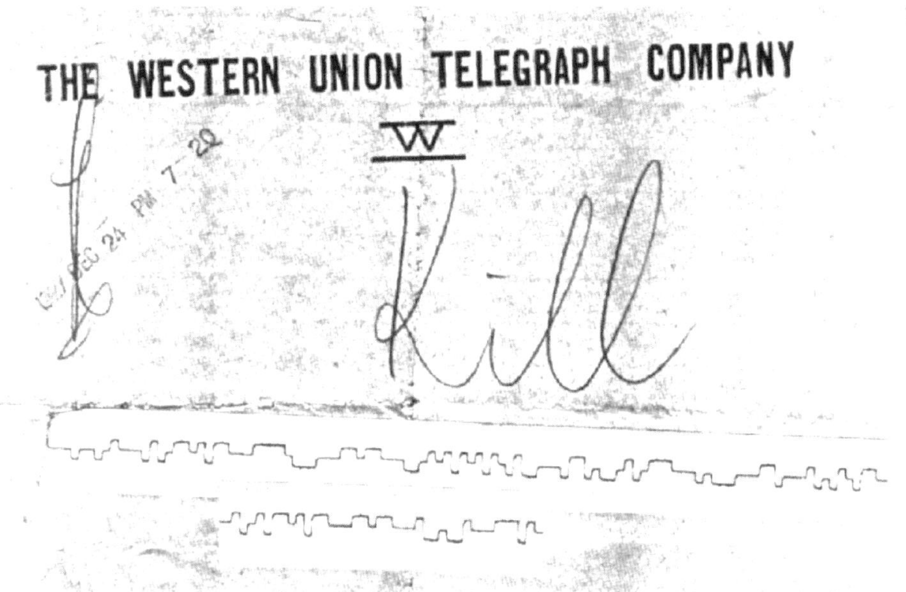

Christmas greetings 1927 sent by Walter Graves in Anzio to Marshall Killen in Horta
Literal translation of cable code: TTE KIL HO II MERRY XMAS TO U AND ALL II WG SN
Long translation: "transmit to Killen Horta (start of message) MERRY XMAS TO U AND ALL (end of message) WG (sender) (end of transmission)"

One disadvantage of loaded cables was the fact that they had to be operated in simplex. It was not possible to produce a loaded artificial cable for duplex working. However with the increased traffic capacity and the effects of different time zones, this did not create too much of a problem. Indeed Western Union's 1928 line from Bay Roberts in Newfoundland to Horta in the Azores was able to relay traffic to/from Spain, Germany and Italy. It is interesting to note that Walter (Wally) Graves , grandson of James Graves and one of the Valentia operators who was replaced by telex in 1922 was involved with the establishment of the new Italian cable from Anzio to the Azores via Malaga in Spain. In 1985 this author discovered a Christmas greeting telegram which Wally had sent to his friend, Marshall Killen* in the Azores amongst a collection of Western Union papers that had been lodged at the Maritime History Archive in Memorial University in St Johns, Newfoundland

* Killen, an Ulster man, was Western Union's station electrician in Horta and was the Superintendent there at closedown

The beginnings of telephone cables

The development of cable loading may have increased traffic capacity across the Atlantic, but in the long term it tolled the knell of telegraphy. With this sort of bandwidth, trans-Atlantic telephony should be possible, at least in theory. Indeed the first moves to establish a telephone link were made in 1928. An application was made to the Irish Government in June by the American Telephone and Telegraph Co. (A T & T). Permission was requested to land cables at points in Co. Mayo and Co. Donegal for a New York-London telephone link. Their intention was to use Ireland as the closest landfall, keeping their cables as far away as possible from existing telegraph cables. They hoped to land cables in summer 1931 and one feature of their request was that all apparatus not manufactured in the Free State should be imported free of duty. Newfoundland had already granted a similar concession. The whole question of a telephone link was viewed with such importance that the Irish Cabinet received a letter from 10 Downing Street on 12 July of that year, encouraging expedition of the application. His Majesty's Government was anxious that it be undertaken under Clause 2 and offered no objection. In the event this note was probably unnecessary. The Irish Administration seems to have become more confident in dealing with such matters. They appear to have been very positive about the proposal. However the records of the Irish State Paper Office do not indicate whether landing rights were ever granted and there is no further mention of the venture.

There was to be no trans-Atlantic telephone link in the 1930's. The causes were many and not related to Irish landing rights. The cable was to be continuously loaded but instead of gutta percha, paragutta was specified as the insulator. This material had been developed at Bell Telephone Laboratories and consisted of a mixture of protein-free rubber, resin-free balata and a petroleum wax as a plasticiser. The manufacturing rights of this superior material were offered to the Telegraph Construction and Maintenance Co. who for various reasons declined. The rights were then offered to Norddeutsche Seekabelwerke, who took an inordinately long time to produce a mere 111 nautical miles of cable for the Key West-Havana telephone.

Changes in the world order of global communications

The technology might have been there (just), but there were many political and economic factors which delayed the development of a trans-Atlantic telephone link until the mid 1950's. The 1920s had been a bust-boom-bust period in the United States and in the midst of this two brothers Hernand and Sosthenes Behn set up and expanded the International Telephone and Telegraph Corporation (ITT). According to Coggeshall, until 1927 ITT was engaged in the exploitation of telephone operation and manufacture in Puerto Rico, Cuba, Spain, Mexico, Austria, Hungary and South America. In 1925 the Behn brothers acquired a large part of Western Electric's international operation. This included International Western Electric in Britain which was renamed Standard Telephones and Cables (STC), whose archive was eventually to hold many Valentia related records. It is not quite clear whether Clarence

Mackay[+] had got cold feet or simply wanted out, but in 1928 he sold his entire operation, including Postal Telegraph Cable Co, Commercial Cable Co, Commercial Pacific Cable Co and the Mackay Radio and Telegraph Co) to the Behns. Thus the Waterville cable station became part of ITT.

Then came the Wall Street crash. In the depression which followed cable communications suffered and all Western Union staff, including those at Valentia, had to take a significant cut in wages and salaries. Of course there were other factors, namely radio. Radio technology had been advancing rapidly. The short-wave service to India was inaugurated in September 1927. The beam-radio network was completed in October of the same year, and with the prospect of loss of traffic to the new medium, cable shares were in free-fall. In an effort to protect such an enormous investment Britain summoned the Imperial Cable and Wireless conference in 1928. By the end of the year there was a set of recommendations in place which effectively halted further expansion of long distance (beam shortwave) radio communications and removed some of what was already there. The Imperial 'All-Red cable routes' were preserved under a new organisation, Cable and Wireless Ltd which came into being in April 1929. The Wall Street Crash followed in October of that year. The world order was certainly changing and the Second World War was only ten years away.

Back to the Kerry stations

Having had a view of the wider political and technological aspects of telegraphy, it is now time to return to the stations in Co Kerry and see how they were progressing after their years of turmoil. In many ways their situation within the Irish Free State had yet to be regularised. The cable landing licenses had expired just before Irish independence (VA on 28 January 1920 and Wv on 31 December 1919). As mentioned earlier, the British Government had granted new licenses which were valid up to 31 December 1924. It is not clear at what point thereafter the matter was resolved, but resolved it was; the successors to Western Union were paying landing fees to the Irish Government up to 1982.

There were also technological developments. While the Valentia cables were never inductively loaded, they were used to maximum capacity in what was now largely a relay station. The station also acquired rotary regenerators and multiplexers. The multiplexer, which was based on the same concept of rotating disks as the regenerator, connected a number of transmitters in turn to the cable. The signal, upon arrival at the other end of the cable, was first regenerated and then distributed to a number of receivers. The phase coherence between transmitting operator and receiving machine was maintained by means of a tuning fork which drove what were called 'phonic' motors. Quite often the transmitter and receiver could get out of phase, even though the tuning forks were maintained in a temperature controlled environment. Regaining synchronism was one of the tasks allocated

[+] Clarence Mackay's daughter, Ellin had married Irving Berlin in 1926. She died in 1988 and her husband was 101 when he died in 1989.

to the station electrician. The process was later automated by means of an additional sector in the arrangement of rotary conductors which could advance or retard one instrument in relation to the other.

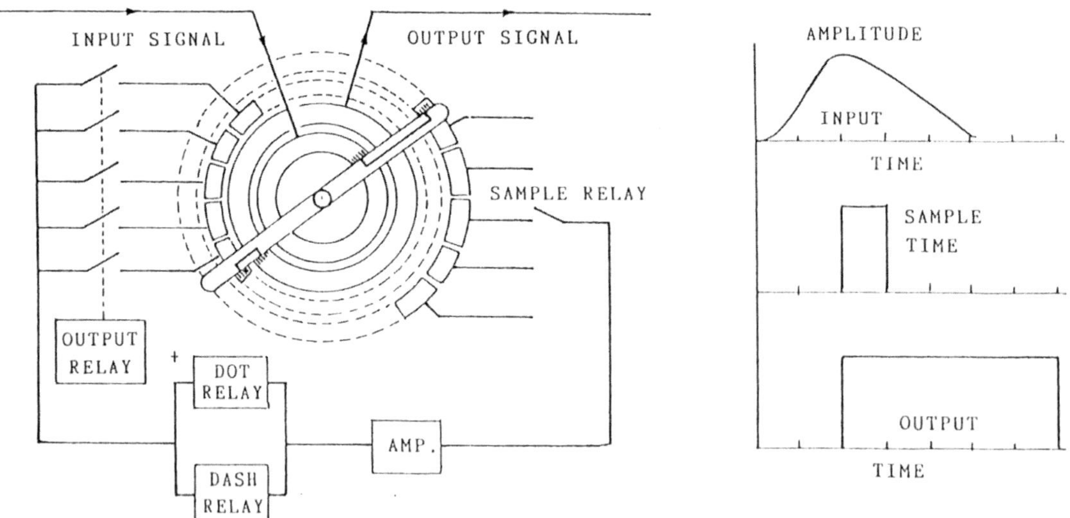

The rotary regenerator comprises a series of metal conductors in a circle with a 'spider' spinning around to distribute contacts. An incoming signal is sampled at the centre of a five-unit time interval. A switch is then closed for five time intervals to relay the polarity of the original signal.

Some of these instruments in the Operations Room of the Heart's Content cable museum (photographed by the author in 1985)

A plan of the Valentia Station at about this time is shown below. It was part of a general survey undertaken in 1926 on behalf of Western Union. It shows as well as can be recalled by those who lived and/or worked there all the different functions of the ground floor rooms. The upper floor was entirely unmarried staff quarters.

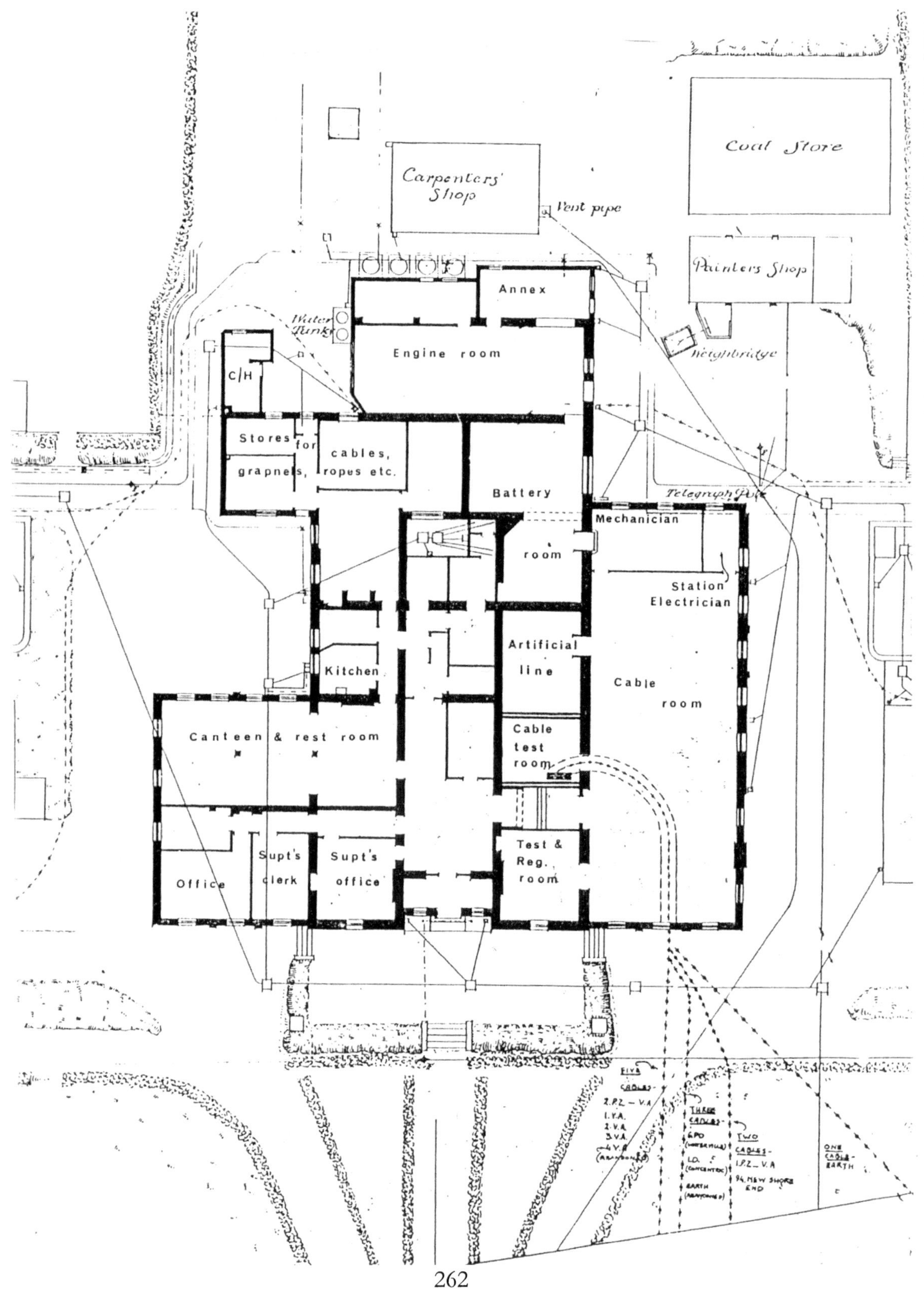
Coal Store
Carpenters' Shop
Vent pipe
Painters Shop
Annex
Water Tank
Engine room
Weighbridge
C/H
Stores for grapnels, cables, ropes etc.
Battery
Telegraph Pole
Mechanician room
Station Electrician
Kitchen
Artificial line
Cable room
Canteen & rest room
Cable test room
Office
Supt's clerk
Supt's office
Test & Reg. room
FIVE CABLES -
2.P.Z. — V.A
1.V.A.
2.V.A.
3.V.A.
4.V.A
THREE CABLES -
GPO
L.D.
(CONCENTRIC)
EARTH
TWO CABLES -
1.P.Z. — V.A
94. NEW SHORE END
ONE CABLE - EARTH

It is interesting to note the route of the cables in from the shore. Three years later the Company decided to reroute them on account of continuing anchor damage. An application was made to the Irish Department of Post & Telegraphs on 7 August 1929. Permission was requested to land six cables via Lacknabau on the north side of the island. Mindful of the delays which had been suffered by the Commercial Cable Co. some years earlier, it is interesting to witness the new-found confidence of the Government. As the distance over which the change was being effected was so small, there seemed to be no reason why the British should be consulted and permission was granted.

The move to Lacknabau was one of the best documented transfers in the history of the Station and was typical of the mode of operation of the Western Union Telegraph Company. The Engineers Final Report consists of several hundred pages of text, maps, contracts, test data, blue prints and photographs. On the recommendation of Superintendent Richards, the Company contracted the Telegraph Construction & Maintenance Co. to raise the shore ends from their existing route and land them instead at Lacknabau as show in the map.

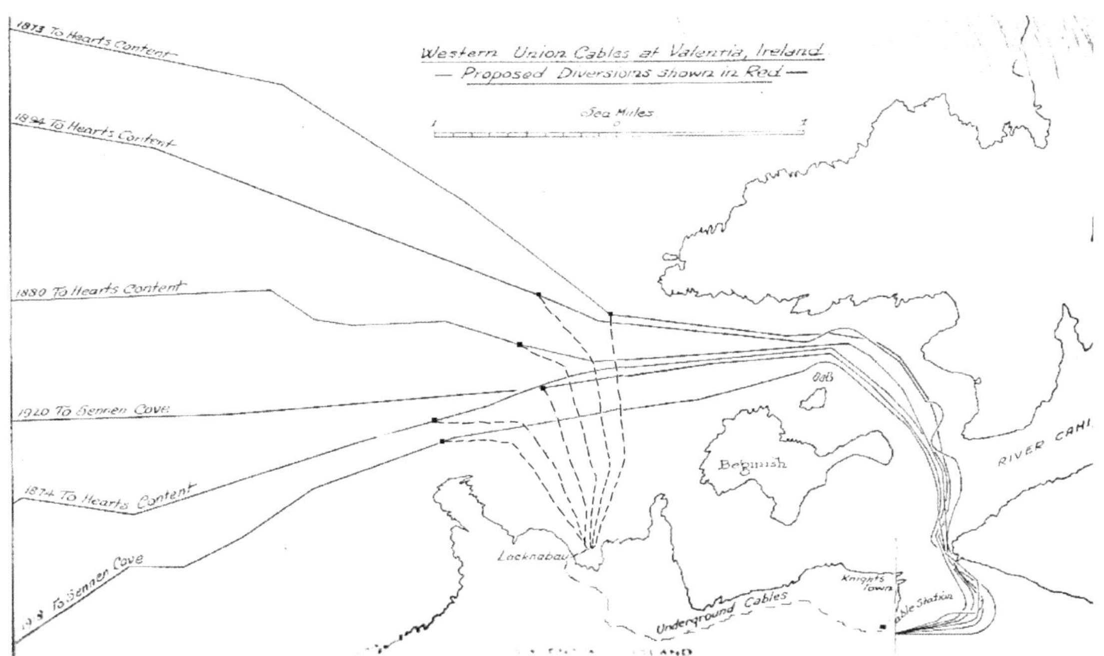

Lacknabau diversion. Solid lines show the original cable routes, while the dashed lines show the proposed new routes. The diversion required trenching to carry the cables from the cable hut at the landing site to the Station

Extensive surveys had shown that the approach was over a relatively rock-free bottom. The transfer also required the construction of a cable hut and the laying of approximately two miles of underground cable. In arriving at this route the Company were weighing economic and political considerations against the alternative all-submarine route which would have involved laying the cable in underwater trenches. Quoting from the Report: "It was felt, on reflection, that if an underground route and cable hut at the landing were likely to be interfered with by reactionary agents*, the same risk affected also the cable station itself. This had been experienced in 1922, and although a repetition was exceedingly improbable, it was not believed that the service could be ensured against interruption merely by eliminating the proposed hut and undergrounds."

There are two interesting features about this document. It is the only place where I have been able to find any official reference to the events of 1922. Were it not for family recollections, I would have been quite ignorant of the implications of the wording in the text. The road map showing the overland route of the cable is the first direct evidence that tri-core cable was being used. This was felt to be necessary due to ground interference from the nearby Valentia radio station. One of the cores carried the message, the other two formed the short and long sea earths respectively. The shore end of each cable consisted of three servings of galvanised iron wire. At a distance of two miles from the shore the short sea earth was connected to the outer sheathing, which was discontinued at that point. The short sea earth was used whenever the cable was in transmitting mode. After another mile the long sea earth was connected to the next serving, which was then discontinued, leaving a standard deep sea cable. The long sea earth was used for receiving purposes.

Between 28 August and 5 September cables 1VA-PZ(1918), 2VA-PZ(1920), 1VA(1873), 2VA(1874), 3VA(1880), 4VA(1894) were rerouted by cs *Telconia* assisted by two smaller vessels, *Cartsburn* and *Alexandra.*

At this time the Commercial Cable Co. was also undertaking many cable changes to improve its services, but most of these were on the other side of the Atlantic. With the expiration of the rights granted to Cyrus Field's original Company, it was now possible to use Newfoundland as a landing place. The Province had undergone considerable development in the interim and it was now possible to use the cross-country railway telegraph, whereas Western Union used the more tortuous coastal route.

Records relating to staff at the station are not as plentiful or indeed as colourful as in previous times. One person who spent some time there during the early 1920s was John Emerson Merrett, and he is still well remembered. He subsequently took charge of the Company's Belfast office, retiring during the early part of the war. Many years afterwards he took up writing in a serious way. *Three Miles Deep*, one of his 12 published works, was an account of the cable history and Valentia. It was published in 1958, many years after he had access to Station documents, and is a credit to his memory. His two chapters on cable failure

* One presumes that they meant Republican activists

and ship watch during repair* have an authenticity which could only be conveyed by someone who had been involved. Merrett recounts a story about James Jolley which also indicates close cooperation between the staff at Valentia and Waterville:

> Jim lived in the Cable Station Mess but went home each weekend to visit his wife (who taught at a school near Waterville) and children, who lived on the mainland twelve miles away. It was an unwritten law that the ferry between the island and the mainland must never prevent one from being on duty at the proper time...... One night, however, when Jim was due on duty at 10 pm, he was marooned. A great gale had blown up fairly suddenly and the ferry was quite impassable. All boats were safely moored between the two stone piers on the island. After some minutes spent flashing lights across the ferry, with no answering beam from the island, Jim set about informing us of his plight. In those days there was no telephone to Valentia Island and it was no good going the three miles to Cahirciveen (the nearest town on the mainland) to call up Valentia Post Office. The postmistress would have gone to bed long since. And so Jim drove twelve miles to Waterville, where there is another cable station - that of the Commercial Cable Company. Naturally the staffs of the two companies knew one another well so Jim got ready acceptance of his request to get a message to Valentia, which he drafted. At that time Waterville had no line to London as New York was working straight through, but once an hour, London would pause on one cable to allow Waterville to send any Irish traffic to New York. During the next pause Waterville passed Jim's note to New York, where the Commercial Cable office telephoned it to the Western Union office. New York (Western Union) then transmitted it to London who in turn passed it to Valentia, just in case VA hadn't spotted it going through. In order to cross half a mile of turbulent water Jim's message had crossed the Atlantic twice and had been telephoned across the City of New York. From the time Jim reached Waterville it took a mere five minutes before Valentia received his note - less time then it took to cross the ferry.

The succession of superintendents has been mentioned before. J.F. Richards had come from Newfoundland to succeed W.T. Scaife and was at the helm during the 1922 troubles. He was also in charge during the diversion of the cables to Lacknabau. Robert Jerram came next having held the post of Assistant Superintendent for many years. 'A real old-world boss' is how many described him.

---

* Mention in Merrett's book of the cs *Marie-Louise Mackay* undertaking cable repairs gives further confirmation to the fact that there was little inter-company rivalry in this matter. It was not unusual for a Commercial Cable Co. ship, if in the area to, repair Western Union cables and vice versa on contract basis. Arthur Hearnden says that the *Marie-Louise Mackay* (belonging to the Commercial Cable Co.) was the most popular of the visiting ships.

Robert Jerram and family

The last link between the Hearndens and the Station was broken during this period. Fred Hearnden, while leaving the Station one night in 1928, slipped on the steps and fractured his hip. The bone took a very long time to mend, but more seriously the accident led to the onset of chronic nephritis, which was eventually to kill him. He was invalided out of the Company and together with his wife and family he settled in Belfast near his relatives. He died there on 5 April 1933. The link with the Graves family was still intact, but had been reduced to one person. Attie Graves still worked there and was in fact to outlive the Station.

The next two maps show the complexity of cables on the Kerry coast in the middle 1930s and their relationship with other cables in UK and the near continent.

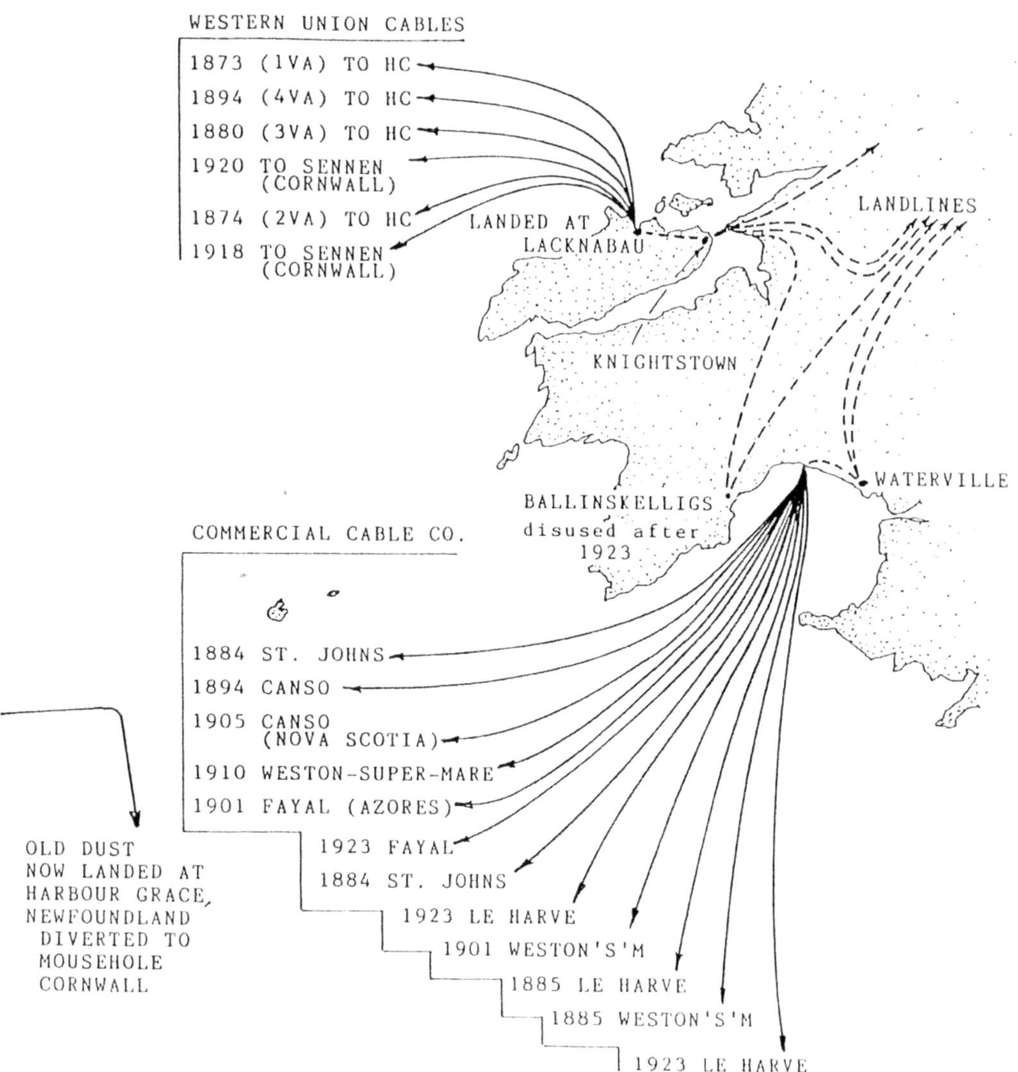
WESTERN UNION CABLES
1873 (1VA) TO HC
1894 (4VA) TO HC
1880 (3VA) TO HC
1920 TO SENNEN (CORNWALL)
1874 (2VA) TO HC
1918 TO SENNEN (CORNWALL)
LANDED AT LACKNABAU
LANDLINES
KNIGHTSTOWN
BALLINSKELLIGS disused after 1923
WATERVILLE
COMMERCIAL CABLE CO.
1884 ST. JOHNS
1894 CANSO
1905 CANSO (NOVA SCOTIA)
1910 WESTON-SUPER-MARE
1901 FAYAL (AZORES)
1923 FAYAL
1884 ST. JOHNS
1923 LE HARVE
1901 WESTON'S'M
1885 LE HARVE
1885 WESTON'S'M
1923 LE HARVE
OLD DUST NOW LANDED AT HARBOUR GRACE, NEWFOUNDLAND DIVERTED TO MOUSEHOLE CORNWALL

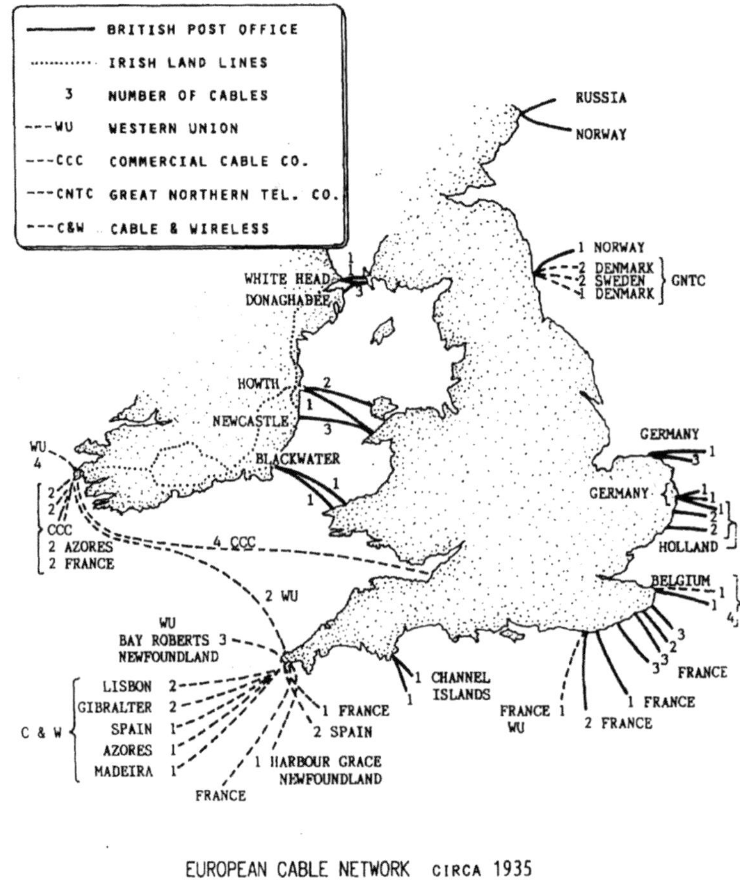

EUROPEAN CABLE NETWORK CIRCA 1935

(NOTE; THE GERMANY - AZORES CABLES HAVE BEEN OMITTED FOR CLARITY. THEY RAN FROM EMDEN THROUGH THE STRAITS OF DOVER TO THE AZORES)

Second World War

The outbreak of war brought some changes, but the overall effect was nothing like that of the First World War. The telegraph stations were put under military guard. This was more to protect them against the possibility of IRA attack. But to understand the context we have to go back a little in history. When Eamon deValera's Republican Party came to power in 1932 it refused to continue the payment of land annuities to Britain. These had been granted to Irish farmers in the 1880s to allow them to purchase their properties. Britain retaliated, and a trade war ensued where the Irish slogan was "Burn everything English except their coal". Attitudes softened in the mid '30s and by 1938 there was an agreement which resulted in the *Eire (Confirmation of Agreements Act)* being passed by the UK Parliament. Under these agreements a one-off payment of £10m was made by Ireland to close the matter on land annuities. Articles 6 and 7 of the 1921 Treaty were rescinded. In effect the 'Treaty Ports' were returned to Ireland and the name 'Irish Free State' was changed to Éire. Thus, when war started deValera declared that Ireland would be neutral. Faced with the realities of war

Britain demanded the use of the Treaty Ports, but this was refused. It can be argued that many thousands of British seamen would had been saved if convoys could have landed in the Ireland and if protective air cover could have been provided from there. The official Irish view was that if such concessions were granted for the period of hostilities, they were unlikely to be relinquished afterwards. However, one must understand the attitudes of the time and the difficult situation in which deValera found himself. In government, he was surrounded by hard-line, anti-British republicans. There was the ever-present threat from hard-line republicans who felt that deValera had abandoned his principles by going into government in 1932. This group is better known as the IRA. And finally, there were bitter memories from the recent 'Economic War.' In this climate it would have been quite impossible for deValera to do anything that might disturb his very delicate equilibrium. In fact Ireland operated a system of sympathetic neutrality and the extent of co-operation with the Allies has remained secret until very recently.

Ireland's neutrality was frequently threatened from within and without. Would Britain invade in order take back the Treaty Ports? Following the fall of France, there was a sudden realisation that Ireland had to take steps to protect herself. An 'Emergency' was declared and almost overnight the army was expanded from about 5,000 men to over 55,000 men, all volunteers. Incidentally, these were mostly provided with British-supplied equipment. Then there was the threat of a German back-door invasion of Britain via Ireland. It seems that the Irish army had two distinct command structures. The brigade structure was to be adopted should the country be invaded by Britain, while the alternative was modelled on the British structure in case both armies had to co-operate in defending against a German invasion. Just before the war there had been agreement to a request by Britain that all meteorological data transmitted by wireless from Ireland would be in Allied cipher (thus denying the Germans access to important Atlantic weather information). Fort Shannon was constructed in a strategic location, using British supplied six-inch guns to protect the Foynes flying boat base. The status of both Valentia and Malin Head wireless stations still remains unclear, but they were operated by the UK Post Office and retained UK call-signs until at least 1949. The Caherdaniel radio beacon was also of strategic importance to the Allies.

The IRA, at all times searching for an opportunity to further their aims, sought to upset deValera's policy of neutrality. A bomb in the Cork telephone exchange on the night of 12 April 1940 was one attempt. There were others, including many direct overtures to the Germans. Such activities led to the internment of known IRA activists. Aware that any appearance of instability could have brought a swift British response, arrangements were made to have vital points such as the cable stations and wireless stations guarded. For example, following discussions in the Irish Cabinet during 1940, the army provided a guard of fourteen men at Valentia. Six guarded the Station itself and four the cable hut at Lacknabau. The remainder were at the wireless station. The maintenance of a guard of this level required considerable backup. The troops were billeted in the single men's quarters on the upper floor of the Station building, and space was made available for a military canteen.

Unmarried Station staff now had to live in digs in the town. The Irish Government also had censors* on the island. It is believed however that they only dealt with messages between Ireland and America.

The whole question of the cable station's continuation was raised at an early stage in the war. The fall of France meant the loss of the Valentia-LeHavre cable, which was diverted into Penzance. During 1940 the Irish Government was approached with a request relating to landing rights. The British Government was putting pressure on the Company to divert all but one of their Valentia cables into Penzance so that they could have direct UK-US links. This was considered by the Irish Cabinet, who felt that there could be no objections on Treaty grounds. They were being left with one cable and if anything happened to that they had wireless. The Cabinet agreed to the request to divert the cables. The cables were never diverted and until now there are no clear reasons why there should have been a change of mind. One can only speculate. One immediate consideration would have been cable speed. By the time of the Second World War the Valentia cables were slow in comparison to the inductively loaded cables from Penzance to the US. The additional distance of diverted cables would have made them even less efficient and therefore less useful. Another and equally likely reason would have been the question of keeping an eye on Ireland itself. With a cable of its own to America, there was no knowing what might have been going on. With the system as it stood before the war, all Irish messages arriving at Valentia were in fact routed to London, so that they could take their place in the queue with UK traffic. Assuming that the British system of censorship was little changed from 1914-1919, all Irish messages travelling by this tortuous route could have been scrutinised.

Britain had security staff who made regular rounds of all facilities in the Irish Free state, including the flying boat base at Foynes as well as the Kerry cable stations. One of the officers was a 'Major' Quintrell., who had been a telegraph operator at the Azores before the war. The late Con. Gillman, a meteorologist at Foynes, tells a wonderful story about Quintrell. Because weather data was transmitted in cipher the cipher-room was under military guard by the Irish army, with a lieutenant in charge. The civilian coding clerks were locked in during their shift, and although they had an alarm bell close at hand, there was much concern about what might happen in case of fire. There was also a military guard inside who had an alarm with which he could call for assistance in the event of any trouble. Gillman recounted a visit by Quintrell to the cipher room at Foynes. The soldier in the ante-room was quizzed on the procedures which were to be used in the event of an unauthorised incursion. There was a bell-push.

"Have you ever used it?" asked Quintrell.

"Yes sir, once sir" replied the guard.

---

* According to Valentia operator James Dennis, these were Ernie Burrows and Bill Giles, whose sister-in-law was Kathleen O'Connell, deValera's personal secretary.

"By Jove, when?" asked Quintrell, suspecting a cover-up.

"It was a test sir" was the response

The late Gen. M.J. Costello (O/C Southern Command during the war) in an interview with the author told a story concerning another security officer, Col. Knaggs. Costello said that the cables into Waterville had been diverted, so in effect the station was not being used. He believed that the staff there would have been aware of this. He had not been told and was furious when he discovered this to be the case as he could ill afford the men to guard the station. Consequently, he withdrew the guard and mined the surrounds. What nobody knew was that he had used dummy mines. This ploy worked very well until he was rumbled late in the war when Col. Knaggs arrived on an inspection, accompanied by his dog. At some point the dog wandered onto the minefield, dug up a mine and survived.

Costello believed that a German U-boat went looking to cut[*] some Waterville cables and when they could not find them they didn't bother looking for those at Valentia. It is well known that Churchill was obsessed with the possibility of the Irish coast being used by U-boats. According to Costello, Knaggs travelled the country offering pints of Guinness in return for reports of U-boat activity. Such an offer could not be passed up and creative reporting abounded! "Of course" said Costello "Britain had a wonderful spy in the writer Elizabeth Bowen, but they would not believe her until very late in the war. We were reading every report that she sent. She was absolutely accurate and had details of the only two U-boat incursions that occurred during the War". Incidentally, the recipient of her reports in Britain is reputed to have been the writer Iris Murdoch.

Once again, it is worth looking at the wider picture to see the factors which had influence on the Irish cable stations. Brendan Scaife is the retired professor of electronic engineering at Trinity College Dublin and is the grandson of W.T. Scaife, fourth superintendent at Valentia. He grew up in wartime London, where his father worked at Western Union's headquarters. He has clear memories of his father coming home and saying to his mother:

"Churchill was in talking to Roosevelt again today."

This author has to ask why, given that he could surely have a link from Downing Street or he could use the US Embassy. Of course, the US Ambassador was Joseph Kennedy, who was not known for his sympathies to Britain and the Empire. Added to this, UK security discovered that there was a 'spy' in the cipher room of the Embassy. At the time it was put about that he was a Soviet spy, but in fact Tyler Kent was a loyal, but disaffected citizen who shared the isolationist views of most Americans. He was aware that much of the actions of Franklin D. Roosevelt (in preparing the US for war) had questionable legality. Even

[*] According to Jack Tranfield the Germans did not cut Atlantic cables early in the war as the dissemination of pro-German news in America was more important to them. In fact any details of German successes in this area appear to have been excised from the records

Roosevelt thought he might be impeached if news of his support for Britain ever became public. Aware of the extent of co-operation, including secret lend-lease agreements, Tyler was making attempts to publicise what he saw as duplicity. He had contacts with various Russians and also with known German sympathisers, who were in fact being shadowed by MI5. When unequivocal evidence was collected it was presented to Ambassador Kennedy who waived Kent's diplomatic immunity. He was arrested, tried in-camera at the Old Bailey and sentenced to seven years imprisonment.

The Western Union superintendents at Penzance, Valentia, London and Liverpool during the early part of the second world war

It is quite clear that the preferred line of communication was the Western Union line from Sennen Cove, Penzance, to Bay Roberts in Newfoundland. The Bay Roberts station, an impressive building, is now a museum, and it certainly boasts that it carried Churchill-Roosevelt traffic during the war. However, Brendan Scaife used an interesting expression when he reported to his father, "Churchill was in talking to Roosevelt again today." The cables between these two termini were inductively loaded and therefore screamingly fast by the standards of the time. Maybe there might have been just enough bandwidth for the two men to actually talk to each other. Scaife couldn't say, because when Churchill and his entourage arrived Western Union staff withdrew (all covered under the terms of the landing licence) and did not return until they had departed. Of course, if Churchill and Roosevelt had spoken via cable, then it is difficult to see how it could have been encrypted[*]. Experiments that were carried out in the US demonstrated that there was significant leakage from cables, and if a German submarine, or a surface ship trailing several miles of cable, could lay this close to and parallel with another cable, then they would have been able to eavesdrop on traffic. For this reason there was a directive in America that all secret messages sent by cable must be encrypted.

We also have some interesting stories about Irish people working cables at this time. Bob Mackey[**], who was the superintendent at Heart's Content when it closed, spent the war working for Western Union at Horta in the Azores. Walter Graves was another. He had been kicked out of Italcable when Mussolini replaced all foreign operators at Anzio by Italians. And finally, Marshall Killen had been the duty electrician and witnessed the exact moment when CS *Mirror* cut the Italian cable when Italy joined in the war. His record is shown below.

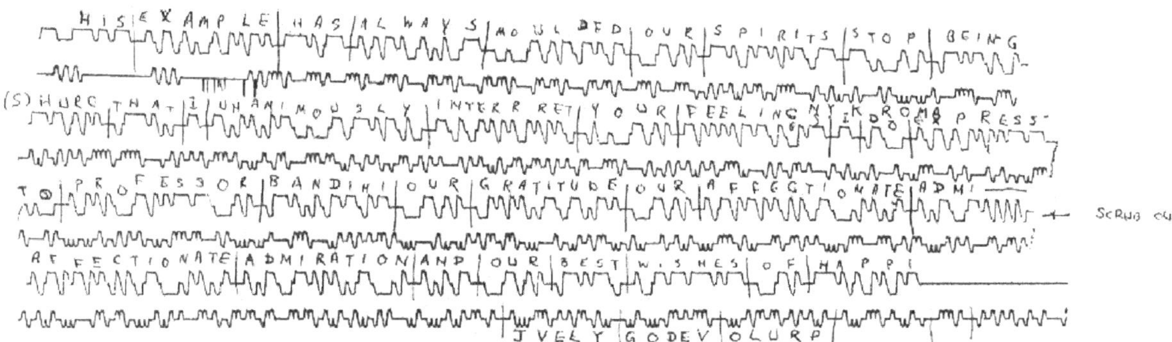

Duplex record of traffic on Italcable 10 June 1940. The upper line (incomer) is from Italy and has not yet undergone regeneration. The line immediately below it (outgoer) is from American and had been regenerated. According to Marshall Killen, who passed it to the author, the incomer was a message from the King of Italy to President Roosevelt. In the middle of the word 'happiness' we can see that the cable has been cut. America is unaware of this and encrypted traffic continues on the outgoer.

---

[*] Later in the war they did speak by wireless using a 'SIGSALY' scrambler

[**] His father had worked for a German telegraph company before the First World War and when the Kaiser visited the island of Yap in 1910, Bob and his brother were the only Europeans in the German mission school there.

An interesting story is told by Fred Mackey, who worked there at the time and was a son of R.B. Mackey mentioned in earlier chapters. According to Fred, once messages had been through the censor their wording was often altered, while the sense of the message was maintained. He gave the reason for this in a brief typed history of the Station which he had prepared. Quoting from this document: "Prior to Pearl Harbour the British cruiser, HMS *Belfast*, was severely damaged by a magnetic mine in the Firth of Forth, Scotland... A few days later a New York paper carried the information ... There was hell to pay at Headquarters, and high-rank brains were racked during many sleepless nights before investigation revealed that an astute news correspondent in London had broken through the security curtain with a very simple ruse. He had arranged with his editor to concentrate on the last word in the texts of a series of messages handed to the cable company for transmission when he sought any important new flash. When the news of the *Belfast* filtered through to London, he got to know it through a confidential source and sent several apparently straightforward cablegrams, each concluding with a significant last word.

However, whatever the official procedures for censorship were during the war, things on the ground could sometimes be quite different. Jack Tranfield reports that he was often left to do censoring in the London office. He was told "anything you don't like wake me up - otherwise stamp it and send it on." He relates that on another night he received a priority message for the Admiralty. The supervisor sent off someone on a motor bike. When he came back he said he gave it to a clerk who said "Don't bother me, put it in the basket." Later on he went with another message and said "the priority cable is still in the basket". The supervisor rang the Admiralty and was told "we must have our sleep and I suggest that you mind your own business."

It is reported that the Irish military guard and censor were withdrawn from the Valentia Station well before the end of the war. It is most likely that this was done once any IRA threat to the neutrality policy had been effectively eliminated.

Desmond Breslin, destined to become Valentia's last, second-youngest, and first Irish Superintendent, arrived on the island in 1943 at the age of 19. One of the old timers there told him that there had always been someone named Sam at the Station. As the last one had now left, he was going to have to be their Sam and the name stuck.

Chapter 13

1945-1972 The End

Following the end of the Second World War, there were several changes affecting the Valentia Station. The link with LeHavre was restored; there was no way that the French were going to tolerate their traffic going via Britain. Ireland distanced herself politically from the UK in 1948 by becoming a Republic.[*]

When Robert Jerram retired in 1943 it marked the end of a line of non-technical Superintendents; men who had been through the service as operators. He was succeeded by Francis Thornton Bateman, who had come with Richards from Newfoundland as Station Electrician.

There are reports that Bateman lost a son with the RAF during the war. War records confirm that on 27 August 1943 Pilot Officer F.W. Bateman (52433), flying a Spitfire Vb (EE768) on a Ramrod operation, did not return to his squadron (133). Circumstances of the aircraft loss are unknown. It is believed that it went down half way between Brighton and LeHavre. He is commemorated at Ste. Marie Cemetery, Le Havre (Div 67, row F, grave 12). He was 27 years old.

As Jerram's successors were men of similar age approaching retirement, their periods of tenure were in each case not very long. Bateman retired in 1950 and was succeeded by Joe Liddicoat. He in turn was succeeded in 1963 by Gus Langland whose tenure was very short. Thus Desmond (Sam) Breslin, who had been senior electrician, became superintendent in 1963 at the age of forty, the youngest person to have held that position since James Graves.

---

[*] According to James Dennis, Valentia Wireless (call-sign GHK) reverted to the new Republic on the last day of 1949. He said that just after midnight British staff at Penzance wireless tried to call them up in Irish, but it seems that nobody at Valentia wireless could speak the language.

Photograph of station staff (February 1949) and a numbered key.
1 Longland or Corbet, 2 is Bateman, 3 is Liddicote, 4 is possibly Cornish, 5 is possibly Grandfield, 6 is Whittlesea, 7 is Edmunds, 8 is unknown at this time, 9 is Breslin.

Discord between Western Union and the Anglo American Telegraph Co.

Meanwhile, the leasing arrangement between the Anglo American Telegraph Co. and Western Union started to show signs of strain. Anglo had been receiving £262,599 in annual rent. Western Union paid the Directors' salaries and made contributions to the Pension Fund under the terms of the lease. However records show that Western Union never remitted the agreed £20,000 pa to the Renewal Fund Account. This payment was conditional on the level of annual expenditure by Western Union for repairs and maintenance of cables and plant. It appears that each year the cost of maintaining the system exceeded £20,000. Under normal circumstances there was a short period between the lodgement of the rent at the bank and the payment of expenses, dividends etc. Up to 1927 the interest accrued by this means had been used to pay occasional bonuses to the ordinary and deferred shareholders. In that year, however, aware of the great changes in cable design (eg loaded cables). the Annual General Meeting of the Anglo American Telegraph Co. voted for a change of policy. A Capital Reserve Account was created to prepare the Company for any major expenditure on the reversion of its lease and all bank interest from rent was diverted into this account. However, owing to increases in income tax deductions and the introduction of the British National Defence Contribution in 1937, the Reserve Account amounted to only £29,906 in 1947.

The National Defence Contribution was to became the sticking point between lessor and lessee. When introduced in 1937, it amounted to a deduction of 5% on all profits made on trade or business carried on in the UK. Western Union took legal advice on the interpretation of the lease; the question being whether it or Anglo should pay the contribution on the rent payable to Anglo as lessors. On the basis of the advice given in 1937 Western Union admitted liability.

The UK Finance Act of 1946 rebadged the National Defence Contribution. It became the Profits Tax, and by the Finance Act of 1947 the rate was increased substantially. Anglo requested its lessees to pay the increased sum, whereupon Western Union decided that enough was enough. A contribution for the period of the war was one thing, but the Profits Tax was likely to become a permanent institution, and the rate payable by Western Union was under the control of the Anglo Co. Consequently, Western Union went to the Courts requesting a legal determination of their liability under the wording of the lease. They lost in the High Court in July 1948, but won in the Court of Appeal in March 1949.

With so much at stake an appeal was taken to the House of Lords in January 1950, but was dismissed with costs, and that effectively finished the Anglo American Telegraph Co, even as an investment company. It is obvious that they made strenuous efforts to reduce the effect of the tax. There appears to have been a takeover in 1951. All the old directors were replaced, the new directors being E.K. and R.W. Hockey, chartered accountants, with Rhodesian addresses. They were also directors of Rhodesian and Overseas Investment Trust. Seven months later the Hockeys went and both Anglo and Rhodesian & Overseas came under the directorship of three Rhodesians, who also held interests in Rhodesia and Anglo American (mining company) Ltd and the Tanganyika Mining & Railway Co. At that point the matter seems to have rested for several years.

The technological developments which had won the war for the Allies were soon going to have their impact on trans-Atlantic communication. As changes in cable design had improved their frequency response, bandwidth had been increased, and they could thus carry more information. Prior to this, time division multiplexing had been used, but with a large bandwidth, frequency multiplexing was possible; each channel occupying a different place in the available frequency spectrum. This mode of operation was to benefit substantially from the introduction of repeaters. A submarine repeater was first used between Anglesey and Port Erin in 1943. At that time, however, the reliability of thermionic valves was such that the improvement obtained by using the repeater lasted for only a short time. Once the valve had failed, it required the lifting of the cable from the sea bed in order to replace it. In 1950 Western Union's cable ship, *Lord Kelvin,* was used to insert the first really effective submerged telegraph repeater. The 1881 cable to Penzance was the subject of this experiment and the results confirmed the viability of such a system. The same year flexible one-way repeaters were used on a twin cable telephone link between Key West and Havana. This allowed twenty voice channels to be used.

In 1952 the American Telephone and Telegraph Co. again initiated discussions with the British Government concerning a trans-Atlantic telephone link. The Post Office Engineers had been working for many years on shallow-water two-way repeaters for use on single cable links, and it was agreed that these would be used for the shallow run between Clarenville (NF) and Sydney Mines (NS). Trans Atlantic Telephone cable 1 (TAT-1) was laid between Oban in Scotland and Newfoundland during 1955 and 1956. Between the two termini there were two cables, the "go" (1945 miles) and the "return" (1942 miles), each with 51 repeaters. TAT-1 provided 48×3kHz voice channels and when it opened for business in September 1956 it was an instant success.

In addition to the use of multiple repeaters, TAT-1 also included another technological innovation: polythene, which had first been available in industrial quantities during the war, was used as the insulating material[*]. The very small dielectric losses meant that the coaxial cable had a significant bandwidth. There was also a commercial innovation. Whereas telegraph cables had generally been single company concerns, the capital required by the new technology ($49.6m) needed a greater spread of investment. TAT-1 was 50% owned by A.T.& T., 41% by the British Government, and 9% by the Canadian Overseas Telecommunications Corp.

Meanwhile, Western Union was facing its own problems. The Company was 'ejected' from France with the termination of its lease in 1958. France had its own direct link across the Atlantic when TAT-2 was opened for business in 1959. In the United States Western Union's expansion had run up against anti-trust law. In the early 1940s it had absorbed its major rival, the Postal Telegraph Co. A legal condition of the takeover was that it should divest itself of its international operations. It is not clear how seriously it took this ruling at first. For one thing there was the problem of trying to find a buyer for an undertaking of this size. Eventually, external factors led them to a change of heart. Technology was about to change and they were in serious danger of being left behind. Radar, which had been developed during the war, was now being used for line of sight microwave telephone links on land. This and the advent of artificial satellite communications heralded a new era of high density trans-oceanic telephony. The days of cable telegraphy were obviously coming to an end. The future would involve the leasing of lines on the new telephone cables and on satellite links.

In the early 1960s it became imperative for Western Union to fulfil the original conditions imposed on it at the takeover of the Postal Telegraph Co.. A.T&T. requested permission from the Federal Communications Commission (FCC) to lease voice channels to the international carriers for transmission of common carrier telegraph and other non-voice services. This was granted in July 1959. Commercial Cable Co was first to take up this option in 1960. They recognised that the

---

[*] The Anglo German cable of 1947 was the first installation where polythene was used for long distance undersea communications.

bandwidth of a single voice channel on a telephone cable would give them more telex capacity than existed on all their telegraph cables. In 1961 they applied to the FCC for permission to abandon all their trans-Atlantic cables (all but the 1884 pair were still in use at that time). Following receipt of approval the Waterville Station was closed, and the cables were taken out of service effective 1 January 1962. In December 1961 Western Union approached the FCC with a similar request, quoting the Commercial Cable Co. as precedent. They obviously wanted similar leasing arrangements, but as Western Union had ignored the conditions associated with the purchase of the Postal Telegraph Co. the FCC refused their request until such time as they complied.

A solution to the problem was devised in 1963. A private company, Western Union International Inc. (WUI), was formed. It would be completely independent and would take over all Western Union's overseas operation. It would, in the future, enter into leasing agreements for the use of voice lines on international submarine cables and trans-oceanic satellite communications.

As part of the formation arrangements, existing cables were to be abandoned and the lease with the Anglo American Telegraph Co. terminated. This would leave WUI free of any contractual obligations. The plan was to buy out the Anglo, wind it up, and pay off the shareholders. Although it may sound simple in theory, the process was in fact to take several years.

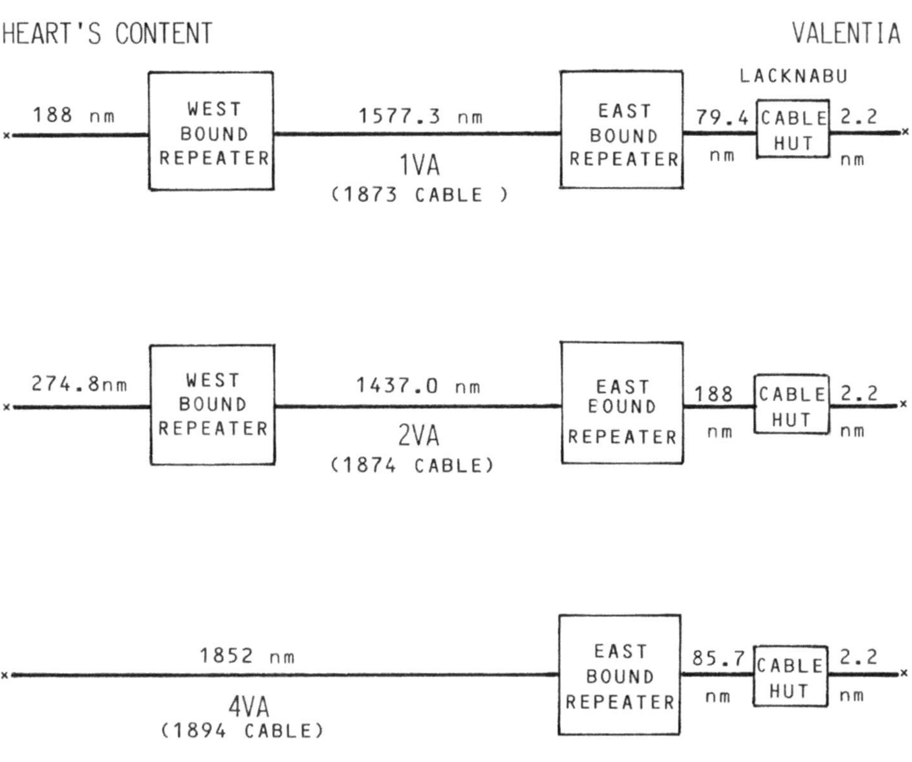

Repeaters on VA-HC cables

In 1963 the Valentia station was now a shadow of its former self. From an all-time maximum of about 200 staff during World War 1, there were now seventeen people employed there. These included Sam Breslin as Superintendent (he had married Bateman's daughter). Des Burke was the station electrician, having trained in the Post Office. Dermot Ring, Mike Sugrue* and Adrian Mackey went to London. With the key clerks long gone there was only the whirr of the mechanical multiplexers and the humm of electronic valve equipment, interrupted by the occasional chatter of a teleprinter. Even the cables were giving up the ghost. The 1880 (VA3) cable went out of service in 1949 and was not repaired. The shore ends at Lacknabau were repaired by the Dutch Government's cable ship, *Poolster* (http://www.shipspotters.nl/viewtopic.php?f=17&t=929) and it is notable for the fact that it was the only case where polythene insulation was used in Valentia cables. Repeaters were added to the remaining cables and also electronics at the receiving ends to shape the incoming signals, but it was all too late. Telegraph cables were now obsolete.

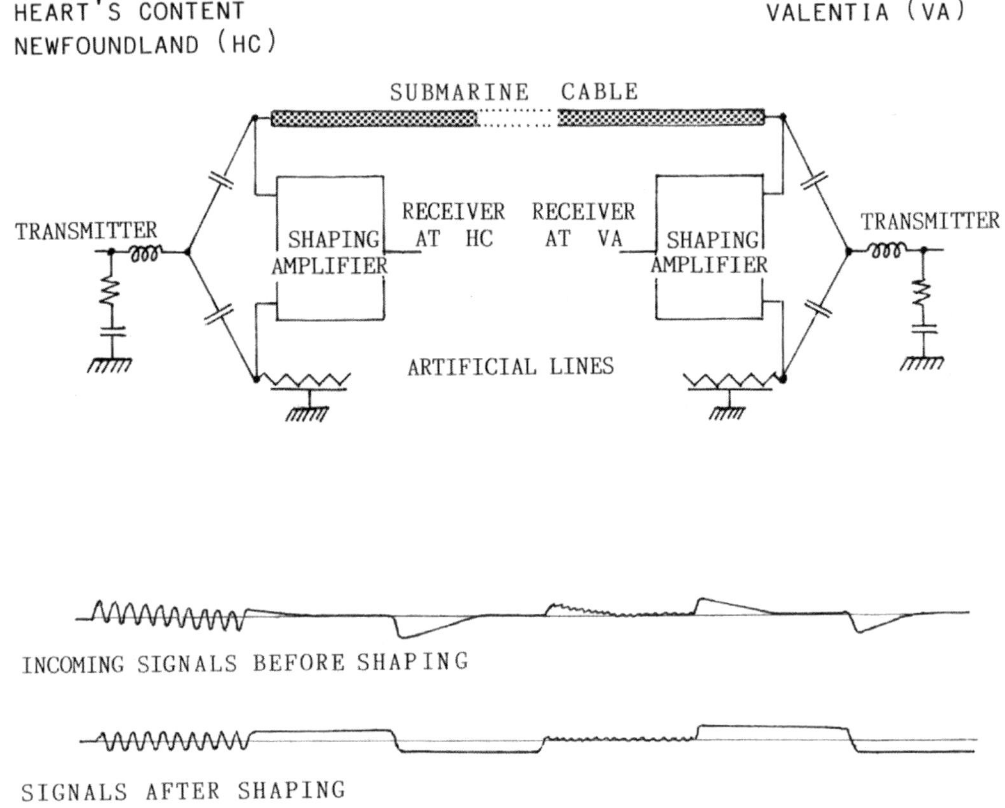

The placement of electronic shaping amplifiers and their effects on incoming signals

* Sugrue's brother had been in charge of the wireless station.

The Valentia station closed in 1966. At the other side of the Atlantic the Halifax cable repair depot was also closed. Sam Breslin had already moved to the London office. The employees were given the option of transfer or redundancy. Contractors moved in to tidy up and ship out anything that was to go. A scrap merchant is reputed to have done very well out of the sale of mercury which had been used as part of the fly-wheels in the rotary multiplexers. There was also the battery lead. There were some cases of police intervention as small unlicensed operators attempted to raise cable for the sale of the copper. There had been similar cases of unapproved salvage when the Le Havre Station had closed. WUI were prepared to license any competent company who wished to raise cable provided it received 10% of the proceeds. A number came forward. However, Dolphin Cable Co is reported to have gone into liquidation after retrieving only a small amount of cable. Difficulties in raising capital, and the lack of approval from British Telecom, which was advising WUI on the question of competence, generally prevented other salvors from moving in.

The long-drawn-out end of the Anglo American Telegraph Co seems to have started at the beginning of the 1960s. Following its takeover by the Rhodesians there was a period of quiet. However, from 1960 onwards there was a series of petitions to Judges in Chambers for reductions in the declared capital. The eventual capital amounted to approximately £2m, a reduction of £5m.

The terms of the Anglo-WUTC agreement of 1911 had specified the return of working cables and a cable ship. With the premature termination of the lease, the Anglo was to receive a substantial cash payment in lieu of working cables. The problem of the cable ship was solved by the formation of a new company, Trans Atlantic Cables Ltd, of Bermuda, who were to purchase the *Lord Kelvin.* The purchase money was paid over to the Anglo and the ship was then sold for scrap, arriving at the breaker's yard in January 1977. This done, Trans Atlantic Cables went into liquidation.

The liquidation of the Anglo itself was started on 10 December 1968 and was handled by Brian C.J. Beckett, a chartered accountant of Nassau, Bahamas. A notification was given to the English courts in 1970 that the final winding up would be delayed for twelve months, pending settlement of the staff pension fund. When the original lease had been agreed with WUTC several classes of employees remained within the Anglo's pension scheme. This of course included the Company Directors, Secretary and secretariat. There were also those like Attie Graves and the Scaifes, who would have nothing to do with the Western Union pension scheme when it was introduced in 1912. Western Union International had taken over WUTC's pension obligations in 1963, but as part of the winding up agreements they were now to take over responsibility for any remaining Anglo pensions. This required locating all surviving Anglo pensioners in order to obtain their agreement to the pension transfer. Naturally this took some time; there were even some pensioners who had worked in the Company's Paris office, which had closed in 1911! The final dissolution of the Company took place on 19 January 1971, ninety five years after its formation as an expedient to ensure the laying of the first successful trans-Atlantic cable.

The year after the Valentia cable station closed down there was a 'scandal' in Britain which had resonances with the recent revelations by Edward Snowden. It will be remembered from Chapter 11 that during the Congressional Hearings in 1920 the President of Western Union had admitted that his company submitted copies of each day's traffic to the UK Post Office and that the British Government blustered a denial. The matter was raised once again in 1967 by the journalist Chapman Pincher, who clearly stated the extent of surveillance of all traffic on private and Post Office cables. The Government of Harold Wilson attempted to gag the story using a D-notice (a supposedly voluntary system whereby publishers would, on request, not publish or broadcast matters which were deemed to affect national security). What was called 'the D-notice affair' backfired on the Government. When Pincher's article was published the Government believed that there had been a breach of the rules, and a committee of enquiry comprising Privy Counsellors was set up. The committee found against the Government. The Government refused to accept the findings and the Secretary of the D-notice committee resigned. All of this made for headlines in the newspapers, but the reaction from America on this occasion was muted. Perhaps they were now actively involved in the same thing

Staff at the close of the Valentia station identified by Anthony O'Connell as
Back Row: Herbert Renwick, Corbett?? Eric Myles Hook, Joe Liddicoat.
Front Row: Herbert O'Sullivan, Tommy Richards, Frank Bateman, Geoffrey Edmunds.

So, finally, at the close of this history there are some strange coincidences.

Valentia's long period of physical isolation came to an end. The first serious moves to establish a bridge to the mainland had been made in 1911, the same year in which both James Graves died, and Anglo's direct involvement in the Station had ceased. Work had not started until the year after the Station had closed, and it was completed the same month as the Anglo American Telegraph Co. went out of existence. It would be interesting to speculate how different things might have been for the island and its Station if work had started in 1911.

Chapter 14

Hindsights

Draft written in 1983

The age of the telegraph is gone. Even TAT-1 has come to the end of its useful life and the thermionic valve, which helped telephony to supplant telegraphy, has now been replaced by the transistor and the integrated circuit. TAT-7, using transistorised repeaters, was laid during 1983 at a cost of $197m. It has 4,200 3kHz channels. In spite of the enormous capital outlay it represents a 22-fold reduction in the cost per channel compared with TAT-1.

Of the original cable laying companies, Siemens are long gone. They amalgamated with the Telegraph Construction & Maintenance Co. (Telcon) in 1935 to form Submarine Cables Ltd., with Telcon maintaining its identity as an independent unit. Telcon itself disappeared in a series of takeovers from 1959 onwards. First the share capital was acquired by British Insulated Callender's Cables Ltd (BICC), who in turn sold it off to AEI (part of GEC) in 1966. On takeover by BICC all submarine cable design and manufacture was transferred to Submarine Cables; the child consuming the parent. On 4 February 1970 Standard Telephones and Cables (STC), which is part of ITT purchased the share capital of Submarine Cables and thereby acquired a large volume of Telcon's archives. STC is still a major cable manufacturer, having produced sections and components for many of the TAT cables.

Western Union International has an office in London and Sam Breslin was still working there in November 1983. Dermot Ring and others have returned to Valentia. Commercial Cable Co. is still in business, now part of ITT. Herbert Hogbin, last Superintendent at Waterville is the European President within ITT. Unhappily, unlike at the Western Union offshoot, little attempt was made to keep the station records at closedown and if this account has appeared to underrate the importance of the Commercial Cable Co. during the telegraph era, it is unintentional, being due only to the scarcity of information.

We are now experiencing another revolution. The development of the integrated circuit has completely changed the size, cost, and capability of electronic computers. This has led to the new science of Information Technology. Since information is only of value if it can be exchanged, the revolution has put a considerable strain on the world's communications systems. In much the same way as the introduction of the word rate for telegrams in the 1870s had a dramatic effect on traffic density, reduction in the cost per channel across the Atlantic has considerably influenced our use of the telephone for long-distance calls. It is no longer unusual for a radio commentator in Britain to call up a journalist or politician in America to comment on some news item. There has also been competition from satellites, which until now have had the monopoly on television linkups. The fact that one can get instant TV coverage of the Olympics and similar events have also affected our concept of distance and has increased our expectations of the world's communications systems. If it was widely felt some years ago that satellites would take over completely from submarine cables, the situation has now changed somewhat. There is the cost of launching a satellite, the uncertainty about its long term reliability, and the fact that the available space, particularly for additional geostationary satellites, is now limited. Submarine cables have proved themselves to be efficient and reliable. Up to 1980 there were 195 routes in service. By the end of 1984 26 new routes will be introduced, adding 36,400 miles to the 1980 total cable mileage of 142,000 miles.

Although not directly related to communications, history is in many ways repeating itself with only minor variations. The Brett brothers laid their cable between Dover and Boulogne in 1851. During 1983-4 massive work is in progress to lay a high voltage DC cable across the Channel to link the national grids of Britain and France. This time considerable effort is being expended to ensure that no "Piscator Ignobile" will have the misfortune to fish up and cut into the cable. It is being buried six feet below the sea bed using specially designed submarine tractors fitted with ploughs.

The line-of-sight microwave links which have taken over from land line telephone wires since World War II have something very old fashioned in concept. They are so like the semaphore and heliograph stations of the past, but of course they are not affected by the vagaries of visibility in the same way. As part of the full circle turn which we are now witnessing, new telephone cables are once more starting to creep slowly under the British landscape. In their way they are as revolutionary as the lines of telegraph which were established by the private companies in the last century. This time, however, the intelligence is carried not by electricity, but by light. The light, which has the information impressed on it by means of a modulated laser, is transmitted along optical fibres, which are no more then a few millionths of a metre thick. Optical fibres have been around for some time, but the difficulties which have beset their use have been little different from those experienced by electricians at the dawn of telegraphy. Attenuation is the measure of reduction in signal strength over a given length of transmitting medium. Not even Faraday was certain that electricity could travel over any great distance along a wire without considerable attenuation. The earliest optical fibres suffered from excessive attenuation, but extensive research over several years has reduced this to acceptable levels. The stage has now been reached where major cities like London and Birmingham are being linked by optical fibres, using an economic number of repeaters along the way.

Approximately seventeen years elapsed between the establishment of inland telegraphy in Britain and the first attempt to span the Atlantic. Much has been learnt since 1857, but we seem set to do much the same again. Tenders for TAT-8, the first trans-Atlantic optical fibre cable, were submitted during summer 1983 and it is intended that it should be in service by 1988.

The past, even the recent past, is now part of history, and there is a responsibility to retain what we can, so that the future can learn of our successes and failures. Ireland's links with telegraphy and thereby with recent trans-Atlantic developments started to break as a result of the problems and uncertainties associated with the formation of the Free State. Regrettably, since the last links were severed with the closedown of the stations, much has been allowed to slip away unnoticed. The ruins of the Foilhommerum station are still visible. The lines of underground cable show up on aerial photographs just like the ruins of ancient fortifications of previous millennia.

The Celtic forts and the megalithic tombs of Ireland are designated as being of national importance. Of relevant recent history, the landing place of Alcock and Brown near Clifden in Galway is one of the few events that is commemorated with a monument*. The telegraph stations on the south west coast of Ireland have played a vital part in 20th century world history, and it would be a pity if they were forgotten.

A large number of documents and memorabilia relating to the era have left Ireland since the early 1960s. What little that remains is in private hands. Enquiries to the National Museum of Ireland reveal that their total holdings on the subject amount to one small length of cable. The museum of the Irish Broadcasting Authority have been more fortunate. They have acquired several private collections, including some relating to the Marconi era. The relatives of Robert Halpin, last master of the *Great Eastern*, have presented his collection to the national Maritime Museum at Dun Laoghaire, Co. Dublin. This includes a scale model of his ship as she was adapted for cable laying. Let us hope that this process of diffusion continues.

On the other side of the Atlantic things have been somewhat different. The Province of Newfoundland, despite its frequent bankrupt status, has taken a more positive approach. The Heart's Content station has now been taken over and preserved as a museum. The accumulation of station documents and records which have survived have been lodged at the Provincial Archives in St. John's.

Draft written in 2015

Looking back to 1984, who would have believed that we are where we are now? Just imagine: smart mobile phones, the World Wide Web and the Internet, WiFi and VOIP. Think of the power of a modern laptop. My first IBM PC XT computer had a 5MB disk-drive. Today 1TB is considered just about adequate. And just think of computing power. The Intel 80386 was new in 1985 and the Pentium in the 1990s.

Okay, so analogue telephony was on the way out since the 1980s and completely disappeared during the 1990s. Heaven knows what TAT we are at now. I thought that a major landmark had been reached with the optical fibre cables TAT12/13, which were laid as a loop so that if one cable was interrupted priority traffic could be re-routed via the other without users being aware that anything had happened. I mentioned earlier that TAT-7 had used transistorised repeaters. TAT12/13 used optical pumping. A laser within the repeater generates light and uses non-linear optical properties of the glass to amplify the signals in transit.

It was the proliferation of cables and the increase in their capacity that led to such a reduction in the cost per bit transmitted. This in turn gave us the Web, and cable laying by private consortia

---

* There is a bronze tablet at Baldonnel (now Casement) aerodrome near Dublin which marked the departure point of the first westward trans-Atlantic flight by Fitzmaurice, Kohl and von Huenefeld.

became a big international business . In this context it is well worth reading Neal Stephenson's detailed account of the laying of the FLAG cable: http://archive.wired.com/wired/archive/4.12/ffglass.html

We have also witnessed the 'dotcom' bubble, and have probably already forgotten its cataclysmic effects.

The UK Post Office's inland monopoly of on telecommunications had been broken in 1981 with the establishment of British Telecommunication (later British Telecom and now BT) as an independent entity. The UK Government sold off its remaining stakes in 1991 and 1993. The BT archive, which contains much material related to Valentia, is still accessible, but the BT museum, with its collection of historic artefacts dating back to the earliest days of telegraphy in Britain, has been dispersed. BT's cable-laying arm (James Graves served on the first CS *Monarch*) is almost forgotten, but this author did acquire a manuscript history of BT Marine by the late Eric Clayton, which he proposes to edit and publish

STC went through a rough patch and was sold to Nortel in 1991. Nortel itself disappeared in 2009. I am assured that the wonderful STC archive which contained so much that was relevant to Valentia is still intact, but is in deep storage and no longer accessible. ITT, the American company which owned STC, Commercial Cable Co, etc., disappeared at about the same time*.

MCI, which had taken over Western Union International, had for a time been the largest communications provider in the US after A.T.&T. It was bought out by Verizon in 2006 and virtually disappeared. Its archives, which contain much that is relevant to the Valentia cable station, had previously been deposited in the Hagley Library at Wilmington, Delaware. You can imagine my annoyance when their response to my enquiry about the WUI/MCI copy of James Graves's Station Diary of 1865 insisted that I sign their copyright form.

There have been even later casualties. As the international subsea cable market expanded a company called Global Crossing was at the forefront. They were a large player during the IEEE Milestones event in Kerry in July 2000. It seems to have disappeared, even if the world cable network continues to expand (see http://submarinecablemap.com).

One of the arguments for using cables as opposed to satellites was the question of security. During the Second World War the Americans had demonstrated that electromagnetic cross-talk could be used to eavesdrop on telegraph cables. This led to US Government cable traffic being transmitted in cipher. At a later date we have the revelations of the US cutting into Soviet cables and the work

* It is still worth reading Anthony Samson's very unflattering account ("The Sovereign State of ITT") which details the way in which this multi-national did its own thing, flouting national laws if they got in the way of its objectives. One wonders whether the situation is any different with today's big names?

of the US Navy Chief Scientist, Special Projects Office, John Peña Craven http://en.wikipedia.org/wiki/Operation_Ivy_Bells. Additionally, I have been informed that obsolete cables such as TAT-1 were subsequently fitted with acoustic transducers to monitor the movement of Soviet submarines. More recently, Edward Snowden has told us how the NSA (US) and GCHQ (UK) engage in giga-scale collection of global voice and data traffic on subsea cables.

All of this has happened since this book (on that most important node in what Tom Standage refers to as 'The Victorian Internet') was first drafted. One wonders where we might be thirty years from now?

INDEX

Printed in Great Britain
by Amazon

45386096R10178